AN EAST END Story

A Tale of Friendship

ALFRED GARDNER

Fonthill Media Limited
www.fonthillmedia.com
office@fonthillmedia.com

First published in the United Kingdom 2013
British Library Cataloguing in Publication Data:
A catalogue record for this book is available from the British Library
Copyright © Alfred Gardner 2013

ISBN 978-1-78155-235-3

Typeset in 10pt on 13pt Sabon LT Std
Printed and bound in England

Contents

No medicine is more valuable, none more efficacious, none better suited to the cure of all our temporal ills than a friend, to whom we may turn for consolation in time of trouble, and with whom we may share our happiness in time of joy.

Saint Ailred of Rievaul

Preface

In the summer of 1998, I finally finished transcribing the war diary of my late and sadly missed friend, David Upson. Shortly afterwards, I found myself writing about the close friendship that I enjoyed with Dave that began when I was a teenager in June 1959. Of course, not all of the incidents and anecdotes are mentioned in this book, but there are enough to give the reader some idea of the kind of relationship that we shared. Included in these memories are indelible experiences of my boyhood in post-war Stepney that I thought might be of interest.

There are no chapters or an exact chronology, but a series of episodes loosely connected.

Alfred Gardner
Isle of Dogs

Acknowledgements

I am most grateful to those individuals listed below who kindly assisted me whenever I contacted them.

Chris Lloyd, Tower Hamlets Local Historian Librarian; Malcolm Barr-Hamilton, Tower Hamlets Archivist; East London Historian Gary Haines; Bob Aspinall, Museum of Docklands Librarian; James Page Roberts, Tom Ash, Dr. Liz Gamble, Jenny Smith formerly of Stepney Books and lastly, Alan Sutton of Fonthill Media for publishing this book.

Every attempt has been made to contact the holders of the copyright images used in this book. Apologies are given to the handful of copyright owners who it has not been possible to trace.

A Fortuitous Meeting

One evening, during that glorious hot summer of 1959, I noticed a woman lying stretched out on the pavement in Commercial Road, Stepney, quite near to my home at Jane Street. I immediately ran across the road to a 'phone booth to call an ambulance, only to be beaten at the door by a Eurasian man who had also seen the injured woman. I recognised the man; he worked alongside several of my old school pals at D&W Ltd, a local handbag factory.

After he made the call, the man and I both went back across the road to stay with the woman, and within minutes a small crowd soon gathered around us. Shortly afterwards the ambulance and a police car arrived. One of the police officers began to disperse the onlookers.

As the Eurasian man and I were no longer needed, we retreated to the nearby Lord Nelson pub for a drink and a chat. From this fortuitous meeting with David Upson a warm, platonic friendship developed that was to last for thirty-seven years until his death.

After introducing ourselves at the bar, we spent the next two hours discussing all sorts of topics, but two things that were mentioned time and time again were women and the sea.

I was fascinated by the sea. The idea of abandoning my job as a garment cutter in a small and cramped workshop in Bethnal Green and joining the Merchant Navy was so appealing that I would seize every opportunity that came my way to obtain information about working on a ship. Seamen and ex-seamen were pestered with endless questions about their experiences. It seemed that my thirst to understand what it was like to spend months at sea was insatiable, so when Dave began to tell me about the years that he had spent working on ships, I was enthralled. Encouraged by my youthful enthusiasm he warmed to the subject.

After spending four years during the war with the Burma Royal Navy Volunteer Reserve, Dave was demobbed in August 1947 with the rank of Midshipman. In March 1948 he was engaged by the Rangoon-based Burma Marine Trawler Owners & Wholesale Fish Merchants, as a skipper of their deep-sea trawler *Khin Khin Lay*. Unfortunately, to his eternal regret, in July 1951 he was laid off when Burma Marine sold the vessel. Unable to find work with the various Rangoon shipping companies and with little money left and no prospects in sight, his situation became desperate. With foresight, he had kept in touch with a few of his former wartime commanding officers, who managed to find him a position with the Imperial War Graves Commission as a roving overseer and caretaker based at Meiktilla Military Cemetery 250 miles north of Rangoon.

Working inland and so far from the coast Dave soon became bored and yearned once more for a life at sea. On 6 June 1953 he resigned from the Commission and proceeded to Calcutta where the chances of finding work on a ship were much greater than in Rangoon. In August, after regular visits to Calcutta shipping offices, he was finally offered a job as an able seaman on the SS *Bangor Bay*.

Seven months later on 23 February 1954 his vessel docked at Birkenhead and he was paid off. Still keen to find another ship, he travelled down to London and stayed at the Seamen's Mission hostel in Dock Street, Stepney.

Because he was unable to find immediate work on an ocean going ship, Dave accepted what he thought would be a temporary position as a deckhand on a Thames dredger, but he enjoyed the work so much that he remained as a 'deckie' for nearly four years until he was made redundant.

Now that he no longer worked on the river, he was politely asked by the warden of the Seamen's Mission hostel to vacate his room. Finding suitable alternative accommodation was difficult. For about a month he stayed in various furnished rooms in the Whitechapel area and he also slept rough for a few days.

Fortunately, his friends Peggy and Henry Johnson came to his aid; they allowed him to rent a tiny bedroom at their home in Buross Street just yards from the Lord Nelson. Although he was now a bench-hand at the D&W handbag factory, he still hoped to return to sea one day.

It was so exciting listening to his stories of the various countries that he had visited. He also spoke about the women whom he had met in Singapore, Hong Kong and Australia.

Dave was able to recall with clarity dangerous incidents on the high seas. He once fought off an attack by a knife-wielding drunken crew member and, much worse, several times he was involved in skirmishes with ruthless pirates when they tried to board his trawler. There was another unpleasant episode ingrained in his memory, when he was asked to leave the bar of the famous Raffles Hotel in Singapore simply because he was a non-European. The formidable and tenacious Upson refused to get off of his bar stool and he created such a furore that the bar manager soon backed down, apologised and subsequently treated him like a visiting VIP. I asked him if he ever kept a diary.

'Sort of,' he replied, 'but unfortunately, Frances, the girl I have just finished with, destroyed many of my old wartime papers and references.'

Recruit 538, David Upson, aged fifteen.

Dave sighed. 'It's true what they say; "Hell hath no fury like a woman scorned"'. ('Heaven has no rage, like love to hatred turned, nor Hell a fury, like a woman scorned.' This famous quote is from 'Act 3, *The Morning Bride*' by William Congrove 1670-1729.)

At closing time, Dave and I left the Nelson's Head and parted company, but not before arranging to meet again so that we could continue our conversation.

The next evening, I met Dave outside the Lord Nelson Head at 7.30 p.m. The lovely June weather was too warm for us to sit in the pub, so I suggested that we should go for a walk instead. It was amazing as we began walking down the Whitechapel Road a succession of people were stopping us in the street and wanting to shake Dave's hand. It was as if they had just been reunited with a long-lost friend. Dave always reacted cordially to these people.

During the following three months, Dave and I met on a regular basis and continued our walks around the East End. No matter where we were, be it down Petticoat Lane at Aldgate or near the Blackwall Tunnel in the east, strolling by the lake in Victoria Park or close to old Wapping Stairs, he was recognised and approached by acquaintances; and when darkness fell we would usually stop and have a drink in one of the more interesting pubs.

Although I drank moderately, perhaps only a pint of beer, Dave was capable of consuming much more. Occasionally during our evening rambles, we would be accompanied by some very attractive girls with whom Dave was acquainted. I could hardly believe my good fortune: besides acquiring knowledge of the Merchant Navy I was being introduced to young women. The future certainly looked promising.

In early September Dave asked me if I would like to visit the Farnborough Air Show with him. He wanted to see the two-stage Black Knight rocket and the Blue Streak long-range missile that were on display. Ever since 1957

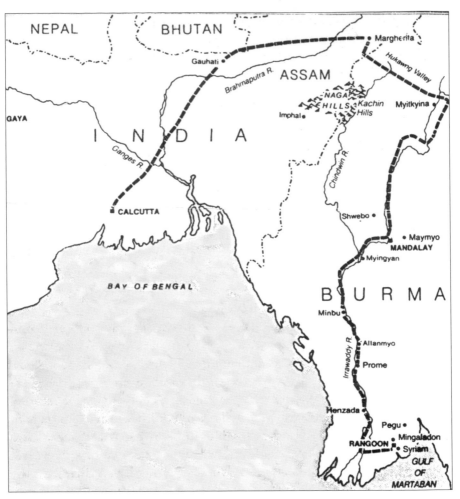

Barbara Upson's Route from Rangoon to Calcutta, 1942.

when the Russians had launched their *Sputnik 1* satellite into orbit, Dave had been fascinated by satellites and rockets. This fascination remained with him throughout his life. My interest in the subject was limited, but I agreed to accompany him. Any excursion with my friend would undoubtedly be most enjoyable and beneficial.

On the train to Farnborough, Dave became involved in a serious but friendly conversation with a group of passengers in our compartment. The group, four men and two women, all seemed to be in their early thirties. They were teachers from Islington, North London and were also visiting the Farnborough Air Show. The conversation began after Dave whispered in my ear 'CND.'

I whispered back 'CND? Who?' One of the members of the group sitting opposite overheard me; my naïvety caused him to grin. He leant forward and spoke confidently.

'We are members of the Campaign for Nuclear Disarmament and we are planning to voice our opposition to nuclear weapons at Farnborough.' Having disclosed his aims, he immediately thrust a 'Ban the Bomb' leaflet into my hands. Not wanting to offend him, I began to read it.

The same campaigner spoke to Dave, who listened earnestly. 'We believe that Britain should ultimately give up her nuclear weapons. We don't need these terrible bombs. If Britain committed itself to unilateral disarmament, it would be a fine example for other countries like France to abandon their nuclear aspirations too.' He also said, 'If that situation did occur, perhaps in time America and Russia would also come to their senses and dismantle their nuclear arsenal.'

I posed a question, 'Are there any active 'Ban the Bomb' movements in Russia or any of the other countries behind the Iron Curtain?'

One of the women answered, 'There are several known active groups in the Soviet Bloc, but unfortunately, because of the strict restriction on free speech, travel and a censored press, the activities of our sister organisations are isolated, monitored and easily controlled.'

Finally Dave spoke. He explained how during the last war, while serving in the Navy, he had witnessed fanatical Japanese kamikaze pilots crash-landing their planes on allied warships and that these suicide missions resulted in thousands of casualties. 'The Japs weren't prepared to surrender; they were determined to prolong the war. Had the Americans not dropped their atom bombs on Hiroshima and Nagasaki, millions of soldiers and civilians on both sides would have been killed by the continued fighting. Moreover at least twenty five million Russians lost their lives between 1941 and 1945 and had the Germans possessed atom bombs in 1939, the war between Germany and Russia might never have occurred. The Russians, rather than be annihilated, would have had no alternative but to surrender to the German demands.'

The second woman campaigner remarked, 'Surely, with the end of the Second World War, nuclear weapons had no further use?'

'Not so, according to the Americans and eventually the Russians too,' replied Dave, adding 'while mutual distrust exists, America and Russia will never give up their atom bombs; by keeping their nuclear arsenals intact these two countries are able to deter a military attack on their homeland.'

Another CND campaigner remarked, 'We believe that possessing nuclear weapons, far from diminishing the threat of war, actually increases the possibility of war. There is always the danger that either America or Russia could have a secret plan to strike first with their atom bombs if war loomed between the two countries.'

Dave intervened. 'There is another important factor to consider that I think people tend to overlook. Conventional bombs can be just as lethal as atom bombs. You only have to reflect on what happened to the German city of Dresden that was obliterated by high explosive bombs and incendiaries in

Manning the ship's guns, 1944. David Upson is in the foreground.

1945, as many civilians were killed in Dresden as in Hiroshima and Nagasaki combined.'

Just prior to our train arriving at Farnborough, Dave decided to have one final word with the campaigners. 'I am aware that the majority of people genuinely believe that the world would be a safer place if all nuclear weapons were deactivated, but we have to be realistic. Atom bombs are, unfortunately, here to stay and there is not one iota that we can do about it and the tragedy is, in the future, other countries like France and Israel will also have the bomb. The question is can we avoid a nuclear apocalypse in the future? I for one just don't know.'

I felt a little sorry for the CND campaigners; even before arriving at Farnborough to hand out their leaflets they had to defend their arguments to an articulate and intelligent man who while sympathetic to their aims had raised important and relevant points.

Dave became disappointed at the Farnborough Air Show; his main interest was to see the star attraction, the Blue Streak long-range ballistic missile, but only a five-scale model was on display. After just one hour we left the air show enclosure and returned to London. (France tested her first atom bomb in the Algerian desert on 13 February 1960. Although Israel is reluctant to reveal details of her nuclear capability, it is widely believed, that the country has an arsenal of two hundred atom bombs.)

It was a Saturday evening. Dave and I were walking past Stepney Green Station when suddenly we were startled to hear a man behind us shouting, 'David, David, *mio amico.*' We turned around and were confronted by a scruffy, limping man of about 40.

'*Ciao* Alberto,' said Dave, with a welcoming smile. I realised that the man needed to speak to my friend in private, so I moved a few paces away and leant on the pavement railings. After a few words were exchanged, Dave took a pound note from his pocket and gave it to the man, who promptly limped away.

Sensing that I was curious to know who Alberto was, Dave explained that he had known him for about five years, ever since they briefly shared a 'cold, smelly room in a Spitalfields doss house.' Alberto had been in the Italian army during the last war, but was captured by British forces in North Africa. As a prisoner of war in England he was sent to work on various farms. After the war ended, rather than be repatriated to Italy where he had few relatives, he chose to stay in Britain. Life seemed to be going well for Alberto; he found employment as a nurseryman's assistant in Bedfordshire and became engaged to a former Land Army girl. I interrupted my friend with a puerile remark, 'Do you think they frolicked in a haystack?'

'Probably not,' said Dave with a grin. 'Italian men prefer their brides to be virgins.'

Before continuing, Dave pointed to the distant and aptly-named Hayfield Tavern. 'Let's stop by for a quick half. I am parched.' As we walked along the busy and noisy road my friend told me that 'at a single stroke' Alberto's plans for marriage and a family life were shattered. Just prior to the wedding, Alberto's fiancée apparently changed her mind about marrying him. 'Poor Alberto,' said Dave sadly. 'The man went to pieces. When he eventually recovered he came down to London and found labouring work on Stepney building sites, but, to add more salt to his wounds, he fell from scaffolding and badly damaged his leg, hence the limp.'

Inquisitive as ever, I persuaded Dave to tell me more about Alberto's life. My friend pondered for a moment before saying, 'Well, as far as I know, he lives in the Salvation Army hostel at Middlesex Street and does casual work around Whitechapel. I have seen him pushing market barrows and helping the traders set up their stalls. You know, Alf, I don't think the man has ever had more than two half pennies to rub together.' Dave did not disclose why he gave Alberto a pound, but in all probability it was to buy food.

As we went inside the Hayfield Tavern, I chuckled before remarking, 'I hope it's not going to be our last drink.'

'Why is that?' he replied curiously.

Still chuckling I remarked, 'Well, there is an unexploded German bomb still buried deep in the ground just outside the pub. The bomb disposal squad decided that as the bomb was far too dangerous to remove, it was safer to leave it alone; they hoped that in time the bomb would render itself harmless.'

Dave listened with interest before remarking, 'One day Alf, I will tell you about my own close shaves with unexploded Japanese bombs and shells.'

Rather than sit down we stood drinking at the bar, where we had a clear view of the pretty barmaid's long legs. Our voyeurism was soon curtailed by the sudden appearance of the barmaid's tall and well-built boyfriend, who promptly sat on a stool next to us. His arrival was effective; we left the bar to sit by the windows. Sitting there, a thought entered my mind: could the heavy rumbling from the traffic outside cause the unexploded bomb to ignite?

'That's highly unlikely,' replied Dave, when I put the question to him. 'There must be hundreds and hundreds of unexploded German bombs throughout East London and probably in the Thames too. Provided mechanical diggers don't pierce them during the widespread slum and bombsite clearance that's taking place at the moment, the bombs will eventually disintegrate.'

Fortunately for the people of the East End, not a single German bomb unearthed during the massive post-war building programme exploded. On several Stepney bombsites that I played on as a child, powerful unexploded bombs were later discovered during excavation work. Had the huge landmine that was raised from the Millwall dock in 1958 gone off it would have flattened a nearby block of council flats, though as a precaution, before the disposal squad began their delicate and dangerous task, the residents had to be evacuated.

Besides Alberto, I was soon to witness Dave giving pound notes to other acquaintances. Maurice, an elderly Jewish widower, patronised the Lord Nelson pub. Dave explained that the old man was once a well-off property speculator who had lost his entire fortune gambling. Most evenings, Maurice would sit alone in the Nelson sipping a glass of lemonade. Other regular drinkers avoided him because of his persistent habit of cadging money. He cadged 10 shillings from me during my second visit to the pub. Not that I cared; it was worth giving him the money, especially after listening to his appraisal of my new friend. When Dave went to the bar to buy more drinks, Maurice left his seat, came over and sat next to me.

His voice was shaky, 'Good evening young man.'

Just before Dave returned with the drinks, Maurice quietly said, 'Your friend David is a real gentleman, he never ignores me and he is always polite, doesn't swear and above all he has a good, kind heart. Believe me, my boy, it is a privilege to know the man.' He added, 'David always slips me a few *shekels* whenever I am short and never once does he ask for it back.' He looked at me and asked, 'Have you got a few *shekels* to spare for my gas meter?' I discreetly slipped him a 10 shilling note, which he tucked into an old wallet that had lost its sheen.

Midshipman Upson aged eighteen.

Mary, a young Irish-born mother also received financial assistance from Dave and not for the first time. It was a Friday evening when Dave and I met her standing outside Sam Goldstein's fish and chip shop in Cannon Street Road. In between rocking a young baby in her arms she was trying to push two restless toddlers against the wall, fearing that they would step into the busy road. Mary had every right to be fearful; that section of the road was notoriously dangerous; over the years many pedestrians, including children, had been injured attempting to cross it. Late-night drinkers who staggered out of two nearby pubs, the Golden Lion and the British Queen were particularly vulnerable. Tragically, in 1952 my childhood playmate, Ann Prince, was killed outside Goldstein's when she ran into the road and was struck by a passing brewer's lorry.

'David, David, I am so glad to see you,' said Mary.

'What is the matter Mary?' replied Dave sympathetically.

'David, I am so sorry to ask you again, please help me, my bleeding old man Sean is on the booze and he hasn't given me any money.' Her swollen cheek was an indication that her husband was also violent. Without saying a word, my friend instantly gave her a pound. Mary's eyes filled with tears as she thanked him. After muttering 'God help me,' she opened the fish shop door, and followed her two small children inside.

Dave once told me that he was almost run over by a fire tender in Cannon Street Road, but he blamed himself for being so irresponsible. He had left the Golden Lion after a heavy drinking session and had fallen into the road. Fortunately, the tender stopped just in front of his prostrated body and he received a severe ticking off from the angry fire chief.

Leaving pubs at closing time could be hazardous for Dave. Besides being struck by a car when he attempted to cross Commercial Road, he also had a near miss with a trolley bus and on another occasion he was knocked over by a motorbike combination in Cable Street. The unsympathetic rider was more concerned about possible damage to his combination than Dave's badly bruised leg.

Before riding away he growled at my friend, 'That will teach you not to walk in the road.'

David Upson did indeed have 'A good, kind heart.' Throughout that Indian summer of 1959 other needy people would benefit from Dave's altruism. One of those beneficiaries was Claude, a thin Anglo-Indian seaman who looked consumptive. Claude, who had known Dave for several years, was standing on the pavement near the Seamen's Mission in Dock Street trying to sell his gabardine raincoat to passing pedestrians. Rather than purchase the coat, Dave gave him some money instead. 'Claude needs the cash to buy some vests and pants,' whispered Dave.

As we turned into Cable Street my friend recalled with amusement the time when he was short of funds whilst staying at the Mission. 'I didn't have a raincoat to sell when I stood on the pavement, but what I did have was a watch, a jack-knife and an almost new pair of boots.' Dave managed to sell his watch and his boots, but thankfully not his jack-knife, which today, is one of my prized possessions.

It was an exceptionally warm evening. Dave and I were walking down Stepney's Johnson Street on our way to the Prospect of Whitby at Wapping when suddenly a gaunt man with thick grey hair emerged from Wilson Carlile House, a Church Army hostel, and nearly collided with us. 'Good grief David, how are you, old boy?' The man spoke with a middle-class accent. Dave instantly introduced me to Raymond, a former Army officer. After we shook hands, Raymond insisted that we should be his guests and join him for a tipple at the Crown & Anchor in adjacent Harding Street. I was not happy with this unexpected intrusion, but Dave did not seem perturbed, so I made no comment. Linking our arms with his, Raymond pulled Dave and me around the corner.

For reasons that I have never been able to establish, the Crown & Anchor was known by local dockers as the 'Chain Locker.' This pub was unusual; it was exceptionally small with a very low ceiling and unlike the majority of East End pubs was not situated on a corner. It may have originally been a house before being converted into a pub.

The landlord kept a large pet Alsatian that he allowed to roam around the bar. As soon as a customer entered the pub, the dog would trot over and sniff at his clothing. Dave recounted an embarrassing experience when he had taken a girl into the pub, only to be confronted by the dog that began a prolonged sniffing session around the crotch area of his corduroy trousers. On entering the Crown & Anchor, the dog sniffed at Raymond, Dave and me in quick succession. Having decided that our scent was acceptable, it curled up in a corner.

At the bar, the landlord asked Raymond if he had finally finished writing '*that* novel.'

'Almost,' declared Raymond confidently.

'You said "almost" two years ago,' remarked the landlord, mockingly.

Raymond sighed. 'Please don't chide me landlord, I guarantee, that in the not too distant future, my book will be published, and you will be one of several local publicans who will receive a free signed copy.'

As Raymond's guests, I had thought that Dave and I were to be offered a tipple, but no tipple was offered because our host had suddenly realised that his wallet had been left in his room. I held back from suggesting that he should perhaps nip back to the hostel and collect it. Payment for our drinks was left to the ever-obliging Dave. He also bought the second round of drinks and I paid for the third round.

While Dave and I drank half pints of beer, Raymond's preference was double gin and tonic. After I gave Raymond his drink, I asked him if he would like to briefly talk about his unfinished novel. He reacted by giving me an inquisitive stare that soon changed into a smile. 'How very kind of you Alfred to be interested in my work.' Then in an instant he produced a folded sheet of notepaper from the top pocket of his jacket. 'Believe it or not, Alfred, I just happen to have the synopsis with me, but before I begin, something tells me Alfred that you have done a little writing yourself. Is that true?' I explained that when I was a fourteen year old at school, I had enjoyed reading Robert Ballantyne's *The Coral Island* so much that I decided to write a boy's adventure story. Three months later my 120-page manuscript was finished. Raymond's eyes opened wide with amazement. 'Good heavens Alfred, how extraordinary for somebody so young to complete a book in three months. That certainly is a remarkable achievement; surely your parents tried to get it published?'

I shook my head sideways before saying, 'My parents never knew that I had written a book, although one of my teachers read the manuscript; she was impressed and offered to send it to a literary agent for an assessment, but I refused.'

'You refused, why on earth did you refuse?' said Raymond irritably.

Dave answered for me, 'Because at fourteen, Alf was more interested in girls than creative writing.'

Raymond did not ask me what eventually happened to my manuscript. In fact for the last six years the manuscript had been hidden under a layer of dust alongside a pile of old *Beano* and *Dandy* comics in a disused cupboard at my home.

Raymond spent a moment reading his synopsis before carefully folding the notepaper and replacing it in his top pocket. He claimed that his novel *Descent into Darkness* was very loosely based on an actual incident. 'I suppose you could say it's a tragic tale. A post-war but still-serving Army officer named Cartwright who, during a brief period of fragility, committed gross indecency with a young corporal. As a result of this single unfortunate incident, the officer was dismissed from the service; in fact he was lucky not to have been incarcerated. Not only was his promising Army career ruined, but his family and friends heartlessly distanced themselves from him. The following years were extremely difficult for Cartwright; he was unable to find suitable employment or adequate accommodation. When his final savings were spent, the poor fellow became so depressed he threw himself off Tower Bridge and was drowned.'

Our host said that he would welcome any criticism of his synopsis, favourable or negative. I wasn't prepared to give an opinion, but Dave was quite keen to do so.

'If you don't mind me saying so, Raymond, I am not happy with the suicide of Cartwright. I can see that your novel is about rejection and lost hope, and I can fully understand why Cartwright felt so isolated especially after being abandoned by his family and friends, which must have been particularly painful, but don't you feel that you owe it to your readers, especially those readers who might find themselves in a similar predicament to Cartwright? Perhaps, like Cartwright, they feel that life has been so cruel to them, that suicide is a far better option than their sad existence. My point is, I believe that your novel would be of some value if it could illustrate how an individual in the utter depths of despair manages to summon that last vestige of inner strength and cling to hope, rather than allow hope to slip away. I would like to see Cartwright, though suicide is always on his mind, somehow begin to come to terms with his awful life. And by persevering he eventually finds a path of recovery. Let your novel have a happy ending. Explain how Cartwright manages to attain a worthwhile job and suitable accommodation and how he acquires new friends and possibly even a new family too.'

Raymond seemed to be nodding agreeably as Dave gave his opinion. 'Well, David old boy, thank you for your well-constructed analysis. You certainly have given me a great deal to think about. Maybe you're right, perhaps my novel should not be a tale of lost hope, but of hope regained. Who knows, I might finally be able to finish the novel. Of course, writing is always a laborious and costly task for me, especially after two years of working full time on the plot without any regular income.'

As we stood up to leave, I notice Dave discreetly hand Raymond a pound note. Although Dave and I were sober, Raymond was by now noticeably fuddled. Fearing he might fall over, we walked back with him to the entrance of the hostel before continuing on to the Prospect of Whitby for a quick half before closing time. Dave was somewhat concerned about Raymond. He thought that his novel might be autobiographical. The same thought had entered my mind too.

'If that is the case,' said my friend cautiously, 'and Raymond does finish writing the novel but is unable to find a publisher, would he, like the rejected

Throughout his teenage years Dave had a crush on pretty Diane Von Bock, the youngest sister of his brother-in-law. He wrote to her continually while he served in the Navy, hoping one day that she might fall in love with him but his dreams of a romance were shattered when she told him that she could only consider him as a friend. I believe at this point he put on hold any thoughts of looking for a suitable wife and having children. He decided that for the next ten years or so he would stay single, enjoy himself and concentrate on having affairs with any women that would fall for his considerable charms. One of his liasons at this stage was the attractive, young, neglected wife of a middle aged American Ambassador. Shortly afterwards he narrowly escaped with his life when he was shot at by the outraged husband of one of the women he was pursuing. 'She told me that she was separated and that her husband was working abroad.

Instead of her waiting for me at my shack, when I opened the door I found myself facing a snarling stranger armed with a shotgun.' 'What happened? How did you get away?' I enquired. 'He asked if my name was Upson. When I said no it was Jennings and that I was an acquaintance of Upson, he then lowered the gun and demanded to know where he was. At this point I bolted and ran toward the bush. That was when he fired and thankfully he missed but it was close.'

Cartwright, feel compelled to make his way to Tower Bridge?'

The only answer I could give was, 'Hopefully not.'

Besides paying rent to his landlady Peggy Johnson, Dave from time to time would give her extra money 'to help to pay her way.' Peggy's husband Henry, a mixed-race ex-seaman from West Africa, was sometimes unemployed. During these unemployed periods he drank heavily. With three young children to care for and an unreliable though loving husband, Peggy often struggled to meet her commitments. Dave would never ask or expect repayment.

I am sure my friend was reasonably content living in Buross Street during the late 1950s. Everything he needed to make his bachelor life style comfortable was at hand: the Lord Nelson pub was at the top of his street and the more popular Refiner's Arms was at the bottom. D&W Handbags where he worked was situated in nearby Cannon Street Road and the Palaseum cinema and Watney Street market were just a few minutes' walk away. With a succession of girlfriends available and with just enough money to enjoy himself, he had no cause to complain.

In 1959 Dave bought a Francis Barnett Light Cruiser motorbike that he kept parked outside Peggy's house. Several times that year I saw him riding around the East End with a pretty girl on the pillion with her arms around his waist.

I remember one Sunday morning during the late summer standing alongside my pushbike with my mouth watering at the sight of a girl's shapely legs mounting his motorbike. Shortly afterwards and to his loud shout of 'Davy Crocket, king of Commercial Road!' they rode off to Southend-on-Sea.

Although Dave had no cooking facilities in his room, Peggy would sometimes cook him a meal, but usually he made use of the local Maltese cafés. Eating was never a problem for Dave because his appetite was so small and it was not one of his priorities. Dave thought that I had a voracious appetite. While I devoured a large spaghetti bolognese at Buttigieg's café in nearby Backchurch Lane, Dave just had coffee and a boiled egg. After I finished the meal he remarked, 'If only I could smoke and drink less, I am sure that I would eat more.'

Dave's readiness to assist friends and acquaintances financially, albeit with small amounts of cash, was admirable. Never once in my presence did he react rudely, impatiently or dismissively when asked for money. Even though he rarely had much money to spare, he would still dip into his pocket and give gladly.

The only people whom Dave and I side-stepped were the numerous 'meth-drinkers' who were often to be seen begging along the Whitechapel Road. David Upson simply amazed me. I have never met anybody before or since that June day in 1959 when I first met Dave who was genuinely liked by so many people of different backgrounds. The key to his popularity may have been, besides his obvious kindness and generosity, the tolerant attitude he always adopted towards people. I am sure that he was blessed with a unique understanding of human nature.

I had noticed over the years how he always reacted differently to each person he came into contact with. Somehow he was able to detect instantly what their strengths and weaknesses were and to know how to respond to them and act accordingly. He would often modulate the tone of his voice when talking to acquaintances, sometimes speaking faster and more firmly, at other times quieter, or with the elderly slower and more gently. Always tactful and circumspect, his speech was never cold or impersonal but warm and reassuring. His wit and ability to mock at his own misfortune and to make you laugh was a joy to witness.

'How do you know so many people?' I once asked him.

He thought for a moment before saying, 'Mostly in the pubs and clubs and down the markets I guess.' The more I got to know and like this unique, friendly and interesting man the more I wanted to find out about his background.

2

Family Background

Sitting one evening on the same riverside balcony at the Angel pub at Rotherhithe where the American painter J. A. M. Whistler had been exactly a hundred years previously and had produced one of his famous Thames etchings, Dave told me about his family life in Burma, where he was born in 1927. Daood (Donald) Upson, his father, was of Portuguese, English and Indian extraction. Originally a Roman Catholic, at an early age Daood became disillusioned with Catholicism and converted to Islam. Eventually he became an enthusiastic follower of his new faith. Entering journalism as a young man, the talented Daood was soon on the editorial staff of the *Bombay Chronicle*. A few years later he became editor of the nationalist and congress paper, *The Independent and the Nation*. As editor, he campaigned zealously for Indian independence. After resigning his editorship, he accepted a post as an academic at the Jamia Millia Islamia (the National Moslem University). He also embarked on an extensive visit to Persia and Turkey; his brief was to obtain first-hand information about these Islamic countries and to explain to his leading Moslem contacts what he considered to be the true aspirations of India. Whilst touring these countries he regularly posted interesting and colourful travel articles under the heading 'Lands of the Crescent' to a leading Indian newspaper.

Tragically, in 1928, at the young age of thirty-six, and just prior to visiting Afghanistan, Daood Upson succumbed to pneumonia. David was just one year old at the time of his father's death. After Daood died, David's mother Doris who was a former governess was left to bring up David and his elder sister, Barbara. With hardly any income, life became so precarious that Doris was forced to sell her late husband's correspondence with T. E. Lawrence (Lawrence of Arabia) to Macmillan, the London publishers. Following several years of widowhood, Doris moved to Rangoon where she formed a relationship with a senior civil servant, who was able to financially support the Upson family. David was not totally happy with this new domestic situation; he believed that his mother's boyfriend disliked him.

For much of the mid-1930s, Barbara spent nine months of the year at a boarding school in India whilst David attended local schools in Rangoon.

David was twenty-one when he became skipper of the 46-ton, deep-sea trawler *Khin Khin Lay*. He found it amusing that the original name of the Australian-built boat was *John Thomas*, a name that he was familiar with having read *Lady Chatterley's Lover*. The three and a half years that he spent on the trawler fishing in the Andaman Sea was the happiest period of his life. He would speak so affectionately of 'my ship' that he had to struggle to hold back the tears, and by the expression on his face I could see that the memories of those far off days were ever constant.

Although he proved a diligent pupil his preference was for sports, particularly boxing, at which he excelled.

Temporarily separated from his mother in March 1941, when she went to stay with friends in the country, David was sent to live with Barbara on a small farm on the outskirts of Rangoon that was owned by her fiancé's parents. These were halcyon days for David; he loved working on the farm after school. He fondly remembered feeding the pigs, milking and grazing cattle and picking fruit in the orchards. It was in one of these orchards that he had his first sexual experience with a local girl.

With his beloved mother now living close by he was extremely happy and contented, but his idyllic life was about to change. On 21 December 1941 the Japanese Air Force ruthlessly bombed Rangoon, killing over two thousand people. This bombardment caused a mass exodus of four hundred thousand civilians, almost the entire population of the town. When the bombers returned two days later Rangoon had virtually been abandoned.

David and fellow shipmate Ferdy, Liverpool, February 1954.

The Japanese were now bombing the area day and night. With the markets closed and few shops from which to buy food, and the animals on the farm either eaten or stolen, desperate measures were needed to survive. Dave smiled when he recalled making regular trips to a RAF station on his pet donkey Benny, and pleading with the personnel for bread for the animal. Little did the servicemen realise that the bread was also sustenance for the Upson family.

At this time, he kept a school notebook in which he would record the times and dates of the Japanese air raids, what damage had been done by the bombing, and how many aircraft had been shot down. He also visited the crash sites to collect parts of the planes as souvenirs.

With the Japanese land forces now marching towards Rangoon it was time for the Upson family to evacuate themselves. So on 19 February 1942 David and his Mother left Rangoon by ship for India, arriving in Calcutta three days later. Barbara who had recently married her fiancé, a top civil servant, stayed behind in Rangoon while her husband was ordered to help with the destruction and torching of government buildings. With the enemy increasingly close, Barbara fled north by car to Mandalay. On reaching Mandalay, she had to hide in a cemetery while the Japanese bombers flew low overhead. She later met up with her husband and they continued their journey north to the little town of Myitkina with its tiny airstrip; but their hopes of being airlifted out of the country were dashed when they were told by airport staff that it was now far too dangerous for the RAF to land and take out any more civilians.

Shortly after his mother Doris arrived in London in the summer of 1961, David took her on a sightseeing tour of the West End.

Unsure of what the outcome would be if they took the advice of a British Army officer to make their way to Fort White, Barbara suggested to her husband, 'Look, we are young and still fit, so let's walk to India.' Walking to India would be a marathon trek even for the hardiest. Not only was India 300 miles away, the refugees would have to pass through the notorious dense jungle of the Hukawng Valley, commonly known by its more sinister name, 'The Valley of Death'. For Barbara and her husband and the thousands of other refugees the journey became a nightmare. The more resourceful refugees managed to survive by eating roots and tiny fish that they caught from the edge of the rivers, but tragically the sick and the elderly soon expired in the harsh conditions.

During the trek, Barbara discovered a dying young refugee. The girl was lying under a tree and being eaten alive by a mountain of red ants. Other refugees went to her aid, but they were unable to save her.

Fortunately, the refugees were shown mercy by the fierce Naga tribesmen who dwelt in the valley. Although known 'head-hunters' the tribesmen remained unseen, but occasionally threw small packets of rice wrapped in leaves onto the paths of the trekkers. Eventually food was dropped by aircraft too, although for many it came too late. Nobody knows how many people died on the trek; incalculable numbers were decimated by exhaustion, disease and starvation. Out of Barbara's group of twenty, only five survived the trek including her husband, now stricken with malaria.

The journey lasted for forty-two days until at last they reached the little town of Margherita in Northern Assam. From there they were taken by train to Calcutta where Barbara was reunited with her mother and David who

Above left: David's mother Doris wearing her wartime airforce uniform.

Above right: Barbara Upson, David's sister in 1972.

were staying in emergency accommodation. A few months later Mrs Upson had to leave Calcutta to take up an appointment in Bombay so Dave moved in with his brother-in-law's family, the Von Bocks.

When Dave left school in the summer of 1942 and in between looking for work, he spent much of his spare time 'loafing around' Calcutta's docks watching the shipping and dreaming of becoming a sailor. During the autumn he applied to join the Merchant Navy, but due to a lack of vacancies his application was turned down. Terribly disappointed, he was forced to accept a low-paid job at the workshops of Clayhall-Supercraft, a boat-building company. The restless David had no intention of remaining a 'landlubber' indefinitely. If he was unable to join the Merchant Navy, there was an alternative. Although still underage, he applied to enlist in the Burmese Royal Navy Voluntary Reserve.

The following year, in February 1943, pretending that he was eighteen and after several failed attempts to join the Burma Royal Navy Volunteer Reserve (BRNVR), the fifteen-year-old David Upson was finally accepted and became Recruit 538 in Burma's tiny but rapidly expanding navy. His mother Doris was soon to be in a uniform too; she became a sergeant in the air force.

For me, having remained within the periphery of the East End for most of my eighteen years, listening to Dave's stories and adventures was a godsend and made me keener than ever to join the Merchant Navy. Dave and I left the Angel pub and walked eastwards down Rotherhithe Street. We past the row of eighteenth-century river-fronted houses with their rear balconies and patios full of potted plants, a picturesque scene so loved by Wapping artists

There is no known photograph of David's father
Donald Upson, only this undated drawing from
the 1920s survives.

on the opposite side of the river. The long time closed Jolly Waterman pub
at number 59 was then the home of Tony Armstrong Jones who was soon
to marry Princess Margaret. A few years later the local council, for reasons
of its own and despite a campaign to save them and many signatures of
support collected, including mine, ruthlessly went ahead and demolished
these historical houses. A priceless legacy of Rotherhithe's heritage was now
lost forever. One solitary building that housed the offices of Braithwaite &
Dean, the lighterage firm, was spared and is still there today now completely
restored.

We continued walking down Rotherhithe Street that led us into the wide
alley with its nineteenth-century warehouses on either side. Suddenly, the
aroma of spices filled our nostrils. It was the same gorgeous aroma that Dave
and I enjoyed whenever we were in the vicinity of the Travers Spice Mill at
Wapping. At the end of the alley, we arrived at the little church of St Mary
the Virgin built in 1714 on the site of a medieval church. According to a sign
on the churchyard's railings, the body of Christopher Jones, Captain of the
Mayflower, the ship that in 1620 carried the Pilgrim Fathers to Massachusetts,
lies buried in its neglected cemetery. I wondered what marvellous stories of
the sea and the new world Captain Jones would have had to tell when he
returned to Rotherhithe.

Dave suggested a quick half in the small, ancient riverside pub directly
opposite St Mary's church. This white-painted pub sandwiched in between
Victorian warehouses was formerly known as the Spread Eagle, but with
the arrival of the first tourists in the 1950s, it was renamed the Mayflower.
The cheerful barman who served our drinks claimed that despite the ever-
increasing number of visitors from abroad, the Mayflower was still popular

Above left: The former offices of Braithewaite & Dean, the Thames lighterage firm, that backs onto the Thames at Rotherhithe.

Above right: Dave and lady friend outside the Mayflower Tavern, Rotherhithe, 1994.

with local dockers and mill workers. He also mentioned that British and American postage stamps could be purchased at the Mayflower and that no other pub in the country had been allowed this concession.

When the barman began to serve other customers, Dave turned to me and said, 'You might not be able to buy stamps in Cable Street pubs, but what I did witness were sailors openly selling hemp, watches, jewellery, coshes, daggers and even loaded revolvers and, believe it or not, a shrunken human head.' Outside on the riverside terrace, I overheard a small dapper man of about ninety reminiscing to a group of Americans about his life as a cabin boy in the 1880s.

Of all of the riverside taverns that Dave and I visited over the years from the Dove in Hammersmith, to The Pavilion in North Woolwich, none of their interiors would give you a sense and a link with the past like the Mayflower could, although the Samuel Pepys restaurant in the Prospect of Whitby and the little Dickens room in The Grapes at Limehouse have remained unchanged for generations.

Leaning over the balcony of the Mayflower and watching the mass of barges bumping together by the wash of a passing ships, Dave told me how much he missed his mother and sister whom he had not seen for over six years and how he dreamt of the day when he would meet them again. My friend had to wait for a further two years before they would join him in London.

The Upson family with
a long side-burned
Alfred Gardener.

Metropolitan Wharf,
Wapping Wall. These
old warehouses stacked
next to each other
seemed to go on forever.
During the 1950s
and '60s , Wapping's
dockside was a hive of
activity, but at nightime
it became peaceful and
quiet and was always
welcoming.

Oliver's Wharf, Wapping High
Street.

After leaving the Mayflower Dave agreed to my suggestion that we should
walk to Greenwich, but when we reached the nearby bascule bridge at the
entrance to the Albion Dock basin, heavy rain caused us to change our mind,
so we turned around and went home walking briskly through the noisy and
fumed-filled Rotherhithe Tunnel.

It was by this same bascule bridge 20 years later that a fat, middle-aged
drunken gypsy blocked my path. He appealed to me to try and rescue
Nelson his one-eyed pet Alsatian that had fallen from the stone stairs into
the Thames. In my haste to help, I slipped on the wet slime-covered steps and
nearly joined the drowning dog. After a few minutes I managed to grab his
collar and haul him out. The whimpering dog, thin and neglected, resembled
a starved greyhound. Of course the dog had no qualms about soaking me
when he shook the water from its fur. Without a word being said, his owner
substituted a greasy rope for a lead and dragged the poor animal away.

3

'To Sir With Love' – Really?

As Dave seemed genuinely interested in my background, I decided to loan him a recently-published book *To Sir With Love*, the supposed memoirs of E. R. Braithwaite, a black teacher from Guyana who had spent several months in 1953 teaching in what was described as a 'tough East End school'. This so called tough school was my school St George-in-the-East in Cable Street, Stepney, where I had spent four happy years from the late summer of 1952. My three sisters and younger brother also attended St George's.

Knowing that I was very interested to hear his opinion of the book Dave returned it a few days later after reading it over the weekend. That same evening, Dave and I sat opposite each other in The Nelson's Head. He had made a few notes on the back of an envelope and was ticking them off as he spoke. He said the book reminded him of the American film *The Blackboard Jungle* that he had seen two or three years previously. He also thought that, 'Braithwaite, despite suffering racial discrimination from prospective English employers and landlords, takes up the challenge to teach undisciplined and mainly white East End children. Faced with opposition and rejection he steadfastly refuses to be worn down and driven away by the unruly pupils. Braithwaite's tenacity paid off and in due course he earns the pupils respect and trust'. Dave had thoroughly enjoyed the book. He believed that the teacher was caring and dedicated and that he came across as an honest writer.

As I had reservations about the authenticity of *To Sir With Love*, Dave was curious to know why. So I spent the next ten minutes reminiscing about my schooldays at St George's, recalling the time when Braithwaite, a tall and humourless disciplinarian with a fiery temper, first arrived at my school. Although Alex Bloom, the head master, had banned corporal punishment, Braithwaite ignored the ruling. On several occasions, I saw him manhandle a boy in the gymnasium. Besides teaching PE, Braithwaite also taught geography, but these lessons were often restricted to tales of his background in Guyana. A typical story was of when he and his father went hunting in the jungle. To reach the hunting grounds, they travelled up-river by canoe. The sport went well and they shot a wild pig. Fearing that the pig's heavy carcass might cause the canoe to capsize, they tied a rope to the carcass, lowered it into the river and attached the other end of the rope to the stern of the canoe. Once secured, they set about rowing home. When the father and son eventually disembarked, they discovered that only the pig's head remained at the end of the rope; the body and legs had been devoured by piranhas.

In the classroom, Braithwaite was very strict. He was also prone to throwing missiles at pupils whom he thought were not paying sufficient attention to the lesson he was giving: keys, chalk and wooden-handled blackboard dusters or any other object that was handy on his desk would be hurled at us. In my class twelve-year-old John Smith was lucky to avoid being injured. Braithwaite had thrown an inkwell at him with great force. Fortunately, John saw the inkwell coming towards him in line with his face and instinctively he lifted the lid of his desk to act as a shield.

Dave interrupted me. 'I did not read about that incident in the book.'

'Of course not,' I replied. 'Braithwaite obviously did not want to reveal that part of his uncontrollable temper, but I can assure you it was true.' Dave was puzzled. 'Do you think it's possible he did not really like teaching East End kids?'

'Braithwaite did not like the St George's boys, it seemed plainly evident at the time and we certainly did not like him. It was mutual resentment. He neither approved of me nor the poem that I had written about him. There was also a rumour that some of the older girls felt uncomfortable near him.' Dave shook his head in disbelief, 'He seems to me to be bad news.'

I recalled how a teacher Mrs Dymphna Porter taught me to write poetry, and when it was suggested that I should write some poems about the teachers and then read them out on stage at the end of term concert, I enthusiastically agreed. I explained to Dave how all the teaching staff, with the exception of Braithwaite, found my poems amusing and they laughed and applauded along with the pupils. I glanced down at Braithwaite when I had finished reading the poems to see his reaction. He sat at the back of the hall at the end of the row of teachers, unsmiling, silent and aloof. His cold, penetrating stare sent a shiver down my young spine.

As Dave and I sat chatting in The Nelson's Head, we were interrupted by the sudden arrival of Bridget, a former Liverpudlian prostitute. Bridget was now working respectably as a clothing machinist in a local factory. I assumed that Dave would be spending the night with her, so I made an excuse and left the pub.

'A teacher affects eternity, he can never tell where his influence stops.'
Henry Brooks Adams 1838-1918

Had Bridget not sat down at our table, I would have spoken at length to Dave about St George's great head master, the marvellous Alex Bloom, who

Alex Bloom was a popular headmaster as this photo proves. The snap taken at our school summer camp in Chichester in 1953 shows a relaxed Alex Bloom with some of his teachers. The headmaster had spent the last thirteen years of his life working tirelessly to make his school a success. He was deeply admired by his staff and adored by most of his pupils. He may have been afflicted with what some describe as unattractive physical features but not by us – we saw no ugliness. (*P. R. Edwards*)

was revered by both pupil and teacher alike. This short unflinching man with his deformed spine, slightly twisted face, brown leathery complexion and hair like silver wire was almost grotesque in appearance, but within his tiny frame beat a heart of pure goodness and I was extremely fond of him.

It was late in the afternoon when Mr Bloom called me to his office. He had been informed that I had inadequate footwear. When he saw my broken old sandals he was visibly moved. I was immediately sent to the shoe shop in nearby Watney Street market, where new shoes were purchased for me with money from his own pocket. Now, if Alex Bloom had done that for me, who knows what assistance he must have given to other poor children, for there were many at the school which was situated in a disadvantaged East End and surrounded by large bombsites and abandoned blitz-damaged houses.

The school that was divided into just eight classes had a maximum of twenty boys and girls in each class. In my sister Mary's class there were just fifteen pupils. A high percentage of the eleven to fifteen year old pupils had, through no fault of their own, inherited many of the hardships associated with poverty. In my own large family there was never enough money for food, coal or clothing.

Alex Bloom, who became headmaster of St George's in October 1945, believed that these children, who came from a poor environment with food still heavily rationed, could hardly be expected to achieve high academic results by attending a school that offered limited opportunities. Two years later Alex Bloom seconded a call by the National Association of Head Teachers to the Labour government to release papers and other materials to overcome an acute shortage of books which resulted in some London schools being reduced to writing on slates.

The headmaster was well aware that the majority of his pupils were keen to leave school at fifteen, find work and earn some precious money. He was also aware that once their schooldays were over, very few former pupils would be in a position to make use of further education. Like their parents and grandparents they were destined to spend their working lives in the local factories and docks. As Alex Bloom could not change the traditional pattern that most of the pupils were born into, he was determined with what resources and facilities he had to try to offer each pupil a reasonable education, albeit a basic one, that would stand him in good stead after he had left school.

Alex Bloom was adamant that a prepared curriculum was not the best policy for St George's School. He believed that it was pointless forcing pupils to study subjects that they did not like or understand. To overcome this obstacle, he devised a plan that would encourage unhappy or sensitive pupils to learn, to take part in the school's activities, and to recognise and develop their own potential and become important and valued members of their class. The headmaster believed that the way for his school to progress would be at the start of the autumn term when the pupils moved up a class;

they would be presented with a list of subjects ranging from maths, English, geography, science and the arts. They would then be given an opportunity to choose subjects from the list that they wished to study in the coming year. Usually these 'elective activities' were for afternoon periods only. Providing that their choice was well balanced and the teachers were in agreement, they would have his consent.

Another novel idea that Alex Bloom introduced was the extremely popular 'Weekly Review.' Every Friday morning, pupils could, with impunity, write about their school attendance for the previous week. We were free to criticise or praise teachers, we could say if we were happy or not about a particular lesson that was being taught, and if the lesson was useful, necessary or irrelevant. We could make suggestions that we felt might improve our class study and also recommend places of interests for the explorers group to visit. Among the recommendations accepted were visits to the House of Commons, The Guildhall, The Royal Observatory at Greenwich and even the Peek Freen biscuit factory in South London.

Although unorthodox, Alex Bloom's original ideas worked surprisingly well at St George's. The headmaster was fortunate in having a team of loyal, dedicated teachers whose commitment to the school policies and goals were both positive and absolute.

In late 1954, a newsagent, in nearby Cannon Street Road, 'phoned Alex Bloom and complained that two boys from St George's had stolen sweets and comics from his shop. The headmaster was furious at this accusation. He knew every pupil personally and was so convinced that none of them were thieves, he immediately invited the newsagent to the school. During morning assembly, Alex Bloom stood on the stage alongside the accuser while he scrutinised every pupil. When he realised that the culprits were not from our school, the newsagent lowered his head as if he was ashamed of himself and quickly left the stage.

Peter Reece Edwards may have been the only pupil who did not live in Stepney. His home was at Pimlico. Peter suffered from chronic shyness and also had a hearing impediment. Prior to coming to St George's in 1952 at the age of eleven, Peter's problems had been mis-diagnosed and he was sent to a special school at World's End, Chelsea, which catered for children with learning difficulties. Peter's mother was not happy with this situation. Eventually she took her son to see a child psychiatrist at St George's teaching hospital in West London. After examining Peter, the psychiatrist advised his mother to enrol him at an extraordinary school in Cable Street, Stepney, which had a reputation for accepting children who were shy or introvert.

So from St George-in-the-West, Peter came to St George-in-the-East. Although Peter was extremely nervous and reserved when he first arrived at the school, he soon began to feel at ease especially when he realised that he was being treated no differently from any other child. However, he was still reluctant to converse with the staff and pupils and whenever he spoke to the teachers the conversation was always brief and whispered.

I never knew why I was chosen to look after Peter but I welcomed the commitment. Peter and I sat next to each other in every class from the summer of 1952 until Easter 1956 and we became close friends. Throughout those four years, Peter never uttered a single word to me or any other pupil. In 1953, Alex Bloom felt that Peter would benefit enormously by spending two weeks at St George's summer camp at Chichester. So determined was the headmaster to get Peter to come to the camp, he travelled up to the boy's home and managed to persuade Mrs Reece Edwards to encourage her reluctant son to have the holiday.

Mrs Rose Gamble, a popular staff member (depicted as 'Flinty' in Braithwaite's book) saw that Peter had a talent for painting. With her encouragement and guidance, Peter's well-crafted portraits of world leaders including Churchill, Eisenhower and Chiang Kai Shek, were soon hanging on the walls of the classroom.

I too benefited from close teacher involvement. Not only did Mrs Dymphna Porter show me how to write poetry, she took a keen interest in my short stories and assisted me with the syntax.

Whenever I reflect on my happy schooldays at St George's, I realise how fortunate I was in attending this small vibrant school with its excellent hard working teachers and a headmaster who had tremendous affection for his pupils. I witnessed little bullying or fighting in the playground and truancy and smoking was rare. Free daily milk was available, and thanks to the efforts of Alex Bloom, the huge and wholesome school dinners that were provided, again free in my case, were said to be the envy of the neighbouring schools.

Because of St George's relaxed atmosphere, an absence of strict discipline, regimentation, competitiveness and no prizes being awarded for clever pupils, many of the pupils excelled. Unlike the fictitious children in Braithwaite's book, we were not stupid and certainly not indolent. Many of us were proud of our school and would defend its reputation when questioned by visiting educationalists. In late January 1953, we proved what mature and responsible eleven and twelve year olds we were. As we sat around the classroom coal fire we fiercely debated amongst ourselves why the mentally retarded nineteen-year-old Derek Bentley should not have been hanged at Wandsworth Prison.

There was music too at St George's, for which I am eternally grateful. At the headmaster's instigation, pupils were given a unique opportunity to appreciate music from an early age. Every morning during assembly, and over a four-year period, we listened, many of us enthusiastically, to two recordings of short classical works and operatic arias. A particular favourite of pupils in my class, and often requested, was Reznicek's lively 'Donna Diana' overture.

Although I was not interested in being a member of form panels, the school council or the various staff-pupil committees, I did agree to a suggestion made

The funeral of Alex Bloom, Cable Street, Stepney, September 1955. (*Daily Mirror*)

by Mrs Porter to be the class reporter. In my new role, albeit temporary, I wrote a few short articles about the visits that I had made with the Explorers group. From the stage in the auditorium and in front of staff and pupils I read out these articles. As class reporter, I was invited to attend an important meeting where Alex Bloom addressed parents and visitors. With a notebook balancing on my knee, I sat in the front row of the auditorium and listened and made notes of Alex Bloom's talk. The headmaster confirmed to his audience that as in the past there would be no annual prize presentation for individual pupils; instead several books would be purchased for the school library. The head master believed that by not rewarding clever pupils, the less able pupils would not feel that they were a failure. Alex Bloom explained that many visitors from overseas had recently arrived at St George's. He also mentioned that after the visitors had returned home he had received several letters from them saying how impressed they were of his school's unusual educational policy and by the children's friendliness and self-confidence.

One of my lasting memories of the headmaster is when a group of us pupils sat around him on the beach at Deal in June 1955 listening to his soft mellifluous voice reading us poetry. Just three months after that school holiday, Alex Bloom the great reformer and humanitarian collapsed in his office and died shortly afterwards in the London Hospital at Whitechapel. Mrs Dymphna Porter was by his bedside when he passed away. On the day of his funeral, pupils, parents and a reporter from the *Daily Mirror* assembled outside the school in the rain. We watched the flowerless cortege arrive. In keeping with Jewish tradition, a black cloth was draped over Alex Bloom's coffin. Other cars in the procession were occupied by teachers from St George's and several neighbouring schools. A few days later the reporter's article appeared in the centre pages of the *Daily Mirror* entitled 'Goodbye, Mr Chips' along with photos of the weeping children.

Just before I left school in late March 1956, a group of older children from our school that included Peter and me were escorted by a priest who held a torch and led us on a tour of the dark damp vaults of the nearby St George's church. The smell of decay was appalling; the sight of so many coffins proved too much for some of the girls who made a quick exit complaining that the vaults were the home of Dracula. As children we would peer into the large ground floor glassless windows of the crypt and could see the coffins stacked on top of each other, many of them were within arm's reach. A few coffins had been vandalised revealing their human remains. In the summer of 1954, I watched the police recover a skeleton that had been removed from the vault probably by teenagers and dumped on an adjacent bombsite in Cannon Street Road.

The crypt may have been the home of the dead but that same crypt had given sanctuary to the living. On Saturday, 7 September 1940, the day that the German Blitz on London began, a group of Wapping Christians were returning home from their annual pilgrimage to Chislehurst in Kent where they had visited the grave of Father Lowder, a former and much-loved Wapping priest. As the group were unable to enter Wapping because of the closure of the bridges and the fierce fires that ravaged the warehouses and docks they turned around, crossed the Highway and spent the whole of the night sheltering from the bombs in the crypt of St George's Church.

During my four years at St George's School, only one teacher seemed impatient and often annoyed with the pupils and he was E. R. Braithwaite, whose presence at the school did more harm than good by undermining the order of things. His method of coercing pupils rather than being patient and approachable as preferred by Alex Bloom was better suited for a borstal. Braithwaite remained at my school for just two terms in 1953 and not the seven years as he claims in his famous book. His tenure was not successful and subsequently, to the delight of many of the pupils, he vanished from the school's precincts. Why he left I neither knew nor cared; news of his departure caused several boys in my class to shout euphorically 'good riddance!'.

On his final day at St George's, Braithwaite was given a parting gift inscribed 'To Sir With Love.' The gift was a packet of twenty expensive cigarettes. Not a single boy in my class contributed to the cost. I was surprised to learn later that after leaving St George's, Braithwaite began teaching at Chapman Primary School in nearby Bigland Street where I had attended as an infant from 1947 to 1952. Braithwaite would have felt comfortable at his new school; corporal punishment was on the agenda. The headmaster of Chapman School was the Guernsey-born Christopher Wyatt who was a six

foot six, bald, towering tyrant (who was known as the tallest headmaster in
East London). Wyatt always showed a readiness to cane young boys. I had
been sent to his office to be punished. My grave offence; I giggled during a
lesson. I recall to this day the look of satisfaction on this brutal man's face
as he brought his cane down hard six times across my fingers. Given *carte
blanche* to beat infants, Braithwaite used his knuckles to punch the back of
their little heads. This punch was referred to by the pupils as the 'Braithwaite
Knock.'

My younger brother Brian, a pupil at Chapman Street School during the
mid-1950s, also witnessed Braithwaite's rage. Brian thought that he had
hit the infants because he had become frustrated and impatient with their
inability to understand his Guyanian accent.

Worse than Braithwaite was Miss Dixon, a neurotic teacher who terrified
the Chapman school infants. Like the headmaster, she favoured the use of
the cane, but unlike Braithwaite, who punished only boys, Dixon would
strike girls' fingers with a ruler. Quite often, for no apparent reason, Dixon
would scream out loud; her incessant screaming took place in the classroom,
along the corridors and even in the crowded dining hall; other teachers had
to restrain her. Apparently, her mental condition was caused by the shock of
losing her fiancé on active service during the Second World War.

It could be a testing time for the pupils at lunchtime when Dixon was on
duty in the dining hall. Some of the pupils' behaviour or habits seemed to
antagonise her. If a boy was not sitting upright as he ate his meal, she would
stand behind him, place her arms around his waist and jerk him upwards;
any pupil who was laughing or talking too loud would receive one of Dixon's
vicious stares, sarcastic remarks or a finger pressed hard between their little
shoulder blades. She often singled me out too. I am left-handed when eating
and my 'bad habit' infuriated her; she would grip my wrists very tightly until
I dropped the knife and fork onto the table.

Patty, my shy younger sister, also became one of Dixon's victims. Patty was
so petrified of being shouted at yet again by this cruel, sick teacher, that when
she arrived at the school each morning, she would stand by the gate and refuse
to go inside. My firebrand mother was horrified on hearing of her daughter's
situation; she hurried to the school and attempted to throttle Dixon. At the
age of eleven, Patty left the dreadful Chapman school and spent four happy
years at the wonderful St George's in the East.

Fortunately for East London school children, Braithwaite eventually gave
up teaching and became a social worker for the London County Council. In
1962 he wrote about his new career in a book entitled *Paid Servant*.

On 2 May 2007, Braithwaite gave a talk to the English Speaking Union
at Washington University. He told his audience that St George in the East
School was considered 'unsavoury' and that 'the youngsters who attended
the school were not accepted by other schools, because they were viewed as

undesirable'. Braithwaite also said an English MP described St George's pupils as 'the great unwashed.' Their aspersions were without foundation. Not for a single moment did I, or my brother and three sisters, believe that our school was unsavoury. To put the record straight, we were not refused entry into other schools because we were considered 'undesirable'; we gained entry into St George's School because we lived within the school's catchment area.

In 2011, Keith Harmer an Australian teacher who taught at my school in 1955-56 told me that he thought 'the pupils were well behaved and eager to learn'. Regarding the 'great unwashed', this often quoted remark was never uttered by an English MP to describe St George's pupils during Braithwaite's tenure. In fact the remark can be attributed to the Scottish-born Lord Chancellor Henry Brougham, who died in 1868.

I have always found it sad that millions of people all over the world have read E. R. Braithwaite's book *To Sir With Love*, but very few people have heard of Alexander Abraham Bloom, who in my view was unquestionably the real hero of St George's.

4

Anne

Dave cancelled one of our Saturday evening appointments. He had a date with Anne, a nurse who worked at the Queen Elisabeth Hospital for Children at Shadwell. I was intrigued to know how and where he had met her.

'A couple of weeks ago,' he replied with a twinkle in his eye.

I listened attentively as he explained how he had stopped for a moment outside the hospital entrance to light a cigarette, when suddenly he heard a female voice call from above, 'Smoking is bad for your health.'

He looked up and saw an auburn-haired nurse giggling and leaning out of the window of the staff lounge on the first floor. Dave immediately answered her. 'Smoking is not the only vice I have.'

'And what are these other vices?' she enquired.

'There are too many vices to list here,' replied Dave, who was enjoying the unexpected encounter. Before closing the window, the nurse laughingly accused him of being a 'cheeky devil.'

The cheeky devil would soon meet her again. It was a Sunday afternoon. He had been drinking in the pubs at Wapping. On his way home, he decided to have black coffee at the little refreshment hut in nearby King Edward VII Park. (The park, popularly known as Shadwell Park, was built on the site of an old fish market and opened by King Edward in 1922 for the enjoyment of the people of East London.) To his delight, sitting on the grass and reading was the same nurse whom he had spoken to a few days earlier.

'I am making an effort to give up smoking,' said Dave as he sat down next to her.

'Oh, it's you!' she replied with a smile. My friend who was rarely serious in the company of women, kept her highly entertained for the next hour with his witty remarks and funny jokes. When it was time for the nurse, whose name was Anne, to leave the park, she agreed that Dave could escort her back to the hospital. She also accepted his invitation to join him for a Chinese meal at Limehouse that same evening.

I was soon to meet Anne and her friend Mavis, a nursing assistant. Dave had arranged for us to meet the girls after they had finished their late shift.

The meeting place he chose was the appropriately named Mariners Arms just a hundred yards from the hospital.

I was impressed with Irish-born Anne who was about 5ft 8 inches tall, quite slim, with curly auburn hair, blue eyes and her voice had an attractive lilt. To my regret, pug-nosed Mavis was not one of the pretty lithe nurses whom I had seen wearing bikinis and regularly sunbathing in Shadwell Park. She was rather plain; her hair was dark with a fringe, she lacked height, was a little plump and her Durham accent was so alien to me, I had some difficulty in understanding her.

The Mariners Arms on the Highway and so close to the docks was a popular rendezvous for Royal and Merchant Navy personnel. Fixed to the wall were several warship insignias and a few framed photos of ships. Dave pointed to a large photo of a sailing ship, 'Look, that is the *Cutty Sark*; it's in a dry dock at Greenwich.' The four of us gazed at the photo, but I gazed a little longer than the others. There was something odd about the ship; it could not have been the *Cutty Sark* as Dave had assumed. The *Cutty Sark* had only three masts, but the ship in the photo had four. Before I had time to have a closer look at the photo, Dave, in a sudden spurt of enthusiasm, suggested that the four of us should visit Greenwich Park the following Sunday. 'And whilst there, we can go on board the *Cutty Sark*.' Neither of the nurses had been to Greenwich before, but they readily agreed to the trip.

Dave gave details of his travelling plan. By bus to Island Gardens on the Isle of Dogs; from there we would use the foot tunnel under the Thames emerging at Greenwich's riverside adjacent to the *Cutty Sark*. His keenness to visit Greenwich made me frown, that fortunately went unnoticed. Although I had always enjoyed visiting Greenwich, as it was not then too commercialised, nor teeming with tourists, the thought of having Mavis by my side throughout a Sunday afternoon and trying to elucidate her accent was not very appealing. I would have preferred not to have accompanied them, but felt unwilling to disappoint Dave, so I reluctantly accepted the invitation.

While Dave kept the nurses amused, I left our table and went to examine the photo of the sailing ship. To my surprise, it was the steel hulled *Pamir*. The photo had many signatures of the crew and was dated February 1948, Shadwell Basin, Stepney. Dave and I were well aware of the tragedy of the ill-fated *Pamir*, which was owned by a West German shipping company. Built in Hamburg in 1905, the three-thousand tonne *Pamir* (that had forty thousand feet of sails) was still being used to carry cargo; she was also a training ship for naval cadets. In August 1957, with a cargo of nearly four thousand tons of barley, the *Pamir* left Buenos Aires bound for Hamburg. Her crew consisted of 24 seaman and 52 cadets, most of whom were teenagers. Six weeks later and 600 miles southwest of the Azores, the *Pamir* became trapped in the path of Hurricane Carrie and subsequently sank. Out of 86 souls on board, only four seaman and two cadets managed to survive by hauling themselves onto waterlogged lifeboats.

The following warm Sunday afternoon, Annie, Mavis, Dave and I walked from Shadwell to Limehouse where we boarded the 277 bus that took us to Island Gardens on the Isle of Dogs. As I expected, the narrow Thames foot tunnel was quite busy and extremely noisy with boisterous, shrieking children, running back and forth. Because we were unable to walk four abreast, Dave and Mavis were in front of Anne and me.

Suddenly, above the hullabaloo, Mavis' trembling voice could be heard. 'I don't like it down here, I feel claustrophobic.' Just before we approached the end of the tunnel, Anne slowed down her pace and gave me a small sealed envelope.

Speaking quickly she said, 'Read it when you are alone.' Without answering her, I put the envelope in my trouser pocket.

To my and Dave's dismay, the nurses expressed little interest in visiting the *Cutty Sark* and the National Maritime Museum.

'Perhaps later,' said Anne. It was Greenwich's beautiful and spacious park that they wanted to explore. Anne was to repeat 'perhaps later' when Dave tried to persuade her and Mavis to have a few drinks before going into the park. Not put off by Anne's refusal, my friend was determined to adhere to his regular Sunday afternoon drinking routine.

'Listen, girls, you go on ahead and Alf and I will meet you in about an hour's time by the oldest tree in the park; you can easily find it because there is a door cut into its trunk.' The girls made no objection.

As they were going into the park, Mavis patted her stomach, 'When you come, can you bring some sandwiches?' A few minutes later, Dave and I were relaxing and sitting sipping beer in the riverside garden of the Yacht Inn. Almost to the hour we left the Yacht. While he joined the queue at in his favourite Greenwich café, Anna Abusi's, to buy sandwiches, I waited outside and opened Anne's envelope. What she had written astonished me.

'Alfred, I do not want to give you the wrong impression that I am David's girlfriend. It's true I am very fond of him, but he is about fifteen years older than me and I hope you don't mind me saying so; I really would like us to meet privately. In a week's time, my leave is due and I will be looking after my sister's flat in Cricklewood while she is on holiday in Jersey. Maybe you would like to come and see me there and if you are interested, could you confirm by meeting me outside the hospital tomorrow evening at 9 p.m. and I will give you my sister's address and we can make final arrangements. PS Please don't mention this note to David.'

As I read the note, I became excited. Not only was Anne an attractive and desirable woman, she seemed to like me. I visualised arriving at the flat. Anne would barely have had the time to close the front door when I would have picked her up and carried her straight to the bedroom. An opportunity like this was every red-blooded young man's dream. Only a fool would have refused her offer, and I was certainly no fool.

The feeling that engulfed me after reading Anne's note was so intense I could have danced happily on the pavement. When Dave came out of the café with a carrier bag of the sandwiches and soft drinks, I just managed to conceal my excitement.

As arranged, Anne and Mavis were waiting by the oldest tree in the park. 'Now we can have a picnic,' said the hungry Mavis when she spotted the carrier bag that Dave was holding. While the four of us sat on the grass and ate our sandwiches, I discreetly nodded to Anne who discreetly nodded back. She seemed a little reluctant to make conversation with Dave.

After our picnic was over, we wandered around the perimeter of the park and spent a few minutes in the forecourt of the observatory, but we did not go inside. Mavis and Anne preferred to walk, rather than join Dave and me as we ran down the steep hill in front of The National Maritime Museum. The girls showed no interest in visiting the Museum, but we did persuade them to board the *Cutty Sark*. Dave loved the old tea clipper; he knew every inch of the ship having been a regular visitor ever since she was brought to the Greenwich dry dock in 1954.

In later years, friends would often join Dave and me on board and he would adopt the role of a guide, explaining how the sails worked, the use of wind and tide, how to navigate by compass, the stars and rule of thumb. He knew his art; often visitors would follow in his wake believing that he was a member of the staff.

Unfortunately, our stay on the *Cutty Sark* with Anne and Mavis was brief. We were surrounded and jostled by some ill-mannered visitors in the ship's hold where the cargo of tea was originally stored. Moreover, Mavis complained that her claustrophobia had returned and demanded to be taken off the ship.

Anne thought that the foot tunnel might again prove an ordeal for Mavis. 'Not to worry,' said Dave, 'I know an alternative route back to Shadwell.' The route was ideal; a short bus journey from Greenwich to Surrey Docks, then the underground to Wapping, which was just a ten-minute walk to the Queen Elizabeth Hospital.

Sitting on the bus that took us to Surrey Docks, I began to reflect on the contents of Anne's note and I started to feel somewhat ashamed. Dave was now a valued friend and here was I going behind his back, surreptitiously making a date with Anne, whom he assumed was his girlfriend. Gradually the idea of visiting her at Cricklewood began to seem less appealing.

By the time the four of us had arrived at Wapping underground station, I felt so guilty; I knew that I could not keep my date with Anne. I would just have to forfeit the opportunity of perhaps sleeping with her.

Shortly after Dave and I had said goodbye to the girls at the hospital entrance and we were walking slowly home, my friend remarked, 'Alf, did you notice this afternoon how Anne seemed to be giving me the cold shoulder? In fact, I honestly believe that she fancies you.' It would have been pointless for me to respond to Dave's comments by saying that I did not notice Anne being aloof towards him and that she fancied me. My friend was far too intelligent and observant to believe me. I carefully chose my words, but made no mention of Anne's note. 'I think you are probably right Dave, but I can assure you, I would never contemplate making a date with Anne behind your back.'

'And why not, Alf?' he replied. 'Surely, all is fair in love and war.'

'All is fair in love and war?' I echoed. 'Well I am not sure if that is, or should be the case.'

Dave continued. 'Actually, I agree with you Alf, though perhaps others would disagree. They would argue that when it comes to women and war, there are no rules of engagement.'

Rather than change the subject I said, 'Now, if you had decided to stop seeing Anne, that would be a different situation. Then I might be tempted to make a date with her, but first I would have informed you of my intention.'

Dave gently elbowed my ribs. 'You are a good mate, Alf.'

I never kept my appointment with Anne outside the hospital.

5

Dave's Girlfriends

Dave may not have had a relationship with Anne, but he was certainly having relationships with other women. One of the women was a divorced redhead who lived in Stepney's Jubilee Street. Although attractive, she was not very intelligent, and after just a few drinks she became moody, ill-tempered and constantly made fatuous remarks and liberally used the f-word. Upset with Dave one evening in the Hungerford Arms over his evasiveness to discuss marriage, the redhead left the pub in a hurry after accusing him of only wanting her for a 'quick poke'.

Another girl whom Dave was romancing at the same time was Rosie whom I much preferred than the redhead. Rosie was a reasonably educated, well-mannered country girl who spoke with a slight East Anglian accent. Her face was photogenic with high cheekbones, large brown eyes and perfect teeth. Having pretty features enabled her to obtain some work as a model while she tried to pursue her real interest, which was to enrol at a drama school to study acting.

I can recall Rosie complaining to Dave how demeaning it was to be a model. She despised the 'leeches that controlled the business and the sleazy photographers who are more interested in my body than in my face'. Eventually, Rosie gave up her intermittent modelling work when she was asked to play the part of a 'saucy waitress' in a cheap film that was to be made in a former old vicarage somewhere in Surrey. Dave became alarmed for Rosie's safety. She rented a room in Parfett Street, Whitechapel and had been accosted by alcoholics from the nearby Rowton House working men's hostel. Dave had also seen her in the street being observed by a well-known Maltese pimp from Cable Street.

I thought that my friend was worrying unnecessarily. There was absolutely no chance of Rosie ever becoming a call girl; she was far too respectable, but I did agree with Dave that it would probably be wise if she moved out of Parfett Street. Later, when I suggested that as an alternative measure he should consider setting up home with Rosie, he frowned before saying, 'Alf, your suggestion is impractical, it's just not possible for me to take on that kind of commitment at the moment; besides, where would we live? And there is the problem of Mum; I want her to stay with me when she eventually leaves Calcutta'.

In due course, Rosie gave up modelling work and because she was unable to enrol at a drama school she decided to return to Norfolk for a holiday; whist there she would re-assess her situation. Dave was pleased that she had made the decision and offered to pay the train fare, but to his regret Rosie suddenly postponed the trip after reading about the Theatre Workshop at Stratford.   With her interest in drama rekindled she asked Dave to take her to see *Sparrows Can't Sing*, the latest Joan Littlewood production. Sitting in the Theatre Royal for a couple of hours would have been an ordeal for Dave; he would quickly lose interest and become restless. His poor excuse to avoid accompanying her to Stratford was rejected by Rosie. He even appealed to me to go in his place. However, after a second attempt by Rosie to persuade Dave to see the play, he agreed. His grateful girlfriend gave him a wink and said, 'I will make it up to you afterwards'.

When I asked him the following evening what he thought of the production, an anguished expression appeared on his face and he uttered, 'Never again. It was awful. I must have been stark raving mad to have agreed to take her there, but that's what happens when you have had too much to drink, you make silly promises'.

Having two girlfriends simultaneously presented a problem for Dave. Two or three times he mistakenly arranged to meet them both on the same evening. This was where I proved useful. Because few people had phones in those days, I twice became a messenger and hurried around to where the girls lived with a note cancelling his date. Always aware that he could be exposed as a 'two-timer' and wanting to avoid a possible showdown, he decided to keep a small diary to record his future appointments. As usual, after a few months with the same girlfriend, he would become bored with her company. Discreetly, he would start looking around for other women, but there was always the same problem; Dave always found it difficult to end relationships. He neither had the heart or the courage to explain to a girlfriend that their affair was over. He always preferred the girl to take the initiative and leave him. Fortunately providence was at hand.

In the autumn of 1960 both girls suddenly left the East End. The redhead met a soldier and went to live near his barracks, and Rosie left for Norwich to stay with friends. A few weeks later Dave received a letter from her saying that she had joined a local drama group and was very happy. Rosie's letter gave Dave an excuse not to contact her.

Of all of his girlfriends that I met over the years, Rosie was my favourite; she was intelligent, good-natured and kind. None of the other women in his life had her combined qualities. She could have become an ideal future wife for him, but it was not to be. His desire for endless fleeting affairs would exclude any chances of a warm, loving relationship to develop and become permanent.

It was a most welcome experience for me to be in Dave's company at this time; I was young and very inquisitive about girls and the Merchant Navy, knowledge of which he had in abundance. Because he was by nature tolerant and patient, my endless probing questions did not seem to irritate him. How mightily impressed I was at his popularity with women, but never envious, nor did I try to emulate him. It was not necessary. Just by being in his company I was meeting more and more attractive girls. It seems that Dave's perennial belief in the language of the eyes and acute understanding of human nature paid off. He claimed that by studying women's eyes, he could easily detect what part of his character they found interesting, then nurture that interest to his advantage.

Having relationships with a succession of women whose personalities and backgrounds could not be more different was an ongoing challenge and delight for Dave. My friend did not have to wait long to become involved with more women after the redhead and Rosie left Stepney. One of these brief liaisons was with 'tempestuous Tina', an unemployed clothing packer from Mile End. Not satisfied with kicking her last employer in the groin for 'touching her up,' and still fretting over being dismissed for her retribution, Tina planned to return to the factory, confront her former employer, and as she put it 'cut him up proper with my Sweeney Todd'.

Dave took her threat seriously. While she was asleep, he removed a cut-throat razor from her handbag. The task of disposing this vicious blade was given to me. The following evening, as I crossed the swing bridge at Wapping Lane, I tossed the blade into the murky waters of the Eastern dock.

In due course Tina's luck changed for the better. She moved away from Stepney and found a new job and a new boyfriend. Dave was glad when she went because he had by then met Jennifer, an idealistic voluntary social worker. Jennifer was writing a thesis on the ever-growing problem of vagrancy and alcoholism in the Whitechapel area. During her field study, Jennifer had followed a drunken tramp clutching an empty bottle to a hardware store in Commercial Road. This store was situated just fifty yards from Dave's lodgings at Buross Street.

Determined to pinpoint and shame East End shopkeepers who were selling methylated spirits to vagrants, Jennifer waited outside the store for the tramp to come out with his purchase. Now having the evidence, she then attempted to persuade customers from entering the store and suggested that they should buy their goods elsewhere. Dave, who had just left the nearby Nelson's Head noticed her having a heated argument with one of the owners of the store. Noticing how attractive she was, he decided to intervene on her behalf. The storeowner was alarmed at the sudden appearance of Dave, who stood beside her with his hands on hips feigning truculence. Jennifer, seeing that she now had a formidable ally became fearsome and Dave found himself having to restrain her from attempting to punch the 'merchant of death.' He managed to calm her down. Shortly afterwards he took her to a local café for coffee.

After leaving the café they then spent the rest of the afternoon walking around the area and chatting. If Jennifer wanted to know more about alcoholism in the East End she was with the right man, for Dave had a considerable drinking problem that would plague him for the rest of his life.

Sitting by the river at Shadwell Park a serious discussion took place. Always pessimistic when it came to matters relating to alcoholism, Dave explained to Jennifer that although there was a difference between a heavy drinker and an alcoholic, it could be difficult distinguishing the two. 'You first have to identify and then treat the underlying psychological problem before you could even think about curing an alcoholic and that is no easy task.' He admitted that he drank regularly and sometimes far too much and if he was not careful, his drinking could get permanently out of hand. Jennifer maintained that although alcoholism was a chronic relapsing illness, with the right treatment it was curable. Although Dave partially agreed with her, he felt that treatment would only be beneficial if drunks and alcoholics possessed the willpower to abstain. He also believed that the methylated spirit drinkers were different; their addiction was so powerful they were beyond help.

When Jennifer told Dave that she planned to interview vagrants on bombsites, he advised her against it, warning her that if she went ahead with her plan and without an escort, she could find herself in dangerous situations. He suggested that she should give up her study altogether, as it was totally unsuitable for a young woman. Dave's sound advice was ignored and Jennifer began to interview vagrants, trying to record their background and present circumstances.

During her wanderings around the Whitechapel area she also compiled a list of the shops that sold the methylated spirits. When the list was eventually taken to the police and the Salvation Army, she was told that they already knew where the spirits was being sold but were powerless to take action. Not disheartened by the negative response she received, Jennifer was determined to continue with her study. Her latest plan was to disguise her looks by wearing dirty old clothes and to mingle with a group of alcoholics who regularly sat around a bonfire on waste ground at Aldgate East.

'And why would you want to do that?' asked a bewildered Dave.

'So I can be trusted and accepted by them and learn a little more about their tragic lives.' Dave emphatically advised Jennifer not to do so and he warned her that the 'meth-men' might beat her up. His warning was not heeded. Two of the alcoholics saw through her guise, suspecting that she was, or might be what Dave termed a 'copper's nark,' and they attacked her with a bottle. Dave, by now romantically involved with Jennifer, was shocked to see her bruised arms. He implored her to avoid any further contact with vagrants. This time Jennifer did listen to my friend. Although still optimistic and keen to finish her thesis, she eventually decided that perhaps it was better to abandon her study and leave it to more able people. She also decided to spend some time at her parent's home in Devonshire. Dave escorted a tearful Jennifer to Paddington Station where she boarded a train to the West Country. He even found the time to answer her letters, but stopped corresponding once she became engaged to a farmer.

Strolling around the East End with Dave was always a joyful experience for me. Although there were building sites everywhere and huge blocks of high-rise flats and many maisonettes being erected, it was still possible to walk down and admire the few remaining old streets and courtyards; but with the council's typical lack of foresight they were bulldozing away whole streets and terraces that should not have been classified as slums.

As young as I was, I felt sad witnessing the demolition of ancient artisan and Huguenot cottages in Bethnal Green. Many of these cottages were easily recognisable with their wide windows that gave extra light to the silk weavers as they worked their looms.

In late April 1960, Dave and I stood amongst a large crowd of local people who had gathered at a Stepney bombsite. A workman had been buried by a landslide of earth and rubble while digging the foundations for a new block of flats on the corner of Bigland Street and Cannon St Road. We were hoping that the man would survive when the rescue team dug him out but sadly, 33-year-old Albert Charles Day of Brixton perished. Somebody in the crowd, who obviously had a grievance against the council's massive building programme said, 'If only that poor devil had known what a slum he was helping to build for the future, perhaps he would never have worked there in the first place'.

Dave and I were extremely fond of the world-famous Railway Tavern that was opposite the West India Dock gate at Limehouse. The pub was generally referred to by its more popular name 'Charlie Brown's'. Charlie Brown 'the uncrowned king of Limehouse' had died several years before. During his tenure as the landlord he amassed a large collection of old curios from all over the world, either sold or pawned to him by stranded or penniless seamen. Many of the items displayed in the 'sailors' bar' included old spears, shields, wooden clubs and weaponry. Ships' figureheads were fixed to the wall and an enormous mural of Port Said completely covered one area. The atmosphere seemed to have been deliberately created for the benefit of the seaman.

A separate bar in Charlie Brown's was reserved for the exclusive use of the heavy drinkers from the Salvation Army hostel in nearby Garfield Street.

In later years Charlie Brown's became very popular with our girlfriends during our regular dockland pub crawls; and despite our concerns of possible scuffles occurring, which they did from time to time, we often drank there.

The customers who patronised the pub were mostly dockers, seamen, and the inevitable few prostitutes and as always, predatory homosexual men on the lookout for possible liaisons.

The writer and television personality and Limehouse resident Dan Farson, who was then at the pinnacle of his career making successful televising documentaries, and the flamboyant labour MP Tom Dryberg, were frequent visitors to Charlie Brown's. Invariably these two men would leave the 'sailors' bar' at closing time with their pick-ups, usually seamen on shore leave.

It could get very colourful at weekends. One evening, Dave and I took two nurses from Poplar Hospital for drinks at Limehouse and visited three pubs in West India Dock Road; the Oporto, the Old Blue Last and finally Charlie Brown's. Inside the 'sailors' bar' a red-bearded Dutch ship's cook politely asked me if the nurse whom I was with would teach him the Cha Cha; she agreed, but insisted that he first remove his orange and yellow flowered clogs. That same evening Dave uncharacteristically floored a toothless Greek seaman with one punch when he caught him trying to steal one of the nurse's handbags.

It was unfortunate that this unique part of Charlie Brown's was not saved when the pub was demolished in 1990. It could, and should have been preserved, perhaps to be later reassembled in the new Museum of Docklands.

Directly opposite Charlie Brown's stood the Asia, a Chinese restaurant that served cheap, fresh food. Unlike the seven other Chinese eateries in the immediate vicinity that barred would-be troublemakers, the Asia, that resembled a shack, had no ban. Consequently, it attracted every drunkard or ruffian who wanted a meal after leaving the Limehouse pubs at closing time. Arguments and fights would periodically occur at the restaurant, especially during the weekends, and often involved seamen or local heavy drinkers.

On reflection it seems amazing that the hardworking Chinese family who owned the Asia managed to avoid serious injury from their sometimes violent customers. Several times over the years Dave and I had to move our plates to another table to avoid the brawls.

Normally, if we were drinking at what was then Chinatown with women, we would never chance inviting them to the Asia with its reputation of being a 'dangerous dump'. Instead, we would dine at the famous and long-established 'Old Friends' opposite Limehouse Police Station.

The two nurses, on hearing of the Asia's wild atmosphere, persuaded us to take them there for a meal on a Friday evening. Within minutes of being seated, there was violence. An ill-advised artist who was sketching by the exit, received a hard blow to his face, which caused him to flee. A lone customer, after being accused of staring at somebody's woman, was pinned against the wall with a knife held to his throat. Two half-drunk prostitutes decided to settle their feud by wrestling on the floor. The cook, now alerted by the fracas, rushed out from the kitchen waving a meat cleaver but quickly went back inside when the two women continued their fight outside on the snow-covered pavement. Despite such risks, Dave and I were fond of the Asia and remained regular patrons until its eventual closure in the mid-1960s.

For a long time, chain-smoking Fay, a plump, cheerful and fearless waitress worked at the restaurant. Fay was impressed with Dave, whom she found charming. She often stopped to chat to him in between serving. Although Poplar born and bred, with a local accent, her voice would suddenly change and sound refined and educated when speaking to Dave, and then instantly revert to its original Cockney when dealing with unruly customers. Always amused by the special attention he received from Fay, but knowing she was a married lady, Dave resisted the temptation to invite her for a drink.

6

The Prospect of Whitby

Of all the endless walks that Dave and I embarked on in those early days, none was more interesting than the journey from Tower Bridge to Limehouse. Our route took us through Wapping and Shadwell, down historical Narrow Street and finally stopping at the door of Charlie Brown's. Usually, to begin this superb walk we would make our way along the Highway to the steps of Tower Bridge. Situated at the foot of these steps was Irongate Wharf where the General Steam Navigation Company had its warehouses and whose ships, moored alongside its quay, were always named after birds. Glancing upwards at the stern notice that was painted on the brickwork to 'Commit No Nuisance' we would embark on our leisurely stroll.

Walking past the huge warehouses that embraced the banks of the Thames was a memorable experience. Stacked next to each other with little bridges connecting their annexes across the road, the warehouses seemed to go on forever. Occasionally small alleys would appear alongside, leading to the river's edge, where old well-trodden stone steps led down to the foreshore. During the day the area was very busy with skilled workers who stood perilously close to open doors set high up in the warehouses, using hoists to lower merchandise on to the backs of lorries.

From the few observation points on the riverside it was possible to see the dockers working on the quays or in the cranes and in the holds of ships and barges. With all of these windows, doors, hatches and holds open, lovely smells of spices and rum would permeate the whole of the area. At night it was so very different, extremely quiet and empty with no traffic and few pedestrians. It was possible to walk the whole of Wapping's riverside without seeing a soul, an ideal place to walk and talk, or just meditate.

Knowing how fond I was of our evening walks, Dave would sometimes park his van or motorcycle near St Katherine's Dock so we could enjoy the half hour walk along Wapping's riverside. Throughout my working day I would look forward to when the factory closed at 7 p.m. I would hurry home to wash, change my clothes, have a quick meal and then dash to meet Dave. These were welcome excursions; Wapping had much to offer me, a tranquil

Challenge about to enter St Katherine's dock, 1973. Dave believed that the figure of a man standing on the edge of the quay was himself. He recalled visiting the Thames dockside several times during the early 1970s, trying to find work on the tugs, but was unsuccessful. After his death I showed this photo to a number of his friends who all agreed that it probably was him. (*Museum of Docklands, PLA Collection*)

riverside, far away from the noisy factory where I worked with its inadequate and artificial lighting. Even my eyes became relaxed, rejuvenated by Wapping's dark and over-casting shadows.

Our pleasant mile long stroll would often end at London's most famous and reputedly oldest riverside tavern, the immensely popular Prospect of Whitby, which was situated at the far end of Wapping Wall. Formerly a notorious eighteenth-century drinking den known as the Devil's Tavern, it was renamed the Prospect of Whitby in 1777 after the three-mast rigger the *Prospect* that regularly brought its cargo of coal from Whitby in Yorkshire to Pelican Wharf adjacent to the tavern.

Stepping inside the pub was like descending below the decks of an eighteeth-century galleon. Ships masts acted as pillars, seasoned timber from old Thames sailing barges completely covered the walls. Wooden barrels were used as tables and chairs and to prop up the pewter bar. Helms and brass bells and old curios from around the world left behind by sailors were permanent fixtures. The well-stoked coal fires and the light from the port and starboard lamps gave out an inviting glow.

Surrounded by this ambience sat the friendly Hawaiian musicians. Les

The Prospect of Whitby at Wapping Wall, reputed to be London's oldest riverside inn.

played a ukulele, Alfie played an electric guitar and Len a Spanish guitar. After Alfie's death in 1962, he was replaced by the popular John Tin. The musicians, who first appeared at the Prospect in 1945, would strum their instruments seven nights a week, to the delight of a large crowd of happily singing customers.

It was at the Prospect that Dave and I mapped out our two-year plan to join the Merchant Navy together and sail around the world. We would sign on with the Union Castle Line. That voyage would take us to South Africa, the P&O Steam Navigation Company to India and the Far East, the Shaw Saville Line for Australia and New Zealand, the Royal Mail Line to South America and finally a voyage with the Cunard Line to North America.

Of course, like most pipedreams they remained just dreams and to my eternal disappointment our plan never materialised, although two years later, I did manage to find work on a ship. I became a scullion based in the galley of the SS *Orontes* that was bound for Australia, a round trip that was to last for three months.

Dave adored drinking at the Prospect as much as I did. We had been regulars at 'our pub' for decades. He first discovered the pub in the mid-1950s when he noticed it from the river whilst working as a deck hand on a Thames dredger. 'It was a dark evening and I could see this enticing light and hear laughter and the loud singings of "Green grow the rushes O". I realised there and then that was the kind of atmosphere I was looking for. Of course I already knew all of the cheeky songs, having learnt them ten years before in the officers' mess.'

The Prospect at low tide.

The pub's fame attracted visitors from all over the world who enjoyed the benefits of singing in unison. The revelry was so exhilarating and fulfilling; when you left to go home at closing time, you were totally satisfied. One former manager was so popular that patrons would regularly hoist him onto their shoulders and to the sound of 'he's a jolly good fellow,' carry him outside and up to the bascule bridge at the entrance to the Shadwell Basin.

There were other advantages on offer at the pub too. It was very popular with the girls, especially nurses, au pairs and students who all loved the party atmosphere. You could, if you really wanted to, meet a different girl every night at the unique Prospect of Whitby. It was at the Prospect that I was to witness Dave's well-tried method of making contact with women. 'You see that blonde girl sitting on the left?' he said, pointing to a small group of people sitting opposite. 'She is giving me indications.'

'And how do you know that?' I asked.

'It's the language of the eyes,' he remarked confidently.

I repeated his words, 'The language of the eyes.'

Dave chuckled. 'Yes, Alf, the language of the eyes. If I get three indications from a girl I put my threepenny bit in.'

I became a little anxious, 'What are you planning to do?'

'I will explain in a moment, by the way, that's the second indication.'

'You are obviously joking,' I suggested.

Dave stubbed out his cigarette and denied that he was joking. 'In fact Alf, I have just had the third indication.'

Having received the required three indications, he took out a pen, and a small tin from his pocket that he opened. It seemed to be full of old bus tickets. Within seconds he had written something down on the back of one of the tickets. 'What's that for?' I asked curiously. 'It's a message for the girl inviting her over for a drink.'

'And what are you going to do with it?'

'I am going to drop it into her lap.'

'Do you think that's wise Dave? She might be angry with you.' He grinned, stood up and walked over to the bar to buy cigarettes.

Before returning to his seat, as planned and unnoticed by her friends, he dropped the folded bus ticket into her lap. I felt slightly uncomfortable; I had a vision of one of her friends, a six-footer with a pugnacious appearance, coming over to us and banging our heads together.

Dave sat down, took a sip of his whisky and nudged me. 'You see Alf, a faint heart never won a fair lady'. I held my breath while the girl read the note. Fortunately, she did not seem annoyed; instead, she gazed at Dave and me for a moment before smiling. After whispering something to her friend she left her seat and came over to join us.

Dave used his novel method many times over the years, often to my advantage, but there were several disappointments too. On one memorable occasion at a pub in Knightsbridge, he mistakenly thought a debutante was making eyes at him. Not having a bus ticket handy, he scribbled a message on an old pawn ticket and dropped it into her lap. I looked away with embarrassment, but only for a moment. The girl, a lovely free spirit, laughed when she examined it.

She immediately gave the ticket back to Dave and said, 'Is that all I am worth, a couple of quid?' Dave knew his bus ticket notes were always accepted with amusement; I never saw any girls who were upset by receiving them. Once the girl read the note and saw his infectious cheeky smile waiting for her reaction, she would never be annoyed.

I remember in 1963 when Dave's bus ticket novelty produced a handsome dividend. A group of singers arrived at the Prospect of Whitby in vintage cars after touring several dockside pubs. Known as the 'Happy Wanderers', they were members of a west London amateur operatic and dramatic society. Every Saturday evening throughout the summer, these singers with their thrilling voices entertained the Prospect's regular clientele. One of the budding sopranos received Dave's bus ticket and soon fell under his spell. Dave was infatuated with the girl and a brief liaison developed. Having no interest in classical music, he resisted her efforts to persuade him to visit the opera; but the girl persisted; eventually, he reluctantly agreed and they went to see Rossini's *Count Ory*. To endure the performance, Dave filled his little flask with whisky that he consumed before the curtain rose. After the performance began, he fell into a deep sleep and started to snore and the poor embarrassed girl spent most of the evening elbowing him in the ribs in an attempt to keep

Interior of the Prospect at Whitby.

him awake. Not long afterwards their romance came to an abrupt end.

Then there was the half-drunk Australian who for a bet dived into the river from the Prospect's balcony in an attempt to swim to Tower Bridge, foolishly egged on by his friends, but discouraged by Dave who understood the river's dangerous currents and eddies. The Australian quickly got into difficulties and had to be rescued by the very annoyed Wapping river police.

'Batman', an ex-Army officer was a regular at the Prospect for several months. It was rumoured that he was cashiered for fiddling regimental funds. Complete with a cloak, cane, top hat and monocle and blessed with a powerful baritone voice, Batman would stand on the stairs and sing, and his opulent tone could be heard outside in the street. To attract women Batman would twitch his moustache at any girl whom he thought was interested in him. One girl was so furious at Batman constantly focusing on her, that she gave his prized moustache such a painful tug it immediately ended his twitching career at the Prospect.

Another time, Dave and I noticed a most beautiful young woman standing at the top of the stairs outside the restaurant, a Grace Kelly look-alike. She was adorned with jewellery and wore an expensive fur coat. Impatient with her escort who was settling the bill, this heavenly one slowly began to descend the stairs. We gasped at her stunning looks and wondered who she was.

'A famous film star,' said somebody.

'A princess,' said another.

Dave, of course, could not resist putting in his threepenny bit as she passed us. Knowing that she would hear him he spoke eloquently. 'In all my years, I have never seen such rare beauty.' The woman stood still for a moment and turned around to face him. Far from being condescending as we expected, she replied in an accent and tone that would have embarrassed even Eliza Doolittle. 'Why don't yer piss off yer f****** old c*** before I kick you in the f****** b******* '. Poor Dave. He was so shocked at this unexpected verbal assault, he immediately rushed up to the bar and ordered a double whisky.

About this time, we became very friendly with a group of fun-loving Australian girls who had arrived in London after spending several months travelling around France and Switzerland. Robyn, the eldest and divorced, was their leader. Nicknamed 'Hooker' because of her large crooked nose, her popularity had kept the five girls together, fulfilling her promise to their parents back home in Sydney that she would look after them whilst they were in Europe. The Australians often invited us back to their large untidy flat in Earls Court for late night parties. Not only were the girls generous with beer and sandwiches, they would entertain us by dancing and singing numbers from the musicals. 'Sweet Charity' was their favourite.

I still recall a very happy Dave sprawled out on cushions on the floor and at the receiving end of half a dozen pointed fingers when they sang to him, 'The minute you walked in the joint, I could see you were a man of distinction, a real big spender'.

Margaret was the youngest of the Australian girls. Although short and overweight she had a pretty face. On the passenger liner that brought her and her friends to Europe she had become infatuated with Claudio, an Italian crewmember. Because the crew were forbidden to fraternize with the passengers Margaret and Claudio had to conduct their romance with great secrecy. As Margaret could speak no Italian and Claudio spoke little English the couple had to use sign language. The older and wiser Hooker told Dave and me that she had disapproved of the relationship. She believed that Claudio was probably married and only interested in seducing the naïve nineteen year old. Hooker explained that Margaret had ignored her concern. 'The sweet kid thinks that Claudio is an honourable man who wants to marry her.'

It was a Friday evening at the Prospect of Whitby where an excited Margaret told me that she had just received a letter written in Italian from Claudio. 'Please translate it for me, Alfie; I know that you speak some Italian.' I explained to her that without the use of an Italian dictionary it would be near impossible for me to give an accurate translation.

With appealing eyes, she held out the letter, 'Please try Alfie. I need to know if Claudio has set a wedding date.' Unable to say no, I took the letter from her and said I would try and translate it on the riverside terrace.

A grateful Margaret gave me a quick hug and whispered in my ear, 'Thank you, Alfie, thank you so much.' In a jubilant state she joined Hooker and the other Australian girls who were happily singing along to the Hawaiian music.

Dave followed me onto the terrace where we sat on the barrel seats. While Dave tried to make eye contact with two Scottish girls sitting close by, I began to read the letter. '*Mia cara, Margaretta, Quanto ti amo.*' My dearest Margaret, how I love you. The second sentence confirmed Hooker's suspicion about Claudio. '*Ma sfortunatamente ho una moglie.*' But unfortunately I have a wife. Because of my limited Italian, I was unable to translate much of the remaining sentences, but there was one sentence at the end of the letter that I managed to decipher: Claudio would be returning to live in Genoa with his family. Dave, who was about to drop a bus ticket message in one of the Scottish girls lap, asked me if the letter contained good news for Margaret.

'I am afraid that it's not good news,' I replied with a sigh. 'Claudio has admitted that he is married and is going home to Genoa to live with his wife and two sons.' Dave instantly tore up his bus ticket and said 'Poor Margaret she will be totally disappointed if she finds out that the Italian has deceived her.'

I was now in a quandary; I just did not have the heart to explain to Margaret the contents of the letter. Dave understood my predicament, for he too would have found it extremely difficult had he been in my situation. 'The problem that you and I have, Alf, we are just not capable of dealing with sensitive subjects.' I asked my friend how I could avoid giving Margaret grief.

He quickly replied, 'Alf, it's Claudio who will give Margaret grief, not you.' He also added, 'No matter what you say to Margaret or how you say it, the fact is, it will not lessen the pain of her disappointment.'

After further thought Dave suggested that I had one of several options. I could explain to Margaret that because my Italian was so poor she should ask somebody else to translate the letter, or I could discreetly whisper in Hooker's ear the contents of the letter and ask her if she would break the news to Margaret, or lastly when I returned the letter to Margaret, not mention to her that Claudio had confessed that he had a wife, but just say that because of family problems he must remain in Genoa for some time and that he will contact her one day in the future.

Out of Dave's three options I thought that the first was the most appropriate. When I went back inside the Prospect, Margaret immediately left her singing friends; she came over to me and said, 'I hope you are going to bring me good tidings, Alfie.' Because her pretty face glowed with anticipation, tact would be required.

'I am sorry, Margaret, but I have not been able to translate your letter. Don't you or any of the other girls have an Italian-speaking friend?'

She answered sorrowfully, 'I only wish we had, Alfie.'

Margaret grasped the letter with both hands, pressed it against her chest and quietly pleaded with me to take the letter away and try and translate it at my leisure. 'It's very important to me Alfie, please, please, do me this one favour.' I reluctantly took the letter and offered to have another attempt the next day and if I was successful I would 'phone her the following afternoon; alternatively I could speak to her at the Prospect during Sunday evening. She preferred the former.

Dave made no criticism of my last minute change of plans and he apologised for not being much help. He suggested that when I spoke to Margaret on the 'phone, delicate as it might be, I should be honest and explain the contents of her letter.

Sitting at my bedside on the Sunday morning and with the aid of an Italian dictionary it took me over an hour to translate the complete letter verbatim. In the letter Claudio mentioned that he would always cherish the memory of their relationship and that his love for her would never die. He had really enjoyed their secret late night rendezvous on the ship's top deck and the fantastic times that they had spent together during his shore leave at the various ports along the route to Europe. His letter ended with, '*Mia cara Margaretta, non ti scordar di me.*' My dearest Margaret, never forget me.

It was most fortunate for me that it was Hooker who picked up the phone when I rang. Margaret had yet to return from shopping. This was a good moment for me to have a word in private with Hooker. I quickly explained to her about the contents of Margaret's letter.

The tone of Hooker's voice was venomous when she replied. 'I always knew that slimy Casanova was married, he is just like the rest of the Ities; they are only interested in a bunk-up.' Her choice of words would have caused Dave to giggle.

What Hooker said next was a relief for me. 'Alfie, don't worry about speaking to Margaret, I will break the news to her; she might be an innocent Sheila, but she has plenty of spunk. We Aussie girls easily get over these trivial affairs.'

When Dave and I returned to the Prospect on the Sunday evening, Margaret took the letter from me and without a word being said, threw it into the fast-flowing Thames. The Australian girls stayed in London for about two years before they packed their bags and left for Spain and Portugal. On their last night at the Prospect, they brought a tape recorder with them to capture the memorable atmosphere.

I am so glad that the Australians, who loved the pub, were no longer around during the late summer of 1969, when an unfortunate incident occurred inside the bar. This incident would curtail the wonderful sing-a-long nights that had been a regular feature for the previous twenty-five years.

All of us were in full voice when a police inspector and a sergeant came into the bar and gently eased themselves through the crowd and made their way onto the riverside terrace. Apparently the local police had been informed that some young boys were hiding on the terrace after being disturbed trying to break into cars parked outside the pub. Satisfied that it was a false alarm, the two policemen came back into the bar and started to make their way through the revellers towards the exit. Suddenly a group of students began chanting,

'All coppers are bastards'. The two policemen remained by the exit. They were absolutely furious at the students' use of offensive language. The inspector immediately ordered the Hawaiian musicians to stop playing.

When all was quiet, he raised his commanding voice. 'I am closing the premises immediately and would everybody leave.' My friends and I were dumbfounded. Nothing like this had ever happened before. We were actually being evicted from our favourite pub.

Five minutes later, dozens of us regulars patiently waited outside on the pavement. We were hoping that the inspector would change his mind and allow us back inside, but it was not to be. As there was no chance of the pub reopening, I parted company with my friends and went home.

A few weeks later, the brewery who owned the Prospect were summoned to court and fined for allowing obscene singing during licensing hours. Because Gary Lacey, the manager of the Prospect, now realised that his livelihood would be in jeopardy if the singing got out of control again, he instantly barred the students who were responsible for the incident. He allowed the revelry to continue but there was to be no rude singing or chanting. The new rules were applied for about a year until Lacey sacked the Hawaiian musicians and replaced them with an unpopular jazz quartet.

Dave lamented, 'The Prospect of Whitby has died a death and will never be the same again.' Although foreign visitors to the Prospect still arrived, many having been told in their own countries about the pub's unique, happy atmosphere, they were to be disappointed, for rather than being able to sing along to the joyous strings of the Hawaiian musicians, they were confronted and deafened by noisy saxophones and clarinets.

During the IRA campaign of planting bombs in pubs in English cities in the mid-1970s, extra vigilance was required by the staff and the regulars at the Prospect of Whitby. Like many famous London pubs at the time, the Prospect had its share of hoax phone calls and false alarms when suspicious packages and bags were left lying around usually by careless customers.

Dave and I were sitting by the Prospect's roaring fire, having come straight to the pub from work. Glancing downwards, I noticed a black plastic bag that had been left by a barstool. The bag looked suspicious. Suddenly, the front door opened and in came a large coach party of noisy middle-aged Italian tourists. The crowd quickly filled up the bar and spilled out on to the riverside terrace. Soon after the arrival of the Italians, another customer also became concerned about the plastic bag. He alerted the head barman, who immediately 'phoned the police. So sure was the barman that the bag contained a bomb that was about to explode, he leapt over the bar and dashed out of the front door and was last seen running across the bascule bridge. This cowardly man had abandoned the customers in the bar and in the restaurant upstairs, his staff and the two cats. The Italians by now had sensed that there was danger at foot and when the loud shout of '*Andiamo, una bomba, una bomba!'* reverberated around the bar, they panicked and fled from the pub.

Soon, a lone policeman arrived and ordered the remaining drinkers off the premises. Regular customers protested.

Dave remarked to the policeman, 'It can't be a bomb it looks too light.' Agreeing with us, but reluctant to look inside, the policeman used a mop and gently pressed the bag that caused it to tilt forward.

'Bang!' shouted somebody.

The policeman instantly backed off. Those of us who were left at the bar stood around in a semi circle and waited and waited. Suddenly one of the Prospect's cats came out of the adjacent kitchen and trotted over to the bag and began to sniff it. As it did so, the bag toppled over and out poured a large pile of men's dirty underwear. The outpouring of the ghastly contents caused the startled cat to jump backwards and run into the nearby kitchen. Followed by cheers and laughter and to the loud shouts of, 'Omo improves even on perfect whiteness', the bag and the underwear were promptly dispatched to the blazing fire.

Throughout the years that Dave and I had frequented the Prospect, we had met people from all over the world, ranging from boring Hollywood film stars and snooty millionaires to the most interesting of all, the men who worked on the Thames: the tug men, lightermen and bargemen whose stories of river life were so fascinating. Although most of these river-men lived at Wapping and neighbouring Limehouse, they, like so many other local folk usually boycotted the Prospect, preferring other pubs in the vicinity that were more family-oriented and where the prices of the drinks were considerably lower than those charged at the Prospect.

I noticed that several of the river-men expressed a feeling of loss and helplessness over the way much of their trade was now being distributed by road transport and air freight and they were deeply concerned that their jobs were in jeopardy and redundancies were inevitable. Moreover, one or two with whom we spoke were extremely bitter that they were being discarded like old clothes. Like their fathers and grandfathers before they had worked on the river or in the enclosed docks all of their lives and had acquired great skills and expertise developed over many generations. As Dave and I always felt an instant rapport sitting and drinking with these proud and tough men, all we could do was to listen sympathetically.

Because the Prospect was crowded most evenings it could be boisterous, although arguments and disturbances were rare. However one tragic incident in November 1966 tarnished the Prospect's reputation as a trouble-free pub. Michael Ferriday, an 18-year-old trainee manager with the Lyons Corner House Group had accidentally spilt some beer on another customer. An argument developed that continued outside in the street; a blow was struck and the young manager fell and hit his head on the pavement. He later died in hospital from his injuries. Although Dave and I and two other friends were at the Prospect that evening we had no knowledge of the tragedy.

When we returned to the pub a few evenings later we were confronted and questioned by the police at the door. Out of our group of four, I was the only one who was asked to go to Limehouse Police Station to be interviewed by the CID and I spent an hour with the police. Apparently, the man who had struck Ferriday drove off in a car, but he was followed by a motorist who had lost him somewhere in the Poplar area. As I lived at Poplar, unlike my three friends who lived at Stepney, the Police had to eliminate me from their inquiries. Relieved to be told that I wasn't a suspect and thanked by the police for my co-operation I was free to go. I left the police station with great haste and rejoined my friends at the Prospect.

7

Bombs Fall on Rangoon and London

Although Dave and I came from different backgrounds, both our families were casualties of the Second World War. Dave, his mother and sister Barbara were forced to leave Rangoon as the Japanese bombing of the city intensified. Likewise, my mother and my brother and sisters Harry, five, Sylvia, two, and one-year-old Mary were evacuated from the East End early in 1940. Our home at Carr Street Buildings, adjacent to Stepney Power Station and near the docks, was a prime target for the German bombers. With my father away in the Army, we were sent to Buckinghamshire, and later spent short periods in Norfolk and Somerset. For the last nine months of the war we were living in West Hartlepool in County Durham.

Whilst we were in West Hartlepool in September 1944, my sister Patricia was born. I was born on 25 February 1941 in Olney, Buckinghamshire. According to my mother, the night I was born, a huge explosion was heard close by.

'You came into the world with a bang,' joked Dave. My brother Harry was found a safe haven with an elderly couple in Cambridge for the duration of the war. He was never to return to us, and remains there to this day.

After the ferocious German blitz on London that started in September 1940 and which was to last for fifty-seven consecutive nights, the raids became less only to resume with equal severity in the spring of 1941. Many evacuated East End families, whose homes were not already destroyed, returned during the lull only to find themselves trapped by this second onslaught.

On the night of 10 May 1941, a huge parachute landmine that had failed to explode struck the railway line at Stepney Station causing an arch to collapse on to the sandbagged Chasely Street shelter below. Nineteen local residents who had taken refuge in the shelter were unfortunately killed including my mother's cousin, forty-six-year-old Elisabeth Hogg, and her three daughters, Annie, twenty, Emily, sixteen and Hida, six. Their home, just a hundred yards away in Salmon Lane, remained intact throughout the raid and was still standing at the end of the war. That night, over 300 German planes attacked London. This was the last big raid on the capital before the Luftwaffe eased off its bombing campaign. The bombers were needed for the imminent invasion of Russia.

The raids on London continued for a further two months but on a smaller scale until finally they ceased altogether on the 27 July.

For five moonlit hours on that fateful May night, the German planes brought death and destruction on a massive scale to the streets of London. 1,436 civilians were killed and 1,792 injured. The casualty rates were the highest recorded for a single raid. Besides the huge loss of life, many public buildings were struck by high explosive bombs. The House of Commons Chamber was destroyed. Westminster Abbey was damaged; so was the War Office, the British Museum, the Law Courts, Mansion House, the Tower of London, St Pancras Station and the Royal Mint. Five livery companies, including the prestigious Mercers' Company lost their great halls. St Clements Danes was one of many famous churches that were badly burnt.

For various reasons many East Enders refused to use the public shelters during the Blitz. Some people were too old and often frail to make the effort to reach safety or they left it too late to leave their homes when the air raid sirens went off. Others no doubt felt nervous in the primitive shelters, or they felt safer under their own roof. Some residents who ignored the sirens and the impending threat of falling bombs stayed at home throughout the blitz and survived unscathed. The decision to stay at home proved fatal for scores of people and they were subsequently killed when their homes were destroyed in the bombing The shelters could be death traps too. Eight public shelters in Stepney received direct hits killing many men, women and children. Altogether, more than 800 civilians lost their lives in the borough from the German bombs of 1940-41 and the V1 and V2 rockets of 1944-5.

The youngest victim was three-week-old Brian Kirby of Lukin Street on the 17 March 1945 and the oldest Elizabeth Templeton, 86, of Yorkshire Road on the 10 May 1941. The last casualty of the London Blitz to be recovered in the East End was at Pennyfields, Limehouse. In January 1964 a workman using a mechanical excavator, unearthed the skeleton of a man lying on an old iron bedstead in the foundations of where several bombed out houses once stood. The body, that was thought to have been a Chinese merchant seaman, had remained there undisturbed for over twenty years.

As a four year old in 1945 my memories of the war years are very limited. However, I do know that in 1943 my mother left Somerset and brought my sisters and me back to our home at Spert House in Stepney. However our return was premature. In June 1944 V1 flying bombs (Doodlebugs) and V2 rockets began to strike the East End. From 13 June 1944 until 25 March 1945 Stepney, Poplar and Bethnal Green that make up the East End were struck by 78 Doodlebugs and 19 rockets. Hundreds of residents were killed during this deadly onslaught.

I can clearly remember during the summer of 1944 being woken by my mother during the night and hearing the air-raid sirens. My family had to leave at once for the underground shelters in the square outside our home, but it was too late and dangerous to cross the open ground so we remained silently pressed up against the wall in the well of the stairs of Spert House whilst loud explosions were heard close by. On another occasion when we did manage to reach the shelter, we had to stand on benches because the floor was flooded. Because of this new danger from the skies, East End families were evacuated a second time. In due course my mother, sisters and me were sent to live in West Hartlepool.

It was sometimes possible for the RAF or the 'ack-ack' guns to shoot down a V1 before it reached its target but not the V2 rocket; at 3,500 miles an hour, it was unstoppable.

On 25 March 1945, a V2 rocket struck Hughes Mansions in Vallance Road Stepney, killing 134 men, women and children. This was the worst single incident in the East End since the Bethnal Green tube disaster two years earlier that resulted in 173 civilians suffocating when a large crowd became trapped on the underground stairs. The Bethnal Green tragedy was caused when local people mistakenly thought that the deafening blasts from the 'ack-ack' gun batteries being test-fired in nearby Victoria Park was a German raid in progress. Widespread panic followed with a rush to reach the shelter of the tube and for so many people, a cruel and senseless death.

Two years earlier and thousands of miles away in Rangoon, the resourceful fifteen-year-old David Upson who was staying with his sister Barbara and her husband, had constructed an underground shelter in the garden of their smallholding. This shelter gave them sanctuary when the Japanese began bombing the town. Although Dave had no formal education, it seems that he was a precocious child. I gained the impression that he had an innate ability to remember facts and figures, and once stored away in his mind, this data could at any time be recalled at will. As an eighteen year old, with a limited education, I was very impressed with his seemingly excellent knowledge of politics, current affairs and religion. Initially, I suspected that he must have studied a great deal to acquire such erudition, but where? He never attended evening classes. The conclusion that I eventually came to was that he must have been self-taught.

When Dave and I first met, he assumed that I was educated and seemed surprised when I explained that like him, I too had left school at 15 with no qualifications. 'You don't talk like an East Ender and you like opera and poetry. How come?'

Being well aware of my limitations and valuing his friendship, my answer had to be honest. 'It's true my accent is not Cockney. Perhaps it's more suburban, but that's the way I talk; it's natural, not cultivated; and regarding the music and poetry, at school we were encouraged to appreciate the arts.'

Satisfied with my explanation he said, 'Coming from the Far East, opera was unknown to me. Dance music was always popular, but my first love is country and western music. I know that the lyrics are corny and the music repetitious, but I always find it easy on the ear, especially when I have had a few drinks.' He glanced across the counter of the Refiner's Arms into the public bar opposite, where a group of revellers began singing and jiving by the jukebox.

He groaned, 'I just can't stand this awful rock and roll music Alf, and it gives me a bloody headache.' When Frankie Ford's popular 'Sea Cruise' was played on the jukebox, Dave and I immediately left the pub.

Outside in the street and feeling self-assured I said, 'Do you know Dave that in a thousand years time, no, ten thousand years, the operas of Verdi and Puccini will still be enjoyed by millions of people all over the world and all of this rock and roll rubbish will be forgotten and not even revived as a curiosity.' Dave probably realised that what I had just said was a well-rehearsed counter-thrust, directed at those ignoramuses who in the past had ridiculed my love of opera. Perhaps he too had been on the receiving end of sarcastic remarks because of his fondness for country and western music.

'And what of country and western?' asked my friend. 'Will my favourite singers like Tennessee Ernie Ford and Slim Whitman, be forgotten too?' Dave's question proved difficult for me to answer. My knowledge of country and western music was very limited. Although I felt slightly nervous in case I was to alienate Dave, I thought that I should at least try to give an answer.

'Because country and western has evolved from folk music, I believe it will continue to evolve, but to what extent, I really don't know, but I think it will survive in one form or another.' I did not think that my answer was very convincing, but apparently Dave did, as he nodded in an agreeable manner.

8

A Wapping Walk

In early March 1960 it came to Dave's attention that Frances, a former live-in girlfriend with whom he had some unfinished business, was working as a barmaid somewhere in Soho. Anxious to find out if it were true he decided to spend several evenings after work searching the pubs off Shaftsbury Avenue in an attempt to locate her. I agreed to accompany him. Whilst in the West End I would stop by at the Royal Opera House and buy a ticket for the forthcoming production of Bizet's *Carmen* beginning on 25 March. Although Dave was very familiar with Soho, I was not, having rarely ventured west of the Aldgate pump, but I did notice from my one and only previous visit to the area it had an established red light district. It was during the early evening on 10 March when Dave and I boarded the number 25 bus at Whitechapel.

The plan was I would disembark at Holborn and walk to Covent Garden and he would continue to Tottenham Court Road. We would then meet later at his favourite Soho pub, the York Minster in Dean Street known by its more popular name the French Pub. My friend felt confident that some of his West End acquaintances would know the whereabouts of Frances. Dave declined my offer to buy him a ticket to see *Carmen* with a definite, 'No thanks, not for me.'

As a country and western music lover, his interest was perhaps understandable. He would have found it highly amusing that the role of Don Jose, the young Spanish soldier, was sung by Hans Kart, a middle-aged grey-haired Dutch tenor with the Nordic looks of a Viking.

After I left the box office with my ticket for *Carmen* safely inside my pocket and with time to spare I began to wander around the theatre's busy foyer. I mingled with a large excited crowd jostling in front of a huge poster advertising the Royal Opera's current production of Puccini's *La Bohème*. The tenor appearing as Rodolfo was Jussi Bjorling. This tenor was unknown to me. Standing among the crowd, I could hear Bjorling's name being mentioned over and over again. Whoever this tenor was, he must have been somebody well known by the opera going public.

As I walked towards the exit, I hesitated for a moment and thought perhaps I should return to the box office and purchase a ticket for *La Bohème*, but the

King Edward VII Memorial Park at Shadwell. The little oasis that divides Wapping from Limehouse.

sight of the long queue now forming caused me to change my mind, a decision that I have regretted ever since. I soon realised that I had missed a once-in-a-lifetime golden opportunity to hear and see Jussi Bjorling, the finest lyrical tenor of the day, arguably of all time, appearing in Puccini's most captivating opera.

It would be several months before I began to listen to the great Swedish tenor's records and appreciate his most beautiful god-given voice that I came to realise my misfortune in not seeing him live at Covent Garden. I was now determined to see Bjorling when he next returned to London, but it was never to be. On 11 September 1960 at the relatively young age of forty-nine Bjorling suffered a fatal heart attack.

After I left the Royal Opera House, I took a slow walk to Dean Street to meet Dave at the York Minster. When I entered the pub I spotted Dave sitting by the window talking to a dark-haired woman who was about his own age. She did not fit the description of Frances. Dave called me over to his table where I was introduced to her. Naomi shook my hand warmly and remarked 'David has just told me about you, you're the boy who likes opera.' I smiled politely, but felt slightly uncomfortable at being referred to as a boy. Because I was unsure of what Dave's relationship with Naomi was, I declined to ask him if he had news of Frances. Naomi reached for a cigarette but changed her mind. With her large brown eyes focused on me she said, 'Tell me, Alfred, how long have you and David been friends and do you live near each other?'

'Dave and I have been friends for about a year; actually we live just three streets apart. In fact our streets are connected by narrow alleys.' I immediately sensed that Naomi was curious about me and like it or not, I felt that I was in for a period of questioning. Dave glanced at me and indicated with a nod that I had his approval to speak freely. Turning to Naomi, he offered her a cigarette which she refused. Perhaps Naomi had noticed my uneasiness, because when she spoke again her voice was softer. 'I have only been to the East End once before and that was for a Chinese meal at Limehouse. Is Chinatown near where you live?'

'Yes, quite near.'

'And do you work in the East End?'

Before I answered her, Dave grinned and winked at me. He was obviously enjoying the mild interrogation. 'I work as a garment cutter in Bethnal Green, although I live in Stepney.' Dave intervened with his usual perfect timing. 'But we drink in Wapping.' His remark caused Naomi and me to laugh. Naomi stood up, took out her purse and insisted on buying the next round of drinks.

Whilst she was at the bar I asked my friend if he had discovered where Frances was. He shrugged his shoulders. 'Nope. She was working in Soho but disappeared two weeks ago and left no forwarding address, but there is a possibility that she might be staying with a relative at King's Cross.'

'What will you do now? She seems elusive.' He pondered for a moment before saying, 'I am not sure; I will have to think about it.'

Naomi returned from the bar and placed whisky and beer on the table. As soon as she was seated and still refusing a cigarette from Dave she focused her attention at me. 'Alfred, do tell me about Wapping where you and David drink. It's a dock area isn't it?'

'Yes it is, very much so,' I replied enthusiastically.

As we spoke two effeminate men entered the pub. They came over to our table and embraced Naomi. She introduced us to her friends. They were both actors and were still wearing their stage make up. Declining to join us, they preferred to drink at the bar.

Whilst Naomi was exchanging pleasantries with the two actors, I appealed to Dave to take over and describe Wapping to her. My problem was, I did not feel confident or articulate enough to talk about the area at length, unlike Dave who was capable of expressing himself perfectly. He also shared my affection for the Docklands and, being a former deckhand on the Thames, he was very familiar with Wapping's riverside and enclosed docks. To my surprise, he flatly refused to cooperate. 'You always wanted to be a Docklands guide,' he remarked with a chuckle. 'Now it's your chance.' As he spoke, he was pushing his packet of cigarettes along the table towards Naomi, who finally succumbed to temptation. But as a punishment, she tugged at his tie and hissed. 'You're a bad influence David; you know I am trying to give up the weed.' I started to feel comfortable with her; she was obviously an intelligent

Charlie Brown's Limehouse, *c.* 1925.
(*Steve Kentfield*)

THE ONE & ONLY ONE *Charlie Brown*

woman with an inquisitive mind, although at first I found her approach when asking me questions a little too direct.

Naomi must have been determined to give up smoking, as she claimed, because after just one inhalation, she snubbed the cigarette out. Dave, who noticed her discard the cigarette, made no comment. Again she turned her attention to me. 'Alfred, you were about to tell me about Wapping.' She raised her eyebrows as if to signal for me to begin. I glanced at Dave in a last attempt for assistance, but he grinned and looked away, seemingly quite content to sit back for the next few minutes and let his young friend take Naomi on a guided tour of 'our patch'. I thought for a moment how to begin. Prompted by Dave, I began slowly and carefully to choose my words.

On reflection, I must have sounded like a bad actor reading from a ten-bob script, starting and stopping after every sentence. 'Wapping is a historical riverside area, um, that lies just east of Tower Bridge and extends along the river to Shadwell, um and it is hemmed in by the Highway to the north, um, it's really a man-made island connected by three or four bridges. Um, sometimes late at night, Dave and I have caught a bridger.'

'What on earth is a bridger?' asked Naomi, glancing at Dave for an answer. He spoke quickly. 'It's when traffic and pedestrians have to wait by a bridge while it is raised to allow a ship to enter or leave the docks; it's very interesting to witness.' Naomi squeezed his hand and said she would like to visit Wapping soon.

Wapping looking west, *c.* 1960, showing how busy it was. Less than ten years later, the last ship had left, the developers had arrived and were soon to be let loose with a vengeance. In due course, all of the historical warehouses in the western dock and the Shadwell basin were demolished. Fortunately, many of the old warehouses at Wapping's riverside were spared and have now been converted to private apartments.

Feeling more confident, I found that my words were beginning to flow more smoothly. I described how the wharfs were lined with huge cranes that lifted cargo from ships moored at the quays and stored in magnificent old warehouses that had been in use for over 150 years. Reminded by Dave, I mentioned ancient Wapping pubs like The Prospect of Whitby and The Town of Ramsgate, which had terraces and balconies that overlooked the Thames. At this point Dave interrupted me. 'Alf knows the area so well, you could blindfold him, take him to any corner and he would know exactly where he is just by the different smells emitting from the warehouses.'

'Really?' said Naomi, apparently believing his joke. I explained that over the years Wapping had become like a magnet, attracting scores of professional and amateur artists. Illustrious names including Turner, Whistler and Dore, had all produced excellent paintings and engravings of the area for future generations to enjoy.

Naomi had read that a seventeenth century brutal judge whose name she had forgotten also had links to Wapping. 'That Judge was the infamous

The Town of Ramsgate at Wapping High Street. The alley to the right leads down to ancient stone steps to the foreshore.

George Jeffreys,' I replied confidently. 'Oh you must tell me more about his infamous activities,' pleaded Naomi. I said I knew little of the exact historical background, only that after the Duke of Monmouth's failed rebellion of 1685, Jeffreys conducted the 'Bloody Assizes' ruthlessly dispatching over 300 rebels to the gallows. 'As many as that?' asked Naomi. Encouraged by her interest, I continued. 'Following the downfall of James II in 1686, Jeffreys fell out of favour with the authorities and tried to leave the country by boarding a ship at Wapping disguised as a sailor, but he was recognised and arrested, according to legend, at the Town of Ramsgate. Imprisoned in the Tower of London, the 41-year-old Jeffreys perished within a year.'

'Phew, you certainly know your history!' remarked Naomi. It was a flattering remark, but I had to admit to her that what I had just explained was printed on a leaflet that was freely available in the bar of the Town of Ramsgate. I livened up the notoriety of the area by mentioning the press gangs and smugglers, and how pirates, including Captain Kidd were hanged on the foreshore at Execution Dock, their bodies left dangling on the gallows until two tides covered them. Later their corpses were taken to the mudflats at Blackwall and left out on gibbets as a warning to others. I described the immensely popular Catholic procession at Wapping that had become an annual fixture, attracting thousands of spectators from all over the East End and beyond. And lastly, I mentioned the halcyon days that Dave and I had spent wandering along Wapping riverside the previous year, when we first became friends.

Naomi wanted to hear more but I had said enough, so I politely refused, preferring Dave to continue; but he still would not co-operate, although he did agree to a future date, when we would take her on a sightseeing tour of Docklands. 'How exciting and thank you,' said Naomi who again squeezed Dave's hand. Naomi suggested inviting her young cousin Daphne to join us. 'As it would be company for Alfred.' Her suggestion was welcome news for me. I glanced discreetly at a grinning Dave, who gave me a wink. Daphne's personal details were now occupying my mind. Was she good looking? How old was she? Did she smoke and drink? Did she have a regular boyfriend? But posing such questions to Naomi might have an adverse effect, so I held back, fearing that if I was too curious, she might change her mind and not invite Daphne.

A little later, Dave and I walked with Naomi to Tottenham Court Road subway where she boarded a train to North London. Sitting on the 25 bus that took us back to the East End, Dave mentioned that although he had never met Daphne, he had seen a photo of her in a swimsuit. 'She was short but nicely proportioned,' said my friend with a mischievous grin.

Several months had passed before we met Naomi and Daphne outside the Merchant Navy and Fisherman's War Memorial on Tower Hill. Naomi threw her arms around Dave and they kissed passionately, leaving a slightly embarrassed Daphne and me to introduce ourselves. She seemed at least two years older than me, about 5 foot 4 inches tall, and like Naomi, had thick dark hair.

As we made our way to the Tower of London's riverside we stopped for a few minutes and joined a large circle of people watching a modern Houdini escape from a thick canvas sack that was chained and held tight by swords and bayonets.   The girls thoroughly enjoyed the show and both placed contributions in a hat that was handed around. We moved away from the crowd and soon arrived by the old cannon guns opposite the Traitor's Gate. A noisy group of French school children who were climbing on the cannons disturbed Dave who was about to take a photo of a cargo ship, possibly Polish, that was moored at Hays Wharf on the South Bank.

Near the Eastern gate we paused for a moment to listen to a guide explaining to her party the tragic story of the two little princes who were murdered in the Tower, supposedly on the order of Richard III. It seemed as if every tourist in London had arrived that day; tall West Africans with colourful robes towered over shorter smiling Japanese visitors, who all seemed to be dressed in dark suits, holding cameras. An overweight beefeater became impatient having to pose too long for his photo to be taken. He gruffly complained that if he stood there for much longer his 'feet would take root'.

The bascular bridge at the entrance to the Shadwell basin. The Prospect of Whitby can be seen in the distance.

I was glad when we went through the Eastern Gate and into St Katherine's Way. The quietness of Wapping was immediate. Naomi took a photo of Daphne, Dave and me with the Irongate Wharf in the background. A little further along St Katherine's way we stopped by the old swing bridge at the entrance to St Katherine's Dock, where all was silent. Never once had I seen a ship in the dock, only barges tied up together.

Ten years later, in September 1970, I stood at the same bridge and watched sorrowfully as demolition gangs pulled down ancient warehouses to make way for what was to be the unsightly Tower Hotel. As we passed the early nineteenth century Dockmaster's house, I almost collided with Bill, a retired local docker whom Dave and I knew. He raised his cap and smiled and chatted with us for a few moments before continuing with his afternoon stroll.

We had first met Bill in Shadwell Park when we sat next to him on a bench during the warm, extended summer of 1959. The hour that we spent in his company was most enjoyable for he was an exceptionally friendly man who was quite willing to share with us his memories of working in the West India docks sixty years earlier, 'just after the outbreak of the Boer war.' Bill told us that he was the son of a dock labourer who had held his head high when he marched during the famous Dockers' Tanner strike of 1889. Without bitterness, Bill described the harsh, sometimes dangerous working conditions in the docks and the poor pay he received, especially before the First World War. Because of permanently inadequate wages, that were never enough to feed or clothe his family, he was forced to take industrial action throughout his working life. He described in detail the causes and outcome of the strikes of 1912 and 1926. His account of how dock labourers received a day's work seemed inhumane and degrading. Each morning he would join a mass of fellow labourers at the dock gate for the 'call on'. The foreman would arrive and begin to choose a certain number of men from the crowd for a day or half day's work. If Bill was lucky he would be chosen; if not, he would try at other dock gates. He was not always successful.

Now widowed, retired and living alone he often saw his two grown-up sons, who were married with families of their own and now living in Essex. Sometimes he would stay with them at weekends and they would regularly visit him at his home. True to East End tradition his family links were strong. The only time he had ever been abroad was during the First World War when he served as an infantry man in France and Belgium. He was content to enjoy his retirement in the East End, spending much time during the summer months in Shadwell Park where he would read, do crossword puzzles and 'jaw to other old contemptibles'.

When Naomi learnt that Bill had spent half a century working in the London docks, she suggested that the memories of ex-dockers were too important to be ignored and should be recorded by social historians. My estimation of her immediately increased tenfold.

Daphne, meanwhile, was impressed with the 1930s-built Matilda House Estate on the left of where we stood. She thought that the planners may have deliberately chosen a light-coloured brick, hoping to soften up the greyness of the surrounding area.

After a little coaxing Dave and I reluctantly agreed to have our photos taken in front of the shrapnel-scarred entrance to the estate. A group of local children decided that they should pose with us, insisting that we bring copies for them when we returned in the future.

We continued walking along Wapping High Street, bypassing the characterless Scotch Arms. This pub was built in 1958 on the site of its namesake that had been destroyed during the London blitz of 1940. I smiled to myself when I remembered how as a 10 year old, a friend and I found a dying sparrow chick that had fallen out of its nest. We substituted a matchbox for a coffin and buried the chick in the rubble where the original Scotch Arms stood.

Further along the High Street, we stopped outside old Jubilee Buildings. These tenements may have been a hundred years old. Although the windows and curtains were clean, at first Naomi did not believe that the buildings, which she described as 'ghastly; resembling a workhouse' could be occupied. Her comments rekindled my own memories of just after the Second World War, when I lived with my parents, three sisters and a brother in a one-bedroom flat in Stepney's Carr Street buildings.

Some young girls who were playing hopscotch nearby were delighted when

The sixteenth-century Turk's Head, Wapping High Street. (*Museum of Docklands PLA Collection*)

Naomi and Daphne took part in their game. A few minutes later Naomi and Daphne hopped to the other side of the road to take a photo of Dave and me with the Jubilee Buildings in the background. Dave glanced up at the buildings and remarked. 'You know, Alf, I would not mind living in these tenements if I had the opportunity, but there's no chance.' As he spoke, little boys raced along the pavement on their homemade wooden scooters. These scooters were exact replicas of the type I made as a boy. To think how my mother would have instantly chastised me, had she known that I occasionally rode my scooter, as did my friends, along the narrow pavement inside the busy, noisy and dangerous Rotherhithe Tunnel.

The girls wanted to be closer to the Thames so I suggested that we cross the bombed site near Colonial Wharf and sit at the river's edge. Here at the Union Stairs lay a wrecked, half-submerged barge, perhaps a casualty of the last war. Dave recalled the time when he worked on the tugs: a fellow deckhand had told him that before the last war he used to drink in the Turk's Head, a sixteenth century riverside tavern that stood on the very spot where we were now sitting. It was said that pirates who were to be hanged at the adjacent Executioner's Dock were first taken to the Turk's Head and offered a last drink of ale before their appointment with the hangman. I was intrigued by the story and was keen to see a photo of the tavern, but it was not until several years later that I came across a print of the building. I discovered it was closed for business on 24 June 1936, on the orders of the local council who considered the building structurally unsafe.

On the evening of the pub's closure the BBC were there to record the last orders. Unfortunately, the vacant Turk's Head, along with several neighbouring historical warehouses, was eventually destroyed during the Blitz.

Dave was starting to feel thirsty. The Town of Ramsgate public house was close by, but he could not persuade the girls to leave. They both seemed quite content just to sit by the river's edge and listen to the waves lapping continuously against the wall. When I mentioned that the Town of Ramsgate had a small, comfortable riverside terrace, the girls stood up and we left the bombsite.

As we passed the Travers spice warehouse on our left, the gorgeous aroma of exotic spices filled the air, Dave, recognising the flavours from his childhood in Burma, promised to cook us a curry soon, using similar spices. We stopped for a few minutes to admire and take photos of the early nineteenth century houses of Wapping Pierhead built on either side of the now filled in entrance to the Western dock.

The Town of Ramsgate was crowded with no free seats either inside the bar or outside on the terrace, so we went down the side alley and sat with our drinks on the top of Wapping's famous Old Stairs. Dave, who had just come through a heavy drinking spell, kept his promise that he would drink no alcohol that day, 'only fruit juice'. Placing his arm around Naomi he squeezed her tight and kissed her cheek. I looked away, but Daphne seemed amused. Because my role that afternoon was as a guide I did not really have an opportunity to speak to Daphne at length and I felt unsure what her appraisal of me was. Avoiding the subject of Wapping, we started to chat about our interests, families and work.

Dave's advice of always telling the truth to girls who were in our company would be adhered to. I gave her an honest account of my background. She too was quite candid about her private life. After a brief courtship she had married unwisely at eighteen, but had left her husband shortly afterwards when she discovered that he was secretly seeing former girlfriends. Her subsequent relationship with a much older man had lasted for about a year, but they drifted apart and he returned to his wife. As a secretary, her job was well paid, but tedious, unlike Naomi, who held a senior position at the same firm and often travelled around the country on company business.

Naomi's father, a property developer, who was Daphne's uncle, had converted one of his large properties in Islington into several flatlets. She lived in the small garden flat at the rear and Naomi occupied the whole of the first floor. Her uncle allowed her to live there for a miniscule rent on condition that she kept the halls and stairs clean and tended the garden.

I asked Daphne what music she liked. Our taste could not be more different. She was fond of jazz and I was obsessed with opera, but there was a common factor. We both disliked rock and roll.

Dave stood up and signalled that it was time for us to leave. We went

The seventeenth-century St John's charity school and adjacent rectory house, Wapping. In the 1950s, these buildings seemed abandoned and near derelict.

outside into the street and spent a moment by the adjacent Oliver's Wharf with all its gothic grandeur. I liked this warehouse; it was totally different from all the others in Wapping. Built in 1870, it resembled a monastery. On the rare occasion when I was in Wapping during the weekdays, I would stand opposite Oliver's Wharf and enjoy watching its hoists lowering tea chests on to the backs of lorries. Ten years later, Oliver's Wharf stood empty, but it was only for a short period. Sold in 1971 for £220,000, it was then divided into units and left for the new tenants to create their own apartments. The wharf became the first conversion in Docklands.

I showed the girls the nearby church of St John that was badly bombed during the war. Fortunately, its clock tower and steeple was still intact, but many of the gravestones in the tiny cemetery were smashed and now partially covered by buddleia. The adjacent late seventeenth century free school and rectory house had been closed for many years and was now boarded up. As a young boy I always found this area slightly sinister and foreboding. Others had noticed the eerie atmosphere too. The rectory was used as the haunted home of Ebenezer Scrooge in the 1951 definitive screen version of Charles Dickens' *A Christmas Carol* starring the incomparable Alistair Sim as Scrooge.

We continued walking along Wapping High Street and entered the little riverside park by old Aberdeen Wharf, where several middle-age artists were busy capturing on canvas the soon-to-disappear picturesque Rotherhithe riverscape. Unaffected by our inquisitiveness, the artists allowed us to stand quietly behind them and peer over their shoulders at their unfinished paintings. Daphne sighed and whispered, 'I wish I could paint. It must be so rewarding especially once your work is finished, to think that you could give your paintings to your family and friends as presents or perhaps even sell them, but unfortunately I don't have the talent.' Naomi who had overheard her protested, 'Yes you do have a talent, a talent for writing good children's stories.' I found Naomi's comment interesting. Daphne had not mentioned to me that she was an amateur writer, when we sat on Wapping's stairs a few minutes earlier. I liked her modesty. It was an attractive quality that was noticeably absent in some of the girls I was friendly with.

Just before we left the park, Dave's eyes were transfixed on a police boat. Due to the fast flowing current the boat was having difficulty tying up to the pontoon at nearby Wapping Police Station. With his eyes still focused on the police boat, Dave explained the various manoeuvres the pilot should or should not be doing.

Naomi stood up on a bench and took a photo of the old riverside houses of Rotherhithe that included the rooms that Tony Armstrong Jones had occupied before his recent marriage to Princess Margaret. As we passed the narrowest point of Wapping High Street, with the massive Gun Wharf on either side of the road that was connected by overhead little bridges, an idea came into my mind, but it would involve a little detour from our route. Because we had found the Wapping spices so pleasant, I thought it would be amusing if the four of us sampled another attractive flavour on offer.

By placing your face at the iron ventilation grills inserted in the dock wall that enclosed the Crescent's wine and rum vaults at the top end of Wapping Lane and taking a deep breath through your nose, you could enjoy an aroma that was so intoxicating you could almost taste the sweetness. However I quickly changed my mind, unsure of what affect it might have on Dave. So far he had behaved impeccably; his little whisky flask had been left at home and he had consumed only fruit juice at the Town of Ramsgate, but a few sniffs at the grill might set him off with us in tow in the direction of his favourite club The Green Parrot in nearby Graces Alley. Drinking all afternoon was not on the agenda.

As we turned into Wapping Wall, Naomi gasped at the sight of the seemingly never-ending row of warehouses. She wondered if our walk would ever finish. Dave chuckled when The Prospect of Whitby came into view. 'This calls for refreshment.' We went inside The Prospect just before closing time. Again Dave kept his promise; he ordered non-alcoholic drinks. It was too late to hear the music of the Hawaiian band that had just finished their session, but still time to enjoy the view of the river from the terrace. A sailing dinghy was tied up along side. Its owners, two middle aged men who had been drinking at the bar, appeared to be somewhat inebriated. When the men climbed down the iron ladder they seem to be experiencing problems trying to get into the dingy. 'Are they mad, where are their life jackets?' gasped Naomi. 'No, just

Wapping Wall, March 1977. Over the years several fine old Dock buildings that stood the test of time were destroyed during the fires of the 1970s. Thankfully the fire brigade always arrived quickly so the neighbouring residences in Wapping were never affected. Built in 1828, Warehouse B in St Katherine Dock was one of the first victims. The last warehouses to be destroyed were those that stood opposite Jubilee Wharf at Wapping Wall, when in March 1977 a huge fire reduced them to a shell.

drunk and stupid,' said Dave, who had witnessed similar scenes in the past. He also remarked, 'Many people are drowned trying to get on or off small craft, especially during rough seas.' It was amusing to watch the men's antics after they managed to board the dinghy. They stood up and then sat down; they changed places. When one of the men tried to hoist the sail, he received a slight knock on his head by the swinging boom. They began to argue, each blaming the other for the delay in casting off. The whole episode was reminiscent of a Laurel and Hardy two-reeler. When a police boat appeared close by they had the good sense to put on their life jackets and wait until the boat disappeared around the bend at Limehouse Reach before sailing away. The two men were fortunate that they had not fallen overboard.

Other sailors were not so lucky. Four years later, after an evening of drinking at the Prospect, 31-year-old Alan Dickson-Johnson and William Reid aged 30, got into their canoe and attempted to row to a yacht anchored fifty yards out on the Thames. Tragically, the two young men never made it to the yacht. The next day, their canoe was found on the foreshore at Deptford. The river police later recovered Jackson's body on the north bank and Reid's body on the south bank.

Our time on the Riverside terrace was too brief; a polite barman informed us that the pub would be closing shortly. A few minutes later we left the Prospect. The bascule bridge just fifty yards from the Prospect was raised and a small coaster was about to enter the Shadwell basin. We walked briskly up

The Grapes, Narrow Street, Limehouse.

to the barrier. Both Naomi and Daphne took photos of the Dutch crew on the deck that smiled and waved at us. After the coaster entered the basin and the bridge lowered, we went into the nearby Shadwell Park. The park was busy. Elderly men wearing their customary white shirts and slacks were playing bowls and the paddling pool was full of children splashing about. Other children were building castles in the sand pit. A decade earlier my childhood playmates and I had spent hours in that same pit.

The friendly blonde lady who owned the tea hut that backed onto Free Trade Wharf, and knew Dave and me by name, made us coffee and, as always, generously-filled sandwiches. Naomi insisted on paying. We sat on a riverside bench close by to enjoy our snack. It was an idyllic spot to observe the passing river traffic, or just to relax and listen to the sound of the waves and the ever-present seagulls.

After consuming the sandwiches, Daphne and I were content to sit there quietly and enjoy the magnificent view, but Dave and Naomi were in a talkative mood. Their attempts to draw us into their discussions were not successful. I was in no mood to argue whether it was right or wrong to execute Caryl Chessman after spending twelve years on death row or to give my opinion of Fidel Castro, and I certainly was not interested in the shooting down of Gary Powers' spy plane over Russia. I whispered to Daphne, 'Let's leave the debating society for a few minutes and go for a stroll.'

As we wandered around the perimeter of the park, we were careful not to bump into groups of excited and happy children who were using our path

Rotherhithe 1937. (*Museum of Docklands PLA Collection*)

as a racing track. I spotted Bill, the retired docker, sitting on a bench and
chatting to local pensioners. He glanced at us and waved.

Daphne took a photo of the coloured tablet of sixteenth century ships at
sea. This memorial was erected in 1922 when the park was opened to mark
the exact location where the Elizabethan sailors Frobisher, Willoughby
and the brothers Stephen and William Burrough had set sail to explore the
northern seas. A look inside the attractive brick-built building that housed the
circular ventilation shaft with its stairs leading below to Rotherhithe Tunnel
proved slightly scary for Daphne who stepped back as she glanced at the
huge rotating fans in its depths. We used my penknife to scratch our initials
on the wall. An unknown man, perhaps a merchant seaman, had also left his
mark, 'Jilted me here in 1928, so goodbye to London'. Standing so close to
Daphne, I was tempted to kiss her, but I hesitated in case she pushed me away.
Rejection might be hard to cope with at that age.

Moments later we joined Dave and Naomi by the riverside. Now their
subject of discussion was the kidnapping of Adolf Eichmann in Argentina by
Israeli agents. Rather than sit next to them, Daphne and I stood opposite their
bench with our backs to the railings. Suddenly Naomi looked at her watch,
realising it was time to for us leave the park; she asked Dave if we should
continue our walk. We left the park and on to the Highway until we came
to Narrow Street. Several of the ancient warehouses were still in use, others
were bomb damaged and abandoned including Old Sun wharf.

At the small ancient iron bridge over the entrance to the Limehouse Cut,

Dunbar Wharf, Narrow Street, Limehouse.

I showed Naomi and Daphne my name that I had carved on the bridge four years previously and was still visible, preserved by a thin layer of dust. The girls liked the Victorian cottages on either side of the lock. 'It's just like a little hamlet,' remarked Naomi. I never fully understood how this particular lock worked, so I left it to Dave to explain the process. For children it was a very dangerous area. The lock only had a low wall surrounding it and I remember as a young teenager leaning over the wall and being chased away by a lock keeper. Sadly a tragedy did occur at the lock. In July 1964 two-year-old Kim Subohon who was the daughter of the resident lock keeper fell into the lock and was drowned.

As we walked down Narrow Street the girls took photos of the Grapes Public House. Daphne asked me if Charles Dickens really had visited the pub. Of course, I could not confirm it, but I did try to give her an answer. 'Because Limehouse had been such an interesting and colourful area in the past it must have attracted many well-known people, therefore it's possible that Charles Dickens, who had connections with Limehouse and even Jack London, who in 1902 wrote about the area in his classic book *The People Of The Abyss*, could have enjoyed a drink at the Grapes.' (Charles Dickens was known to have visited his godfather Christopher Huffam, who lived in nearby Church Row adjacent to St Anne's Church.)

Dave and I wanted to walk through Chinatown and beyond, but the girls had seen enough for one day, so we boarded the bus at West India Dock Road that took us to Mile End tube. We eventually arrived at their home in

Limehouse Wharf, Narrow Street, Limehouse.

Islington about six o'clock in the evening. While Naomi cooked us a meal Daphne, Dave and I relaxed in the garden. Being a well-behaved teetotaller all day, Dave was now offered red wine, which was much appreciated. Later that evening, Dave and Naomi, who both had drank too much, retired for the night.

Just after they left the small dining room, Daphne pulled me up from the sofa and invited me downstairs to her flat, where we had coffee and listened to some of her records. I enjoyed the coffee, but not the music. Her attempts to introduce me to jazz failed. Opera was my music; to me it was the supreme art. Not wanting to offend her and admit that I loathed jazz, I simply said that her music was different to what I was accustomed to listening to. She understood and went over to a cabinet and brought out more records. To my surprise it was Mantovani's lovely music that seemed more appropriate for the occasion. When the gentle sound of 'Three Coins in the Fountain' filled the room we stood up and began to dance. The closeness affected my mind and body. Although I desperately wanted to kiss her, I was still unsure of how she would react, so I held back.

We continued dancing and listening to the strings of Mantovani's orchestra until the early hours of the morning. Her suggestion that I could share her bed rather than sleep alone on the sofa was accepted with a grateful smile, the perfect end to a memorable day.

At the beginning of 1960 Stepney Borough Council decided that Jane Street, Buross Street and the adjacent streets were to be demolished as part of their slum clearance programme. The residents of these streets were to be offered new dwellings on the expanding council estates at Poplar and Bow. The fifty-three houses in Jane Street did not have modern kitchens and bathrooms and their WCs were in the back yard; none had been badly damaged during the Blitz.

It was difficult for me to understand why these houses had to be demolished, when they seemed to be structurally sound. I would have preferred Jane Street and the neighbouring streets to be refurbished in keeping with the original character of western Stepney. Having to move away from an area that I was extremely fond of caused me some grief. Since 1947, my family, though extremely poor, had lived happily in peaceful Jane Street. The street was so quiet, especially on a Sunday morning when the only sounds to be heard were the sentimental Hebrew melodies being played by an elderly wandering violinist. Most of the neighbours were kind, thoughtful Jews. Our house was number 51. The Donns lived at 49 and the Isaacs at 53. I liked Mrs Jenny Donn, who was short, blonde and stocky. She was always grinning, with a permanent cigarette dangling from the corner of her mouth.

In the summer of 1960, Jenny, her husband Archie and son Raymond moved into a two bedroom flat on the top floor of Wickham House, that was a new council skyscraper, adjacent to Stepney Way. The Donns' weekly rent was £2, 11 shillings and sixpence. 'It's worth paying that just for the bath!' said a delighted Jenny. The Queen and Prince Philip, on an official tour of newly-built council dwellings, in the East End, were invited to visit Jenny's flat. 'And when are you going to get spliced?' asked Prince Philip to taxi-driver Raymond, who was with his fiancée Betty. 'We are planning to get married in December,' replied a proud Raymond.

Lou Isaacs, who was my age, was forever challenging me to race him down the street. Never once did he succeed, but just before he and his family moved to Manor Park, I deliberately slowed down my pace and allowed him to win.

Shortly after my family were rehoused to Poplar, I went on a nostalgic stroll down Jane Street and gazed sorrowfully at the abandoned houses. Not a single former tenant remained. Some of the houses had been vandalised and set on fire, others were now occupied by vagrants and squatters. I also saw totters (general dealers) removing discarded furniture from the houses. On the corner at the bottom of Jane Street, and still standing was the long-time closed 'Tradewinds Club'. This fine brown-painted building had a huge mural of a sailing ship on its outside wall. There were also six bullet holes in the wooden entrance. According to Dave, someone in Cable Street had told him that the shooting was the result of an incident that occurred during the end of the Second World War. Apparently, some American GIs were fighting over a woman.

I was determined to have a look inside the Tradewinds before it was demolished, but when I returned to the club at a latter date I was prevented from entering by the demolition workmen on site.

When Dave realised that Buross Street would be demolished, he became apprehensive. As Peggy Johnson's lodger, he knew that he was not entitled to any council accommodation, new or old. Fortunately, Peggy came to his aid. In December 1960 she somehow managed to persuade the council's housing officials to offer him a tiny one-bed-room flat in Old Grosvenor Buildings on Cotton Street, Poplar. His weekly rent was 17 shillings and sixpence and his electricity 'about half a crown'.

I was extremely pleased to hear that Dave had moved to Poplar. We would be neighbours again. Grosvenor Buildings was only a ten-minute walk from my family's maisonette on the newly-built Lansbury Estate. My friend was absolutely delighted with his cosy little flat, that he promptly called 'Davy Jones' locker'. For the first time in his adult life Dave would have a home of his own. He went to the pub to celebrate his good fortune, but got so drunk he had to be half carried home by workmates. Within a short space of time every house in Jane Street, Buross Street and the surrounding streets would be erased, all that remained on the vast cleared site were a few old sycamore trees.

On another sentimental visit to the area, I began to reflect on my Stepney boyhood. As a child, I hardly ever played in Jane Street, nor did my brother and sisters, mainly because few children lived there. We would run around the corner to the junction of Buross Street and Mariner Street where the majority of our close friends lived. It was at this location we would spend hours playing games that were always taking place in the safe car-free streets. Several of the resident children were Anglo-Indian, Maltese or Irish, but most were English and many seemed related.

Street sellers would appear in the summer and at weekends, causing us to throw down our cricket bats and run over to see what they sold, knowing full well that the choice would always be the same: ice cream, honeycomb, candyfloss or toffee apples. If you had some pennies you took your pick, consumed it quickly and returned once more to your game.

As pocket money was so scarce in those days, my school friends and I would seize any opportunity that allowed us to earn some pennies. Besides the selling of rags we turned our attention to collecting old newspapers. Just by knocking on doors and asking the tenants for their discarded newspapers we could accumulate sack loads, pile them on to our homemade wooden carts and sell them at Hough's the paper merchants, at Narrow Street in Limehouse.

Another of our enterprises that proved equally profitable, but only during the winter, was the selling of kindling for tuppence a bundle. Because the majority of Stepney's households relied on coal fires, we had no problem with our sales and obtaining the wood was easy. We had two main sources of supply. Wooden off-cuts from the nearby Chowder Street furniture factory were regularly dumped on an adjacent bombsite. Our second source was the wooden panelling that we removed from the halls of old empty houses that were waiting for demolition. We would drag the wood into the back yard and use big stones or old iron piping to break it in pieces about ten inches long.

One Saturday afternoon in late 1954, I was with my two school friends, Kenny and Brian, removing wood from a semi-derelict terrace house in Philpot Street, which was just a minute's walk from my home, when I decided to explore the small dusty basement. Amongst the hundreds of old letters, receipts and newspapers, I found £7-10/- inside a neatly folded, white paper bag. I had never seen so much money; it was a treasure trove. Excitedly, I ran up the stairs and into the yard shouting to my friends, 'Money, I have found money!' The three of us danced around the yard, for Kenny and Brian knew that our strict code of sharing whatever we found on bombsites or inside abandoned old houses was binding. Being the eldest, at thirteen, I kept £3. I gave £2-10/- to 12-year-old Brian and £2 to Kenny, who was 11. Kenny immediately screamed, 'I am rich, I am rich!' He then took off like a hurdler in a race jumping over the little dividing back yard walls and calling out, 'I am rich, rich and I am going to buy a suit'.

I ran home and gave the £3 to my mother who, despite my protest, decided to take the money to the local police station. I begged her not to do so, fearing that the police would want to interview my two friends and perhaps cause problems for their parents, but she would not listen. I reminded her that when she had taken the £2 I had recently found in the gutter of a neighbouring street to Arbour Square Police Station, she has received no acknowledgement or reward from the Lascar (Indian Seamen) who claimed he had lost the money. Knowing what little money my parents had, I continued to try to persuade her to change her mind, and thankfully in the end she did. So we kept the money, my reward from mum a valuable two shillings.

How resourceful we boys were in keeping ourselves occupied during the school holidays. When not trying to earn a little money or participating in the various street games, we would visit our adventure playgrounds which were the ubiquitous bombsites. From these scars of the Blitz, many of which were now already covered with young trees, bushes and buddleia, we would use branches to make catapults or bows and arrows. Even the thin wire still attached to the discarded cardboard flower boxes stacked on the waste ground behind Kelly's, the florist shop at the corner of Cavell Street, proved useful. We would wind the wire around the blunt tip of our arrows to give them more balance in flight and to bind thick elastic on to our catapults. We could even make a wire loop that enabled us to open the exit doors of the Palaseum cinema in nearby Commercial Road and dodge in. By poking the wire through a thin gap in the centre of the door we could loop it over the crash bar, pull downwards and the door would open, allowing us to sneak in.

Maurice Cheepen, the charismatic and popular Palaseum manager, was usually lenient with us when he realised we had gained entry; providing we made no noise once seated inside, he would take no action. Sammy McCarthy, the young Stepney featherweight boxing champion, often arrived in Mariner Street walking alongside his proud father, who sold fruit and vegetables from a barrow.   Sammy, known as 'Smiling Sammy', was polite, friendly and always impeccably dressed, a role model for us impressionable twelve-year-old boys. A few years later, our same group of boys who crowded around the boxer for his autograph became smartly-dressed Army cadets in the Rifle Brigade and spent two weeks training at a big military camp near Colchester.

My instructor, who lay alongside me on the firing range and showed me how to load and fire a Bren gun, was none other than Colonel Victor Turner VC, one of the greatest soldiers of the 1942 North African campaign. Colonel Turner of the 2nd battalion of the Rifle Brigade was awarded the Victoria Cross following the battle at El Aqqagir, (Kidney Ridge) El Alamein.

After about a year of being a boy soldier my interest waned. I much preferred to play 'kiss chase' with the local girls during the evenings rather than practice boring rifle drill.

'Ginger' Dunne was a rag merchant who had a shop on the corner of Mariner Street and Anthony Street. To us children who had spent hours collecting old rags during the school holidays, which we sold to him, he was a crook who would cheat us whenever he could. Ginger altered the scales in his favour when he weighed our sacks of rags and would often delay payment until a later date and then refuse to pay us when our money was due. (His usual excuse being that he had already paid us.) Ginger's ongoing dishonesty deeply upset his enterprising little rag-collectors, and we desperately wanted revenge.

During a Friday night, thieves broke into his warehouse and stole much of his stock. The following morning his warehouse door was left open by the raiders. As Ginger had not yet arrived, I went into the warehouse and with the aid of a friend, brought out the few remaining valuable sacks of wool. We quickly loaded them on to our carts and hid them on a neighbouring bombsite and later sold them to another rag merchant.

Ginger Dunne was to be taught a further lesson: we quickly collected a huge sack of rags and hid several bricks inside to gain extra weight. As usual, Ginger wanted to defer payment. We protested and refused to leave his shop until he had paid us. Our tenacity paid off. He begrudgingly gave us a few shillings. That evening, the same pile of bricks that we had hidden in the sack was piled up outside his shop.

'Old Mother Segal' lived in Mariner Street. Known to everyone as 'Square Shoulders' because of her peculiar box-shape figure, she sold second-hand clothes from her barrow in Watney Street market. Her front room was piled to the ceiling with old, often smelly clothes.

Each morning this short, old, Russian-born Jewish lady, near blind with cataracts, would load the clothes on to the barrow and push it 250 yards to the market and then in the evening make the same arduous journey home. She managed to push her barrow with some difficulty, when the road surface was level, but there was a problem when she arrived at the slope at Aggra Place at the eastern end of Mariner Street. Going up or down this slope was perilous for the old lady; if she lost control of her barrow it would take off and roll down the hill. If my friends and I saw her struggling we would go to her aid.

It was a Saturday morning when Mother Segal arrived at the top of the slope, but before my friends and I could go over to help her, the heavily laden barrow took off with Mother Segal clinging to it. With her feet dangling about two feet from the ground the barrow gathered speed. It shot down the slope, crossed Bigland Street and struck the kerb in front of the school. Passers-by ran over to her. Amazingly Mother Segal, who must have been in her eighties, was unhurt. We picked up several old stays and brassieres that had fallen off the barrow and placed them back on board; we then turned the barrow around to face the market. Mother Segal thanked us and continued her short journey.

Sylvio and John Lomiglio were two childhood friends of mine who lived in Buross Street. Their parents were Maltese-born, practising Catholics who settled in Stepney in 1938. Unlike their daughter Mary, the two sons suffered from dyslexia. As a young boy I would often sit with the brothers at their home and try to teach them to read, but my efforts were not very successful. Because of the amount of time I was spending with the family I began to learn rudimentary Maltese.

When I was eight years old, Sylvio and I were returning home from the 'threepenny pictures' that were shown twice a week at St George's Methodist Church in Cable Street, when suddenly I almost collapsed from the excruciating pain of pleurisy. My good friend Sylvio picked me up and carried me the 300 yards home. I spent the next few days in the Children's Hospital at Shadwell where a hot poultice was placed on my chest. Fortunately, I quickly recovered and readily followed my mother's instruction to say yes to the doctor when he asked me if I would like to 'go on convalescence'. I had no idea what the word 'convalescence' meant, but I soon learnt. The following day an ambulance took me to the Children's Convalescence Home by the sea at Broadstairs in Kent, where I remained for six weeks.

Mr and Mrs Lomiglio were a very emotional couple who seemed to be constantly bickering with their two sons. It was a highly charged atmosphere at their house, with constant loud arguments that could be heard in the street. Most of the disturbances started in the kitchen where the two boys would often antagonise their parents into an explosive rage. Mrs Lomiglio would respond by whacking them with ladles, rolling pins, spoons or any other utensil that she happened to have in her hand. Even as young adults Sylvio and John were on the receiving end of her fierce temper.

I was standing outside their house when Sylvio ran into the street. Seconds later his angry mother appeared on the doorstep and threw a large carving knife at him. The knife missed Sylvio's head by inches. That same year, I witnessed Mrs Lomiglio, who was obese and suffering from painful arthritic legs, pursuing Sylvio onto the bombsite at nearby Hungerford Street where she aimed stones at him. His misdemeanour was that he had eaten more than his share of toast that morning at breakfast.

Because Sylvio was overweight he was nicknamed 'Fat Migio', but his weight did not prevent him from climbing. During the summer school holidays of 1953, Sylvio was crossing the roof of a local disued garage. Near the centre of the roof, a section of the asbestos sheeting caved in under his weight; he went through the hole and fell twenty feet to the ground and broke his foot. The unfortunate Sylvio had to spend the rest of the summer on crutches.

Sylvio's inability to read or write was well known by local children. Sometimes, while we were playing in the street or on bombsites, a few spiteful children would call him a dunce. This name-calling had little effect; he had learnt to ignore it. However, bullies were another matter. He hated aggressive boys who occasionally tried to take advantage of his passive nature, a mistake many a boy made, for Sylvio was strong, nimble and no coward.

During August 1955, Sylvio and I just left the open air swimming pool at Goulston Street, Aldgate East (the pool had become open air because its roof had been blown off at the height of the Blitz and had never been replaced) when we were confronted in the street by Alan Hogan, a tall, well-built 16 year old, who had a reputation for being a vicious bully. Hogan, who often beat up boys younger than himself, decided that he would like to provoke my friend into a fight, a decision he soon learnt to regret, for Sylvio proved to be a tough opponent. Seeing that there was no chance of beating him in a fair fight, Hogan decided to ignore the Marquess of Queenberry's rules and kick Sylvio's genitals. A sturdy young lorry driver, who was standing on the nearby loading bay of the Brooke Bond tea factory, witnessed the scrap; he was so outraged by Hogan's appalling behaviour that he jumped down from the bay and stood between the two fighting boys and challenged Hogan to a fight, fair or otherwise. As the lorry driver was approximately his own size the cowardly Hogan declined his offer and quickly left the street.

John Lomiglio was three years younger than Sylvio and like his brother he was good-natured and very popular in Buross Street. In early 1959 when John was seventeen, a drunken neighbour, twenty year old Alan Higgins, stabbed him in the chest with a broken bottle. John was rushed to the nearby London Hospital for emergency treatment. Because Higgins had a sly character, the stabbing was thought to have been deliberate, but in all probability it was the result of a dangerous prank that went wrong. Although the incident caused great stress to the Lomiglio family they decided not to contact the police once John was out of danger.

A few months later, I was invited to a house party in Bermondsey. Alan

Higgins and two of his friends had also been invited. At first the partygoers seemed quite friendly, but after about an hour the atmosphere became tense and I started to feel uncomfortable. There seemed to be too many suspicious eyes glaring at Higgins. I began to suspect that our hosts may have become annoyed with Higgins who for sometime had been looming over the drinks table. It seemed obvious that the four of us were no longer welcome, so we said goodbye to the two girls who had invited us to the party and left the house. We were followed by about twenty of the guests who immediately surrounded us in the street. Higgins was then singled out and accused of stealing a bottle of spirits. After admitting the theft, he received a succession of blows to his head. Higgins fell to the ground where several men started to kick him. I tried to intervene but was instantly struck about the face. When Higgins's body was almost lifeless the men fled.

The next day I visited him in Guy's Hospital. Fortunately, there was no brain damage, but his head and face was badly bruised and cut. I suggested that we should contact the police, but he adamantly refused. When Mrs Lomiglio heard the news of the severe beating that Higgins had received in Bermondsey, she was delighted, believing it was God's way of punishing him for stabbing her son. I thought otherwise. Kneeling on the floor and clasping her hands tightly she said, 'Its God's wish, God's wish, thank God.'

Five years later in 1964, John Lomiglio escaped death a second time. While swimming off a Devon beach, strong tides swept him out to sea. The emergency services were alerted and he had to be rescued by helicopter.

9

The Lithuanians

At 5.30 p.m. on Friday 10 June 1960, I left the A&B Hyams Bethnal Green factory where I had worked as a dress cutter for the previous four years. My plan was to try and enlist in the Merchant Navy at the earliest opportunity.

During my final year at Bethnal Green, I had become very friendly with several Lithuanians who lived and worked locally. Many of these exiles were employed in the men's clothing trade, especially the pressing and machining of trousers and waistcoats. Usually at 1 p.m. I would meet my older friend Joe, a Hoffman presser for lunch. (A Hoffman pressing machine is used for pressing mainly coat and jackets). Most days we would dine at the nearby George Tavern, Bethnal Green's ancient public house and occasionally we would visit Tony's Café at the corner of Blythe Street. Tony, like Joe, was a second generation Lithuanian. As Joe's wife Alice worked as a lunchtime waitress at the George restaurant, Joe and I always received prompt service and generous portions of food.

The George was owned by Ball Brothers Ltd, a well-established family business of wine and sherry importers. Huge casks of their noted produce were kept behind the bar and were much appreciated by the pub's regular clientele, especially the old-age pensioners. Built in the early eighteenth century, the George had a wonderful old-world interior. The ground floor was divided by well-preserved oak panelling into three smaller bars. On the ceiling and walls hung polished wooden signs with quotations from famous English writers all praising the merits of the alehouse. One of the quotations by Dr Samuel Johnson, that was written over two hundred years ago, is still relevant today and remains a particular favourite of mine: 'There is nothing which has yet been contrived by man, by which so much happiness is produced, as by a good tavern or inn.'

I enjoyed dining at the George with Joe who was a former Eighth Army soldier. Besides our interesting conversations, there was usually an opportunity to catch a glimpse of Mary, the beautiful eighteen-year-old daughter of the licensees Percy and Joyce Vitler. Percy and Joyce, originally from Bexhill-on-Sea had arrived at the George in 1958. They soon became very popular with their customers that included many of the local stallholders and off-duty detectives from nearby Bethnal Green Police Station. Mary had temporarily given up her student nurse training and was now employed as an assistant at a local chemist. She had no interest whatsoever in her parents' pub. The only time she could be seen behind the bar was for a few brief moments at lunchtime, when she would chat to her mother before returning to work.

Eventually, I became very friendly with Mary. When she celebrated her nineteenth birthday, I gave her a small present for which she was extremely grateful. Later that evening we sat in her bedroom and played classical records. The following Sunday we took a boat trip on the Thames and visited Greenwich Park. Because Mary loved ballet, she eagerly accepted my invitation to see London's Festival Ballet at the Royal Festival Hall.

Neither Mary nor I wanted our relationship to be more than just good friends. At that stage of my life, I certainly did not want a regular girlfriend. Meeting girls for sexual encounters was my priority, or as my friend David Upson succinctly put it, 'sowing your oats'.

Occasionally, I would meet Joe at weekends for drinks in the pubs along Bethnal Green Road, where I met several of his Lithuanian friends. Although Joe was born in London, he had never visited his parents' homeland, but he was aware of its history. It seems that the Lithuanians came to Britain in two waves, and the first immigrant families arrived at the beginning of the century. The second wave, mostly men, came just after the Second World War. Many of these men had been forced to serve in auxiliary units under German control and fight against the Russians. 'We had no choice, if we had refused, we could have been shot,' said Vickinis, a high-class trouser-maker.

I soon began to like these intelligent people, who all seemed to possess excellent linguistic skills. Frustrated by my own slow progress in trying to understand basic Italian grammar, I could not but admire the Lithuanians' flair for languages. I asked one exile, a waistcoat-maker by trade, how he managed to speak, besides his mother tongue, English, German, Polish and Russian. He replied confidently, 'because of Lithuania's unique geographical position. We bordered Poland and Russia and after the German occupation of my country during the last war we learnt to converse in German too.'

During numerous slightly tipsy conversations in Bethnal Green pubs late at night, and more sober, serious discussions at the Lithuanian social club in Victoria Park Road, I became knowledgeable about Lithuania's recent tragic past. I invited David Upson to meet my new acquaintances, but he showed no interest.

Prior to coming into contact with the Lithuanians, I had no idea that Lithuania was a small Baltic, mainly Roman Catholic country and that for the previous fifteen years, against her will, had been forced to become a Soviet Socialist Republic. It was explained to me that Lithuania had originally been a part of the old Tsarist Empire, but had achieved independence in 1918.

The years that followed were of great optimism and progress. Although the country's Jewish minority controlled much of the commerce and industry, the land reforms that had been introduced brought enormous benefits to the semi-literate peasants who made up the bulk of the population. The peasants were allowed to organise themselves and form well run co-operatives that helped to improve the standard of living for the working classes; but tragically, in the summer of 1940 and after just twenty-two years of independence, Lithuania's short period of freedom was extinguished. The Russians, worried that a possible German invasion of their homeland was imminent, appealed to the governments of Lithuania, Latvia and Estonia to allow the Red Army to establish military bases in their countries in order to protect her northern flank from a surprise German attack. The three Baltic States refused Russia's demands. Russia responded by sending her tanks into their heartland. An exile told me that when the Russian tanks had arrived in his city, the only inhabitants who welcomed the invaders were the Jews. Detecting a note of anti-Semitism here, I quietly listened and made no comment. David Upson's sound advice rang in my ears. 'When you are in the company of strangers, avoid mentioning a sensitive subject; or if an emotive issue is being discussed, it's better to remain neutral, never take sides and refrain from making comments; by doing so, you will be accepted and allowed to stay.'

Sitting one evening in the White Hart pub in Bethnal Green Road with Joe and two of his Lithuanian friends, I could not resist the temptation to raise the subject of Russia's invasion of Lithuania. Ignoring Dave's advice I ventured to press the two exiles for more information. I knew that once they started to expound they would not stop. Speaking in impeccable English, the older of the two men said that the effect of the Russian invasion had been terrifying. The communist secret police, who he described as a 'Jewish outfit', had arrived with the tanks. They immediately began arresting the country's intelligentsia, especially people in government, the universities and the army. Those who were not tortured or butchered were deported to Siberia and never seen again. The younger of the two men claimed that as a teenager in 1940, he had witnessed many business people being shot and women and girls being raped and murdered by the GPU.

The older man explained that GPU was the name of the 'dreaded, cruel and sadistic secret police'. I had noticed that other exiles to whom I had spoken in the Lithuanian club had made similar allegations of atrocities committed by the secret police. Most of the exiles blamed the Russian and Lithuanian Jews for the ruination of their homeland. Time and time again, when the word Jew was mentioned by those in our company, it was used derogatively. To these Lithuanian exiles, the very word Judaism was synonymous with communism and terror.

This anti-Jewish attitude was baffling; I had never encountered a subject that aroused so much ill feeling. In the past, a few anti-Semites had approached me in the street. They thought that by accepting their leaflets, I might share their beliefs that the majority of British Jews were 'perfidious, avaricious by nature and have a propensity for fraud', but I had rejected their views. I thought that their arguments were based on prejudice rather than fact. Stereotyping a whole community was absurd. Nor could I accept that thousands of Jews in wartime Lithuania were violent revolutionaries involved in the mass genocide of non-Jewish civilians.

Far from being perfidious, avaricious and fraudulent, the Jewish people whom I knew were law-abiding, hardworking and successful, just like my own employers were. I also thought that these fine qualities could be found in their co-religionist in Lithuania and elsewhere in Europe; although the exiles I came into contact with during the early summer of 1960 were adamant that the events they were describing were accurate and did occur during the Russian occupation of Lithuania in 1940. Of course, I was in no position to ascertain if there was any truth in their allegations, but what was obvious to me, the Lithuanians, a talented and intelligent people, were continually expressing abhorrence of an equally talented and intelligent people: the Jews.

Because I was still keen to learn more of Lithuania and its people, I accepted Joe's invitation to meet him and a group of his Lithuanian associates the following weekend.   Again we would meet at the popular White Hart pub. I asked one exile if he was in Lithuania during the German occupation.

'Yes I was,' he replied. 'And thank God for the German Army, that saved us.' He explained that from the time the Russians invaded Lithuania in 1940 until they were driven out of the country a year later by the German Army; perhaps fifty thousand of his countrymen were murdered by the communist secret police. I asked him why innocent civilians were arrested and killed.

'Why?' he replied, slightly agitated. 'Because the ruling classes, the intelligentsia and the religious leaders were seen as the main obstacle to the establishment of bolshevism in Lithuania, these people had to be liquidated by the GPU. The captives were shown no mercy. When the Russian Army occupied Latvia, Estonia, Poland and Hungry, the GPU massacred all opposition, just like they did in my country; and look what happened to the captured fifteen thousand Polish Army officers in the Katyn forest; the Russian GPU shot every one of those brave soldiers. Thousands of Poland's finest intellectuals were among the victims; and we must not forget it was the Russians who suffered most of all. The state secret police murdered millions of their own citizens, including Tsar Nicholas and his family.'

Another exile at our table told me that had the German Army not invaded Lithuania in 1941 and driven the Russian forces out of the country, the GPU would have executed thousands more of his countrymen. A third man spoke, his eyes ablaze with anger. 'Now it was our turn for justice or retribution, call it what you will. Those Jewish people who were informants, spies or members of the GPU who did not manage to escape with the retreating Russian Army were arrested by our comrades and summarily shot; they were shown no mercy, just as they showed no mercy to the thousands of Lithuanians who were murdered by their communist friends.'

The shocking events that were alleged to have occurred in Lithuania twenty years before was difficult for me to comprehend. Whatever the truth the Bethnal Green based exiles must have lived through a terrible experience.

A few minutes later, whilst in the gents', a feeling of guilt engulfed me and I felt that I had just made a bad mistake. I was a guest of Joe and his friends, it was a Saturday night and a time to relax, drink and dance, but what was I doing, coaxing the Lithuanians to recall bitter wartime memories.

When I went back to the table, I had hoped that the subject would be changed, but it was too late, my hosts knew that I was interested in learning about their homeland. As always, they spoke in an angry tone. They told me that when the Russian Army eventually recaptured Lithuania from the Germans in 1944, the whole process of mass arrests, executions and deportations began all over again. It was during this period, or just before that the Lithuanians with whom I was acquainted had fled their country and arrived in Britain.

In May 1960 Israeli agents kidnapped Adolph Eichmann in Argentina and forcibly smuggled him out of the country and delivered him to Israel. Shortly after the kidnapping, I was drinking in the Lithuanian social club with Joe and his Lithuanian friend Anton, who was an exile from Vilnius. Anton told me that he was proud to have worn a German uniform when he fought on the Russian front in 1942. When Joe mentioned the Eickmann case, Anton began to dominate the conversation. He was totally convinced that Eichmann was a 'scapegoat'. His view was that if Eichmann had been involved in the killing of European Jews, he should be put on trial in Europe, where he had allegedly committed the crimes, and not in Israel which did not exist during the Second World War. Also the climate for revenge in Israel would prevent the accused from having an unbiased trial.

A little later Anton continued his argument by suggesting that even before Eichmann appears in court he had already been pronounced guilty of masterminding the plan to murder millions of European Jews. 'The trial would simply be a formality and useful for propaganda reasons. We all know that here in Britain, a man is innocent until proven guilty, but not in Israel. Their Prime Minister Ben Gurion has already sentenced Eichmann to be shot by announcing to the world's press that, "The man who was responsible for sending millions of Jews to the gas chambers was being held in Israel and will be placed on trial." So you see my young friend that is what you call a show trial.'

Joe and I listened earnestly as he spoke. 'This whole business is a Zionist plot,' he remarked, with a smile that suggested that he had discovered peculation at work. Anton also said, 'Israel needs money. They are so desperate for money to survive that they are prepared to capture an ordinary simple colonel like Eichmann, stage a show trial, produce false witnesses and forged documents and then try and convince the whole world that Eichmann was the chief architect who carried out his plan and sent millions of Jews to the gas chambers. The Israelis know that they can obtain generous rewards from gullible Christians, I think you English people call it rich pickings.'

'Rich pickings?' I replied 'What do you mean?'

He looked at me slightly surprised. 'Don't you understand me, my young friend? Governments and good people all over the world will show sympathy for Israel and feel it is their duty to offer financial and military aid to Israel, of course, at the expense of the Palestinians.'

I wanted to ask him more questions, but he was by now in full flow. 'I guarantee, that in the future perhaps not in my lifetime, that there will be great wars in the Middle East. If the whole world believes that the Jews have suffered enough and should have their own state in Palestine, while disregarding the Palestinians, then the Israelis will forever be at war with the Arabs.'

Just at that moment, other Lithuanians came into the club and joined us at our table. They began to speak in their own language and then in English. Having consumed too much beer and knowing that I had a long walk home, I declined the offer of more drink. After saying goodbye to Joe and Anton, I left the club.

After I stopped working in Bethnal Green, I would never meet any of my Lithuanian acquaintances again. However, later that year, I did visit Joe who was a patient in Hackney Hospital. Whist the worst for drink, he had fallen down the steps outside the Lithuanian social club and tumbled into the basement area below, breaking several limbs in the process.

During the early summer of 1960 I made my first attempt to join the Merchant Navy, but I came away from the Shipping Federation's offices in Prescot Street at Aldgate East extremely disappointed. The federation had temporarily stopped recruiting Merchant Navy staff. David Upson also applied and was advised to return in the spring when there would be vacancies.

Now out of a job, I did what most unemployed cutters did in those days and went around from one factory to another to see if the owners needed staff. I soon found employment at a small dress factory in Leman Street just a short walk from the Shipping Federation.

The factory was typical of so many that I would come to work at over the years. The dirty and smelly cutting room which was in the cellar had no fire escape, extinguishers nor alarms. A single flight of stairs led down to the cellar. At the other end of the cellar, a small trapdoor measuring about eighteen inches square was cut out of the ceiling and was used for lowering fabric into the room. If a fire started on the ground floor, the cellar would be a potential death-trap for the cutting staff, although a cutter, albeit a slim one could, by standing on a stool placed on the cutting-table use the ceiling trap-door to escape.

An added problem was the rats. A whole colony was present having gained access via an adjacent broken sewer that ran parallel with the cellar. Dennis, the other cutter employed at the factory, told me that the rats had created a run from the cellar to 'Italian Lui's' café next door.

During a lunch break in July an ebullient David Upson was waiting for me outside the factory exit. He grabbed my arm and said, 'Come on Alf, we have to go the Shipping Federation, they are recruiting.'

I answered him incredulously, 'Recruiting, are you sure, Dave?'

'Yes, definitely,' he replied confidently.

As we increased our pace along Leman Street, Dave explained that he had met his seaman friend Len Mackenzie the previous evening who had told him the good news. I was surprised at this news. Dave and I had only recently visited the Shipping Federation's offices in nearby Prescot Street to enquire about enlisting in the Merchant Navy and had been advised to reapply in the spring, when there would be vacancies for utility stewards.

Our elation soon expired. At the offices we were told by a less than sympathetic clerk that we were too late. The Federation had stopped taking on new staff earlier that morning.

Noticing our disappointment a West Indian seaman standing nearby said, 'They will take you on in April, man, but pop in meanwhile, you might be lucky.'

Dave did not share my disappointment. Always an optimist like Mr Micawber, he tried to console me. 'Cheer up Alf, don't consider it time wasted, we tried and we can try again.' He smiled and spoke cheerfully, 'Spring will soon be here, mate.' But spring was eight months away and I was becoming more restless by the day. Instead of travelling east to join a ship at Tilbury and sailing away to exotic places around the world, I was heading back to a filthy, rat-infested cellar at Aldgate East.

That same evening, I met Dave for drinks at the Prospect of Whitby. The disappointment that I had experienced at lunchtime was soon forgotten. At the Prospect we met two pretty occupational therapists from Bristol. Enjoying their company we formed a quartet and sang the evening away. This was therapy at its best. At closing time we escorted the therapists to Wapping underground station.

During our walk home, Dave suggested that as we both worked near the Shipping Federation's offices, it would be in our interests to take it in turns to visit the Federation once a week. We subsequently did, over a several week period, but the reply was always the same 'Not at the moment.' As it was probably futile to expect to gain entry into the Merchant Navy until the spring, we made no further visits.

Since Dennis, my fellow cutter, had handed in his notice and had left the company, the atmosphere in the cellar had become less noisy. With only one cutting machine in use, the quietness appealed to the rodents, who were appearing more frequently. One fearless huge rat came out from under the cutting table quite close to where I stood. I tried to kick it, but I was far to slow. With lightning speed it zigzagged in between my feet and disappeared down a hole beneath the sink. Routinely, I would throw various objects at the rats or use a steel yardstick to strike at them whenever they scuttled past. Invariably my aim was poor, but I did manage to hit an unwanted visitor on the snout with the yardstick when it emerged from a large cavity in the wall that was used for storing dress markers.

When Elsie, a West Indian machinist, was confronted on the stairs by a rat, she jumped in the air and tumbled down the stone stairs injuring her back.

It was a Monday morning. As I went down the stairs to the cellar, I followed my usual practice of stamping my feet, hoping that the racket would frighten off any rats that were lurking in the cutting room. After turning on the lights, I had to remain by the door; at least six rats scattered in every direction. When I went inside, there were fresh droppings in the sink and also on top of the dress lay that I was due to cut out. From that moment, I knew it would be impossible for me to continue working in that disgusting, malodorous cellar. Gerald, the boss, had yet to arrive; had he been on the premises, I would have thumped him.

As I strode grim-faced through the sewing room towards the exit, the manageress peered over the top of her spectacles and said, 'Rats?' I answered her with an emphatic nod.

At midday, I telephoned Gerald and demanded that my P45 be ready for me to collect within the hour. He immediately began to complain that I had let him down 'badly'. I responded by replacing the receiver.   A week or so later, I met Gerald's manageress in the nearby Commercial Road. She had good news. Elsie had been discharged from hospital, having recovered from her fall.

Despite the calming influence of David Upson, I was now extremely frustrated and utterly disillusioned with the clothing trade. To make my situating worse, I was unable to join the Merchant Navy until the following year. Outdoor employment interested me, at least until the spring.

In the local newspapers there was a variety of non-clothing factory work being advertised. I considered becoming a postman, an assistant groundsman in a park or even a hod carrier like my father, though I could never match his strength. How I envied my friend Alfie Debono, who was a former disgruntled stock cutter, but who was now working at Wapping River Police Station as a labourer, although he preferred the title 'maintenance hand'.

10

The Grenadier Guards

By chance, in the Refiners Arms on Buross Street, I met a soldier friend Mike Cassidy who was on leave from the Army and visiting old mates in Stepney. My friend, who was nineteen, originally came from the Midlands. About two years earlier, he had left home and somehow made his way to the East End where he had found work as a butcher's assistant. Mike's ghastly bedsit was situated at the rear of a Maltese-owned lodging house in Cable Street. The premises was divided into several bedsits and let mainly to working prostitutes. A single WC situated in the backyard was shared by the occupants of the entire building. Apart from the mice and bugs in Mike's room, the curtains were torn, an old wardrobe leant at an angle and the small wobbly table seemed as if it was about to collapse.

Whist living and working in Stepney, Mike had become bored with his mundane existence. He too yearned for a life of adventure. Joining the Army offered him an exciting life. Soon his regiment would be posted to the Far East.

Mike was wearing a finely-pressed uniform when we chatted at the bar of the Refiners. He explained that his Army training had been extremely challenging, but now that he was a trained infantryman and had joined a battalion of 800 men he was always 'treated with respect'. He explained that because Britain's worldwide military commitments were much less than before, large numbers of military personnel were no longer needed, hence the abolition of National Service. By 1962 the last of the national servicemen would be demobbed and Britain would have a smaller but professional regular Army.

My friend thought that as I had lost interest in the clothing trade I should perhaps consider joining the Army for a few months. He mentioned a new scheme that the Ministry of Defence had just introduced. The scheme was designed to attract volunteers for three, six and nine year engagements with a proviso that if a recruit found that he was not suitable to be a soldier during his initial three-month training period, he could buy himself out of the Army for £20.

'Why not give the Army a try, Alf, at least just for the summer?' said Mike, enthusiastically. 'Volunteer for three years, but just come for three months, do your training and go home. Surely it's worth investing £20? However, you must remember Alf, if you are still in the Army after three months, you will forfeit your right to resign.'

Mike's suggestion interested me. Joining the Army for three months could be beneficial, it might help to cure my acute restlessness and help to pass the time away until April 1961, the magic date when I would be able to enlist in the Merchant Navy.

David Upson and Alfie Debono were the first of several friends to advise me against the idea of being a 'three-month soldier'. Dave thought that it may not be that simple for recruits to resign.

'Alf, read the small print carefully before you accept the Queen's shilling.'

My mother, whose health was declining became upset when I told her of my imminent plans. She implored me to change my mind and not join the Army, but I ignored her tearful pleas. I also made the stupid mistake of not explaining clearly what my intentions were in signing up. To this day, I have never forgiven myself for causing my mother unnecessary grief.

About a week after meeting Mike at the Refiners, I visited an Army recruitment centre near Charing Cross and volunteered for three years Army service. On 3 August 1960, I packed a few belongings in a carrier bag and left Stepney for the Brigade of Guards depot at Pirbright Camp in Surrey. A soldier driving a jeep spotted me whilst I was waiting at the bus stop by Brookwood Station. He stopped and offered me a lift to Pirbright Camp.

As we drove along, he surprised me by saying 'I have twenty-eight bloody days and one hour left in this outfit.' When I did not reply, he slowed the jeep down and said, 'Have you been called up, or are you a volunteer?'

I preferred not to mention to this stranger that my plan was to resign within three months. Instead I stated, 'I have volunteered for three years.' My answer caused him to apply his brakes.

After he parked the jeep at the side of the tree lined lane and with the engine still running, shouted, 'You must be mad! You're throwing away the best three years of your life and for what? While your mates back home are out boozing and partying with tarts, you will be confined to the barracks, scrubbing your kit or watching a load of rubbish on television or having to jump every time one of the officers appears. If you want some good sound advice, mate, chuck the Army at the earliest opportunity!' As I was getting out off the jeep near the entrance of Pirbright Camp, the soldier looked at his watch. 'I now have twenty-eight days and 45 minutes left, and then I am free.'

In my barrack there were twenty-four other recruits who came from all over England. At first, I found it a little difficult to understand some of their regional accents, particularly the Newcastle dialect, but I soon became accustomed to different voice tone. I was intrigued by recruit Moyle's Camborne timbre, amused by Fynon's Manchurian vowels and I liked O'Connor's soft euphonious Yorkshire dialect, but I found the Eton-educated officers accent unpleasant; their accents seemed to me to be redolent of elitism.

A sergeant and a trained soldier were in charge of our squad. The two men had quarters in the centre of the barrack. Sergeant Harrison was a brawny, often scowling, ex-master builder from Matlock in Derbyshire. During one of his rare moments of friendliness, Harrison proudly told the squad that his wife bore a strong physical resemblance to the Queen. Trained soldier 'Nosher' Bains was a former fireman who came from Southampton. Without question, Bains was an unremitting bully who derived much pleasure from roughing up recruits, especially those who were the last of the National Servicemen.

I quickly adapted to the camp environment. I excelled at drill and weaponry and was proficient on the assault course, but a disaster at 'spit and polish' and it would cost me dear. The next bunk to mine was occupied by Oilles who was twenty years old and one of the last men to be called up for National Service. As a civilian, he had sold wallpaper in a shop at Grimsby. It was a pleasant surprise for me to discover that Oilles loved music and shared my passion for opera. Oilles was totally unsuited to be a soldier. It seemed peculiar to me that he had been sent to Pirbright Camp to be trained as a guardsman. Although excellent at keeping his kit immaculately clean and polished, he was useless on the parade ground, during manoeuvres or exercising in the camp's gymnasium. Being in the gym was a terrifying experience for Oilles. The mere thought of doing a simple forward roll would cause him to become nearly hysterical. I soon became concerned for my friend and hoped that he would never contemplate suicide. I felt that it was only a matter of time before Bains singled him out.

During the early hours I was woken by a very distressed Oilles who was worried about having to do exercises in the gym later that morning. I quickly ordered him into the washroom to try and calm him down. After a few minutes of taking slow and deep breaths he began to relax. He even forced a smile when he realised I was prepared to help him. I quickly suggested an idea that would have mutual benefit. If need be, I would spend the rest of the night showing him how to do a forward roll and in return he would help me with the cleaning of my kit. He agreed wholeheartedly.

We went outside the barrack and I laid my ground sheet on the damp grass. I then spent over an hour demonstrating the forward roll until I became too giddy to continue. After endless coaxing, he finally managed to do it himself and seemed reasonably confident in the gym a few hours later.

I was thankful for Oilles' expert help with the polishing and blancoing of my kit, for Bains was no longer kicking it around the barrack floor.

Just after breakfast, our squad began preparing for a route march with Sergeant Harrison. As we did so, a thin new recruit arrived to join our squad. The lad seemed to be about seventeen years of age and very anxious. Bains, who was in a foul mood, was looming over him as he unpacked his kit on the bunk. I dreaded the thought of what would happen to the recruit once our squad had left the barrack and he was alone with Bains. Within minutes we were ordered outside and marched away. When we returned several hours later, as I expected, the lad had absconded.

I thoroughly enjoyed drill practice and I soon became an accomplished marcher. We often marched quickly, though I preferred to slow march, especially when the band played Handel's delightful 'Scipio'.

Sergeant Harrison, impressed by my marching skills, embarrassed me by barking at the squad. 'Swing your arms shoulder high, just like Gardner.' Following this order he barked even louder. 'As usual, it's always Gardner every time who is showing the rest of you how to march properly.'

My ability on the parade ground was recognised by a drill sergeant who had a reputation of being a martinet. Our squad was called to attention by this sergeant, who was standing just in front of me. I brought my knee up so high, it accidentally knocked the baton out of his hand. Instead of retribution, which I thought was inevitable, the sergeant picked up his baton that had landed several feet away and yelled at my fellow recruits.

'You useless mob, why don't you follow Gardner's example and lift your bloody knees up?'

I abhorred this unwanted and ongoing praise. Fortunately, none of the other recruits thought that I was an exhibitionist. Oilles reassured me, 'Don't worry Alf, we all know that you're not a show-off.' Our marching seemed to be ever-increasing, which pleased me.

We were marched to the parade ground, to church service, the canteen and even the gymnasium and baths. In the tiny cubicles of the bathhouse, we were allowed just a ridiculous ten minutes to undress, bathe, dry off and get dressed. I quickly solved the problem of having to put my uniform back on when I was still wet; I often avoided taking a bath. For several minutes while Harrison continually banged on the cubicle doors and shouting 'Get a move on', I would just splash the water with my hand. My deception always worked. I asked Oilles how much time he thought that the officers would spend having a bath. He replied with a tinge of jealously 'A minimum half an hour'.

There was sport available at Pirbright Camp which was much appreciated by the recruits with the exception of Oilles. We were encouraged to take part in boxing bouts, but the matching of opponents was laughable. My opponent towered over me and he was at least a stone and a half heavier. I went the required three rounds, but lost on points.

During cricket practice, I had inadvertently annoyed Lieutenant Tedder. Tedder, who was perhaps a year or two older than me, ordered us recruits to form a wide circle. After taking up our positions, we were to throw the cricket ball hard at each other and hopefully catch it. I loved throwing cricket balls. At school sport events, I had held an unbeatable record for throwing a cricket ball the furthest. With great force, I hurled the ball at Tedder who was standing about fifty feet from me. He managed to catch the ball, but instantly dropped it. After rubbing his painful hands together, he glared at me and raised his voice, 'Gardner, don't you ever throw a ball like that again at me, you could easily have damage my fingers!'

I and several other recruits in my barrack were assigned to the butts of a rifle range. The seventeen year old standing alongside me in the butts was the youngest and shortest youth in the barrack. For his clumsiness in lowering and hoisting the target, he was repeatedly hit about the head by the tall and thickset sergeant Walker who was in charge of the butts' squad.

Within a few weeks of arriving at Pirbright Camp, I had heard rumours that suicides and attempted suicides had occurred at the camp. If the rumours were true, I could only surmise that these tragedies might be the result of young National Service recruits finding Army life unbearable or were being bullied with impunity by thugs like Bains and Walker.

I am unsure if senior officers like Major Ratcliffe and Captain Abel Smith were aware of the bullying, as they seemed to me to be spending much of their time sitting behind a desk. Oilles had a theory that I thought ludicrous. He believed that because trainee officers at Sandhurst Military Academy were never subjected to brutal bullying, they were incapable of realising that ill-treatment would be inflicted on ordinary squaddies.

Perhaps one can make allowances for Ratcliffe and Abel-Smith seeming obliviousness, but not the junior officers Lieutenants Larken and Tedder. These two young subalterns, who were closely involved with our training programme, must have been incredibly naïve if they had not noticed that a grazed cheek, a cut lip or nervous speech, might be signs that a young recruit, who in all probability had never left home before, was being ill-treated.

I received a letter from my sister who wrote with worrying news. Our mother had been admitted to hospital. After I read the letter I promptly made a request to see Captain Abel-Smith about obtaining twent- four hours compassionate leave. To my surprise Abel-Smith was devoid of compassion. He coldly stated, 'I can not grant you any leave.'

Lieutenant Larken had a kind-looking face, but an unkind nature. It was during the early evening when Larken came into the barrack and immediately ordered our squad to find a pencil and paper. We were to make notes on a brief talk he would give on the history of the Grenadier Guards. Because I and another recruit were unable to find pencil and paper within the few seconds that we were allocated, Larken instantly ordered us to run ten times around the parade ground. I was puzzled by Larkin's motives; what on earth did he expect to achieve by this unwarranted punishment? I could not see how he could expect recruits to have any respect and confidence in their commanding officers if they were being victimised in such an unjustifiable manner. The only conclusion that I could arrive at was that Larken was acting out of spite.

The recruit who ran around the parade square with me was an ex-coal miner from northern England. During our run, he had made a decision.

'If t' f**king toff (Larken) finks 'e can push me around, 'e is f**king wrong, 'e can have my twenty quid, I am going back to t' pit.'

A little later he added, 'Ah fink thee should go 'ome too, matey.'

My low opinion of Lieutenant Larken soon became even lower. It was during rifle drill. Sergeant Harrison had become exasperated by a recruit's inability to shoulder his rifle correctly. Placing his mouth just inches from the recruit's ear Harrison bellowed an order. The nervous recruit was to lift his rifle high above his head and shout three times, 'I am a c**t.' As the recruit did what he was ordered, Lieutenant Larken, who was walking close by and witnessed the incident, made no attempt to reprimand Harrison or place him on a charge. I thought that Larken's nonchalance was deplorable. The recruit whose ear was blasted by Harrison's mouth promptly bought himself out of the Grenadier Guards.

Our barrack room squad, which at the start of the training programme numbered twenty-four, was now reduced to just fourteen. Nine recruits had paid their £20 and left the Army and recruit Fynon was hospitalised following a bad fall on the assault course. Harrison threatened to 'brain the next man' who wanted to resign.

After eight weeks of intense training, I received two letters: one from David Upson reminding me that the three-month deadline was not far away; he also included a photo of himself with his arms around two smiling and pretty girls. The letter also included a PS: 'The blonde is a petite wood nymph and she is reserved for you.' The second letter was from my close friend Alfie Debono whom I had written to a few days earlier. In my letter, I had asked Alfie if he would kindly send me £20; I urgently needed the money to buy myself out of the Grenadier Guards.

I had no money. Most of my Army pay was sent direct to my mother to help her with the family bills and the £20 discharge fee that I had brought to Pirbright Camp had been stolen. I was on fatigue duty in a camp kitchen when the theft happened. Although recruits had been warned to be vigilant, as there was occasional pilfering at the camp, I had foolishly left my tunic top that contained the money in a small changing room adjacent to the kitchen. It was only during the evening that I discovered that the cash was missing. I decided not to report the theft to Sergeant Harrison. Losing the money was my own fault. I should never have left the cash in my tunic.

Inside Alfie's registered letter there was the £20 and a note suggesting that once I had been discharged and had found a job I could repay him the loan at £5 a week.

My time in the Army was almost at an end, or so I thought. Ignoring the danger of being 'brained', I immediately contacted Sergeant Harrison with a request to see the Commanding Officer, so that my application for discharge could be immediately processed. The sergeant was not happy to see me. 'You are making a mistake, Gardner, you show promise and you have the makings of a future drill instructor.'

His words had no effect. I was determined to leave the Army within the next few days. My stance caused him to frown. He said that I was the ablest recruit in the squad and probably would be awarded the best recruit's cup if I remained in the Grenadier Guards, but again I said that I wished to leave the Army; suddenly his mood changed, he became impatient and ordered me to return to my bunk, hinting that he may not allow me to apply to resign.

Harrison's threat had to be taken seriously. I was now a worried man; the three-month deadline was just a few weeks away.

The next day, I contacted Harrison again to see if he had forwarded my request, but he was not prepared to listen to me. He merely said the CO would see me soon. I now suspected that there were dirty tricks at work, perhaps Harrison and others were in collusion trying to keep me in the Army. That evening, as I sat on my bunk cleaning my kit, a black mood descended over me; I was deeply concerned that I might have to spend the next three years in the Army. I cursed my stupidity for not taking the original advice of David Upson and other friends against volunteering.

Suddenly, Lieutenant Tedder came into the barrack and approached my bunk. I immediately sat bolt upright to attention. Tedder, like Larken, was disliked by several recruits in my squad. 'Gardner,' he sneered. 'I understand that you wish to leave the Grenadier Guards, is that so?'

'Yes sir.'

With the corner of his upper lip still curled, he said, 'All I can say is that you're a weakling.'

'No sir.'

'It's obvious to all of us in 14th Company that the training is too tough for you; is that not the case?'

'No sir.'

'I repeat, the training is too tough for you and that you are a weakling.'

'That is not the case, sir.' I suspected that Tedder was trying to provoke me. If I had retaliated orally, I could have been charged with insubordination or if I had attempted to strike Tedder my actions would have had been so disastrous I would have had no chance whatsoever of buying myself out of the Army.

Tedder continued with his tirade, but my composure remained intact. When he finally finished haranguing me, he momentarily glanced at the rest of the squad before turning around and leaving the barrack.

The following morning, I was still annoyed at having been insulted by Tedder. His provocative behaviour was unwarranted. He knew that I was in no position to defend myself. At least Sergeant Harrison and the rest of the squad never regarded me as a weakling. Time and time again I had proved that I was a model recruit. I tried to analyse what had caused Tedder to seek me out when he had ignored the other nine recruits in my squad who had bought themselves out of the Army. It was unlikely that Tedder was still angry with me for hurting his fingers. In all probability, he must have been informed, perhaps by Sergeant Harrison who had somehow detected that I never had any intention of being a professional soldier and because I had wasted the Army's valuable resources, it was an opportunity for him to teach me a lesson. My punishment was to be humiliated in front of the other recruits. Tedder's decision to shame me may have been his prerogative. I did not agree. I thought that I had acted in accordance with the recruitment officer's guidelines which stated unequivocally that volunteers would be under no obligation to serve the full three years with the colours if they decided that during their twelve-week probation period Army life was not for them.

To be absolutely sure and to clarify an important point, I had mentioned to the recruitment officer that, 'in all honesty, I would only be interested in doing basic training'. He listened carefully as I spoke. Aware that there were more senior officers nearby, he leant forward at his desk and lowered his voice to almost a whisper.

'You're still welcome to join us lad. Who knows we might get you to change your mind and stay on.'

I had carefully prepared my locker for inspection when trained soldier Bains suddenly entered the barrack. He stood akimbo by the stove. His contemptuous glare was an indication that he was ready for mischief. After moving away from the stove he began to inspect the shelves of our narrow steel lockers. If soap, comb or razor were not placed correctly and neatly on the shelves as he demanded, he would throw these items out and push the lockers to the floor. Not satisfied with pushing a scared young recruit's locker over, he grabbed the recruit and pushed him against the wall. Bains then strode arrogantly towards my locker and looked inside. Seconds later my locker was pushed over and I too was shoved hard against the wall.

Bains soon released his grip from my throat. Pointing his finger aggressively to within inches of my face he assigned me to a regular daily duty. I was to become the barrack latrine cleaner. How I wished at that moment I had had my bayonet with me. Disregarding the repercussions, that would have meant a life-long prison sentence, I would not have hesitated for a moment in stabbing this monster.

Shortly after Bains left for the canteen, Oilles, who had escaped his wrath, leant across from his bunk. He spoke dismally. 'It's pointless, Alf, complaining, about Baines. These officers don't give a hoot about us; they are only interested in their careers.'

When Oilles was called up for his two year National Service, he had volunteered to serve an extra year 'for more allowance'. Now, two months later, my friend was determined to get out of the Army which he had come to loathe. He had been informed by another recruit that there was a loophole that he could take advantage of. If a National Service recruit had volunteered an extra year service, there was a possibility that he might be eligible to buy himself out of the Army under the £20 scheme.

'By hook or by crook, I am going home to Grimsby,' he remarked confidently. 'And I miss playing my opera records,' he lamented.

I understood exactly how he felt. Oilles also commented on Tedder's attempts to goad me the night before. 'You did the right thing mate, by taking it on the chin.'

Later that morning, I was detailed to clean the inside of one of the churches in the camp. Working there alone was just what I needed; the church was empty and peaceful. Amidst the tranquillity, I began to plan my next move to leave the Army. I thought for a moment; should I not desert? But I quickly discarded the idea, realising that ultimately deserting would be a mistake. Perhaps I should contact a senior NCO from another squad or even go and see the medical officer who seemed approachable? Surely there was somebody who could help me? Suddenly the door opened and Major Growbecker, a tall, slim Army chaplain, entered the church. He came over to me.

I instantly put down my mop and stood to attention; he smiled warmly before saying, 'That's all right, stand easy.'

The chaplain was exceptionally friendly and humane, unlike other officers who treated us recruits with disdain. He asked me what squad I was in, whereabouts in London I came from and what was my job as a civilian and was I happy with Army life.

Seizing the opportunity, I replied, 'No sir, I am not happy being a soldier. I originally and mistakenly volunteered for three years service, but now I want to buy myself out of the Army for £20 under the three-month clause, but I seem to be prevented from seeing the CO who must accept my application for discharge.'

'That's rather odd', said the Major quizzically. He took out his notebook, quickly wrote down my name and number and said, 'I will have a word with the Camp Commandant in the mess this evening and see what I can do for you.'

My God, I thought, what luck! What bloody marvellous luck! I thanked the Major and stood to attention. He smiled, turned around and went into a small room near the altar.

The next morning our squad took part on a strenuous route march. When we returned to the barrack I was ordered to appear in front of the CO. The good Major had kept his promise and had spoken on my behalf. With my teeth clenched and heart beating at a fast rate, I placed four £5 notes on the CO's desk. For a brief moment, the CO stared at me indignantly before signing my discharge papers. I saluted, turned around and was marched out.

The next day I was free to leave the Pirbright Camp for I was no longer a soldier. Wearing my old and now ill-fitting suit that I wore when I arrived at Pirbright Camp in early August, I strode briskly away from the barracks. I felt fit, lean and alert.

Although I had only been in the Army for about ten weeks it seemed much longer. I had missed my family and friends immensely. Despite the bullying, in a way I was grateful for my Army experience and had enjoyed the comradeship and accepted the discipline without complaint. The training may have been rigorous, but rigorousness was an absolute requirement if young civilians were to be moulded into tough, fearless soldiers.

At the camp I had witnessed human nature at its best and unfortunately at its worst. It was a privilege to have met Major Growbecker who was so kind and helpful (Geoffrey Frank Growbecker was later to become the Senior Chaplain to the British Army) and I was glad that I was able to assist Oilles to overcome his terror; but the memories of Bains' and Walker's cruelty, Larken's spitefulness, Abel-Smith's heartlessness, and Tedder's provocation remain vivid to this day.

Fifty years after my brief Army tenure, I raised the subject of bullying with my brother-in-law Mac who had served in the Brigade of Guards from 1945 to 1948. Mac could not recall a single instance of bullying during his basic training at Caterham and Pirbright Camp. He said that the conduct of the officers and non-commissioned officers was 'exemplary' and he seemed surprised when I explained about the maltreatment of recruits at Pirbright Camp fifteen years after he was based there. In my brief ten week Army experience at Pirbright Camp, I thought that exemplary conduct was often lacking. To this day, I cannot ascertain why this was the case. However, what I am certain of is that in 2012 there must be several elderly men that have bitter memories of being ill-treated at Pirbright Camp during that late summer of 1960.

Celebrating my homecoming from the Army, David Upson had arranged a little drinking session at the Tiger Tavern on Tower Hill. He brought his current girlfriend, attractive Louisa to the pub, accompanied by her younger friend Elaine. I recognised Elaine; she was the blonde 'petite wood nymph' in the photo Dave had sent to me whilst I was at Pirbright Camp. Louisa was in her mid-twenties. Her dark features indicated that she might be of Italian or Maltese origin. I thought the Tiger Tavern an odd venue, but Dave was fond of the old pub that allegedly had a secret tunnel in its cellar that led to the nearby Tower of London.

'Beefeaters would use the tunnel to sneak out for a drink,' joked the barman.

With typical generosity, Dave insisted that he would buy our drinks that evening. Within the hour, we had left the Tiger and were sitting in a taxi on our way to the Prospect of Whitby at Wapping. My best friend was keen to 'round off the evening with merriment'. When we arrived at the Prospect, I offered to pay the taxi fare.

'No, no,' said Dave, as he reached for his wallet.

'No, no, no,' argued Louisa. 'I insist on paying.' Dave snatched her purse. Louisa laughed as she tried to retrieve it. The taxi driver was becoming a little impatient. I moved foreword to settle the bill, but Elaine, unnoticed by Louisa

The back of this postcard simply reads,
'David I Love you. Betty xxx'.

and Dave, darted in front of me and thrust some money into the driver's hands.
He smiled and tapped his cap.

We entered the Prospect to the familiar sound of a hundred voices singing
'On Ilkley Moor baht'at'. The pub was as busy as ever and it took some time
before Dave was able to get served. We gently squeezed ourselves through
the happy revellers to a corner where the Hawaiian musicians sat. Friendly
groups of London medical students and a contingent of Australian and South
Africans were trying to out-sing each other. As usual the rivalry was good
humoured.

At 10.30 p.m., the last orders were called. Following 'Auld Lang Syne'
which was sung with great gusto we left the Prospect. Outside in the street,
Dave offered to foot the bill for a Chinese meal. Happily we linked arms and
set out on foot for the twenty-minute walk to Chinatown at Limehouse.

We soon arrived at Narrow Street. Although our throats were still hoarse
from too much singing we managed to give a hearty rendition of 'Lloyd George
knew my Father' to the tune of 'Onward Christian Soldiers'.

After a sumptuous meal at the Old Friends, a popular Chinese restaurant,
paid for by Dave, we hailed a taxi that took us to Victoria Park at Hackney.
Both girls lived with their parents near the park. This time I paid the taxi fare.
For a dare, the four of us climbed over the park's fence and raced across the
open grass. Dave soon disappeared into a wooded area with Louisa. Shortly
afterwards I led Elaine into the same thicket. My friends' description of Elaine
was apt; she was indeed a 'wood nymph'!

In the early hours of the morning we climbed back over the fence and within ten minutes Dave and I had escorted the girls to their homes. With no buses available and not a taxi in sight, we had no alternative to walk home. As we strolled down the long Burdett Road, Dave asked me if I had made any plans to keep myself occupied until the spring when we could join the Merchant Navy. My immediate plans were straightforward. Besides trying to entice Elaine back into the park at the earliest opportunity, I would have to look for a temporary stock cutting job. Dave agreed with my first priority. He pondered for a moment before suggesting that as I had become disillusioned with garment cutting, I should consider learning a second trade. More curious than interested, I asked him why. Pragmatic by nature, he outlined what he thought was a sensible idea.

'Look, Alf, you're intelligent and adaptable, if you did learn another trade, it could be useful, especially once you are in the Merchant Navy. Just imagine, if you are on shore leave and are in no hurry to return to sea, you could have a greater choice of finding work to keep yourself busy for a while.'

I assumed correctly that this new trade he had in mind was handbag manufacturing and that I should apply for a vacancy at D&W Handbags Ltd where he worked as a framer.

The following Monday morning at 8 a.m. I met Dave outside the handbag factory in Cannon Street Road. The factory had been converted from a large Victorian house. Dave cautioned me. 'Take note Alf, if Alex my boss offers you a job as a trainee framer or a clicker, you must expect the salary to be low compared to what you can earn as a clothes cutter, but once you are on piece-work your wages will increase.'

Alex, the managing director was speaking on the telephone when we entered his office. He clasped his hand over the mouthpiece and spoke quickly to Dave. 'Take your pal around the factory David and show him the setup. If he is interested in working here, bring him back to the office later.' Dave closed the office door and gave me the thumbs up sign. I tried to muster a little enthusiasm by giving a satisfactory nod.

Dave soon proved to be an excellent tutor. He seemed to know every aspect of the trade. At each workbench we would stop for a few moments and he would explain the various stages of production from the initial cutting to bench work, machining and framing. We stood and watched the young workforce busy at their benches. Several of the workers were former old school friends of mine who lived at nearby Mariner Street. It soon became apparent to me that many of the bench workers and framers, especially the taller ones, appeared to be toiling away in an awkward stationary position. With their heads lowered they hardly moved from where they stood. As a garment cutter, these working positions seemed alien to me. I was used to spending hours every day walking up and down at the cutting table laying fabric. Even when cutting out the garments I was still moving about.

After my conducted tour of the factory was over, Dave asked me if I would like to learn the trade. Having decided that I had no intention of working there, but a little concerned that I had wasted his and Alex's time, I made an excuse that I needed a little time to think it over. Dave of course immediately detected my lack of interest.

'Okay Alf,' he said sympathetically. 'I will let Alex know that you will 'phone him in a day or two, but don't worry mate, he is a reasonable boss. If you feel that you are unable to fit in here, he will understand.'

Later that afternoon, I 'phoned Alex and explained that I thought it wise that I should return to garment cutting, which I was trained for. He thanked me for 'phoning and wished me the best of luck, agreeing that I had probably made the right decision.

In October I began working as a stock cutter at the Wills dressmaking factory that was situated on the corner of Stepney's Commercial Road and Albert Gardens. The basement cutting room was almost an exact replica of Gerald's cellar at Aldgate East. It had poor lighting and was airless and dusty. The ancient and loose fitted wooden staircase began to move the moment you stood on it. As expected there were no fire exits or extinguishers.

My perennial fear of being trapped by fire in an underground cutting room was not unfounded. Stan the other cutter was a heavy smoker who constantly threw matchsticks onto the floor, some of which were still lit. We soon began quarrelling when he realised I did not approve of his smoking in the basement.

The inevitable soon occurred. Just prior to leaving the basement at lunchtime, Stan had lit a cigarette. A few minutes later I was forced to switch off the cutting machine. A small but rapidly spreading fire was raging at the foot of the stairs. Fortunately I had the prescience to keep a bucket of water by the cutting table and was able to dowse the fire, but because the irresponsible Stan refused to stop smoking permanently in the basement I had no choice but to hand in my notice.

11

Father Joe Williamson and Cable Street

'Too much has been said of the heroes of history, the strong men, too little of the amiable, the kindly and the tolerant.'
Stephen Leacock (Essays and Literary Studies)

Now that Dave and I had moved to Poplar, we began frequenting the pubs of nearby Limehouse, but Dave being a man of regular habits still returned time and time again to drink and socialise in the western end of Cable Street where he was well known. At the end of the 1950s, cosmopolitan Cable Street, which was extremely popular with seafarers, had acquired a reputation for being a notorious club and vice district on a par with Soho.

Situated in Cable Street were Yugoslavian, Czechoslovakian and Somalian cafés and many late nightclubs and brothels. I never really felt comfortable drinking there, having witnessed several fights involving punters who were being overcharged in the clubs; and I had never forgotten that six years earlier two young men had been stabbed to death in a Maltese café. One of those killed was nineteen-year-old Francis Bezzina, the eldest brother of one of my school friends.

Francis, a National Serviceman, was on leave from his regiment at the time of his death. There were other victims of violence in the Cable Street area. Noel Morgan, a drunken Scottish sailor, received fatal stab wounds after becoming involved in a fight with staff at Abdullah's Somalian café. Dave too had several fights in Cable Street. In an inebriated state, he fought jealous rivals of the women he was pursuing, but more often the fights were the result of having to defend himself late at night when thugs attempted to rob him.

'They thought I was easy prey, because I was drunk.'

Getting drunk in Cable Street could be costly for Dave. After leaving the Brown Bear pub, he bumped heavily into a policeman; as a result of this collision he was 'carted off' to nearby Leman Street Police Station where he had to spend the night in a cell. The next day he appeared at Thames Magistrate Court and was fined for being drunk and disorderly. After subsequent fines for similar offences, Dave was placed on probation for a year.

Besides being a red light district, Cable Street had scores of multi-occupied slums. Many of the slums, situated just a stone's throw from St Paul's Church, were unfit for human habitation. There were also dozens of bombed houses in the locality. Without doors or windows, they attracted vagrants who used them as latrines, night shelters, and for methylated spirit consumption; they also became places to dump rubbish. The putrid smell that was emitted was awful. Sometimes the occupants of these hovels would be loitering on the pavement in a drunken stupor and they could be abusive and even violent if you refused to give them money.

While passing through the North East Passage that led to Wellclose Square, Dave was approached by a group of vagrants who demanded money; when he ignored them, they spat at his face and threatened him with a broken bottle. My friend was wise to walk quickly past the group. They may have been the same violent vagrants who pushed over and kicked a young artist as she was sketching alone in the square. It was a Sunday afternoon when Dave and I found her wandering aimless and confused in nearby Ship Alley. She declined our offer to take her to Leman Street Police Station but agreed that we could escort her to Aldgate East Tube.

My former classmate George Platt lived at the junction of Graces Alley and Wellclose Square that was just yards from Cable Street. George's family might well have agreed with the author Ashley Smith, who in 1961 published a book entitled *East Enders; A Social Enquiry of the East End.* Smith described the west end of Cable Street as 'the filthiest, dirtiest, most repellently odoured street in Christendom; an offence to the eye and the nostril, a menace to the health and the happiness of its unfortunate inhabitants and a standing reproach of criminal dimensions to any authority that has the power to pull it down, burn the ground clear of the foulness, rehouse its people'.

Usually, if Dave and I were drinking at Cable Street, we would visit three clubs, the Green Parrot, the Rio and Black Rose's Café Bar. Rosetta Jackson, an African woman, was the mighty proprietress of the café bar. Fearless and pugnacious, she looked very strong with a wide v-shaped back and muscular arms. Rosetta had to be tough, especially when dealing with the aggressive unemployed seaman who would intermittently sneak unnoticed into her bar and pester customers for drinks and money. The atmosphere could be tense at Rosetta's with sinister Maltese men coming and going. Drugs were being openly sold and prostitutes bartered with the clientele.

Dave eventually suggested that we should boycott Rose's Café Bar. He suspected that a regular smooching couple were undercover police officers engaged in a surveillance operation. 'The last thing we want Alf, is to be here if the police raid the joint.' His observation may have been accurate. The police did raid the premises and Rosetta was arrested for possessing 42 packets of hemp and a loaded revolver.

It was during the evening when Dave and I were drinking at the Green

Father Joe Williamson.

Parrot club in Grace's Alley (the club was next door to the long-time closed Wilton's Music Hall that was then being used as a rag warehouse) when in walked Father Joe Williamson, the Anglican Vicar of St Paul's Church in adjacent Dock Street.

Father Joe or the 'Good Samaritan,' as Dave called him, was an outstanding and courageous, Poplar-born vicar. In 1958 he had established a refuge for young homeless girls and prostitutes at Church House in Wellclose Square. He was also engaged in the sometimes precarious task of personally rescuing girls from the seedy clubs in the vicinity.

Earlier, Dave had spoken briefly to the vicar in the alley. He was accompanying two teenage girls to his refuge. My friend thought that the girls were probably prostitutes. He described one as looking emaciated and the other as having a nasty black eye. Father Joe asked the proprietors of the Green Parrot, a small, serious-looking Greek and his large, buxom, blonde wife, a Mae West lookalike, if they had seen a young Scottish girl in their club. The girl, who had recently arrived in Cable Street after having been given a lift by a long distance lorry driver, was thought to be sleeping in bombed houses.

The proprietors were unable or unwilling to assist the vicar. Although the 1959 Street Offences Act was in force, prostitutes could still regularly be seen soliciting in Cable Street and its adjoining streets with impunity. On numerous occasions, Dave and I saw these ladies of the night emerging with their clients from quiet alleys and dark recesses, but many were now operating from the dozens of clubs that flourished in the area.

Dave had become an acquaintance of Father Joe in 1954, shortly after taking up residence at the Seamen's Mission in Dock Street that was adjacent to St Paul's Church. As he wandered around on foot to explore the area, my friend had confused Swedenborg Gardens with nearby Wellclose Square. 'So much for my navigating skills, I lost my bearings.' Father Joe who happened to be passing by noticed that the stranger was lost. He approached Dave and gave him directions.

As Father Joe was about to leave the Green Parrot, the vicar recognised Dave and me; he gave us a warm smile and came over to our table and sat down. Father Joe, whom Dave had introduced me to at the club a few months earlier, was very interested when I mentioned that my family had recently moved from Stepney to Cordelia Street at Poplar. He said that he had been born in neighbouring Arcadia Street and had many happy memories of growing up in Poplar. Our conversation inevitably turned to the problems of the vice trade, a subject which he had already discussed with Dave in the past. The vicar and Dave knew, as did the police, the social workers and the local residents, who were responsible for the unremitting growth of prostitution in the area. It was exclusively in the hands of the Maltese pimps.

The vicar spoke of his dreams of seeing the dilapidated slums in his parish being demolished and local people having an opportunity to move into new and affordable dwellings. He was also determined to continue with his campaign to force the local authorities to close down the brothels that had bedevilled Cable Street. Only then, he predicted, would the despicable profiteers 'and exploiters' of young girls be driven out of the borough.

Father Joe's battle with the ubiquitous pimps would last for more than a decade. The police fully backed his campaign. Hardly a week went by without yet another local Maltese man being sent to prison for living off of the immoral earnings of prostitutes, but there were always other ruthless pimps moving into the area to take their place. During the first six months of 1962, twenty-eight Maltese pimps in Stepney received prison sentences.

That same year a Maltese 'madam' was also brought to trial. This mother of five children stood in the dock of Thames Magistrates Court on Saturday 26 May 1962 and was charged with operating a brothel in a dilapidated house that was owned by her husband who was languishing in prison. The woman pleaded guilty; she was fined £100 and jailed for six months. One of the dingy rooms in the brothel was let to three prostitutes for £16 per week (equivalent to about £400 in 2012). After the madam received her sentence, it was revealed in the court that she had been convicted in the past for soliciting and in 1957 she was sent to prison for two years and six months for controlling prostitutes.

Not only were the pimps regularly appearing in local magistrates courts, so were the prostitutes too and in ever-increasing numbers. In 1946 just two Stepney prostitutes were fined for soliciting; in 1949 the figure rose to nine, but in 1956 convictions for soliciting in Stepney reached an incredible five hundred and eighty five. Besides controlling the majority of the local vice trade and subjecting their wretched prostitutes to regular beatings, many of the Cable Street Maltese were ruthless slum landlords.

When a rundown house came into their possession they would quickly convert it for multiple occupation. Fire escapes, extinguishers and alarms were non-existent. The landlord's only concern was to extract exorbitant rents from their tenants.

In the early hours of 1 January 1955, a fire occurred at a Maltese-owned lodging house in Wilkes Street, Spitalfields. The four-storey house had been divided by wooden partitions into seventeen tiny bed-sitters. The fire, that seems to have been started by an unserviced oil stove in the basement, quickly spread upwards. The majority of tenants managed to escape the blaze by jumping twenty feet out of the windows. Miraculously, none of those who jumped were seriously injured, but tragically three tenants, Lillian Bisson aged thirty-six, James Noble, forty-two, and Selina May Knight, forty-four, all lost their lives when they were overcome by fumes on the upper floors.

'Malteseism' was indeed flourishing in parts of western Stepney a decade before 'Rackmanism' was coined in the mid-1960s. Peter Rackman was a notorious, Polish-born landlord who owned approximately eighty houses in West London. When Rackman's tenants could no longer afford to pay the high rents that he charged, he resorted to using terror tactics to evict them. It was alleged that these tactics included threatening behaviour, violence and the intimidating presence of Alsatian dogs. Rackman first came to prominence because of his friendship with Mandy Rice-Davies, a key figure in the Profumo scandal that upstaged the Conservative government of 1963.

Although Dave had fixed views on why the Maltese dominated the East End vice trade, I remained puzzled why they did so. The Maltese families I knew who had settled in Buross Street and neighbouring Hungerford Street, namely the Lomiglios, Spiteris, Debonos and the Buttigiegs, were of a different class. They were decent law-abiding people. I enjoyed their company, was made welcome in their homes and for a short period I even had a Maltese girlfriend.

Because so many people living in Stepney automatically associated the Maltese community with prostitution and racketeering, my Maltese friends believed that they were being unfairly demonised. I sympathised with them.

I knew that my friends genuinely despised and distanced themselves from the pimps and slum landlords of Cable Street. Mrs Frances Lomiglio was so ashamed of her fellow-countrymen's involvement in the vice trade and the misery that it caused young girls that she would always insist to her neighbours that she was an Italian lady.

'But you're Maltese, Maltese, Maltese!' shouted a furious Sylvio at his mother. For his impertinence Sylvio was struck with a ladle.

As I had Maltese friends from childhood, especially the Lomiglio brothers and Alfred Debono, I had learnt a little of their language, which I found intriguing. The Maltese language which is a blending of Semitic and Italian words seemed to produce a peculiar, agitated tone. More so, whenever they spoke in English, their accent always sounded quite anxious.

I asked Father Joe if the legalisation of brothels might be the ultimate solution to an ongoing problem. He thought carefully for a moment before saying, 'Possibly in the future, but only in certain designated areas like Soho. Brothels must never be allowed to be established in Stepney.'

Fortunately, there were few customers in the Green Parrot as the three of us spoke, so there was no problem with eavesdropping, but even so, the proprietor behind the bar at the far end of the club had begun to glare at us disapprovingly.

'I believe he wants me to leave,' remarked the vicar.

'Oh just ignore him,' replied Dave, who was content to continue with our discussion all evening. I was well aware that Dave had been a willing and regular member of the local café society ever since he first stayed at the nearby Seamen's Mission Hostel seven years previously. He had drunk, ate, gambled and met women in the Cable Street clubs more times than he could recall. Besides being acquainted with several of the local pimps and sleazy landlords, he knew a smattering of the Maltese language too.

Preferring not to smoke because of the presence of the vicar, Dave pulled his chair closer to the table and spoke quietly to our guest. 'Don't misunderstand me Father Joe. As I said to you in the past, I am far from condoning the activities of the pimps. These people have absolutely no conscience whatsoever about exploiting women for profit; after all, they have been doing so for the last hundred years, ever since the Royal Navy created a base and dockyard in Malta. The Maltese of Valetta had large families to feed and with little or no income they sometimes had no alternative but to supply women for the sailors. In many cases the women were their own wives and daughters. So what you are seeing now in Cable Street and Soho, is a continuation of a tradition that the Maltese have made their own. And another important point to remember, if there were no prostitutes in this part of East London, there is a danger that local women and girls could be accosted, propositioned and even attacked on the streets.'

Father Joe immediately countered Dave's argument by stating, 'that situation is already happening. Because Cable Street is a recognised vice district, many of the men coming into the area looking for prostitutes seem to believe that any woman walking along the pavement is advertising her body. Several of my parishioners, including teenage girls, have been approached by strange men and asked if they were looking for business.'

At this point I said, 'Now that the word Maltese is synonymous with poncing, respectable Maltese living in the borough feel humiliated.'

Both Dave and Father Joe agreed that it was most unfortunate that they were being victimised. I told the vicar that I had seen some of the pimps emerge with the crowds from St Mary and St Michael's Catholic Church on a Sunday morning after mass.

'These are evil and heartless men,' he replied bitterly.

The continuing looks of disapproval by the proprietor of the Green Parrot and the cleaning of our little table by his wife were signs that they wanted our conversation to end immediately. The vicar recognised the signs too. He stood up, waved to the now-smiling proprietors and said goodbye to Dave and me and left the club to continue with his search for the homeless Scottish girl.

A few minutes later, the entrance door of the Green Parrot was pushed ajar and in swarmed about a dozen, noisy American GIs all eager to sample the not too cheap beer and spirits. Shortly afterwards several young prostitutes arrived, none of whom had Scottish accents. The prostitutes were probably tipped off by the club proprietor who was on a retainer from their pimps. When the relayed music became louder and the wild dancing started, I suggested to Dave that we should move on to the nearby Somalian café that served a superb curry; also I wanted to see Jean who sometimes worked as a barmaid-cum-hostess in the basement club beneath the café.

I had met Jean few months earlier when I went to the opera at Covent Garden and noticed her selling programmes in the foyer. Because Jean was poised, articulate and seemingly well-educated, I was at a loss to understand why, with these advantages, she needed to supplement her income by occasionally being a call girl. Nor was I prepared to ask her; although she did hint to me that she was saving money and would like to buy an open-top sports car and tour Italy.

After we had finished our meal we went downstairs to the near-empty club. Jean leaned over the bar to hug me and in between serving us our drinks she was enthusiastically praising the tenor Charles Craig whom I had recently seen singing 'Cavalleria Rusticana' at Covent Garden.

'Who is Charles Craig?' enquired Dave. When I explained that he was a new English singer beginning to make a name for himself in the opera, Dave shook his head disinterestedly before remarking, 'Alf, you know opera is not for me, give me Slim Whitman and country and western any day.'

Dave and I never know if Father Joe had managed to find the Scottish girl before she fell into the clutches of the pimps, but he did rescue many other

Edith Ramsey MBE. David admired Father Joe Williamson and Edith Ramsey who both worked tirelessly in Cable Street trying to rescue young girls from the clutches of the evil Maltese pimps. When he introduced me to Edith in 1959, I was amazed that she actually recognised me from four years earlier when she sat in the audience at Toynbee Hall and saw me playing the lead part in our school play *The Man in the Bowler Hat.*

homeless and endangered teenage girls who happened to find themselves stranded in Cable Street.

From the time I had met the intrepid Father Joe Williamson I had taken a keen interest in his work and also the work of the formidable and much loved Presbyterian voluntary social worker Edith Ramsay. Besides Edith's social work, she was a local councillor and, for a long period, the principle of the Stepney Evening Institute.

Whilst Dave was living at the Seamen's Mission Hostel in Dock Street, he had met and befriended Edith during one of her periodical visits to the hostel. Dave was impressed with her knowledge of the problems that faced single, lonely men, especially seamen. He admired Edith immensely. He told me that it was so easy to talk to her. He was also a welcomed visitor to her flat, which was on the ground floor of Gwyn House in Turner Street, Whitechapel. Edith's flat was an open door to many people in need of advice and assistance. At the flat, Dave and Edith had several long discussions. Knowing that whenever he called at her flat it would only be tea and biscuits offered, he would first pop into the Good Samaritan pub adjacent to Gwyn House for a quick drink and tease Kathy the ever-smiling little Irish barmaid.

Edith, sometimes referred to as the 'Florence Nightingale of the Brothels', had like Father Joe helped many a young girl in distress to escape from a life on the streets. She was also a tireless campaigner to clean up the Cable Street area. Throughout the late 1950s and early 1960s, Edith and Father Joe, both in their late sixties and united by their compassion and Christian faith, continued with their perennial struggle to expose to the nation the terrible housing conditions of the Cable Street area, the plight of young prostitutes and homeless girls and the ever-increasing problem of dope peddling. They constantly wrote letters appealing for help and action to the Prime Minister, the Housing Minister, MPs, London County Council, local authorities, the police commissioner, archbishops and bishops.

Father Joe and Edith Ramsay were interviewed by many reporters and they also spoke at public meetings. Father Joe even visited my friends the Kemp family, who lived in the Sander Street tenements that stood directly opposite some brothels. The vicar hoped that the Kemps would be prepared to appear alongside him on television and describe what it was like to live in a ghastly vice-ridden little street, but the family refused to cooperate, fearing that exposure on television might invite reprisals from the local pimps.

Walter Edwards, Stepney's Labour MP, had also played a leading role in the past in trying to rid the East End of its prostitutes and pimps, but Father Joe had little respect for the MP when it came to local housing matters. Although 'Wally' Edwards was a resident of Wapping and his home was within walking distance of St Paul's vicarage at Dock Street, the MP never made a single effort to visit Father Joe.

During the First and Second World Wars, Edwards served as a stoker in the Merchant Navy. In 1943 he left the navy, and two years later was elected MP for Whitechapel following Labour's landslide victory in the general election. In due course, Prime Minister Clement Attlee promoted Edwards to Lord of the Admiralty. As a ten year old during the 1951 general election campaign, I enthusiastically joined other Stepney children in the street to sing this little ditty. Very few of us really understood what we were singing about.

Vote, vote, vote, for dear old Edwards.
Punch the communists in the eye.
If they want a war, kick Churchill in the jaw.
Roll me over, lay me down and do it again.

Father Joe had hoped that Edwards, now an opposition MP, would wholeheartedly support his ongoing campaign to rehouse several poor Stepney families who were living in some of the borough's worst slums. An appointment was made for Father Joe to meet Edwards in a bar at the House of Commons. The vicar came away from the meeting extremely disappointed; Edwards was disinterested, unsympathetic and offered no assistance whatsoever; he even refused to look at the photos of the shocking housing conditions that were published in *The Pilot*, St Paul's church magazine. The only advice that the honourable Member of Parliament was prepared to give was a suggestion that his guest should write and state his case to the Housing Minister.

On 13 February 1961, Father Joe and Edith Ramsay were invited to address the London Diocesan Conference at Westminster and speak about Stepney's worsening housing conditions and gutter-level vice. Father Joe, outspoken as ever, told his audience that because cosmopolitan Cable Street was now a firmly established red light district, tourists could be seen roaming the streets. He explained that only a few weeks before, a coach had arrived in Ensign Street; the American guide led his coach party into a club, assuring them whatever they wanted was available inside.

Pulling no punches, the fiery vicar continued unabated. 'The slum landlord's object was to fill every flat and put up the rents. An exposé of the purchase of property and the rents charged would sicken the country, and right now, I would move the unemployable, the impotent and the weak-minded not back to Malta, or Jamaica, or Africa, but to internments around the Houses of Parliament and in Lambeth Palace Gardens and such other places. Let Parliament enjoy a bit of Sophia Town under its nose.'

The conference was a resounding success and a resolution was passed calling on Mr Henry Brooke, the Housing Minister, to ensure that slum clearance in Stepney be given top priority. While addressing the delegates, Father Joe had invited the same minister to join him for a cup of coffee in the East End and then to be taken on a guided tour of the area to see the terrible housing conditions. 'He would be shocked,' stated Father Joe.

Needless to say, the Housing Minister declined his invitation. However, Sir Percy Rugg, leader of the opposition on the London County Council, did accept a similar invitation from Father Joe. Sir Percy was first taken to Church House to inspect the pioneering work done by the vicar's small dedicated team. He was very impressed when told that since the hostel had opened its doors two and a half years before, one hundred and fifty women and girls had been given sanctuary. Father Joe seized the opportunity to escort his guest around the dismal streets. Eventually, they arrived outside the brothels at Sander Street.   Even though Father Joe was wearing his cassock and biretta, it did not stop him, nor Sir Percy, from being solicited by the prostitutes sitting at open windows. Sir Percy was amazed at what he witnessed and even more amazed when he was told that the buildings that housed the brothels were owned by his own LCC.

On 2 July 1961, Father Joe stood in the pulpit at St Paul's Cathedral. Again he described the awful housing conditions that prevailed within his parish. He told the congregation how he had recently visited the Parker family, who had ten children and had been living for the last thirteen years in a terrible, damp, bug-infested, two-bed roomed flat at Royal Jubilee Buildings in Wapping. The top floor flat had no roof. The family living there had to use a weighted tarpaulin to keep out the elements.

Father Joe then moved onto the subject of prostitution, the problem that had plagued his parish for many years, and the reason why his church had committed itself to trying to assist young girls to escape from a life of vice and degradation. As expected, he criticised the Church of England, accusing it of neither fully understanding, nor being willing to involve itself in important social issues.

'The church has slipped into a wet and weak attitude and is in danger of losing sight of its vocation. Literally, our hands are too clean and we are too damned respectable. As things are, can we imagine an archbishop or a bishop finding time to live for one week in the toughest parish of his diocese without a shield around him.'

Before Father Joe stepped down from the pulpit, he made a passionate plea to his congregation. 'I conclude with an appeal from this cathedral pulpit to all people of goodwill to back a material, practical and most Christian action. Almost without exception the one hundred and fifty three women and girls who have come to us have said, "I never had a chance." We accept that, but we reply at once, "You can never with real truth say that again, because here is your chance." I know that many hundreds of our British girls are living in slavery, under men who are living off their immoral earnings. They are living in this country of ours, often under threat of razor and gun. I call on these girls to come out of it and go to the nearest police station and claim protection. Assistance must be offered to them by the churches. Up and down the country we have thousands of friends of Church House; we also have moral welfare branches in every diocese. Open your house and your hearts to these girls. I call upon the archbishops and bishops to back this church work with vocal support and material help. Christians must not allow any girl to be enslaved by an evil man. We must offer these girls shelter and a way of escape. Practical help in this way is the Lord's own work and is priceless, and so very close to the saviour's heart, who was so kind and good to women.'

The Church's reaction to Father Joe's controversial sermon was predictable. Some bishops were upset that he had criticised the Church. Other diocesans praised him for what they perceived as being a courageous and necessary sermon. The press, namely *The Times*, and the *Daily Mail* gave him good coverage, which resulted in the vicar again appearing on television and broadcasting on the radio.

The Housing Minister, who a few months earlier had declined Father Joe's offer to accompany him around the run-down areas of Stepney, suddenly felt the need to meet the vicar at Royal Jubilee Buildings where the Parker family lived.

Unfortunately, the long-overdue changes in Cable Street did not occur following the publicity of Father Joe's sermon. Several years would pass before local people would witness the slums, the grubby cafés, brothels and the late-night drinking clubs that blighted the area being demolished and the prostitutes and pimps being driven out of the borough.

In late 1962, Dave and I decided to drink less in Cable Street in favour of Limehouse, which was nearer to where we lived. Limehouse was also less threatening than Cable Street and its pubs were always full of interesting and colourful characters. During one of our final visits to the cable Street area, Dave and I had left the Brown Bear in Leman Street following a disturbance at the bar. Shortly afterwards, I saw Father Joe being forcibly evicted from a Somalian café. After he straightened his biretta he attempted to go back inside the café, but was prevented from doing so by several men at the door. Undeterred, the vicar tenaciously stood his ground. Suddenly, a teenage girl, either drugged or drunk and unsteady on her feet, came out of the café. The vicar immediately gripped her arm and she was whisked away.

Just before Christmas 1963, I returned alone to Cable Street. I was hoping to ask Father Joe to sign my copy of his autobiography which had just been published. Unfortunately, he was visiting friends in the country. One of the priests on duty at Church House kindly invited me to join the Christmas party that was in progress. After a hearty meal, I agreed to take part in a carol service. At the end of the service, the same priest who had invited me to the party tried unsuccessfully to persuade me to be a member of St Paul's Church choir.

In 2011, Father Joe's son Cannon Tony Williamson told me that a man who may have been a pimp went to see his father at the vicarage. Once inside, the man attacked Father Joe and literally threw him across the front room. Father Joe chose not to publicise this dangerous incident.

It was in the Good Samaritan that Dave and I often met our mutual friend Alfred, an affable Ceylonese. Alfred's complexion, a reddish tan, was unlike any I had ever seen and possibly a symptom of his chronic heart condition. He claimed that the shock of having his arm trapped in an elevator door had damaged his heart. By refusing to diet and cut back on his occasional but excessive drinking his health had deteriorated alarmingly.

After serving for five years with the British Army during the last war and seeing action in the Far East, Alfred settled in Stepney with his second wife Mary, a gentle, polite Maltese woman. Their small attic flat in an awful tenement block in dreary Christian Street was cramped, cold and extremely draughty. Although Alfred was quite intelligent he worked as a low-paid warehouseman at the well-known Houndsditch Warehouse.

Whenever the three of us met in the pub on a Sunday afternoon, Alfred would insist on inviting us back to his flat for lunch. Dave and I never refused his offer. The Indian food that Mary prepared was excellent. Either in the pub or at his home, Alfred would attempt to involve Dave and me in short but serious discussions, mainly on politics and various current news items. Unlike Dave, I often become bored if the conversation was restricted only to politics. Topics which would have aroused my enthusiasm, like the Merchant Navy, or the Second World War, were hardly ever mentioned. There were occasions when I tried to coax my two older friends to talk about their wartime experiences, but I usually received a negative reaction.

Late one Sunday afternoon after we had finished a mouth-watering meal and consumed far too much wine at Alfred's flat, my two friends began discussing the Indian Army's recent annexation of Portuguese Goa. Usually they would simply state their views and opinions, rarely disagreeing or feeling the need to emphasise a particular point. However, this time their language was unusually sharp. When they moved on to the subject of General De Gaulle's Algerian policy they started arguing profusely. Attempts by Mary and me to calm them down were unsuccessful.

Suddenly, Dave got up from his chair and said, 'I am leaving.'

As he moved towards the door, Mary pleaded with him to sit down, to which he replied, 'I will stay only because of you.'

On hearing Dave's answer, Alfred lost all control of himself. He stood up and shouted, 'What did you say? "Stay because of you?" Remember this, David Upson, you are a guest in my home.'

Dave did not reply; instead he put on his coat and left the flat. I tried to follow him, but was held back by Mary who implored me to stay.

Alfred, whose head was now lowered, burst into tears. 'Oh my God, I have upset David, upset David.' Mary and I tried to comfort him; she held his head to her body and gently rocked him like a baby. It was a sad scene to witness; a sick, distressed man living in appalling conditions. When he eventually became quieter and after I had agreed to apologise to Dave on his behalf, I went home.

Later that evening I met Dave; he too was inconsolable, blaming himself for annoying Alfred. 'I can be so bloody stubborn Alf; it always happens when I drink the crazy wine.'

Fortunately, the two men were soon friends again and the incident was quickly forgotten and Alfred was to enjoy Dave's continued friendship once more, until his heart finally gave out a few years later.

12

Soho

My twentieth birthday on 25 February 1961 was on a Saturday. Dave suggested that we should celebrate by spending the evening drinking in Soho. Generous as ever, he insisted that not only would he pay for all drinks consumed, he would also pay for our meal at the West End's only Burmese restaurant. Dave was familiar with the pubs and clubs around Soho's Dean Street. He had first visited the area shortly after arriving in London seven years previously. Periodically, he would leave the East End; travel up to Soho and seek out old acquaintants that drank in the Golden Lion and the nearby York Minster. Sometimes, I would accompany him up west, but unlike Dave I had little interest in Soho's pubs, which I thought lacked excitement. I found the atmosphere grey and enclosed. Few women were to be seen in this all male-domain. Moreover, there seemed to be an absence of young people. I much preferred the vibrant pubs of Wapping and Limehouse that were always full of laughter, song and dance and, above all, frequented by an abundance of fun-loving young females.

The French pub in Dean Street was the most famous of Soho's pubs; a popular rendezvous for writers, painters, alcoholics and many homosexuals; other patrons were well-known faces whom I had seen on television and in films. There seemed to be a common factor among the clientele: they were exclusively middle-aged. The pub's popularity was probably due to Gaston Berloment, the jovial host. Tolerant and affable, he attempted to make everybody feel that they were valuable customers.

In 1959 when I entered the French for the first time, Gaston who was serving behind the bar called out, 'Hello, David, we don't see you much nowadays!'

Dave promptly introduced me to Gaston before ordering our drinks; he also ordered a further drink which he took over to a solitary, elderly woman who was sitting by the door. She mumbled something to him and then kissed his hand. I wondered who she was.

Dave noticing my curious expression when he returned to the bar whispered, 'She was once an artist, but her work was never appreciated.'

Dave's presence was certainly appreciated by several of the drinkers at the French. I stepped quietly aside as my friend was surrounded by at least half a dozen people. And so, as in the past, I was to witness the same warm affection that all and sundry showed towards him. No matter where we were, he seemed to draw people to him like a magnet and with the greatest of ease he brought a smile to their faces. David Upson was without question a panacea. I would stand just a few feet away and observe with great interest Dave's ability to chat confidently with the writers and intellectuals of Soho, and then a few days later repeat the same performance with some unsavoury characters in the Limehouse pubs or clubs of Cable Street's red-light district.

Dave was not gregarious by nature, but with his customary politeness, he would entertain his acquaintances until they drifted away. With the passing years, my friend lost interest in Soho. His visits to the area became less frequent as he preferred to stay contented within the confines of Stepney.

Sitting on the number 25 bus that was took us to the West End, Dave gave me my birthday card. Inside the card there was a ten-shilling note. My friend's kindness was infinite.

At the Golden Lion in Soho, Dave recognised a slim, pretty woman sitting on a bar stall. It was Harriet one of his former casual girlfriends. Harriet, who was in her mid-thirties, lived in Soho and worked as a part-time hostess at a local drinking club. The Maltese who owned the club were former Stepney brothel owners. Dave had spoken about Harriet once or twice in the past. He knew little of her background, but he thought that she may have spent much of her childhood in a Catholic home for orphans and probably arrived in London from Ireland when she was a teenager. He had no knowledge of how or why she had become a hostess.

Although Dave was a great listener, he rarely asked personal or leading questions. However, his reluctance to probe did not prevent him from being candid when asked by curious acquaintances or even strangers about his own background.

Dave was convinced that Harriet was never a prostitute; her role as a hostess was to entertain and dance with customers and encourage them to buy expensive drinks; if there were occasions when she did sleep with customers from the club, he said, 'it was certainly never for money'.

Two or three years earlier and on a Friday evening, Dave had gone alone to the club where he bought whisky at four times the cost of what he would have paid at the Prospect of Whitby. Realising that the club was a rip-off joint, but too polite to complain, he decided to finish his drink and make a hastily departure. Just as he was about to leave, Harriet sat down at his table and introduced herself. Entranced by her prettiness, he changed his mind about leaving. When he left the club a couple of hours later, he had spent his entire week's wages. All what remained in his pocket were a few shillings, which was just sufficient to pay for the bus fare back to the East End.

At a later date, Dave made a second visit to the club and again spent the majority of his wages, but this time, he did get a much better and unexpected return than 'just Scotch whisky'. When the club closed, he walked with Harriet to her nearby flat where he stayed the night. Dave could not recall if anything happened, 'because I was too tanked up with whisky', although on subsequent meetings 'it did happen'. Dave's relationship with Harriet would last for several weeks.

Seated at the bar with Harriet was Henri, a pleasant middle-aged French businessman who spoke perfect English. Henri immediately bought drinks for Dave and me. When Dave told Harriet that it was my birthday, both she and Henri and much to my embarrassment sang 'Happy Birthday To You'. Fortunately, they only sang the first verse just once.

Dave and Henri soon discovered that they had a mutual interest in space travel. While they chatted enthusiastically, Harriet leant across to me, smiled and said, 'Boys will be boys!'

I returned a smile and said, 'Maybe we have a common interest too.'

After her martini was placed on the bar, she lit up a cigarette and politely asked me if I ever found time to read books. I explained that I occasionally did read books, especially poetry, but that usually I preferred newspapers. Harriet stated that she was an avid reader of 'well-written' current novels. She was fond of poetry too 'especially the poems of Moira O'Neill'.

After taking a sip of martini and inhaling her cigarette she said, 'Because I only work at the club on alternative evenings, I have ample time to browse through the second-hand bookshops along Charing Cross Road, and I usually buy at least one book a week at Foyle's.'

To my question as to what books she was reading at the moment, she replied, 'One of them is *Lady Chatterley's Lover*.'

I grinned and asked, 'The censored or uncensored version?'

Fluttering her eyelashes she remarked, 'The uncensored version of course.' Harriet said that she had only bought *Lady Chatterley's Lover* after reading about the Penguin Books trial the previous year. 'I can't see what all the fuss was about,' she remarked, 'I thought the novel quite dull.' In 1960 Penguin Books at great risk published an unexpurgated edition of *Lady Chatterley's Lover*. Following the publication, attempts were made to prosecute the publishers under the 1959 Obscene Publication Act. After a well-publicised trial in which several noted authors and literary critics were called by the defence, Penguin Books were acquitted.

I had not read *Lady Chatterley's Lover*, but I had seen an English sub-titled French film adaptation. However, Dave had read the book nearly a decade before and he found it humorous that the Australian-built fishing trawler he captained in the Far East had its name changed from the 'John Thomas' to the Burmese 'Khin Khin Lay'. (In *Lady Chatterley's Lover* a 'John Thomas' is a sobriquet for the penis.)

Not only did Harriet appreciate books, but she appreciated opera too. Just a year before, Henri had taken her to Covent Garden to see Bizet's *Carmen*;

it was her first experience of seeing live opera and she was thrilled that they were shortly to visit the same opera house to see Puccini's popular *Madam Butterfly*. By coincidence, I also had a ticket to see the same production. Harriet mentioned that she had recently seen *La Bohème* and *Tosca* at Covent Garden; again by coincidence I had seen the same superb productions. No doubt as Henri was wealthy, he and Harriet always sat in the stalls; I was never so fortunate, all I could afford was a seat in the upper slips with restricted views.

After Harriet glanced at Henri who was still conversing with Dave, she said, 'I just love '*Vissi d'arte*' from the second act of *Tosca;* so melancholy, yet so beautiful.' She glanced at Henri a second time, it seemed as if he and Dave had forgotten that Harriet and I were in their company.

Harriet finished the last of her martini and said in a wistful tone, 'I have a recurring dream Alfie; I dream that one day Henri and I will have an opportunity to see Maria Callas sing *Tosca* at Covent Garden.'

Perhaps Harriet's dream did come true. In January and February 1964, Maria Callas gave six wonderful performances of *Tosca* at Covent Garden. I was unable to purchase a ticket for any of these performances, but I did manage to listen to a live broadcast on the radio.

Harriet intrigued me; she was well spoken, polite, amiable and articulate, the complete opposite to the gum-chewing, semi-literate Soho hostesses whom I had met briefly in the past. As she sat on the bar stall wearing a grey skirt and matching cardigan, I found it difficult to visualise her at the Maltese club, attired in a low-cut dress, and inducing customers to buy expensive drinks. Because I was enjoying conversing with Harriet, I asked her if she and Henri would like to dine with Dave and me at the Burmese restaurant. I knew that Dave would approve. Her response to my invitation was immediate as she smiled and thanked me for the invitation.

After stubbing out her cigarette and finishing the residue of the martini, she tapped Henri gently on the shoulder and said, 'Are you two would-be-spacemen ready to tuck into some exotic Burmese food?'

'We most certainly are!' replied Henri smacking his lips.

When the four of us left the Golden Lion and stood outside on the pavement, Dave looked to his right, and then to his left; he seemed perplexed. I asked him, 'Which way, left or right?'

'Actually, I am not sure, Alf,' remarked my friend as he scratched his head. 'I can't quite remember now where the restaurant is situated.' Harriet said that she was not aware that there were any Burmese restaurants in the surrounding area. Suddenly, Dave stopped scratching his head and he began to smile. 'Ah yes, I remember now, I think it's in New Compton Street.'

We followed Dave as he headed in an easterly direction. Within ten minutes we had arrived in New Compton Street, but to his dismay the only eatery to be seen was the Bombay, an Indian restaurant. Dave frowned, 'Sorry folks, it looks like my navigational skills have gone haywire.' Looking glum, he admitted that he had only been to the Burmese restaurant once before when former shipmates had taken him there after an evening of drinking in Soho.

Fortunately, Harriet and Henri were not displeased that Dave's sense of direction had failed him and they agreed, as did Dave, to my suggestion that we should dine at the Bombay instead.

After we finished our excellent curry and rice and were drinking beer, Dave and Henri decided to resume their conversation that had began earlier in the Golden Lion. Neither Harriet nor I found the subject of rockets and satellites particularly interesting, but we politely listened as our friends enthusiastically discussed space exploration. From their conversation, I was to learn that a few weeks previously the Americans had launched a Mercury space capsule with a chimpanzee named Ham strapped on board. The capsule ascended to a height of nearly two hundred miles. Henri was quick to inform Harriet that Ham was brought safely back to earth. Shortly after the American success, the Russians propelled their seven-ton *Sputnik 5* into space where it fired a rocket towards Venus.

Henri also mentioned that although only in its infancy France had its own space programme too, and just a few days before, his countrymen had successfully launched the Veronique rocket. The rocket that was carrying a rat reached a height of one hundred miles. Henri had no information if the rat survived the flight.

I said to Harriet, 'Just imagine, if the poet Shelley were alive today and he had had a second profession.'

'And what might that second profession be?' replied a bemused Harriet.

'He was an astronaut.'

Still bemused, she said, 'Why an astronaut, Alfie?'

Before answering her, I took another gulp of the refreshing cool beer. 'I think that if Shelley was able to take his hands off the controls just for a few moments and had peered out of the satellite window, I am sure he would have found the loveliest of words to describe the universe.'

'Just like his poem about the moon,' remarked Harriet.

I was quite surprised that Harriet was familiar with Shelley's haunting but enchanting poem of the moon. In unison we quoted the poem:

> *Art thou pale for weariness,*
> *Of climbing heaven, and gazing on the earth,*
> *Wandering companionless,*
> *Among the stars that have a different birth,*
> *And ever changing, like a joyless eye,*
> *That finds no object worth its constancy?*

Dave firmly believed that the Americans would be the first to send a man into space; Henri disagreed, he was absolutely convinced that it would be the Russians. Dave argued that the Americans had the money and vast resources.

'Maybe so,' replied Henri, 'but the Russians have the technical edge.'

With tongue in cheek I said, 'Why don't the pair of you bet on who will be the first man in space; obviously it's going to be either an American or a Russian.'

Dave and Henri responded by agreeing that it was a good idea. Terms of the bet were suggested by Harriet. If Henri should lose the bet, he would pay for the four of us to have a meal at a posh Soho French restaurant and if Dave should lose he must seek out the elusive Burmese restaurant and arrange for us to dine there.

Unfortunately for Dave, he lost the bet. Two months later, the Russians sent their Vostock satellite into orbit with Major Yuri Gagarin on board. Three weeks after this historical flight, US Navy Commander Alan B Sheppard Junior seated inside a Freedom 7 capsule and fired by a Redstone rocket achieved a height of one hundred and fifteen miles.

Dave and Henri finally ended their extended discussion on space travel.

Harriet discreetly muttered to me, 'Thank God for that.'

Unable to find her cigarettes, she emptied the contents of her shoulder bag onto the table; alongside the compact set, hairbrush, comb, keys and a small jar of tablets was a book entitled *To Kill A Mockingbird*.

'That's an unusual title.' I remarked.

'It's an excellent new book,' she said, 'though fictitious.' She raised her voice so that Henri and Dave could have her attention. 'I don't suppose you two spacemen have read *To Kill a Mockingbird*? Her supposition was correct.

Now having our attention, Harriet told us that she had recently obtained the book, written by a woman called Harper Lee, because it had been well received by the critics.

'What is the book actually about?' asked Henri curiously.

She placed the book back inside her shoulder bag before answering him. 'Well, its about a white liberal lawyer in 1930s Alabama who defends a black cotton-picker who is accused of raping a poor, illiterate white teenage girl. In those days, rape was a capital offence.'

'And did he rape the girl?' said Dave quizzically.

Harriet shook her head sideways. 'No, he was totally innocent; in fact, it was the girl who had enticed the cotton-picker into her home with a request that he help her to repair an old door that had loose-fitted hinges; but her real intention was to seduce him. Apparently, she had picked the wrong man. The cotton-picker was well aware that in Alabama it was considered taboo for a black man and a white woman to have a carnal relationship, and fearing the harsh inevitable consequences of such a liaison, he instantly rejected her advances and fled from the house.'

While Harriet lit up a cigarette, Henri, Dave and I sat quietly and waited for her to continue. After exhaling the smoke, she said, 'It seems that the girl was so humiliated that her offer had been rejected, she complained to her father and the local sheriff that the cotton-picker had raped her.' Epithets followed suit.

'Good grief, the nasty bitch!' uttered Henri.

'Hell has no fury like a woman scorned,' remarked Dave, cynically.

Harriet explained that it was the chapter on the subsequent trial of the cotton-picker that she found most spellbinding especially the defending lawyer Atticus Finch's summoning up speech.

'And was the accused found not guilty?' I asked.

'Unfortunately no.' replied Harriet. 'He was found guilty.'

She quickly added, 'Although the novel is fictitious, does anybody here honestly believe that in 1930s Alabama, where black men were being lynched by the Klu-klux-Klan, a poor cotton-picker would get a fair trial in front of an all-white bigoted jury? When it came to black defendants there was always a deliberate miscarriage of justice.'

After listening to Harriet's appraisal of *To Kill a Mockingbird* I decided that this was a book I must read.

'I presumed they went ahead and executed the man,' said Henri.

'They might just have well,' exclaimed Harriet. 'After the trial, the cotton-picker was placed temporarily in the county jail to await sentence and while he was in the exercising yard, he attempted to escape by climbing over the fence, but he was spotted by the guards who shot him dead; the poor guy had seventeen bullet holes in his body.'

Harriet felt that the book would make an excellent stage play or even a film. 'Of course there is only one actor who could play the part of the lawyer Atticus Finch and that is my favourite, the Irish-American Spencer Tracy.'

In 1962 *To Kill a Mockingbird* was made into a successful film. Perhaps Harriet was not entirely disappointed that Gregory Peck rather than Spencer Tracy was chosen for the leading role. Peck's brilliant portrayal of Atticus Finch won him a long-overdue academy award.

The four of us would spend the remainder of the evening discussing crime and punishment which was a subject that Harriet felt exceptionally passionate about. Henri fully supported capital punishment and the use of the guillotine, France's traditional method of execution. 'If you take a life, you must be prepared to give up your own. In France the guillotine has proved to be an ideal deterrent.'

As Harriet listened attentively to Henri, she shook her head disapprovingly before declaring, 'Ever since I was a young girl, I could never accept the argument that capital punishment was necessary; I believed it then and I believe it now, that hanging people is a medieval and ghastly practice and the sooner that this awful method of executing people is abolished the better!'

Despite Henri's belief that the guillotine was a deterrent, he admitted that not all criminals were terrified of the oblique-edged blade. 'Even Doctor Petiot, who was one of France's most notorious mass murderers, had no fear of losing his head.'

Dave asked a relevant question. 'Was this murderer Petiot brave, or did he believe that he would never be arrested by the authorities?'

Henri said he was unsure of Petiot's state of mind when he was killing people; he only knew about the crimes that the doctor committed. As Harriet, Dave and I had never heard of Doctor Marcel Petiot, Henri was only too pleased to explain the doctor's notoriety. During the last war, Petiot was a practising doctor in German occupied Paris. He also had a lucrative sideline selling heroin, performing illegal abortions and ostensibly aiding wealthy people to clandestinely leave France. Petiot's paid agents, who were usually petty criminals, enticed would-be émigrés to his mansion on the assumption that the doctor would smuggle them out of the country, but once inside the mansion the unfortunate people were killed, robbed of their possessions and their bodies disposed of by the means of an incinerator and quicklime.

'And how many people did he actually kill?' asked an astonished Harriet.

Henri believed the figure was about 70 including at least one child.

'Good God, how could he kill a child?' gasped Harriet.

'Well he certainly did,' remarked Henri. 'Fortunately, the cunning doctor's two year reign came to an end, he was arrested, put on trial, found guilty and guillotined in Paris some time during May 1946.'

Collecting her thoughts, Harriet said, 'I know that you probably believe that Petiot deserved to be executed for the terrible crimes he committed, but surely you see my argument that capital punishment, even one as barbaric as the guillotine, is not a deterrent.'

Henri interrupted her before she continued. 'My dearest Harriet, you misunderstood me, I did state that although the guillotine is a deterrent, it is not an absolute deterrent, but I most certainly believe that capital punishment does prevent many criminals from committing murder and for that reason alone, I think that the death penalty should remain on the statute books in France and in Britain too.'

Dave asked Harriet if capital punishment was abolished, what should be the alternative punishment. Her answer was instant, 'Locked up for life, without parole.'

Henri said, 'Perhaps many of these murderers would prefer to be executed rather than spend the rest of their lives in prison.' Harriet chose not to answer him.

Dave and I also had entrenched views on crime and punishment. We both strongly favoured the reintroduction of corporal punishment, especially the birch and the cat-o'nine-tails that we thought should be used against violent street robbers, bullies and child abusers, whom we particularly despised.

Our attitude towards the death penalty was similar too. We would exclude crimes of passion, as in the Ruth Ellis case, but approve the hanging of child murderers and ruthless killers like John Christie.

Harriet reminded us that there had been terrible miscarriages of justice in the past, which was another reason why she thought that capital punishment should be abolished. To reinforce her argument, she mentioned that Timothy Evans and Derek Bentley were judicial victims. Evans was hanged in 1950 and Bentley went to the scaffold in 1953. Although only nineteen, Bentley had the mental capacity of a nine year old. (In 1966, Evans was posthumously pardoned and, in 1992 after an unremitting campaign that was to last for four decades, Bentley was finally granted a posthumous but limited pardon.) I thought that Harriet had made a valid point.

'But these cases are extremely rare,' asserted Henri. Dave thought that in the future, miscarriages of justice would be averted because of the advance of forensic science. Though I was in favour of capital punishment for certain crimes, I too was aware that in murder trials there was always a remote possibility that a miscarriage of justice might occur. This awareness was heightened after the 1960 'winkle-picker' murder case that left me disturbed. In fact to this day I still remain somewhat disturbed.

'Winkle-picker, I have never heard of this English word,' said Henri when I briefly mentioned the case. I explained to the Frenchman that 'winkle-pickers' was slang for pointed Italian shoes that were fashionable in the late 1950s. Dave knew of the winkle-picker case, but not Harriet, who may have been in France with Henri at the time of the trial that took place at the Old Bailey during the autumn of 1960.

'You and David must explain to me about this case,' insisted Harriet. As I had taken a greater interest in the case than Dave and was more familiar with the facts, my friend thought it appropriate that I should explain. Neither Harriet, Henri nor Dave would utter a single word while I related the tragic events that began on 25 June 1960.

On that fateful Saturday evening, four young Hounslow men, Norman Harris, twenty-three, an unemployed van driver, Christopher Darby, also twenty-three, a coalman, Francis (Flossie) Forsyth, eighteen, a roofer, and seventeen year old Terrence Lutt, a labourer, consumed a great deal of beer at their local pub. At closing time, they left the pub. As they walked home, Harris, who seemed to be the leader of the coterie suggested that they should break into a nearby scrap yard and steal any items of value; he also suggested waylaying and robbing passers by.

The gang soon arrived at the isolated scrap yard where they began to loiter on an adjacent towpath. Not long afterwards, Edward John Jee, a twenty-three year old trainee engineer who had become engaged just the day before, appeared on the towpath. As he passed the four men, Lutt said to him 'Hello darling.' Jee ignored the remark. Suddenly Lutt punched Jee hard in the face;

the blow caused him to fall over. Whilst he was lying on the towpath he pleaded to be left alone. Ignoring his pleas, the gang savagely punched and kicked him. When Jee ceased to struggle and was motionless, the gang fled, but not before rifling his pockets. It was thought that the victim had no more than a ten shilling note in his wallet.

A little later, a passer-by found the unconscious Jee; he immediately 'phoned the police and called for an ambulance. Tragically, two days later, Jee died of a fractured skull. It seems that some of his severest wounds were the result of being kicked by somebody wearing pointed shoes; winkle-picker shoes had been worn by Forsyth.

Harris and his three friends were quickly arrested, and in due course were put on trial at the Old Bailey. As I read the reports of the trial in the daily press, I became convinced that the four defendants were obviously guilty of robbery with violence, which had resulted in the tragic death of Edward John Jee, but I did not quite believe that the gang really intended to murder Jee. I had always interpreted murder as being when you deliberately intend to kill someone. (A prime example was John Christie.) I also felt that the gang had been influenced by the large amount of beer that they had consumed. Had they been sober that evening, I don't believe that they would have attacked Jee.

The jury at the Old Bailey soon reached a verdict. I expected the verdict to be manslaughter, but I was wrong. The three men were found guilty of murder and the sentences were harsh. Harris and Forsyth were sentenced to be hanged by their necks until they were dead. Darby was sentenced to life in prison and sixteen-year-old Lutt would be detained at the Queen's pleasure.

Following the announcement of the verdicts, a campaign to reprieve the two condemned men began. Two thousand people signed a petition for clemency that was handed to the Home Secretary, RA (Rab) Butler. William Bentley, the father of the executed Derek, persuaded the forty-one members of the London County Council to sign a petition, but it was to no avail; the Home Secretary refused to grant a reprieve.

On the morning of 9 November 1960, Norman Harris was hanged at Pentonville Prison and Francis Forsyth, was hanged at Wandsworth Prison.

Henri was the first to comment, 'As far as I am concerned, justice had been done; the two perpetrators of a brutal murder were hanged, so what?'

Harriet immediately hissed at him. 'Henri, how on earth can you say that, they were just young men.'

'The poor victim was a young man too,' retorted Henri.

'Remind me again, Alf, how old was Forsyth?' said Dave.

I explained that he was only eighteen when he was hanged.

'Good God!' sighed Harriet. 'How on earth could the British government, in the middle of the twentieth century, execute a young lad? Is there no humanity, no compassion in this world?'

I totally agreed with Harriet. Although Forsyth's crime was unforgivable, he was just too young to be executed. I was aware that in the nineteenth century it was customary to execute eighteen- and nineteen-year-old murderers, and in the eighteenth century children as young as thirteen and fourteen were hanged for stealing just a small item like a loaf of bread; but this was 1960 and the government was still allowing teenagers to be executed.

Henri realised that his uncompromising views had upset Harriet and quickly decided to make amends. He gently squeezed her hand and said, 'My dearest Harriet, of course, we who favour executing convicted murderers are losing the battle. I am sure that within a few years, capital punishment will be abolished here in Britain and maybe in France too.'

Henri's prophecy was correct as capital punishment was abolished in Britain in 1965 and in France in 1977.

13

Madeleine

In April 1961 I made one of my regular fortnightly visits to the Shipping Federation at Prescot Street. The friendly official behind the counter whom I recognised from previous visits beckoned to me.

'Persistency pays off,' he grinned. 'You're in the Navy now.'

The official wrote down my name and told me to return at the end of the month to accept a vacancy as a utility steward, 'Probably on a P&O ship'.

I had no idea what the duties of a utility steward were. An elderly seaman, who was about to join a queue at the counter kindly explained, 'Kitchen portering, serving at a hot plate and potato peeling; all galley work mate, not a bad job and plenty of grub too.'

Whatever the work entailed, no matter how menial the position, I would not complain. At long last, my dream and maybe David Upson's dream too of joining the Merchant Navy would now be a reality.

During the evening I searched the Wapping pubs for Dave. I could not wait to tell him the good news. I eventually located him walking up Wapping Lane with Madeleine who was one of his occasional girlfriends. 'Maddie', as Dave would affectionately call her, had arrived from Manchester two or three year's earlier. Despite being well educated and with a degree in English, she seemed happy working as a waitress in a West End restaurant.

Dave would sometimes visit her 'boudoir' near Aldgate East. Propped up in her bed, with the inevitable glass of whisky in one hand and a pencil-thin cigar in the other, my friend would become increasingly aroused as he listened to Madeline's sensual voice reading to him her beloved Shakespeare sonnets.

Dave and Madeleine were somewhat surprised to see me when I caught up with them by the swing bridge. Both were slightly intoxicated. Madeleine put her arms around my neck and kissed me on the cheek.

'Watch it, mate,' joked Dave. 'Why aren't you in the pub?'

Madeline gently prodded him in the ribs. 'Behave yourself Davy Crocket; you just leave Alfred alone.'

Dave winked at me as he lit up a cigar. 'Keep Saturday night free, mate.'

I was very familiar with his winks; on this occasion it was an indication that he had acted on my behalf. Whatever he had planned, I knew that it would involve girls.

Madeleine also noticed the wink and immediately imitated his voice. 'Yes, keep Saturday night free, Alfred.'

Dave and I laughed at her near perfect mimicry. Suddenly, Madeleine gripped my arm; her voice was slurred as she spoke.

'Alfred, how would you like to meet my nice friend Lucy?'

Dave answered for me. 'Yes, he would, very much so.'

Madeleine again prodded him in the ribs. 'Just you be quiet, Davy Crocket; let Alfred speak for himself.' Dave did what he was told and playfully clamped his hands over his mouth.

Never letting an opportunity pass me by when it came to meeting women, I responded gleefully. 'Yes, I would love to meet Lucy.'

'Good,' replied Madeleine. 'David will bring you along to my place this Saturday evening and we can have a little party.'

'And will Lucy be at the party?' I replied with enthusiasm.

Madeleine yawned; she looked tired and her voice was fading when she spoke. 'Yes, Lucy will be there.' Turning to face Dave she said, 'And don't forget to bring some wine.'

Dave reacted by giving her a prolonged smile. 'Of course Maddie, of course.' His answer was followed by another wink which he directed at me.

I walked with my friends slowly up Wapping Lane towards the Highway. When Madeleine rested her head on Dave's shoulder, he began to recite the poems of Omar Khayam; always a sign that he was relaxed and at ease.

Obviously, this was not the ideal occasion to discuss serious matters with Dave, so I decided to postpone telling him the good news that I had received from the Shipping Federation until the following evening when we would be alone in the Green Parrot.

Once we reached the Highway, Madeleine was too weary to walk on to Aldgate East. The three of us stood chatting until I managed to hail a passing taxi. Once Madeleine and Dave were in the cab, I turned around and began my long walk home to Poplar. As always, my favourite route was via Narrow Street at Limehouse.

The next day, I was sacked from my job as a blouse and skirt cutter. Chris, my Greek-Cypriot employer, gave me three hours' notice. No reason was given for my dismissal. Just four words were said; 'Alfos, you finish tonight.'

I knew exactly why I was dismissed. A few weeks after I began working for Chris, he had engaged his son-in-law Nicos, who had arrived from Cyprus to be the top cutter. Rather than pay wages for two cutters, Chris obviously decided that his less experienced son-in-law was capable of cutting the garments and that I must go.

Chris's decision to employ Nicos would prove to be an irreparable and very costly mistake. Nicos completely ruined 600 shirt blouses.

Whist working at the Greek factory, I befriended Glynis a Barbadian born presser. Middle-aged Glynis was deeply religious. Whenever there was a break from the bouzouki records that were constantly played on an old radiogram, Glynis would quietly hum and sing gospel songs. I soon began to appreciate her sweet voice, especially when she sang 'Swing Low, Sweet Chariot' and 'Sometimes I feel like a Motherless Child'.

Glynis invited me to watch her choir practice at a Hackney church. Politely, I refused, but became interested after she offered me a sweetener.

'The choirmaster has two very attractive daughters.'

David Upson and I wore smart clean clothes when we were introduced to the daughters at the church. Glynis must have been myopic; far from being attractive, the sisters, both overweight sopranos, were hideous. It was unlikely that the excuses that Dave and I gave to leave were believed: I had a stomach upset and Dave felt faint. We quickly left the church. Once outside in the churchyard we bolted and within fifteen minutes we were drinking in Dirty Dick's pub.

Because I had been accepted into the Merchant Navy, being dismissed from the Greek-owned factory meant little to me, but my joining the P&O ship would not take place until early May, which was three weeks away. With time to spare I had two choices, either take a short holiday or find temporarily employment. It was an easy choice to make. I 'phoned Marco Gowns of Bow. This manufacturing company were advertising for an experienced dress cutter. The conversation was brief.

'How long have you been a cutter Alfred?'

'For five years.'

'When can you start?'

'This Monday morning.'

'Good, be here by 8.30 a.m. We are situated at Paton Close, directly behind Poplar Civic Theatre.'

'Thank you, Mr Marco.'

Now that I had secured a job for the few weeks I could relax.

That evening I made my way to Cable Street to meet Dave. For 'nostalgic reasons' he wanted to visit the Green Parrot Club. The club was very busy. Young and middle-aged prostitutes were drinking and dancing with Scandinavian and African sailors and some American servicemen were showing off their jiving skills. Even though the club was at full capacity, Dave and I managed to find comfortable seats and were just able hear each other above the revelry.

As we sat there, I thought it was inappropriate to mention that I had been given the sack. That episode was of no importance, but what was important and urgent was the necessity for Dave to visit the Shipping Federation and enlist in the Merchant Navy.

His reaction to the news that I had gained entry was lukewarm and, in a way, not totally unexpected. 'Alf, I don't want to disappoint you, but I think that I should postpone joining the Merch until later in the year.'

'But Dave,' I replied. 'There is no guarantee that there will be any vacancies whatsoever in the autumn.'

Swirling the remaining whisky and ice in his glass he said, 'I do realise that, but I am prepared to take a chance.'

Questioning my friend would be pointless. I assumed his lack of enthusiasm was in part due to hedonism. With an abundance of women available, a stable job and enough money to keep himself well supplied with drinks and fags, he was unwilling, for the foreseeable future, to stray too far from the East End. Also, his movements would now be restricted; Doris, his elderly mother had recently arrived from Calcutta and was staying at his flat. But I was different; the call of the sea was so powerful that it felt like a magnet. I just had to fulfil my childhood ambition to become a merchant sailor and circumnavigate the globe.

We left the Green Parrot. It took us twenty minutes to walk to the Prospect of Whitby.

The following evening, Dave and I, with our bottles of cheap wine, travelled by bus to Aldgate East. As there would be much drinking at Madeleine's place, Dave had wisely left his motorbike at home. Earlier he had told me that Madeleine had planned to vacate the furnished flat the following day and would move in with Lucy and her sister who occupied a small house in Fulham. Lucy would be bringing her car to help Madeleine remove her belongings that included a large collection of books.

Because he had other women available, Dave was not unduly concerned that Madeleine would be leaving the East End. The pattern was always the same; once a girlfriend moved beyond the Aldgate pump, he invariably lost interest and would make little, if any, effort to contact her again.

Dave had met Lucy on a previous occasion. His description of her being 'pretty but gawky' intrigued me.

A wide-eyed Madeleine was waiting at the doorstep when we arrived. She warmly hugged and kissed us and her voice was welcoming.

'Come in, come in.'

We were guided to a well-worn and frayed sofa. Once seated, she gave us full glasses of white wine. I gazed around the room; it was small, bright and clean. A framed poster of Cambridge and a smaller poster of Manchester were hanging on the wall. Some hockey sticks and a tennis racket were stored in an umbrella stand by the coat rack. With the exception of a well-polished bookcase, heavily laden with hard and softbacks, the rest of the furniture was old, although in good condition.

Madeleine went over to the bedroom door and opened it slightly; she poked her head inside and called out, 'They are here Lucy.'

Feeling a little apprehensive, I took a deep breath, but instead of a pretty, gawky female emerging from the bedroom as I expected, a huge Alsatian trotted out and stood in front of Dave and me. It towered over us and instantly showed its authority by growling and revealing a mouth full of menacing teeth. Dave and I sank deeper in the sofa. For a moment I thought, surely this intimidating hound can't be Lucy?

As Madeleine knelt down to stroke the dog, I glanced sideways at my friend. He too looked astonished. 'Whose pet?' whispered Dave, anxious not to speak too loud, fearing that his unfamiliar voice might provoke the beast. Madeleine smiled when she answered him.

'Lucy has brought Rex to stay for the weekend. Don't worry boys, he is not aggressive at all.'

I was not so sure if that were the case; Dave and I were strangers to him and we were on his domain. Moreover, I had never trusted the breed, especially after a reputedly friendly Alsatian had bit and scratched me several years previously.

Madeleine soon lost interest in stroking Rex who had been enjoying the attention.

She glanced at her watch and remarked, 'Where is that girl?'

After taking another sip of wine, she placed her glass on the coffee table and hurried into the bedroom. Her departure seemed to be a signal for Rex to come closer. Thankfully, its vicious teeth were now replaced by a less threatening protruding tongue. Lowering his head, the dog sniffed my and Dave's shoes; it seemed as if his left eye was focused on me, and the right eye on Dave. We obeyed Rex's instruction to sit perfectly still.

Suddenly, Madeleine and Lucy came out of the bedroom. They immediately burst out laughing at the sight of Dave and me transfixed on the sofa. Lucy ordered Rex to lie down in a corner before apologising for her pet's behaviour.

Dave was mistaken. Lucy was not pretty, she was beautiful; a tall natural blonde, with blue-grey eyes; her accent middle class. Apologising again, she explained that Rex belonged to her parents, who were visiting friends in the country and would be gone for the weekend.

'So I am looking after him. Rex is very docile and he never bites.'

Dave and I soon vacated the sofa, preferring to squeeze into the tiny kitchen where the girls were making sandwiches. Rex, who had smelt the food, decided to join us. Lucy promptly shooed him away. He quietly returned to his corner and started to sulk, but not for long; a small plate of cold sausages was offered to him, which he quickly consumed.

A worktop in the kitchen was substituted for a bar. Amongst the bottles of wine, Dave spotted a half-bottle of whisky, which he jokingly claimed was for his own consumption. Madeleine responded by playfully pointed a carving knife at below his belt with a warning to behave himself 'or else'. I shuddered at the thought of what she had in mind. My friend must have shuddered too, because he instantly replaced the bottle, having decided that he valued his manhood above the whisky.

Madeleine and Dave edged slightly away, deliberately giving me an opportunity to chat to Lucy, who proved to be an enthusiastic conservationist.

An hour passed by very quickly. I soon learnt that Lucy was in her mid-twenties and had been a close friend of Madeleine ever since they met at university in 1957. Her time at university was short-lived; she had found her subject too difficult to complete.

'I was a bit dim in those days,' she sighed. 'Not like Madeleine, who is exceptionally brainy.' Pondering for a moment, she said, 'You know Alfred, life is really amazing. I failed miserably at university, yet today, I have a well-paid job at a merchant bank and Madeleine, who has a first-class degree in English and would make a fine tutor, is working in a restaurant. She really is wasting her talents.'

'But is she really?' I remarked. 'Perhaps, by being a waitress she is trying to gather material to write a novel or a play; no doubt she has plenty of stories to tell about the customers and staff and who knows, she might be able to knock Arnold Wesker off his perch.'

A mischievous expression suddenly appeared on Lucy's face. Leaning sideways, she tapped Madeleine on the shoulder; her voice was teasing. 'Is it true, Madeleine that you are recording your experiences as a waitress, so that you can eventually write a great literary masterpiece?'

''Fraid not, Lucy. The only kitchen drama I will write about in the future is the one I am having right now with Davy Crocket.'

Dave had resumed his interest in the half-bottle of whisky and was involved in a gentle tug-of-war with Madeleine. She had one end of the bottle and he had the other end.

Lucy listened with interest when I mentioned that my garment stock cutting days were soon to be over. She asked me what my future plans were after leaving the 'profession'. Describing garment cutting as a profession caused me to smile.

'Why are you smiling Alfred?' she remarked curiously.

I stopped smiling and explained that stock cutting was a trade and could not be described as a profession. With her arm around my waist and pressing her body against mine, she whispered, 'Oh, you are just being pedantic.' My limited education failed me; what on earth did pedantic mean?

Again Lucy asked me about my future plans. I spoke of finally achieving my boyhood dream of enlisting in the Merchant Navy, but felt embarrassed at having to describe my on-board duties that included kitchen portering, washing up and potato peeling. Fortunately, I was spared this uncomfortable ordeal by Rex who suddenly stood up, facing the door.

'He is telling me that he wants to be taken outside,' said Lucy.

I followed Lucy into the street. Aldgate East and Whitechapel were not safe areas on a Saturday evening. Even though Lucy would be accompanied by Rex, her powerful bodyguard, there was a risk that she could be propositioned, or worse, forced into a car.

As we were leaving, Dave who had lost the tug-of-war with Madeleine, began to prepare a punch. Over the years at various parties, he would sometimes be persuaded to make a 'Dave's punch'. He had his own secret recipe that he guarded religiously. Whatever the ingredients were, I was never to know, but his concoction was always delicious and much appreciated.

Lucy and I were soon walking briskly down the Whitechapel Road. A few prostitutes could be seen shivering in doorways. A car stopped alongside and one of the prostitutes spoke to the driver before getting into the car that quickly drove off. The whole transaction took just seconds.

I remarked to Lucy that what we had just witnessed could not occur in Maidstone, her home town. 'Not so,' was her reply. She herself had been accosted in the town centre and even once as a schoolgirl in broad daylight. 'That was a disadvantage of being tall; I always looked older than I was.'

We continued walking east until we came to Black Lion Yard, where every shop was occupied by a jeweller. We took a short cut through the narrow thoroughfare. Approaching us, but on the opposite side of the yard there was an elderly man with a small mongrel on a lead. As a precaution Lucy held Rex by the collar, but she had neither the strength nor the command to restrain him; Rex darted across the yard and attempted to snap at the mongrel. The elderly man managed to protect his little pet by scooping him up from the ground. Lucy and I grabbed Rex's collar. We pulled him back across the yard and apologised to the mongrel's furious owner. He responded by calling me a 'stupid idiot' for not having more control of my dog. So much for Rex's docility.

When Lucy and I turned into Old Montague Street, the biting wind penetrated our clothes. Lucy felt cold and wanted to return to the warmth of Madeleine's place.

As we hurried along, loud music and laughter could be heard coming from the old tenements on our left. A West Indian party was in progress. 'Those poor neighbours,' whispered Lucy. 'This area is horrible; thank goodness Madeleine is leaving tomorrow.'

A slightly anxious Madeleine opened the door. 'We were beginning to worry, what happened to you?'

'There was no need to worry. Jack the Ripper is long dead,' replied Lucy.

'But not his successors,' quipped Dave, who reminded us that a year or two earlier 'Big Audrey' was stabbed to death in nearby Brick Lane

Madeleine and Lucy had never heard of Audrey Hamilton, but I had. Audrey, who originally came from Eastwood in Essex, had a wasted, tragic life and was only twenty-eight when she died. As a teenager, she formed a relationship with an American serviceman; later she bore him a son. As she was unable to care for the little boy, he was adopted. During the late 1940s, Audrey left Eastwood and settled in Brick Lane. Whilst living there she met and married a West Indian; but the marriage was not to last and they were soon divorced.

Audrey, known as 'Big Audrey' because of her obesity, had spent most of her social life in the ubiquitous cafés, clubs and pubs of Aldgate East and Whitechapel, where she befriended many men. In due course, she went to live with Barat Ulla, a local Pakistani man. While staying with Ulla, she began an affair with another Pakistani, Panglam Gopolan. Audrey ended the affair when she met Anthony Attard, a thirty-nine-year-old Maltese cook. Although Audrey had only met Attard a few weeks previously, the couple planned to marry the following December.

On the evening of Friday 26 September 1958, Audrey was chatting to her friends in Giorgio's Maltese café at 164 Brick Lane. She was waiting for Attard who worked in the kitchen to finish his late shift. Her back was facing the café's entrance; suddenly Gopolan, her former lover, ran into the café and plunged a knife into her back; the blade penetrated her left lung and aorta. Gopolon fled from the café, pursued by several of Audrey's friends and the café's owner Joseph Myzzi. The pursuers caught up with Gopolan on a nearby bombsite, where he was struck to the ground.

Attard, rather than comfort his dying fiancée, who had been carried out of the café and was lying on the pavement, ran straight to the bombsite, where a half-crouching Gopolan was cornered. Attard picked up a piece of concrete and used it repeatedly to smash Goplan's skull.

The slaying of Gopolan was regarded by some local residents as a lynching; perhaps it was, but it seems that the jury at Attard's trial at the Old Bailey a couple of months later thought differently. Attard was able to convince the jury that he had not intended to kill a violent and armed Gopolan, only to try and restrain him until the police arrived. Attard was eventually found not guilty of manslaughter and discharged.

After Dave and I briefly related the details of the incident to a curious Madeleine and Lucy, we sat around the coffee table sampling Dave's excellent punch. I soon began to feel the effects of too much drinking. Determined to avoid a painful hangover, I tucked into the sandwiches; so did the two girls, but not Dave, who seemed unaffected by the alcohol.

A little later, a less than sober Madeleine announced that she would entertain us by reciting some poetry. After standing up too quickly and almost losing her balance, Madeleine swayed across to the bookcase and selected a little volume of verses. I wondered if she had chosen the Shakespeare sonnets that Dave had become familiar with, but no, her choice was *The Seasons* by Edmund Spenser and John Keats' lovely *Ode to a Nightingale*. How strange, I thought; it was only few months before when I began to read Keats' poetry for the first time. So appreciative was I of Keats' exquisite sonnet *I stood tiptoe upon a little hill*, I read it continuously until I could recite the fourteen lines by memory.

Madeline explained that Keats was probably influenced by Spencer, and that Keats and his famous contemporary and friend Shelley, both died tragically young in Italy.

Madeleine took another sip of punch, stood with her back to the fireplace and then bowed to her audience of three. Dave raised his glass. Madeleine responded by blowing him a kiss. I noticed that there was a tinge of slurring in her voice when she slowly delivered her brief prologue.

'Now, I know that Lucy's favourite poet, or should I say poetess, is Elizabeth Barrett Browning and David is fond of Omar Khayyám and even Alfred can write a verse or two, so I am in good company.'

Dave started to clap followed by Lucy and me. Our clapping aroused a sleeping Rex, who started to bark. Lucy offered him a half-sandwich as a bribe to keep quiet. The dog needed no coaxing to accept the bribe. The sandwich was swallowed almost whole. He soon wanted a second helping, but Lucy refused and promptly scolded him for being greedy.

Once Rex had settled down, Madeleine began reciting the Spencer poem. The slight slur in her voice seemed to have disappeared. Her tone was now clear and melodic, ideal for reciting this most beautiful poem. Rather than applaud her when she had finished, fearing our clapping might cause Rex to bark again, the three of us raised our glasses. Madeleine bowed and sat down, having decided that she should postpone reciting the Keats poem for the time being.

It was now after midnight. The four of us had consumed a great deal of wine and punch. I ate the last of the sandwiches in the hope that a full stomach might help in preventing a possible and dreaded hangover. Inevitably, it would be Madeleine who was the first to start yawning. The rest of us followed soon afterwards.

Just before Madeleine finally dozed off and like a dying heroine in a Puccini opera, she opened her eyes and spoke softly. 'O Morpheus, truly a son of Hypnos, please come to me tonight.'

Dave waited for a moment before picking her up. He carried her slowly into the bedroom and closed the door.

I was puzzled, who on earth were Morpheus and Hypnos? I repeated these Greek-sounding names to Lucy who thought that they might be Greek Gods. Curious as ever, I quickly turned the pages of Madeleine's dictionary for an answer. Lucy was correct. In Greek mythology, Hypnos was a God of sleep and Morpheus his son was a God of dreams. Satisfied that I had increased my knowledge, I replaced the dictionary in the bookcase and joined Lucy on the wide sofa.

As I did so, Rex who was lying on the floor raised his head. I had noticed throughout the evening whenever I got close to Lucy he became a little protective and would sometimes growl; but to my surprise, just after a few minutes of my sitting with Lucy, he lowered his head. All was well; I had finally won his approval. Perhaps he sensed that sleep was on my mind and not seduction.

Lucy and I held hands and quietly chatted. She gave me her phone number and suggested that I should give her a call when I returned from the sea. Within minutes, we stretched ourselves out on the sofa; my duffle coat was substituted for a blanket. It was uncomfortable lying there and a little cold. Lucy quickly fell a sleep and I followed soon afterwards. At dawn, I felt my face being licked, but unfortunately it wasn't Lucy's tongue, but Rex's.

I immediately got up and splashed cold water on my face. It felt good and thankfully there were no after-effects from my heavy drinking the night before. Lucy was not so lucky and had a slight headache. I suggested to her that we should take Rex outside for a walk, adding that the fresh April air might help to lessen her pain. She promptly agreed.

When we returned some twenty minutes later, Madeleine was preparing eggs and bacon and Dave could be heard snoring in the bedroom. He soon joined us at the table; declining to eat, he was content with just 'coffee and fags,'

By 7 a.m., we had finished our coffee. An hour later, Lucy's car was filled to the brim with Madeleine's belongings; the roof rack proved invaluable. After Dave and I had hugged and kissed the girls and patted Rex they got into the weighted down car and drove away.

It would be more than two years before I spoke to Lucy again. By then she and Madeleine were both married with young babies.

I was to spend the next three weeks at the Marco Gowns factory. Alfie Hart, the senior cutter at the factory was an extremely pleasant natured man who was instrumental in making my short stay so enjoyable. He was disappointed to learn that as a skilled cutter I was about to leave the trade and join the Merchant Navy, but he also realised that I needed to see 'a bit of the world.' He hoped that I would return to work at the factory one day; he also gave me his East Ham address, insisting that during my next shore leave I should stop by at his home and tell him all about my visits to foreign countries.

A few years later, I did try tried to contact my erstwhile friend, but sadly it was too late as Alfie had passed away.

At the end of April, I said goodbye to family and friends and boarded the bus at Poplar that would take me to Tilbury. How I wished David Upson was sharing my adventure.

14

SS *Orontes*

Fastened to a quay was the twenty thousand ton *Orontes*. She was one of the P&O shipping company's oldest liners. Now at the end of her lifespan, this huge old lady of the sea was due to make one or two more voyages before being broken up.

In an excited state, I strode up the gangplank. A deckhand standing by the gangway gave me directions to locate the second steward's office. It took me about ten minutes of wandering along a maze of narrow corridors before I found the tiny office. The second steward was writing at his tiny desk by the open door. When he saw me by the doorway a sickly smile suddenly appeared on his face; it could have been mistaken for a smirk.

His voice sounded very feminine. 'Come in, please sit down.'

I sat down at his desk and handed him my documents.

As he examined them I said, 'You must excuse me; this is my first voyage, so I am not familiar with the procedure.'

He looked up at me and sighed before remarking, 'Familiarity breeds contempt my dear.'

No doubt he was referring to his past relationships.

After retaining my seaman's record book, he stood up and we went into the corridor where he instructed a passing crew member to escort me to the crew's quarters that were situated in the depths of the ship. I was to share a cabin with seven other men.

The conditions in the cabin were sparse; no tables or chairs, just bunks and lockers. Choosing a top bunk in a corner was a good choice, as it offered a little privacy.

I unpacked my kit, which included several books on English history, a subject that I was teaching myself with a view to sitting for the GCE 'O' Level examination in 1962.

Gradually, the other crew members with whom I was to share the cabin arrived. It seemed that none of my new companions had been to sea before. As we chatted, a head chef came into the cabin and explained what our duties would be, starting that very evening. Hugh MacDonald a London-based Scot and the two Maltese men would be kitchen porters. The two Glasgow lads, both my age, had the unenviable job of potato peeling. A seventeen year old from Belfast was to serve on the hotplate, and Alan, a tall slender youth from Brixton, who claimed that he had considerable experience of cooking in the kitchens at Guy's Hospital, would become an assistant vegetable cook. The two vacancies for scullions were allocated to me and Graham 'Daisy' Day, a slightly-built South London teenager who bunked in an adjacent cabin.

After every sitting Daisy and I would be responsible for cleaning and stacking away the chef's cooking utensils, which included huge heavy pots, saucepans, frying pans and ladles. Our working hours would be divided into three shifts: 7 a.m. to 10 a.m., 12 p.m. to 3 p.m. and 6 p.m. to 9 p.m. At the end of the day, the scullery had to be hosed down. We would have to repeat this work pattern seven days a week.

Daisy soon revealed his sly nature; he did his utmost to avoid work. Throughout the three-month voyage he constantly made excuses that enabled him to be absent from the scullery. At first I resented his deviousness, but gradually as the weeks went by I accepted and even welcomed his absenteeism. By working alone and with great speed it was possible for me to complete my duties before the end of the shift. I took pride in my work and kept the scullery spotlessly clean and tidy.

The entire galley was inspected weekly by senior officers including the Captain and the medical officer who insisted that at all times a strict code of hygiene was maintained.

In between shifts, many of the ship's crew would relax on the forward deck that was reserved for their private use. I often avoided the forward deck during my breaks, preferring instead to study in the cabin. Although it was quiet in the cabin, the atmosphere was always hot and stuffy due to our quarters being located directly above the engine room and below the galley. With inadequate portholes and a constant flow of sickly, stale air emitting from the small adjustable ventilators, I too would sometimes be forced to seek refuge on deck.

Never a sun lover, finding a cool or shaded spot could be difficult with so many seated and stretched out bodies occupying every available space. Often my reading on deck would be interrupted by a bored or homesick crew member wanting to engage me in conversation. Usually, I would tolerate these interruptions and soon I had made several acquaintances.

Jock, a thirty-year-old kitchen porter from Dundee, always carried a small book of Robert Burns' poetry in his pocket. Aware that I was fond of poetry, he would often perch himself next to me on deck and read out loud the verses, much to the delight of his fellow Scots, but to the annoyance of the 'sassenachs'.

Not only did Jock have a passion for Burns, he also had a passion for beer. After finishing the evening shift, he would retire to the Pig & Whistle, the crew's tiny bar, and gulp down as many pints as he could during its limited opening hours. As he reeled half-drunk back to his cabin, his singing voice with its rolling rs would echo down the corridors; it could only be the Robert Burns song 'O my love's like a red, red rose'.

Jock considered himself to be an 'outward bound' drinker.

'You do?' I said, not realising what he meant.

'Aye, most definitely,' was his instant reply. 'I've sailed on the *Oronsay*, the *Orion* and the *Orcades* and I drink regularly on board, but the moment the ship turns around and is homeward bound, I never touch another drink until we reach Tilbury; and that's what I am doing here on the *Orontes*. Under no circumstances will I drink on this ship once she leaves Sydney and is homeward bound. I am a man of discipline who always keeps his word. You will see, laddie, you will see.'

Jock did keep his word. He was never seen in the Pig & Whistle after the *Orontes* left Sydney. In fact he never made the return voyage. The Australian police arrested him when he was involved in a drunken brawl in Monty's (The Montgomery), Sydney's world famous dockside pub and he was promptly jailed.

A tall, handsome young Irish cook named Michael also befriended me. We often met on deck during the afternoon break. He had joined the Merchant Navy to escape from the clutches of his strict Catholic parents who wanted him to enter the priesthood, a calling that he had no enthusiasm for.

Michael claimed that as a young teenager a Jesuit priest who was a close family friend had attempted to molest him. 'It would have broken my parents' hearts if they had known that this so-called servant of God was a disciple of the devil.'

Michael seemed to have regarded me as a willing and patient listener. He admitted that he was confused by his sexuality and sought my advice. I explained that I was in no position to give advice, but I would try to answer his questions.

'No, I did not condemn homosexuality, although I thought sodomy was an unnatural practice.'

'No, I had never been attracted to men, only women.'

'Yes, I had sex with several girls.'

'No, I hade never knowingly been with a prostitute.'

My friend confessed that he was considering visiting brothels with other crew members when the *Orontes* docked at Piraeus in Greece, but what concerned him deeply was his virginity. He had no idea what to do if he 'went with a prostitute' or whether he would enjoy the experience. He said any advice I could give him would be appreciated. My advice was quite simple. If he did decide to go whoring in Piraeus, it was essential that he used a French letter and not to worry about knowing what to do because the prostitute, as I delicately explained, 'would soon put him straight'. He laughed nervously at my tongue-in-cheek remark.

At the last moment, Michael changed his mind and did not go ashore at Piraeus. He did however, eventually lose his virginity with a fifteen-year-old prostitute in Bombay. He wisely followed my advice to take precautions.

I too went ashore at Bombay. Unlike Michael, I chose to take a camera with me rather than a packet of three. It was a pleasant surprise for me as I wandered around the city to discover how genuinely friendly the local people were, but I was shocked at the sight of so many child beggars and pickpockets. Earlier, I had declined my shipmates' invitation to accompany them to see a 'live show' at a Grant Street brothel in the heart of Bombay's notorious red light district. The thought of watching women copulating with animals was disgusting and not for me. However, the two Maltese kitchen porters went to see the show. Later, they were persuaded by the brothel's owner to spend a 'short time with the girls upstairs'. In due course, these two fools had to pay a price for their folly as they both contracted gonorrhoea.

For the older Maltese it was a disastrous voyage; besides the venereal disease, he was beaten up following a dispute with his fellow kitchen porter, the pugnacious Hugh Macdonald and, much worse, he was later nearly killed when he stepped into the open lift shaft that led to the ship's hold. The screaming man just managed to cling to a rail by his fingertips.

Another crew member who occasionally interrupted my studies on deck was 'Soapy'. He would always arrive late in the afternoon, shortly before I returned to the scullery for my evening shift. Soapy was a greaser/donkeyman. Never once did I see him in the crew's canteen, the Pig & Whistle or the recreation room. It's possible that he ate his meals in the engine room and may have even slept there too. Soapy would emerge on deck like a rescued miner from a collapsed coalface; he looked and smelt awful. His hands and face were covered in grime and he wore the same filthy jeans every day; his torn t-shirt, originally white, was now a dirty grey.

Like me, Soapy came from Stepney. He knew the Dockland pubs I was familiar with and by coincidence he had once met David Upson at the Seamen's Mission Hostel at Dock Street.

Soapy and I were chatting on deck, when suddenly he gazed upwards and pointed to a group of passengers who were leaning over a rail on the upper deck.

He spat out the chewing gum and said, 'Alf, you see the blonde girl to the right wearing sun-glasses?'

'What about her?'

'What would you say if I told you that she was my bird and I was knocking her off?'

His bragging caused me to utter, 'You wish, you wish!'

Anxious to convince me that he was speaking the truth, he produced a photo of himself and the blonde drinking at a bar. The girl was stunning and resembled my current favourite pin-up girl, the British actress Belinda Lee, who tragically was about to die in a road accident in San Bernando, California.

'Wow!' I said enviously. 'She is beautiful.'

Soapy smiled before snatching the photo from my hand. He immediately kissed it and quickly tucked it back into his wallet.

Incredulous as it seemed, he was obviously telling the truth. After I had promised that our conversation would be private, he proceeded to tell me how he had met the blonde and several other girls on previous voyages.

By remaining in the engine room all day and only appearing on deck for brief periods, camouflaged by grease and grime and rarely mixing with the crew, he found that he could use his anonymity advantageously. Late in the evening after he came off duty, Soapy would shower, groom himself, put on clean clothes and wander up onto the passenger decks, which were strictly out of bounds to all crew members. Masquerading as a passenger he remained unnoticed by the patrolling Master-at-Arms, and mingling with the passengers in the bars, he would seek out any female who seemed available.

I was tempted to take up Soapy's offer of joining him on one of his evening excursions to the forbidden passenger decks. During fire drill, when we crew hurried to the top deck to man the lifeboats, I had seen many attractive girls amongst the passengers. Soapy was very persuasive; he also mentioned that the blonde girl had several female friends on board.

'But what if I am recognised? I asked.

He brushed my cravenness aside. 'Don't worry, chum, nobody will recognise you, trust me! Look, if you wear a nice shirt, doll yourself up and carry a book, you will definitely pass as a passenger.'

He sounded confident. Impersonating a passenger may have been easy for him, but not for me. I would be a novice and lacking in confidence.

Although there were about a thousand passengers on the *Orontes*, most of whom were emigrating to Australia, none would have known me, but there was still a slight possibility that I might be recognised and exposed by a crew member who worked on the passenger decks. An added problem was the ubiquitous Master-at-Arms. If I was spotted and questioned by these patrolling sergeants, would I just be cautioned and ordered back down to the crew's quarters or would I be apprehended and put on a charge? Appearing in front of the Captain and being fined on my first voyage, with the probability of the misdemeanour being recorded, might place my new career as a merchant seaman in jeopardy. Sneaking up to the passenger decks with the aim of meeting females was not worth the risk. It was common sense for me to remain patient until I returned to the East End on the 1 August. No doubt David Upson would be waiting to introduce me to new women.

Disappointed that I was too 'chicken' to take a chance, Soapy returned to his engine room. But to my surprise, he again resumed his efforts of trying to persuade me to venture up to the passenger decks. I was curious to know why he needed my company, when he seemed to be a successful lone operator. Soapy explained that he wanted to help me to 'find a bird' because he owed my best friend David Upson a favour. He claimed that Dave had lent him money when he was desperate. He also claimed that he had repaid Dave at the agreed time. His reason may have been genuine; Dave had lent money to several hard-up seamen whilst he was a resident at the Seamen's Mission at Dock Street. Sometimes the loan was paid, but invariably it was not.

My greasy acquaintance remained persistent. Eventually, to stop him pestering me, I agreed to accompany him to the passenger decks on just one occasion and no more.

He patted me on the shoulder. 'Believe me chum, you won't regret it.'

The next evening as the *Orontes* steamed south-east across the Indian Ocean, Soapy led the way up various flights of stairs until we reached the passenger decks. I trailed nervously behind him clutching a copy of *The Adventures of Tom Sawyer*. Sitting near a bar, Soapy wasted no time in trying to draw the attention of passing unescorted females. When a redhead returned his smile, he followed her to the nearby bar with a panache that reminded me of David Upson's method of pursuing females. I watched intensely as Soapy introduced himself to the girl, who accepted his offer of a cigarette and a drink. He guided her to a vacant table where they sat down. Once they were sitting comfortably, Soapy discreetly winked at me.

Feeling relaxed and encouraged by Soapy's successful contact, I decided that I would follow his example and smile at any young female who headed in my direction. Unfortunately, none came my way, but who did appear and walking towards me was one of the Masters-at-Arms whom I knew casually from below decks.

I quickly picked up my book and pretended to read it and in the process cursed my stupidity and bad luck. Spending the night in the brig did not appeal to me at all.

Incredibly, the Master-at-Arms failed to recognise me as he slowly walked past, but he did say just three words, 'Good evening, son.' I did not look up or answer him.

A moment later, I signalled to a startled and opened-mouthed Soapy that I was leaving. With great haste I left the deck and made my way back down the stairs to the crew's recreation room, vowing never to listen to the greaser again.

The following morning, while I was busy cleaning the pots in the scullery, I was paid an unexpected visit by the same Master-at-Arms who had come so close to feeling my collar the previous evening. He stood at the doorway with his cap high on his forehead and began eating custard from a small bowl. My heart increased its pace. Never did I scrub those pots so furiously.

The sergeant neither looked in my direction nor spoke a word. Instead he walked over to the porthole and looked out. After taking a couple of deep breaths, he turned around and faced me. His penetrating stare was a grim reminder of the same kind of focused stare that I had received up close from the Army drill sergeants at Pirbright Camp the previous year.

He spoke quite loudly. 'You know sonny, they say every one of us has an identical twin somewhere.'

Before I could answer him, he exchanged the empty custard bowl for one of my study books that was lying on a shelf. As he glanced through the pages he said, 'English history. I prefer English and American literature myself, particularly nineteenth century authors like James Fennimore Cooper and Mark Twain.'

My God, I thought, Mark Twain – he has recognised me. Now I am for it, but instead of being led away as I expected, he placed my book back on the shelf and started to walk towards the door.

He stopped by the door, turned around and said, 'Sonny, have you ever read *The Adventures of Tom Sawyer*?'

'Yes, sarge,' I replied meekly.

'I thought you might have.' He said with a grin. Straightening his cap, he left the scullery. I was reprieved.

Although I would now avoid Soapy, I could never avoid 'Queer Antonio', a carefree Italian-born bedroom steward. Tony, with his ready smile and likeable nature, was a joy to chat to. Grasping this opportunity to improve my Italian, I asked '*Il mio amico*' if he would kindly give me an occasional lesson or two in basic Italian grammar.

He responded warmly. '*Volentieri, Alfredo, volentieri*.' (Gladly, Alfred. Gladly.)

Unfortunately, Tony was not well educated; consequently, he had a limited knowledge of grammar. He constantly combined English and Italian words whenever we spoke. This habit made our conversations confusing and difficult for me to construct simple sentences, but I did make use of a most important rule: that every Italian vowel must be pronounced very clearly.

Tony soon realised that there was absolutely no chance of a '*relazione intima*' (intimate relationship) with me. Our friendship would be strictly '*plantonico*.' (Platonic.)

My friend explained that he had a longstanding relationship with Alistair, a rich businessman living in central London, 'nearer the Marble Archer.' A second '*innamorato*' (lover) worked in the *Orontes*' galley. I also learned that Tony had other boyfriends who were based at various locations around the world. San Francisco was his favourite port, '*una bella citta dell amore*.' (A beautiful city of love.) He also mentioned the wonderful times he had spent there whilst on shore leave, but from his inability to recommend any places of interest that might be worth visiting, I could only conclude that he probably never ventured too far from the various waterfront bars, clubs and bath-houses.

Tony kept a '*diario picolo*' (small diary) of his worldwide contacts. With his customary openness, he explained that these wealthy '*innamorati*' were given descriptive '*nomignoli*' (sobriquets). There was a 'Hercules' in Gibraltar, a 'Pimpo' in Marseilles, and 'Silver-tooth' and 'Dwarfo' were residents in Hong

Kong. Noticing my smile when he recalled a 'Pinocchio' caused him to look up to the heavens and make the sign of the cross. '*O dio mio, povero* Pinocchio, his *nosa* was bigger than his *pena*.' My smile immediately turned to laughter.

Tony and I were sitting on the deck chatting when we were disturbed by the arrival of a group of seamen who had just come off duty. They sat around us. Cards and dice were produced. The loud swearing and cacophony that followed upset Tony.

Knowing that the seamen were unlikely to understand Italian, my friend snapped, '*Alfredo, questi uomi sono porci*.' (These men are pigs.) Regaining his composure, he whispered 'Andiamo, Alfredo.' (Let's go.) We stood up and managed to find a quieter part of the deck.

Tony was keen to explain to me what his future plans were. He was desperate to leave the Merchant Navy. Alistair, his rich London boyfriend, wanted to sell his business and purchase a hotel on Italy's Adriatic coast and Tony would be made a partner. Effusively, he made the sign of the cross on his chest and said, 'I will settle downer with Alistair.' He also promised that as I was his '*Amico*' (friend) I would be allowed to stay at the hotel free of charge.

Tony was missing on deck for a few days. I eventually saw him one evening; he was standing alone, leaning on a rail and staring out to sea. When he looked briefly in my direction, I noticed that his cheeks was badly bruised, an obvious indication that he had been beaten up. I called his name, but he was either too embarrassed or ashamed to face me.

Veteran seamen had already told me that it was a regular occurrence for homosexual staff to be attacked by jealous or discarded lovers and in some cases by 'queer-hating' crew members.

I strode across the deck and stood alongside Tony, but he refused to explain what had happened to him. 'Alfredo, I must forget the *episadio*' (episode).

I learned later that Joe, one of the Maltese kitchen porters, had witnessed the incident. Too scared to intervene, Joe explained that as Tony stepped out of a shower cubicle, he was grabbed by two drunken men who may have been deckhands. Apparently, the thugs had held my friend down and tried to force him to commit indecent acts on them. When he refused, he was struck about the face.

Following this vicious assault, I hoped that Tony would leave the Merchant Navy much sooner than he had planned.

Tony quickly recovered from his beating. The bruises were concealed by make-up a few days later when he appeared on a makeshift stage during one of the crew's evening variety concerts that were regularly held on deck. His song and dance sketches, combined with two other effeminate stewards, were professionally performed. Not once did the trio rely on crude gyrating or smuttiness.

'Yorkie', a chef from Leeds, followed their act. He possessed an excellent, but untrained tenor voice. Years of imitating his idol, the late American singer

Mario Lanza, had given his voice a striking similarity. As he sang 'Be My Love' and 'Because You're Mine', Lanza's hit ballads from the early 1950s, a crowd of passengers assembled on the upper deck and began jostling for a position to appreciate Yorkie's fine *bel canto* singing.

Tony was not the only friend of mine who was attacked by cruel bullies. Alan, the tall unassuming vegetable cook who bunked in my cabin, was another victim. It was rumoured that Alan was a secret homosexual. If he was, the rumour should hardly have raised an eyebrow; at least a quarter of the SS *Orontes* 400-strong crew were of the same inclination.

Alan's sexuality was his own affair and nobody else's. Whatever his preferences, he certainly did not warrant the pain and humiliation that he was to endure during the early hours. I was woken by a loud commotion and just caught a glimpse of three seamen running out of our cabin. Alan was lying on the floor naked and in a daze. The intruders had crept in, gagged him pulled him out of the bunk, ripped off his pants and forcibly inserted a toothbrush into his anus. Alan and Tony refused to report these cruel bullies to the Master-at-Arms.

Because I was constantly chatting to an array of crew members on deck, I found that my studies were being neglected. There were other distractions too. Schools of dolphins would often arrive and demonstrate their wonderful agility by leaping out of the sea in front of the ship's bow. Flying fish would skip along the waves and the occasional shark could be seen.

When the *Orontes* docked in Colombo, Ceylon, fresh water was brought on board. Prior to arriving in Colombo, the crew's drinking water was awful; it tasted rubbery. Never did water taste more refreshing than the Colombo water did and shore leave was most welcome, a necessary break from the mundane cleaning in the scullery.

I preferred to explore Colombo unaccompanied. At a street market, a skinny rickshaw owner stood next to a woman who was selling fruit from a barrow. I assumed she was his wife. The rickshaw man offered to take me for a cheap ride, to which I agreed. Although short and probably weighing no more than eight stone, he was quite strong. He soon gathered speed and we seemed to travel in a wide circle. The little man's sweating and panting caused me to feel embarrassed and slightly guilty. When we eventually returned to the fruit-barrow, I felt compelled to pay the rickshaw man double his fee. He was extremely grateful and pleaded with me to wait for just a moment while he turned his rickshaw upside down. He pointed to a serial number engraved on the axle and insisted that I write down the number so that when I was in Colombo again I could seek him out and receive a discount on my next ride. I assured him that it was not necessary for me to make a note of the number, as I would recognise him.

He smiled and said, 'Thank you, boss.' As I was about to leave, he grabbed a large pineapple from the fruit-barrow and thrust it into my hands.

After the *Orontes* left Colombo, we were at sea for at least six days before we reached Fremantle in Western Australia. Our duration there was short-lived, but I did manage to spend several hours walking around the city. Twenty-four hours later we sailed. When we arrived in Adelaide in South Australia, Hugh MacDonald and I went on a sightseeing tour of the city.

A few days later the *Orontes* docked in Melbourne in Victoria. During shore leave in Melbourne, I had found an expensive camera on a park bench. I handed it in to the police station on my way back to the ship. When I eventually returned to London, a little parcel of gifts that included a decorative ashtray was waiting for me, sent from Australia by a Miss Vicars, the grateful owner of the camera.

Whilst in Melbourne I was curious to sample the famed Victorian bitter, but going ashore with Jock was a mistake as he insisted that we visit several of his favourite pubs in Collins Street. The pubs that Jock and I visited were full of noisy but well-behaved crew members from the *Orontes*. We joined their company and I soon realised that I had drunk no less than five pints of the superb Victorian bitter. Five pints was much more than I had ever consumed before in one session. Dreading the thought of the painful hangover that would surely follow after sleep, I left Jock leaning on the bar quoting Robert Burns poetry to a disinterested barman. I needed to get back to the *Orontes* and drink plenty of black coffee.

As I staggered up the gangplank, I tripped and fell to my knees. David Upson's words echoed in my ears; 'Many people are drowned trying to get on and off small craft especially during rough seas.' The *Orontes* may not have been a small craft, but in my drunken state I could quite easily have fallen off the gangplank and into the water. The coffee was effective. When I woke up the next morning, my inevitable hangover was just bearable.

Our final destination was Sydney in New South Wales. The *Orontes* would be berthed there for at least five days, which was ample time for me to explore the city.

Jock tried unsuccessfully to get me to meet him for drinks at Monty's, but I politely refused, having already made arrangements to meet my close friend Alfie Debono. Alfie had recently emigrated to Sydney from London's East End and was staying with relatives in the suburbs. I was surprised to find him a little depressed when we met in a café. He spoke sorrowfully.

'I don't know the reason why, Alf, but my cousins don't seem to like me.' He explained that since arriving in Australia several weeks before, he had tried unsuccessfully to find work. Unfamiliar with Sydney, he had wandered into a red light area just as the police were mounting a raid. 'Suddenly, police vans appeared from every direction.' Not only Alfie but every other male pedestrian who happened to be in the street was apprehended by the police and forcibly shoved into the vans. At the police station, Alfie vigorously complained to a desk sergeant that he was not trying to pick up a prostitute, but was just passing through the street.

Unfortunately for my friend, the unsympathetic sergeant replied, 'It would be in your interest and a lot less trouble, if, when you appear before the magistrate, you just plead guilty to the charge that you were looking for a prostitute and don't worry, it will only be a small fine.'

Alfie spoke woefully, 'Now I have a criminal record too.'

Whilst in Sydney, I spent an evening at the Tivoli, a wonderful old Victorian theatre, to see a production of Sigmund Romberg's *The Student Prince*. I was very familiar with the operetta and had seen the film of the same title many times. Back home in London, amongst my music collection, I had recordings of all the songs from *The Student Prince*, sung by Mario Lanza. Lanza was originally cast as the Student Prince, Karl Franz, in the planned Hollywood film of the operetta, but after disagreements with MGM executives and soaring weight problems that would have made him look ridiculous on the big screen as the dashing young prince, Lanza pulled out of the production. His replacement was the handsome and slim British actor Edmund Purdom. As Lanza had pre-recorded the songs, his voice was dubbed on the screen.

When I glanced around the Tivoli's auditorium, I noticed there were fewer than a hundred people seated. I also spotted a smartly dressed Yorkie sitting a few seats away to my right. This emptiness seemed puzzling to me. How could a country like Australia that was continually producing so many world-class opera singers who were appearing on stage at Covent Garden and Sadlers Wells have so few theatre-goers at the Tivoli?

Yorkie thought he had the answer, which he explained to me as we walked back to the docks after the performance had ended. 'The trouble with the Aussies, lad, it's that they just don't have any interest in culture. They prefer beer and the beach.' I thought his answer was unsatisfactory and probably wrong. Obviously, he was not a patron of the two London opera houses.

Yorkie responded to my enthusiasm for the evening's superb performance by promising that as a special favour to me, he would sing the 'Serenade' from *The Student Prince* at the next crew concert. A few weeks later he kept his promise.

Sadly, two tragedies occurred during our homeward voyage. A baby died in the ship's small hospital, and one of the *Orontes* engineers, last seen leaving a bar after a heavy drinking session, was lost at sea.

When the *Orontes* docked at Bombay, a large party of Indian students bound for London came on board. A local chef was hired to cook their curried meals. His slight bloated face was an indication that he drank regularly. Because my scullery was close to where he worked, we soon struck up a conversation. Within the hour the chef had asked me where the Pig & Whistle was situated, the prices of the drinks and the opening times. I explained that the Pig was a tiny saloon and the bar, a former broom cupboard, was only open for a couple of hours during the evenings to sell beer.

'What, no whisky sold there?' he asked disappointedly.

Realising that many Hindus were passionate about whisky, I replied sympathetically, 'I am afraid not.' The chef looked glum when I informed him that it was the P&O Company's policy to try and discourage drinking among the crew. The company stipulated that only beer and no spirits of any kind could be sold at the bar. There was another strict rule. No pint glasses would be supplied. If a crew member did not own or borrow a pint glass, he would not be served at the bar. Consequently, glasses became valuable items that non-drinking crew members who possessed one could barter with. I had guarded my old dented pewter mug ever since I had found it hidden in a broken pot in the scullery. No doubt it belonged to my predecessor. When not paying my occasional visit to the Pig my mug would remain concealed in the pot.

I thought it inappropriate for me to mention to the chef that the beer sold at the Pig often tasted as if it had been watered down. If a malpractice was in operation, it would not be unusual; malpractice was a daily occurrence amongst several of the *Orontes* catering staff.

Because of the paucity of the crew's meals, we were often hungry, especially during the evenings. For a small fee one of the obliging chefs would supply you with sandwiches or a cooked supper. Not possessing a pint glass and faced with the prospect of no drinking when he came off duty, the curry chef made me a proposition that seemed reasonable. In exchange for the use of my pewter mug, each evening he would cook me a special curry dish of my choice. When I paused for a moment to consider the deal, he offered to include chapattis as well. As he seemed sincere, I agreed. We shook hands to bind the deal. That same evening and in between cleaning the big pots I discreetly ate a superb lobster curry.

If the curry chef had become dissatisfied after drinking beer at the Pig, it was unlikely that he would complain. Like so many other crew members who drank there, he too would be culled into silence by the enormously strong barrel-chested 'Tarzan' who singularly managed the bar.

Towards the end of the voyage and while Daisy was sunbathing on deck, the Captain, accompanied by the Chief Steward, the head chef and a Master-at-Arms visited the scullery. I put down my scrubbing brush, wiped my wet hands and stood to attention. The Captain's smiling face was a refreshing change from his usual slightly austere countenance. He was the only man who spoke.

'We would like to congratulate you and your partner's magnificent efforts in constantly sustaining a high standard of cleanliness.'

I nodded and replied, 'Thank you very much, sir'.

The Captain asked me if I would be on the next voyage.

Rather than admit that I was unsure, I gave him the answer he wanted. 'Of course, sir, most definitely.'

After smiling yet again, the Captain tapped his white cap, turned around and left the scullery with his entourage.

When the *Orontes* arrived at Tilbury on 1 August, as a parting gift I gave the delighted curry chef my pewter mug.

15

Homecoming

Tucked safely inside my pocket was £122 that was 95% of my earnings for the three-month voyage. The money was useful. I gave £30 to my mother, which covered the loss of the £2.10s a week I would have given her had I been working and living at home. I also gave £30 to my sister Sylvia, who following the break-up of her marriage had returned to live at home with Danny her five-month-old baby. I also paid off the outstanding hire purchase for some small items of furniture.

After just a few days relaxing at home, I had become bored and was keen to start work again, but not on the *Orontes*. I had already decided that I would miss her next voyage, and rejoin the ship in November for what was probably to be her last trip. After 36 years at sea, the *Orontes* would be broken up.

There were two reasons why I chose to remain ashore for the next few months. The first was women. Having had no contact with the opposite sex during the previous three months, they were now constantly on my mind. The second reason was that I was determined to sit for my GCE 'O' Level in English History at the earliest opportunity.

I soon found low-paid work in several East End clothing factories. My tenure at these factories rarely lasted longer than a few months.

I had arranged to meet David Upson at the Prospect of Whitby. My walk to Wapping would take me through Narrow Street at Limehouse. As expected the area was tranquil, devoid of traffic and pedestrians. I could never pass down Narrow Street without a glance at the Victorian Dunbar Wharf, which backed onto the inlet of Limekiln Dock. Dunbar Wharf was very busy during the day with its hoists and cranes endlessly lowering and lifting merchandise, but now as dusk approached, the wharf was silent with its chains and ropes secured for the night. (Thirty years later, I stood opposite old Dunbar Wharf and sadly witnessed its commercial activity finally coming to an end after 150 years of continued use. A crane was lowering onto the back of a lorry sacks of juniper beans that are used for the flavouring of gin.)

The huge Taylor Walker's Barley Mow brewery, which was situated on

Orient Wharf,
Wapping High
Street.

my right, had ceased production the previous year. Now, abandoned and in darkness, the brewery would soon be demolished.

A light was on in Dan Farson's flat above the Woodward Fisher barge-repair yard and an elderly woman dressed entirely in black was leaving The Grapes, Narrow Street's historical riverside tavern. She may have been a widow. I looked over my shoulder at her as she slowly walked along the pavement clutching a bottle of stout. Her swaying from side to side suggested rheumatism, not intoxication.

As I passed Stepney Power Station and Hough's Paper Mill, where my grandfather had worked as a labourer, I could hear the faint drone of machinery coming from both buildings; the evening shift was at work.

There was an air of stillness by Ma Follen's Lockside café and the adjacent lock keeper's cottages alongside the little iron bridge.

I continued walking and approached the characterless swing-bridge at the entrance to the Regents Canal dock. This bridge was only a few weeks old. I preferred its predecessor; though ancient, it was part of Limehouse's heritage.

Probably the old bridge had become too costly to maintain. Inside the dock, there were several coasters and barges whose holds were covered by tarpaulins. I crossed the bridge and passed old warehouses; some were derelict, casualties of the Blitz, but others survived and were still in use.

Shipwright House at the far end Narrow Street came into view. This isolated block of council dwellings that were built in the mid-1930s seemed incongruous alongside gracious Victorian warehouses. The wailing of a disturbed child and a fierce argument taking place on the top floor caused me to look up at this hideous building, but the only movement I could detect was the flickering lights of television screens from inside darkened rooms.

I turned quickly onto the Highway and walked briskly past the conveniently situated dock workers' urinal outside the Free Trade Wharf. It was at this location a few years later, with me on the pillion, that David Upson lost control of his motorbike. We mounted the pavement, Dave braked, but it was too late; we crashed into the urinal and were both thrown off the bike. Fortunately, our injuries were only minor bruises. We picked ourselves up and examined the bike; it was slightly damaged.

'Not to worry, it can easily be fixed,' said a confident Dave.

How we laughed at our predicament.

My friend spoke facetiously, 'I can just see the headlines if we had been killed here. "A motorcyclist and his pillion rider were fatally injured when they collided with a urinal."'

It was now dusk. 'Friar Tuck', the friendly, rotund park-keeper, was about to close the gates of Shadwell Park, but he hesitated and allowed me a few minutes to take a short cut across the grass. I emerged at Glamis Road and joined other pedestrians by the barrier of the raised bascule bridge. I had stood at this spot by the entrance of the Shadwell Basin dozens of times in the past.

Within a few minutes a ship had passed through and I was inside the Prospect of Whitby. As usual the pub was crowded. A group of Royal Navy personnel were dominating the singing. From a position on the stairs, I soon spotted David Upson amongst the revellers. His prominent forehead was just visible above the bobbing wrens' caps.

When the Hawaiian musicians took a short break and the singing stopped, I squeezed myself through the throng to join him. With a wink and a grin, he introduced me to two pretty wrens; they both had Liverpool accents. Before I had an opportunity to put my threepenny bit in (trying to create an impression) the music started; conversation would now be impossible, so along with scores of raised voices, I taxed my vocal cords and sang 'Ten Green Bottles'.

After nearly two hours of drink and song, the last orders were called. Fifteen minutes later Dave and I linked arms with the wrens and left the Prospect. Outside in the street, we accompanied the wrens and their still-singing shipmates to Wapping underground station. The wrens agreed to meet Dave and me the following evening. They thought it appropriate that when they met us they would wear civilian clothes.

In the autumn of 1961, Stepney local Labour Exchange found me a job as a stock cutter at Sclare & Lee, a thriving Jewish family business that manufactured medium-priced dresses from their modern first floor factory on Rampart Street. Fortunately for me, the D&W Handbag factory where David Upson worked was situated in Cannon Street Road just a minute walk away.

Occasionally, I would meet Dave at lunchtime either at blind Mo's café in Rampart Street or the nearby Golden Lion pub. As always our conversation would be about girls, planning pub crawls or airing our views on the major news stories of the day. We discussed the Hanratty murder trial that was then progress at the Old Bailey. James Hanratty had been accused of shooting dead Michael Gregsten as he sat in his car near the A6 at Bedford. Gregsten's mistress Valerie Storie was dragged from the car, brutally raped and shot; she survived the shooting but was left permanently paralysed. Even though Hanratty was ultimately found guilty and hanged in April 1962, there are people today who still believe that he was innocent.

Dave was adamant that Hanratty was guilty. I was not so sure; it seemed to me that there was a slight element of doubt. I pointed out to my friend that the accused was handicapped by having a sinister sounding surname that did not help his case.

Dave dismissed my argument remarking, 'His name is irrelevant; the evidence that is going against him is overwhelming and will prove his guilt.'

At the beginning of November, I left Rampart Street one lunchtime and hurried to the P&O Shipping Office at Leadenhall Street in the city. I was interested in rejoining the *SS Orontes* for her last voyage, but the thought of working again in the scullery did not appeal to me at all, whereas serving on the hotplate did. Even more desirable was the prospect of becoming a bedroom steward. This valued position was highly recommended by Soapy the greaser 'for meeting the birds'.

Unfortunately, I had arrived at the P&O offices a few days too late. There were none of these preferred positions available on any of the company's ships. The only vacancy on offer was for a potato peeler to work on the *Orontes*. Being a potato peeler for the next three months was a job I had no enthusiasm for; it would be equivalent to Army fatigue duty.

I was very familiar with the *Orontes* antiquated potato-peeling machine. It had been installed in 1926 next to the entrance of the scullery where I had previously worked. Besides the contraption's unreliability, the monotonous and repetitious loud 'tcha tcha tcha' sound that it emitted could be extremely irritating.

The two utility stewards, or 'spud barbers' as they were known, who operated the machine started their long day by descending into the depths of the ship, where the stores were kept. Then, like coal-heavers, they would carry the heavy sacks of potatoes to the lift. Once inside the galley, they would place the sacks by the scullery entrance. After the machine was filled with potatoes, it would be set in motion. When the noisy spinning eventually stopped the potatoes would be removed and their 'eyes' scraped out. The cleaned potatoes would be dropped into huge pots half-filled with water that were later collected by the cooks. Meanwhile, a new batch of potatoes would be emptied into the machine and the whole cycle would start again.

Another reason why I decided not to be a spud barber, there was a possibility that my partner for this unpopular and tedious work might be Graham 'Daisy' Day or a similar artful dodger.

I left the P&O Shipping company's offices a little disappointed, but not unduly concerned. As a registered merchant seaman, I could return again at any time and I could always visit the nearby Shipping Federation at Prescot Street, to see what vacancies were being offered.

With great haste I made my way back to the Sclare & Lee factory.

After working at the factory for four months, I had become bored with the daily, mundane routine and began to look for a more worthwhile job; also my intention to rejoin the Merchant Navy was beginning to wane, which was partially due to my interest in attending evening classes. I had recently passed the GCE 'O' level in English History. Encouraged by this little self-taught achievement, I decided to turn my attention to studying maths, English and Italian grammar and to see as much live opera as I could.

During the autumn of 1961, I frequented The Royal Opera House and Sadler's Wells where I saw *The Barber of Seville, Rigoletto, Ill Trovatore, The Flying Dutchman, Aida* and *Madam Butterfly*. Although I thoroughly enjoyed these superb operas, I was disappointed with Offenbach's *Orpheus in the Underworld* and Stravinsky's *The Nightingale* and *Oedipus Rex*.

After handing in my notice at the Sclare & Lee factory, I found an interesting job as a stock cutter at Pridewear Ltd, which was a dress manufacturing company based in Dalston.

I was still not ready to rejoin the Merchant Navy. My evening classes were going well and my social and sex life was excellent, mainly due to David Upson who would never miss an opportunity to chat up unescorted girls during our dockland pub visits.

'He who hesitates is lost,' was his motto.

Perhaps my motto was, 'You lead and I will follow.'

The Eastern Hotel, situated at the junction of the West and East India Dock Roads at Limehouse, was one of our favourite pubs. Although there were dozens of bedrooms on the upper floors, the Eastern had ceased being a hotel several years previously. In its heyday and because of its close proximity to the docks, the hotel was very popular with sea passengers and ship's captains. The famous novelist and master mariner Joseph Conrad wrote about the Eastern and is believed to have briefly stayed there.

Following the hotel's closure during the 1930s, the pub on the ground floor remained open and was regularly patronised by seafarers from all over the world. Like other pubs at Limehouse many of the customers at the Eastern were local dockworkers, prostitutes and homosexuals.

The interior of the Eastern had fine wood panelling and reminded me of a lounge in an ocean liner. The large room at the rear that may have been a former restaurant was now used for music and dancing. At weekends, the atmosphere at the Eastern was vibrant. There was always a motley crowd of happy people singing and dancing. I had seen tough-looking dockers dancing with pretty Scandinavian waitresses from the ships moored in the West India Docks or with fun-loving debutantes out 'slumming' at Limehouse. Groups of transvestites, tall, elegant and slim would make fleeting appearances. Sometimes they prolonged their visit to dance with lesbians wearing pin-stripe suits.

Dave enjoyed dancing at the Eastern too. Although reluctant at first, he was once persuaded to perform his hilarious solo 'organ grinder' dance. The floor was cleared and for the next few minutes he entertained a large crowd and was rewarded with a thunderous applause.

The trio of musicians who regularly played at the Eastern consisted of a drummer, a trumpeter and a banjo player. Their off-key music was so awful, it was amusing just to sit there and listen to them performing. The trumpeter, an objectionable little character, would leap from the tiny stage every ten minutes and thrust a collection box under your nose; if you refused to make a contribution, he would unleash his vicious tongue. Inevitably, his provocative habit did upset some drinkers. I had seen the trumpeter being struck across the head by a handbag-waving harridan, punched on the nose by a Scottish sailor and having his foot stamped on by an outraged prostitute. However, these repercussions did not stop him from demanding money.

'Assaulting him is like water off a duck's back,' remarked Dave.

Taking non East End friends to the Eastern hotel was an occasional enjoyable activity for Dave and me. Our friends were curious to see riverside characters and invariably they were not disappointed. One of the characters who frequented the Limehouse pubs was a soft-spoken elderly peddler who was known as 'Ruski'. John Hastings, the resident landlord of the Eastern, allowed the peddler to sell his wares inside the pub. Ruski would roam slowly around the bar wearing a huge raincoat complete with half a dozen poacher's pockets. If he thought that you were a potential customer, he would stand in front of you and quickly open his coat like a flasher and display his wares that included cheap watches, trinkets, pens, diaries, maps and magnifying glasses. David Upson once bought a diary from him, only to find that a least a third of the pages were missing and I purchased a ballpoint pen that dried up after just one letter. The peddler probably obtained much of his merchandise from local jumble sales.

It was rumoured that the peddler, who bore an incredible resemblance to Bulganin, the Soviet leader, was a Russian émigré. John Hastings foolishly suggested to me that Ruski was probably Buganin's exiled brother.

Another local character was 'fat, flatulent and fifty, mad Maggie'. With an outstretched hand she would stand up close to you and sing in full voice her regular song, 'I Left My Heart in San Francisco'. Maggie's voice sounded dreadful. The dreadfulness was made worse by her lack of front teeth. Ignoring the catcalls, innuendoes and sarcastic remarks of her critics, usually dockers, she was determined to continue singing in an attempt to extract a few shillings from you; often she succeeded. Contrary to being mad, Maggie was sane and quite clever; she knew that customers would give her money just to silence her.

The atmosphere could sometimes be a little rowdy at the Eastern. I had witnessed a few heated arguments and one serious brawl in the saloon. Fortunately, John Hastings, who was extremely strict, would not hesitate to bar those whom he considered troublemakers.

John, a heavy smoking northerner, was short, overweight and suffered from chronic bronchitis; he was also prone to histrionics. His two beautiful, blonde, blue-eyed stepdaughters were typical English roses. Sylvia was a teacher and Pamela a nurse at the Royal Free Hospital.

I became quite friendly with Pamela and we met on several occasions, but my attempt to introduce her to opera on 30 November 1963 was a disaster. Instead of inviting her to see Puccini's *Madam Butterfly* or perhaps Bizet's *Carmen,* which would have been an ideal introduction for a newcomer to the opera, I mistakenly took her to Sadlers Wells to see Kurt Weil's three act opera *The Rise and Fall of the City of Mahogany.* The performance was terrible, the singing amateurish and the music tuneless. It soon became embarrassing sitting in an almost empty auditorium. After the second act and along with other opera goers we left the theatre. I am sure Pamela must have been permanently put off visiting the opera.

It was a Saturday evening. David Upson and I were thoroughly enjoying ourselves at the Eastern Hotel. We were being entertained by a crowd of inebriate dockers, seamen and local females who were attempting to rock and roll. Also enjoying the hilarious scene and sitting near the stage were two mysteries. The girls, attractive and in their mid-twenties, were all alone.

When the musicians eventually played a cha-cha-cha, Dave became a little impatient. He feared correctly that the opportunity to make contact with the two girls would be lost to other predatory males who were poised to pounce.

He quickly stood up and whispered, 'Come on Alf, a faint heart never won a fair lady.' Grabbing my arm, he almost dragged me over to where the mysteries sat. At their table Dave politely asked the girls if they would like to dance. They instantly agreed and joined us in front of the stage. Neither could cha-cha-cha, but they were pleased to learn. Within minutes, they had grasped the simple steps. After the dance was over the girls readily accepted our offer of drinks and to my surprise they invited us to sit at their table.

The girls freely explained that they were unhappy working as chambermaids at the Tavistock Hotel, which was in the West End. Apparently, an elderly guest at the hotel, who was a retired Merchant Navy officer, had given them wrong information. He had advised the girls to enquire at the Eastern Hotel at Limehouse 'as they were always looking for maids'. The girls were disappointed to find that the Eastern was no longer a hotel, but their journey east had not been in vain as they had been offered positions as restaurant staff at a local seamen's hostel.

So, with Joyce from Aberdeen and Megan from Pontypridd, we formed an on-and-off attachment that was to last for several weeks.

Joyce and Megan were particularly interested in exploring the East End. They visited the Whitechapel Art Gallery, walked along the Limehouse Cut towpath to Victoria Park and were fond of the Sunday markets at Petticoat Lane and Club Row. While they toured the two busy markets, Dave and I went drinking in the pubs at nearby Spitalfields. I rather liked Spitalfields, which was an area that I was very familiar with, especially Artillery Lane and the adjacent narrow Artillery Passage. In the early 1960s I had worked briefly at a garment factory at Artillery Lane. In those days the lane was full of ancient houses and small workshops. Crammed next to each other were gown manufactures, tailors, furriers, tie and cap makers, wholesale warehousemen and an artificial flower maker. Other trades included bookbinders and quilters.

In Artillery Passage there were two cafés, the Siesta and The Little London and the Ninepins club. The lane and the passage were extremely busy during the day, but after dark they became totally deserted. Halfway down the passage is the tiny Parliament Court. During the 1960s the court, that in fact is an old alley, was always poorly lit, sinister looking and often smelly. It was possible that Jack the Ripper might well have used Parliament Court as an escape route.

Often late at night, after David Upson and I had been drinking at Dirty Dick's opposite Liverpool Street Station, we would stroll down Artillery Passage on our way home. Sometimes, shadowy figures could be seen in Parliament Court, which seemed to have a dual purpose: these figures were either prostitutes with their clients or heavy drinkers from the Salvation Army hostel in adjacent Middlesex Street using the court as a latrine.

Situated directly behind Parliament Court is the Provident Row night shelter. Constructed in 1860, the night shelter originally housed a hundred women and twenty men. Mary Kelly, the last of the Ripper's victims, stayed at the shelter in 1885. Three years later she had moved out and rented a room in nearby Millers Court where on the night of 9 November 1888 she suffered a cruel death. The infamous police photograph of her disembowelment by the Ripper is regarded by many as one of the most horrific images of barbarism ever recorded.

In the 1950s the Providence Row night shelter was administrated by the Catholic Sisters of Mercy and used as a temporary sanctuary for destitute families. It was at the sanctuary during the summer of 1957 that my friend Alfred Debono and his mother and sister sought refuge from his violent father.

A two-minute walk from Artillery Lane stands Christ Church, designed by Nicolas Hawksmoor and built in 1714-29. The church gardens had probably remained unchanged ever since the American writer Jack London's visit during the early 1900. Because of the habitual use of the gardens by vagrants, this little green acre was referred to as 'Itchy Park'. Whenever I glanced at the elderly vagrants continually scratching themselves on the benches, I would wonder if it was just possible that they were some of the original prostrated figures amongst whom a shocked Jack London walked when he entered Christ Church Gardens all those years ago. The following extract from *The People of the Abyss*, Jack London's famous 1902 social study of the East End poor and homeless, makes compelling reading:

> We went up a gravelled path. On the benches on either side arrayed a mass of miserable and distorted humanity, the sight of which would have impelled Doré to more flights of fancy than he ever succeeded in achieving. It was a welter of rags and filth, of all manner of loathsome skin diseases, open sores, bruises, grossness, indecency, leering monstrosities and bestial faces. A chill, raw wind was blowing, and these creatures huddled there in their rags, sleeping for the most part, or trying to sleep. Here was a babe, possibly of nine months, lying asleep, flat on a hard bench, with neither pillow nor covering, nor with anyone looking after it. Next, half a dozen men, sleeping bolt upright or leaning against one another in their sleep. In one place, a family group, a child asleep in its sleeping mother's arms, and the husband or male mate clumsily mending a dilapidated shoe. On another bench, a woman was trimming the frayed strips of her rags with a knife, and another woman with thread and needle sewing up rents. Adjoining, a man holding a sleeping woman in his arms. Further on, a man, his clothes caked in gutter mud, asleep, with head in the lap of a woman, not more than twenty years old, and also asleep.

Gustave Doré, 1832-83, was a brilliant French artist. In the 1870s he arrived in the East End where he produced many fine lithographs. His work extends from the sardonic and grotesque to the grim and harrowing, especially his lithographs of night shelters and the homeless.

This terrible scene of despair, so vividly described by Jack London, was not just restricted to Spitalfields. At the turn of the century, many destitute people who were too poor to afford the five pence a night for cheap lodgings or had been turned away from the workhouse would sleep in the open. Throughout the night, in all weathers, 'distorted humanity' gathered and slept in parks and open spaces that stretched from Aldgate East to Limehouse.

An investigative journalist, who visited the poverty-stricken Limehouse Fields area in 1884, that very same area where my grandparents were then living at the time, penned a graphic, horrendous account, arguably even more shocking than what Jack London had witnessed and recorded. The unnamed journalist's article entitled 'Travels in the East' appeared in *All The Year Round,* a popular weekly periodical that Charles Dickens founded in 1859:

> Also we went into a cellar, which, some while since, was famous; a poor woman who had lived there, having died of sheer starvation, after bringing into life a miserable babe. This place was ten feet square and exactly six feet in height. It contained a biggish bed, wherein slept father and mother while Jane and Charley somehow lay crosswise at the foot. In a small bed by the window slept a big lad of fifteen; while the eldest girl, who owned up that she was "going on for twenty" slumbered somehow in a corner, with a child "not quite three" and a sister "turned sixteen". In the backyard, which seemed common to the row of meagre tenements, I observed two little figures who recalled to me the pair of wretched, abject children who were introduced by the Ghost of Christmas present to Mr Scrooge by the names of "Ignorance" and "Want". Stunted and half starved, uncared for and unkempt; with one scanty bit of sackcloth to serve in lieu of clothing; with pale though filthy faces and bare legs reddened with rough usage and well-nigh black with dirt; they stared at me half savagely and then scampered to some hiding place like two small, scared beasts. Poor wretched little creatures! Who would be their keeper? They were the saddest specimens of civilised existence I had ever met with in the East End; and as I went upon my way for I could find no entrance to the hole where they were hid. I reflected that the School Board would find fit work to do with pupils like these. Moreover, I reflected that if living human creatures were constrained to stay in styles, it scarce needed Circe's art to turn them into brutes.

(In Greek mythology, Circe, the daughter of Perse, the sea nymph and Helios, the sun god, practised witchcraft. By chanting magic spells and the use of potent substances, she could turn human beings into animals, including pigs.)

Of course by 1962, the situation was vastly different, but overcrowded conditions still existed in the East End. Father Joe Williamson, the vicar of

St Paul's Church in Stepney's Dock Street, writing in his parish magazine the same year, described how a local family the Caddens, eight in total, were forced to live in two rooms. The parents slept in the living room, while a daughter of seventeen and a son of fifteen and four younger girls slept in two beds in the other room. The family had been on the council housing waiting list for fifteen years.

Because Britain was now a welfare state, nobody who found themselves destitute in Spitalfields would be allowed to starve, sleep on the grass or be denied medical care, but the area still attracted scores of 'bestial faces'. Many of these 'meth-drinkers' suffered from chronic physical and mental illnesses. Even though, over the years, hostels and night shelters were made available to them, including a 24-hour clinic that had been established in the crypt of Christ Church and was staffed by a team of dedicated medical volunteers, many of the vagrants and alcoholics chose to avoid these agencies, preferring instead a life of roaming the streets, sleeping in doorways or derelict houses. An added attraction was Spitalfields Market where they could rummage through the rubbish after the market had closed, eating discarded old fruit and vegetables and collecting wooden boxes for their bonfires.

David Upson once told me that in 1958, after moving out of the seaman's hostel in Dock Street, he embarked on a three day 'bender' and found himself sleeping rough with some Whitechapel vagrants. 'I was taken to this bombed house, where there were maybe ten other men on the bottle. We were in a smelly cellar that stank of urine and methylated spirit. Just before I passed out, I remember seeing some of these characters fast asleep, crouching in line and dangling by their armpits over a thick rope that stretched from wall to wall.'

16

The Irish Sisters

I arranged to meet Dave in The Mackworth Arms, an Irish pub in Stepney's Commercial Road. A small cut above his eye suggested that he had recently been involved in an incident. Usually, Dave was reluctant to talk about his personal problems; he always maintained that his friends had enough of their own problems without wanting to know about his, but on this occasion he was quite explicit when I asked him how he had received the cut.

Dave explained how he had made an enemy at D&W Handbags; a fellow worker was stealing handbags. My friend had previously warned the worker to stop thieving because it cast suspicion on the other staff and could jeopardise their jobs. The thief ignored him and continued pilfering until Dave approached him a second time. Following an argument between the two men they started fighting. Knowing that his time was now up, the thief fled the building before the police were called. As I knew many of the workers at D&W Handbags, I was curious to know who the thief was, but my friend refused to name him. However, I did learn later that the thief was none other than Alan Higgins, the same Higgins who had stabbed John Lomiglio two or three years earlier.

Dave's remorseful expression indicated that he was sorry that he had become involved. In an attempt to console my friend, but not thinking clearly, I unwisely remarked, 'I know that you have only worked in one factory, Dave, but I have been employed in several and have witnessed pilfering on three or four occasions.'

He seemed surprised. 'You have Alf? I did not know that.'

I mentioned that when I worked at a Whitechapel men's jacket factory we had a similar problem with a thieving employee who had become greedy and daring, but also careless.

'It sounds familiar,' he replied with a deep sigh.

I also said that none of the staff were prepared to expose him because they knew that it was inevitable he would be discovered. The boss did eventually notice that some of the expensive jackets were missing, so he decided to set a trap and try and catch the thief. Fortunately, the culprit was soon caught and promptly sacked.

Dave's tone suggested contrition when he spoke. 'I know that I should have turned a blind eye too. I don't need this hassle, Alf.'

I suddenly realised how tactless I was. Far from consoling, I had made him feel worse by implying that he should have minded his own business. I cursed my naïvety; I should not have attempted to offer comparisons to Dave who when not drinking was more than capable of grasping the rights and wrongs of any situation and acting with the soundest of mind. I did not know what to say next, he seemed to have become sullen and sighed continually.

I looked around the saloon bar hoping to pick up ideas to start a fresh conversation that might distract him. If only acquaintances would come in and join us, or the Irish musicians still drinking on the stage would begin their music. Dave declined my offer of a drink, which was rare for him. Even my latest jokes had no effect.

Suddenly, as if some magic wand had been pointed at us, a remedy was provided that would instantly draw Dave out of his despondency. Two young women, obviously sisters and Irish, came into the bar; they ordered their drinks and sat just a few feet from us. What good fortune I thought, no matter how bleak a mood Dave was in, the mere sight of a pretty woman would be a rejuvenating tonic. Within seconds the blank look on his face had disappeared to be replaced by a cheeky grin. His foot was tapping to the sounds of the long-awaited music and he was egging me on to chat up the two Irish women. But chatting up women was no easy task for me. I was never quite sure of what to say and always feared that I might blurt out something stupid. I much preferred my friends to do the groundwork and start the conversations.

'He who hesitates is lost,' remarked Dave impatiently.

'Should I ask them if they are Irish and do they come here often?' I joked.

Looking aghast and half believing me he said, 'Don't be a clot Alf, offer them a drink.'

When I noticed one of the sisters looking obliquely at Dave and me, I needed no further encouragement. As I leant towards the sisters' table, I misjudged the distance and slid onto the floor. Dave instantly burst into song, substituting, 'It's a long way to tickle Mary' for, 'it's a long way to Tipperary'.

The sisters burst out laughing at the two clowns at the next table. I quickly got up from the floor, forced a smile and said to the older sister, 'It's my friend's birthday and we are out celebrating.' Although untrue, I had made this remark in the past and it had been effective.

The two women raised their glasses at Dave and wished him a happy birthday.

'Smart move,' whispered Dave. 'Keep up the momentum.'

Feeling more confident I said, 'My friend would like to buy you a drink.'

'That's very kind of you,' said the slightly younger sister. 'Could we have gin and tonic please?'

Dave instantly went over to the bar and ordered the drinks. When he came back he placed the drinks on their table and politely asked them if they would allow us to join them at their table.

'Please do,' replied the older sister.

It was good to see my friend in high spirits and the sisters proved excellent company. Dave even managed to have a dance with Anne, who was younger than Eileen; she was also two months pregnant and unmarried.

After an hour or so the sisters left to visit some friends who lived locally. Just prior to leaving, Anne explained that she and Eileen would return to the Mackworth Arms the next evening to have just a couple of drinks before departing for a house party that was to be held in nearby New Road. Eileen suggested that if Dave and I had no other plans we were welcome to come along to the party.

The following evening I met Dave at the Mackworth. It was one of those occasions when we were smartly dressed in our rarely worn suits. As expected, Dave had been drinking earlier. He promptly gave me his usual excuse. 'Unless I have a few drinks first, my brain does not function.' I had noticed that if he was cold sober, he could be exceptionally formal and overbearingly polite, especially with new girlfriends, but once the whisky took effect he would, to quote his words, 'loosen up'. However, this loose state could not be maintained; eventually he would succumb to tiredness and a desire to sleep.

Dave realised that he had drunk far too much already; so in an attempt to keep tiredness at bay for the rest of the evening, he decided to avoid the whisky and only drink light beer at the Mackworth Arms. When the sisters came into the bar they refused Dave's offer of a 'quick half'. Eileen insisted that as they were late, 'We should leave immediately.'

The party had already begun when we arrived. The guests were mostly Irish and several were elderly. By coincidence, I had been to the house three years previously with my friends Alfie Debono and Brian Miah, when we had attended a spiritualism meeting that was held in the basement. In charge of the circle was Mrs Nerva, a Jewish medium. Mrs Nerva had had her hour of fame during the last war, when she assisted the police in a murder enquiry. The medium had supposedly pinpointed the exact location in South London where the body of a strangled woman was found in an air raid shelter.

The girls' party was most enjoyable; besides the soft music, there was plenty of food and drinks available and thankfully little smoking. Throughout the evening, I began to dance more and more with Eileen, who was probably 15 years my senior. With a good figure and a pleasant smile she was frequently asked by several of the other male guests who wanted to dance with her. Eileen never refused an offer to dance but she always came back to me.

Anne had now sat down in an armchair and was reluctant to dance. Perhaps her pregnancy had made her tired. Dave had also stopped dancing. For the previous hour he had been sitting on a sofa quietly talking to a middle-aged woman whose son had recently died. I noticed how tearful she had become. When Dave looked in my direction, I could see he had also shed a tear. For some time the woman's hands were clasped in his. Although Dave was a stranger, she appeared to be at ease with him. I never learned what their conversation was about.

When the party was over the sisters stayed the night at the house and Dave and I walked home to Poplar. Earlier at the party, Eileen had invited me to stop by at her basement flat at Mornington Crescent, near King's Cross Station, an invitation I readily accepted. Apparently her flat was previously occupied by a young Julie Andrews, long before she became a famous musical film star.

Eileen, an office worker, was very independently-minded and self-assured; she led an uncomplicated lifestyle, enjoyed dancing, gin and tonic and was fond of men, preferably younger than herself. When I left her flat early on the Sunday morning, I had a smile on my face. I had never met a mature sensual woman before and found the whole experience of sleeping with her exciting.

Eileen looked forward to my Saturday night visits, which went on for several weeks. Our relationship could never be serious; neither of us would have wanted it to be.

Suddenly and unexpectedly, Eileen had to return to Ireland to look after her mother who had been taken ill. When she returned to London a few weeks later, I did not call on her, nor did she try to contact me. While she was away, I had affairs with two women, one of whom I also met in the Mackworth Arms. The second woman, a vivacious redhead, was separated from her husband.

She spoke blithely, 'Let him sleep around, that's his choice, so he can't complain if I follow suit'. Of course, I didn't complain either.

Dave congratulated me on my ongoing success with women. He also admitted being a little envious, but this did not last. The vivacious redhead introduced Dave to her divorced sister.

I was pleased with my 'ongoing success' with women and I welcomed the fact that I had become exactly like my best friend, who was only interested in indulging in brief liaisons rather than permanent relationships.

Dave's words were ever constant, 'Always be like a ship passing in the night.'

I readily accepted the advice from this perennial Lothario. Not for one moment did it enter my mind that womanising and hedonism was wrong. I was only twenty-one years old and I regarded myself far too young for serious love or marriage; and it was particularly sad for me to see the discontented look on the faces of some of my former classmates who were already trapped in loveless marriages. It made sense to me to enjoy myself while I was still young. Providing I never try to take advantage of a girl or harm her in any way, I would continue to follow in Dave's footsteps for the foreseeable future.

Now that my affair with Eileen was over, Dave became friendlier with her and they started drinking late at night in Cable Street. I thought this unwise; Dave would only have to turn his back for a few unguarded moments and Eileen could find herself being propositioned, molested or, worse, assaulted.

He dismissed my concern with his customary, 'Don't worry, Alf, everything is okay', but I remained unconvinced and baffled as to why he was acting so irresponsibly, considering that we had only recently agreed to spend less time drinking in Cable Street. Dave admitted to me that it was Eileen who had persuaded him to take her to Cable Street for after-hours drinking. I warned him a second time that he was playing with fire.

I was aware that Eileen was curious to know more about the area. A few weeks previously, she had asked me if that part of the East End was really as notorious as the newspapers claimed.

'Much worse.' I replied. I explained that the Cable Street's pubs and clubs were a haven for pimps, prostitutes, perverts and villains and, like Soho, it was a red-light district that respectable women avoided.

Eileen seemed disappointed with my negative description of the area and to my surprise she jokingly remarked, 'Not being a "respectable woman" I should feel at home there.'

In a further attempt to discourage her from visiting Cable Street, I mentioned how Dave and I had to offer assistance to the young artist who was set upon by vagrants while she was sketching in nearby Ship Alley. My warnings did not deter Eileen; she seemed keen to visit some of the area's bars at the earliest opportunity.

It was inevitable that sooner or later an incident involving Dave and Eileen would occur if they continued to drink late at night in the clubs there. Of all of the dens of iniquity in the East End that Dave and I frequented during the 1960s, none was more unwelcoming than The Black Door that was situated at Buckle Street, just a few minutes walk from Cable Street. Several of the drinkers congregating around the bar had hard immobile faces and some had razor-slashed cheeks. It soon occurred to me that The Black Door might well be a rendezvous for members of the underworld.

I suggested to Dave it was essential we avoid eye contact with the clientele, better still, finish our drinks and leave. Dave agreed; he had been drinking heavily all evening and was ready 'for a good night's shuteye'.

Ignoring intuition, I reluctantly accompanied Dave on a second visit to The Black Door. That decision proved to be a mistake. While at the club, a man who proved to be a psychopath somehow gained entry. He produced a pistol and placed a single bullet in the chamber and after spinning the chamber he pointed the weapon at each of us standing at the bar and pulled the trigger, not once but twice. Fortunately, he was overpowered before he could try again; the pistol was immediately confiscated and he was forcibly ejected.

I whispered to Dave, 'If we became regulars here, we would be courting trouble and could soon find ourselves in the line of fire again, be it bullets, knives, fists or even petrol bombs!'

I was adamant that we should not patronise The Black Door, it was just too dangerous. My friend thought that I was overreacting; he argued that he had been drinking in local bars and pubs for over seven years and had never really felt afraid.

'Of course, there are occasional outbreaks of violence, but this is a dock area and it is to be expected; I know that in the past, it was stupid of me to get involved in fights, but nowadays, providing that I behave myself, nobody will harm me and if there is a hint of trouble, I would make a quick exit.'

'And what if that mad gunman returns?' I asked.

'That's highly unlikely,' he replied dismissively.

Dave may have been content to spend the rest of the evening drinking at the club, but I was not. Within minutes, I had left the premises and was walking home.

As I walked down the long Commercial Road I began to wonder why Dave had taken so little notice of my not unreasonable concern to avoid visiting the club. It was obvious to me that for once his perspicacity was clearly flawed and it might prove costly.

A few weeks later Dave foolishly returned to The Black Door with Eileen. Throughout the evening, they made a risible exhibition of themselves, dancing erotically and kissing in front of the bar. Two men sitting there, whom Dave later described as 'a pair of jealous, sulking hounds', provoked him into a fight.

The fight was more serious than his previous scrap with the thief at D&W Handbags. A terrified Eileen fled from the club during the mêlée and Dave, with his two badly blackened eyes, was left to stagger outside.

Dave's attempts to contact Eileen again were unsuccessful. She refused to see him again or venture back to the East End.

Following this assault, Dave finally decided that he would never visit the Black Door again.

I had witnessed a similar incident involving a man with a gun two years previously. I was playing table football with my friend Sylvio Lomiglio at the nearby Vincent Maltese Club in Batty Street. The club, ostensibly a social club, was in reality a front for illegal late night drinking

Our game was suddenly interrupted by a laughing thug who came into the club armed with a pistol. The thug aimed the pistol at a small group of customers and pulled the trigger. Fortunately no bullet was discharged. Meanwhile, Sylvio and I crouched behind the football table and other customers fled to the WCs. Still laughing the thug attempted to fire the pistol again, but it still did go off. The remaining customers must have realised that the pistol had jammed or was not loaded because they rushed foreword and tried to restrain the thug, but he broke free and ran out of the club.

Maltese-born Vincent Farrugia, the proprietor of the Vincent Club, soon found himself appearing at Thames Magistrate Court. He was charged with selling alcohol outside the permitted hours.

At the court, Chief Inspector Thomas of Leman Street Police Station told the magistrate Mr Leo Gradwell that, 'the Vincent Club was frequented by prostitutes, men living on their earnings and people with criminal records.' He added, 'Farrugia, in my opinion, is an unmitigated villain. He is a man of extreme violence and a profligate of the worst type; the club itself is an iniquitous den and is patronised by people I can only describe as the lowest possible.'

Chief Inspector Thomas was hoping the magistrate would close the club indefinitely, but he was to be disappointed. The Magistrate ordered the club to be closed just for a year; he also fined Farrugia and his partner Joseph Zammit each £100, with 50 guineas costs for selling alcohol outside the permitted hours.

Dave asked me to meet him during the evening at the Brown Bear that was just a hundred yards from the Seamen's Mission Hostel in Dock Street. The Brown Bear had an awesome reputation of being one of the roughest pubs in Docklands. On Friday 24 November 1973 a seaman, Hohn Gale, who had a grudge against two men who drank at the Brown Bear, poured a gallon of petrol on the saloon bar floor and set it alight. One of Gale's intended victims was badly injured in the inferno, but two seamen, one Scottish and the other Somalian, were burnt to death. Besides the fatalities, several of the clientele received serious burns. However, during my own visits to the pub, I rarely witnessed any brawling or altercations. This absence of trouble was because Dave and I usually avoided drinking there at weekends and only visited the pub during the beginning of the week when the atmosphere was quieter and disturbances were less likely to occur.

The middle-aged prostitutes who often gathered at the Brown Bear bar seemed more interested in drinking with merchant seaman from West Africa than meeting customers. Dorothy 'Dolly' was past fifty, overweight and now semi-retired after spending thirty years on the game. Her habit of greeting me with a forceful hug was embarrassing and I was further embarrassed when she explained to her friends at the bar that I looked exactly like her son. Dolly claimed that she preferred 'mature and refined gentlemen from up west'. This was hardly the description of the scruffy little punter I saw her with in nearby Grace's Alley.

A few days after I was paid off from the *Orontes*, Dave and I visited The Brown Bear. Seated at the bar was Dolly who complained that I had broken a promise and failed to bring her back a present from my voyage to Australia. I had made no such promise. My attempts to pacify her with several whiskies had little effect, but when I gave her the nice decorative Australian ashtray (my reward from Miss Vicars of Melbourne) a few days later, she grinned, and hugged me; all was forgiven and I was now back in favour.

When I arrived at The Brown Bear at the appointed time to meet Dave, he jumped up from his chair, came over to me, grabbed my arm and pulled me towards his table. 'Thanks for coming, Alf. I want you to meet an old friend of mine.'

His friend, a girl of about my age, had short fair hair with a parting that gave her a slightly boyish look. She smiled, shook my hand and said, 'Hi, I am Terri. Any friend of Dave is a friend of mine.'

This was Terri, an ex-prostitute Dave had told me about. He had befriended her two years earlier when she stepped in front of him late at night in Cable Street and offered him a 'short time'. When he declined her offer, she asked him to lend her half-a-crown to buy a sandwich. Noticing how poorly she looked, he offered to buy her a hot meal instead at the nearby Somalian café.

Sitting in the café, Terri must have realised that this stranger with his gentle manner was no threat to her. Hesitant at first and in between falling asleep at the table she spoke about her background in Birmingham. As a child her stepfather had sexually abused her. At fourteen she was raped twice, first by schoolboys and later by two men in a car. On her sixteenth birthday she ran away from a remand home, eventually arriving penniless in London.

Sleeping on the benches at King's Cross Station the inevitable happened, a Maltese predator named Joseph picked her up. He brought her to Whitechapel. After seducing her, he forced her to work for him as a prostitute in Soho and Stepney. Like so many young girls in similar circumstances she would receive a beating if her takings were low. Unable to continue with her life as a prostitute which was making her ill, and afraid that Joseph might beat her yet again, she somehow managed to break free from his control and had spent the last two days roaming the streets looking for somewhere to stay.

When Dave and Terri left the Somalian café, Dave suggested that he accompany her to Father Joe Williamson's sanctuary in nearby Wellclose Square where she would be offered temporary accommodation.

To his surprise she replied, 'No, it's too risky; Joseph would find out I was staying there.'

My friend tried to persuade her to change her mind, arguing that it would only be for a week or two, but Terri was not prepared to listen.

She replied tearfully, 'I have messed up my life.'

Dave now found himself in an unexpected predicament, unable to offer her shelter and unwilling to give her money. He was unsure what to do next, but he knew that he would never forgive himself if he just walked away and left her all alone at midnight in Grace's Alley.

As they wandered past Leman Street Police Station, Dave suddenly remembered Zaid, his elderly Egyptian friend, who lived alone in a basement room in East Tenter Street directly behind the police station. Zaid, woken at midnight by somebody banging on his door, was relieved to see that it was Dave. He invited Dave and Terri inside and made them coffee; he also agreed to Dave's request to allow Terri to stay in his room for the time being and sleep on the couch. Dave offered him money for his inconvenience, but Zaid refused.

'Daveboy, no offend me, we friends, five years past, still friends five years future.'

After seeking an assurance from Terri that she would not work as a prostitute while staying at Zaid's room, Dave left and went home. He returned the following evening and subsequent evenings to see how she was.

The ever-obliging Zaid would often disappear to the pub for a few hours leaving Dave and Terri to talk. During the next few weeks Terri spent her days looking for accommodation and trying to find work. She adhered to the promise that she had made to Dave and ceased being a prostitute. She also avoided Cable Street through fear of coming into contact with Joseph or his associates.

Her determination to start a new life was successful. Much to Dave's relief and delight, Terri's application for a vacancy as a chambermaid at a West End Hotel was accepted. Although the salary was poor, the position included food and accommodation at the hotel's staff quarters.

On their last night together in the East End, Dave and Terri returned to the Somalian café for a late night meal. It was an unwise decision as there were several Maltese men in the café, one of whom was a relative of Joseph, her former pimp. Ignoring her pleas to leave at once, Dave was in a defiant mood, insisting that they would leave only after they had finished their meal. Unfortunately for my friend, he was to pay a high price for associating and helping Terri. On a Saturday evening a few days after Terri left the East End, Dave was walking past the Whitechapel Bell Foundry when a car stopped nearby. Three Maltese men got out of the car and beat him to the ground. It was unlikely that Terri knew of the beating that Dave had received.

Listening to their conversation, I was to learn that Terri had 'phoned Dave at work the day before and had asked to meet him in The Brown Bear 'for old time's sake'. Being introduced to Dave's former lovers and acquaintances was always a pleasant experience for me. It usually guaranteed that interesting little anecdotes and episodes that involved him in the past would be referred to and I would learn something new about my genuinely modest friend, but on this occasion Dave and Terri's conversation was about the present; the past was not mentioned at all. Dave explained to Terri how happy he was that his sister would soon be arriving from Calcutta and would probably be staying permanently with him and his mother at Poplar. He also mentioned his unfulfilled dream of rejoining the Merchant Navy. Terri had much news too. She was no longer a chambermaid but now a housekeeper. She was also engaged to a young banker whom she had met when he attended a business conference that was held at the hotel. She spoke enthusiastically of her forthcoming marriage and the prospect of living in New York.

At closing time, we left The Brown Bear and walked with Terri to Aldgate where she hailed a taxi to take her back to the West End. As Dave and I sat on the bus that took us home to Poplar, he leaned his head against the window.

'You know, Alf, not once did Terri mention Zaid this evening.'

He paused for a moment and almost whispered, 'Nor did I for that matter.'

Before I could answer him he said, 'How easily we forget our old friends. When we want something from them or need their help we seek them out. Later, when we have made use of their services we often discard them like old shoes.' He concluded by adding, 'Maybe it's a part of human nature to take our friends for granted.'

I thought he was unfairly criticising himself. I had met Zaid in the past. During a quieter moment, he had told me that he was extremely fond of Dave, who had defended him when he was being attacked by local vagrants.

'If Daveboy no come, me dead man, me always thankful for Daveboy.'

Throughout much of the 1960s, I was a customer at Nat Shine's tiny corner shop in East Mount Street adjacent to the London Hospital at Whitechapel. Usually I would stop by at the shop in the evenings after work. Nat not only sold sweets and cigarettes, he also had a profitable trade in selling condoms to the hospital's doctors and medical students. Other items for sale, which were kept in two glass containers, included antique paperweights, little pieces of jewellery and collectors' cigarette cards. Periodically, Nat would attempt to persuade me to buy some cheap trinkets from the display.

Nat loved chatting to his customers, but his greatest love was medium-dry sherry. Each day he would consume at least a whole bottle, but never once did I see him inebriated. Customers were often offered a tipple; more favoured and regular customers were invited into a little room at the rear of the shop for drinking sessions. I was a willing participant.

Dave accompanied me a couple of times to the little room, but he took a dim view of Nat, whom he thought had a devious nature and was 'not a man you could trust'.

Eventually, Nat's back room developed into an unofficial drinking club; the only requirement for entry was a bottle of medium-dry sherry. Sometimes, student nurses, still in uniform, and a few local girls were invited by Nat to step into the little room for drinks. Molly was one of the local girls who would partake in the drinking sessions; nicknamed 'Molly the Plater' because of her expertise in the practice of fellatio. Even Nat, who was well into his sixties, made use of her services, as did a few of the regular drinkers. I found these sexual activities sordid and would have no part of it. I was never sure if money was offered to Molly, but it was certainly a possibility.

For a while the police became suspicious of Nat, believing him to be allowing his premises to be used as a brothel or meeting place for crooks and their molls. The CID secretly observed Nat's shop and assigned a handsome young detective to woo Molly. Having three young children and no husband, money or social life, she welcomed the attention, the meal in the restaurant and a visit to the cinema. Molly was not naïve; she quickly realised her 'bloke's true motive'. The detective was to be disappointed when he tried to coax a little information from her about the 'goings on' in the back room of Nat's shop.

'There are no goings on,' insisted Molly. 'Just a few friends go there for a private drink.' The CID soon lost interest in Nat and called off their operation.

It was an early Friday evening. I was standing at the front of Nat's counter when a short elderly hospital porter came into the shop. There was a poppy in his lapel. After he made his purchase Nat offered him a sherry. The porter politely refused the drink and explained that he was still on duty. With his customary inquisitiveness, Nat began to ask the porter questions about the nature of his job, the hours he worked and whether he lived locally.

Several times in the past, I had witnessed Nat tactlessly trying to obtain customers' personal details. In most cases people were prepared to reveal a little

David Upson and lady friend,
1995.

about themselves; only once in my presence was he told, quite aggressively, by a red-beaded Scotsman to 'piss off', although I suspect that Nat must have received similar responses over the years.

Noticing the porter's poppy, Nat wanted to know if he had been a soldier in the First World War. The porter replied that he was indeed an ex-serviceman who had served for nearly four years in the Rifle Brigade on the Western Front. Having been a former Army cadet in the same regiment in 1955, it was an ideal opportunity for me to mention that I too was in the Rifle Brigade, but only as a cadet. A sudden feeling of shame prevented me from recalling my three-month period with the Grenadier Guards.

The porter seemed quite willing to stay and have a chat. He explained that thousands of East End men had served in his regiment during the Great War and many were young teenagers. At just eighteen he was in uniform and after basic training had been sent to France. I asked the porter if he had ever met Colonel Victor Turner VC, also of the Rifle Brigade, who, at an Army base near Colchester in August 1955, had taught me how to fire a Bren gun. To my surprise, he said he had indeed met Colonel Turner several times. He went on to say that the Colonel had been awarded the Victoria Cross in North Africa in 1942.

The porter looked at his watch before adding, 'And I was awarded my Victoria Cross at Ypres in 1917.' Both Nat and I gasped in astonishment as he spoke. Suddenly, this diminutive man seemed to be ten foot tall.

Following a brief moment of silence, Nat, who had either been too young to serve in the First World War or too old for the Second World War or had deliberately avoided military service (which was the most likely) sounded humble when he spoke. 'You actually won the Victoria Cross? Listen, my friend, you must be my guest and have a small sherry,' but the porter again refused and repeated that he was still on duty.

Before he returned to the hospital, Nat and I managed to persuade him to give a brief account of his bravery that had taken place all those years before. He explained how, on open ground at Ypres at 1917, he single-handedly charged at a German machine post that was firing at his comrades; he had killed the gunner, retrieved the machine gun and carried it to a new position where he fired it again at the enemy troops. When German reinforcements arrived, he left his position. Aided by two riflemen he managed to get behind these reinforcements where they killed six soldiers and took about thirty prisoners.

After the porter finished relating this incredible act of bravery he quickly looked at his watch and said, 'I have to get back to work now.' He turned around and quickly left the shop.

Unfortunately Nat and I failed to obtain the name of this war hero, but I would never forget the privilege of having met him.   Several years later, through research, I discovered he was none other than William Francis Burman VC who was born at Mile End Old Town in 1897. In 1915 Burman became a private in the 16th Battalion of the Rifle Brigade (Prince Consort's Own). The following year, he was promoted sergeant in the field. On 20 September 1917, at the age of twenty, he was awarded the Victoria Cross for gallantry at Ypres in Belgium. In August 1918, the Mayor of Stepney, Councillor Jerome Reidy, presented Sergeant Burman with a Bayonet of Honour and £200 in war bonds. The money had been donated by the people of the East End. In 1974, at the age of seventy seven, William Burman VC died at Cromer in Norfolk.

David Upson's warning not to trust Nat Shine proved correct. Nat tried to embezzle a small amount of money from me. When I threatened to notify the police he panicked and immediately returned the cash that I had lent him.

Just prior to this incident in 1966, I had become friends with Vic Clarke who lived and worked in Whitechapel. Clutching his bottle of medium-dry sherry, Vic too ventured into Nat's back room. It was surprising how much Vic and I had in common; we were of a similar age, working-class stock with no formal education. Vic was a machinist who worked for his father who owned a small men's trouser making workshop in Whitechapel. Vic's father was proud that he had once made trousers for Sir Winston Churchill.

Vic and I had similar interests too, girls, pubs and opera. We admired the tenor voice. Vic's favourite singer was Enrico Caruso; he was also very fond of Gigli, Schipa and Joseph Schmidt, but Vic was adamant that Caruso was the greatest tenor who ever lived. I thought differently; to me, Jussi Bjorling was unquestionably the finest tenor of all time.

During the late 1960s and the early 1970s Vic and I were fortunate to see in concert and recital several illustrious singers including Di Stefano, Correlli and Gedda, but sadly these singers' careers were by then almost at an end. In the mid and late 1970s we visited Covent Garden to hear the fine singing of Pavarotti, Domingo and Carreras. During the 1990s Vic lost interest in visiting Covent Garden, but I continued to attend, especially when the gifted 'Fourth Tenor' Roberto Alanga was appearing.

Vic's father liked opera too and he would never tire of listening to Richard Tauber's recordings. He believed that no other famous tenor was capable of singing from the heart like Tauber could. It is unlikely that any serious opera lover would have disagreed with Mr Clarke.

Being sympathetic to his son's musical interest, Mr Clarke allowed a record player to be installed in a spare room at his house. Vic and I would spend hours on a Sunday afternoon listening to our operatic recordings. For a long period my entire Bjorling collection was kept in this room.

Although my friend and I had very limited knowledge of music, we sometimes attempted to compare Caruso and Bjorling's singing. First we would play a Caruso aria and then play the same aria sung by Bjorling, but it was a wasted exercise – their voices were beyond comparison. Caruso's timbre was dramatic and with the passing years had acquired a light baritone quality, whereas Bjorling's voice was a lyrical spinto. Vic and I were too musically naïve to realistically compare top Cs, B flats, pitch, or any other facet of our idols' singing. However, this lack of musical knowledge would in no way inhibit our preferences. To Vic 'Caruso was gold and Bjorling silver'; of course I thought the reverse was true.

On 23 March 1968, the Canadian tenor Jon Vickers was a guest on the BBC's long running series 'Desert Island Discs'. Each week the presenter of the programme, Roy Plomley, would ask a well-known personality which eight gramophone records he or she would like to take with them if they were a castaway alone on a desert island.

I was disappointed with Vickers' choice of music; I did not expect him to choose Mantovani, Bing Crosby or Cole Porter, but there were compensations; Vickers included 'Crimmond' sung by the famous Glasgow Orpheus Choir, and two items by Bach. Caruso sang an aria from Halevy's *La Juive* and finally Bjorling's beautifully sung *Salut! Demeure Chaste Pure* from Gounod's *Faust*.

After the Caruso record was played Vickers explained why he loved listening to Caruso's and Bjorling's records, but what he said next must have been very painful for Vic to hear, for I knew that my friend would be listening to the programme as he sat working at his sewing machine. Vickers thought that Caruso never possessed Bjorling's vocal technique, saying that 'Bjorling's ability to stay in a legato line, and the way he handled the extremities of his range of voice, to me is absolutely exemplary'.

When I met Vic at his home the following Sunday afternoon, he told me that he too had listened to the 'Desert Island Discs' broadcast. Unable to resist temptation, I quoted verbatim Jon Vickers assessment of Caruso and Bjorling. My friend responded by saying that he did not recall hearing Vickers saying 'those exact words'. Vic suddenly seemed a little perplexed; he thought that I had deliberately misquoted Vickers. I assured him that I had not. It was possible that he did not quite hear Vickers comments; I know from personal experience that when you are working in a busy clothing factory with noisy sewing machines switched on, although you can normally hear the music on the radio, it is sometimes difficult to hear the spoken word.

Satisfied that I had said my piece, I quickly changed the subject. During the remainder of the afternoon and in between playing our choice of records, I noticed that Vic had become a little quieter and was reluctant to talk.

For the next couple of years Vic and I would refrain from comparing Caruso and Bjorling's voices; the subject was just too sensitive to discuss as our opposing opinions might jeopardise our friendship. Unfortunately this period of mutual restraint did not last indefinitely.

Vic and I attended a Carlo Bergonzi recital at the Royal Albert Hall on the evening of 23 April 1972. The great Italian tenor was at the peak of his power and regarded as the finest Verdi singer in the world. I had twice seen Bergonzi sing before at Covent Garden. The first time was in 1962 as Don Alvaro in *La Forza del Destino* and in April 1971 when he appeared as Gustavo in *Un Ballo in maschera*. I can never forget Bergonzi's singing that evening. His glorious voice reverberated around the entire theatre. After he sang *Di To Se Fedele* from the first act, the appreciative audience gave him a thunderous two-minute round of applause.

This 1972 recital at the Royal Albert Hall was exactly what one expected from a famous Italian *primo tenore:* operatic arias and Italian and Neapolitan songs. Bergonzi was in superb voice; his delicate soft singing pianissimo, smooth middle range full of tone and colour and soaring fortissimo sent his audience into raptures. One over-excited young woman ran up to the stage where a smiling Bergonzi knelt down and hugged her.

Unfortunately the programme of seventeen arias and songs ended all too soon. The capacity audience shouted for more. Unlike Jussi Bjorling who was often over-generous with his encores, Bergonzi restricted his encores to just three: *Ch'ella mi creda, Core'ngrato* and *E lucevan le stele*. The audience still refused to allow him to leave the stage, but a somewhat tired Bergonzi would sing no more; he bowed, smiled at the vast audience and bade his farewell.

After Vic and I left the Royal Albert Hall, rather than exchange our views on Bergonzi's marvellous recital, the old Jon Vickers 'Desert Island Discs' programme was mentioned. I cannot recall if it was Vic or me who raised this sore point, but it was obviously a mistake; within minutes we were having a fierce argument that continued unabated in the car as we drove home to the East End. By the time we reached Stepney, the pair of us had come to our senses. It was ridiculous and futile to arouse such passions; we just had to respect each others fixed opinions. Vic would never change his belief that Caruso was the greatest and neither would I ever alter my view that Bjorling was the finest.

Fortunately for my old friend and I, the truce remains unbroken to this day. However, I will point out that in a '*Classic Magazine*' poll in 2000, twenty-eight music critics voted Jussi Bjorling the best singer of the twentieth century.

17

Reunion with Mark Windsor in Greenwich Park

The two nubile Swedish girls with whom Dave and I were friendly asked us if we would take them to visit the beautiful Church of All Hallows by the Tower. I knew the church well and had once met the incumbent, the Reverend 'Tubby' Clayton who for many years had kept the spirit of Talbort House, a Christian fellowship alive. In 1915 at Poperinghe in Belgium, Army Chaplains N. Talbot and P. T. B. Clayton opened Talbot House as a church and social centre for soldiers on short leave from active service. Talbot House, known as TOC H by Army signallers, was dedicated to the memory of Lieutenant Gilbert Talbot who was killed in action.

The girls wanted to see the famous All Hallows' crypt with its remains of a Roman pavement. Part of a wall in the crypt was still blackened by fire from the fierce battle that raged there between Queen Boudicca and the Romans.

The guide who showed the four of us around the crypt took an instant dislike to Dave who unfortunately had been drinking and was in a mischievous mood. The situation worsened when my friend kept asking irrelevant questions of this pompous guide. The guide finally lost his patience with Dave whilst he was explaining the meaning of some Roman words scratched on a wall.

He overheard Dave whispering to one of the girls, 'This is the place where Boudicca cut off her left breast so she could target her arrows more accurately.'

The joke brought a gasp from me and a giggle from the girl, followed by a cold pernicious stare from the guide whom I thought for a moment he would pick up a heavy crucifix from a nearby table and whack the troublesome Upson.

Dave suddenly realised that he had upset our host, but the damage had been done. Anxious to make amends, Dave unwisely attempted to offer the guide a donation, 'For the church funds.'

Ignoring his offer, the guide, whose fragile equanimity had disappeared at the start of the tour, replied vehemently, 'We don't need your money here. Would you please leave this church at once.'

As we were leaving, Dave began to remonstrate with the guide, trying in vain to persuade him to accept the donation. He soon had the guide pressed against a pew and was searching his jacket for a pocket to deposit the cash. An elderly women tourist, who had just walked into the church, was shocked, believing that she was witnessing indecency taking place. She tut-tutted, turned around and marched towards the exit uttering to me as she passed, 'Disgraceful, absolutely disgraceful!'

I was feeling mischievous too; I remarked to the woman in a loud voice, 'You are quite right, madam. These perverts should be locked up!'

After this episode, I thought it would be better if we were to cancel our planned visit to the Tower of London Armoury. Dave was in a buoyant mood and still swigging whisky from his little flask and I was unsure how he would react when we were confronted by Henry the VIII's huge suit of armour with its large protruding codpiece. He probably would comment on it, but he certainly would not be crude; his behaviour usually depended on how much he had to drink. If he had just consumed two or three whiskies he could be marvellous company and extremely funny, as those who know him would attest, but more than this and he might become a little outlandish. Only people afflicted with pomposity like the All Hallows' guide would have found his sense of humour insufferable. So, fearing the worst I decided to play safe and suggested that the four of us should postpone our visit to the Tower Armoury and hop onto a motor boat and spend the afternoon in Greenwich instead.

At Greenwich's riverside, the girls enjoyed exploring the *Cutty Sark* and the hour we spent in the National Maritime Museum.

With the sightseeing over we climbed the steep hill in the park and sat on the grass and listened to the music being played by a brass band. During the band's intermission Dave had a quick cuddle with one of the Swedish girls, but his ardour had become deflated by too much whisky and the warm weather. Stretching himself out on the grass and with his head resting on the girl's lap and lulled by the melodies of *My Fair Lady* and *Oklahoma*, he soon drifted into a deep sleep.

We stayed in the park all afternoon and then spent the evening in the Old Yacht Pub. After finding seats in the beer garden overlooking the then still busy river we tucked into our tuna sandwiches and scotch eggs. The girls seemed relaxed and contented and, an added bonus for me, the elderly, classically-trained pianist inside the bar was playing selections from the Puccini operas.

As we gazed at the endless river traffic passing by Dave spoke ominously, 'Enjoy the view while you can, Alf; one day, in the not too distant future, all of these ships, tugs and barges will disappear and a whole way of life that's been around for generations will be lost forever.'

I was somewhat baffled by what he was saying. The river still seemed so busy with about 28,000 dockers employed in the Port of London, 6,000 barges, and 350 lighterage tugs distributing much of the cargo on the river and in the docks.

Noticing my confused expression, Dave remarked, 'Unfortunately change is inevitable, Alf, so try not to be too disheartened. Besides, what do you want out of life, you're still young! Look, we have two pretty girls for company, food and drinks and reasonably good health. Well, at least you have; I am not so sure about me, having a perforated liver. What more is there?'

'Going to sea?' I suggested.

He paused for a moment before answering. 'You're right, the sea. I understand that, but for the time being let's settle for the next best and enjoy the river.'

We continued to see our new-found girlfriends during that summer. Once or twice they stayed at Dave's tiny flat in Poplar and cooked us strange Swedish dishes. In late December, much to our regret, engulfing us in hugs and kisses, they returned to Sweden.

As Dave predicted, six years later the Port of London Authority began their inexorable dock closure programme. The first dock to close was the East India Dock in 1967; the following year the Surrey Dock was also closed for business and in November 1969, Wapping's Western and Eastern Dock including the Shadwell Basin lowered their bridges for the last time.

The main reason why these ancient docks were closing was because they had become obsolete and were no longer economically viable; they did not have the facilities to accommodate the big container ships. Another contributing factor was the dockers' readiness to resort to industrial action to settle disputes. There were rumours that the royal group of docks, which consisted of the King George V and the Victoria & Albert Dock, were to be modernised to handle containerisation, but it was not to be. These docks at Silvertown, along with the West India and the Millwall docks on the Isle of Dogs, would close. By 1981 the last of the London docks had closed.

Following the closure of the London docks, the small Tilbury Dock 25 miles downstream on the Essex coast was expanded and modernised to cope with the ever-increasing container trade that the old London docks could not facilitate.

Dave and I spent a great deal of time in Greenwich in the early 1960s. Our visits were usually on a Sunday during the summer. The routine was much the same. First we would have a few drinks at the two riverside pubs followed by a sandwich in Anna Abusi's café in Greenwich High Street. Before wandering into the park, we would pay our usual visit to either the National Maritime Museum or the *Cutty Sark*. In the afternoon, after finding a comfortable bench in the park and in between observing the females passing by, we would invariably discuss the latest news. Occasionally, Dave and I would stand by the statue of General Wolfe high up on the hill and gaze into the distance. Across the Thames we could see the Millwall and West India docks. Their big cranes cluttered together resembled a small forest. From this famous location Dave would sometimes repeat himself when he spotted a ship as it made its way around the bend at Blackwall reach.

'The sea is like your first love. You always remember her with affection.'

I wholeheartedly agreed. For single men, Greenwich Park was an ideal place to meet young women. With a large nurses' home at the foot of the park and a teacher trainer hall of residence close by, it was guaranteed that with a little bit of pluck you could strike up a conversation with some of the nurses and student teachers who were relaxing or sunbathing on the grass.

It was in the park in 1962 that Dave met Sid Smith, a self-confessed confidence trickster whom he had known in Calcutta and more recently in Soho. Before settling in London, Smith had spent a brief period in the Merchant Navy. Smith, now known as Mark Windsor, regarded himself as a ladies man whose *raison d'être* was to meet rich, lonely women, usually middle-aged, widowed or divorced. Once he gained their confidence he would then set out to try and 'gently deprive them of a small portion of their wealth'. Windsor claimed that in recent years he had accumulated a sizeable fortune by way of expensive watches, gold cigarette cases and generous gifts of cash. He bragged that he was a frequent guest at Knightsbridge house parties and was often invited by his lady friends to spend fabulous holidays in the Caribbean and the South of France.

If Windsor's stories of being a gigolo were true, it meant little to Dave or me. We were not impressed and found it difficult to understand why he showed no remorse for the vulnerable women whose trust he misused.

Having now learnt of Windsor's antics, I would have preferred to have walked in the opposite direction whenever he approached Dave and me in the park, but Dave was too polite to deliberately avoid him. My friend assured me that Windsor would eventually lose interest in Greenwich, and return to his natural habitat the Marble Arch area.

'The sooner the better,' I muttered.

It was during a warm sunny afternoon that Dave and I bumped into Windsor by the Royal Observatory. He insisted in joining us when we sat down on a nearby bench. Once seated, he produced a huge gold ring for Dave to examine.

'A present from a lady friend, and I have had a good week with more to come,' he boasted.

'And how exactly do you meet these rich women?' I enquired.

He gave a confident answer. 'Oh it's easy, boyo, with the aid of Bepe.'

'Bepe your little dog?' gasped Dave.

'Yes, Bepe, my little poodle,' replied a smiling Windsor.

'Oh, really, you don't say,' I remarked, trying to imitate his refined Welsh-sounding accent.

Ignoring my sarcasm he smiled again. 'It's very simple and effective, boyo. You see, I have trained Bepe to distinguish women from men in Regent's Park. He has a special ability, just like a border collie.'

I thought this claim was nonsense and was about to tell him so, but hesitated; I suddenly remembered an incident the previous weekend when Dave and I, whilst chatting to two Irish girls on the grass, were disturbed by the unexpected arrival of Windsor, who decided to impose himself on us. His little dog instantly demanded and received attention from the girls who tried in vain for several minutes to calm down the excitable poodle. When one of the girls coughed shortly afterwards, Bepe climbed on to her lap and attempted to lick her face. Dave received no friendly lick when he coughed after lighting up a cigarette; the poodle went into frenzy and barked furiously at him.

To my regret when Dave and I got up from the bench by the Observatory, Windsor stood up too. As the three of us descended the hill, Windsor said, 'Just to conclude what I was saying, as soon as I let Bepe off his lead in Regent's or Hyde Park, he has his orders and will always run towards the women who of course love to stroke him. I quickly move in and thank them for rescuing my precious pet and bingo I have made a hit. Of course the unsuspecting women are so naïve they don't realise that they are actually being picked up. It always works.'

I immediately pointed out to Windsor that with or without his dog he was wasting his time in Greenwich Park as there were no 'rich pickings available, only impoverished students'.

'That's alright by me, boyo,' he replied smugly. 'Having young lamb will be a refreshing change from mutton, don't you agree?'

I did not agree with Windsor about anything and was becoming increasingly annoyed with him and also with Dave for tolerating this fraudster.

'Be patient, Alf,' whispered Dave who had sensed my disapproval. 'He won't be around too long.'

My friend was mistaken. Windsor was a frequent visitor to Greenwich Park that summer, and was always with his poodle. Even if Dave and I were strolling around other areas of the park, he would seek us out assuming that because he was an acquaintance of Dave's he had an automatic right to join us. After a few weeks, my initial resentment of Windsor became less severe and I forced myself to accept his presence, although his persistent habit of telling 'unnecessary fibs' as Dave called them remained a sore point.

From the time I had become friends with Dave three years earlier, I had adhered to his strict instruction of always trying to be honest with the women we were pursuing. He maintained that it was essential to tell the truth otherwise it might be difficult to remember our fibs especially once we had had a few drinks.

When I asked Dave if he thought Windsor might be a lonely man and needed male company, he replied, 'No, not at all. I have two or three theories about his motives, the most plausible being that Mark has had little or no experience of meeting young ladies; even in Calcutta he was always to be seen with older women. Perhaps by joining our company and knowing that we are reasonably successful with younger women he might be hoping to learn something about our methods and adopt them himself.'

I thought it was unlikely that young nurses or teachers would find Windsor attractive. Although only in his early thirties he spoke and moved around like a much older man. His clothes were a handicap too. Wearing a trilby hat, tweed jacket and thick corduroy trousers might be acceptable to the mature Knightsbridge ladies, but a were a turn off for the girls here in the park where slacks and short-sleeve shirts were ideal.

Dave and I were picnicking with Ann and Mary who were nurses from Lewisham hospital. As we sat on the grass by the children's boating lake, I suddenly spotted Windsor heading in our direction. As soon as he saw our group, he let Bepe off his lead and the little dog raced towards us. Ignoring Dave and me the dog leapt on to Ann's legs causing her to spill some lemonade on to her dress. Windsor sat down, apologised for his pet's behaviour and promptly scolded Bepe who was placing his nose too near the jam tarts.

Dave, as expected, introduced Windsor to Ann and Mary, who accepted this sudden and unexpected intrusion with slight bewilderment. I glanced at Dave disapprovingly. He responded by grinning and shrugging his shoulders as if to say 'what can I do?' which of course was true. Dave was just too lenient and kind to ask him to leave.

Windsor would probably now be in our company all afternoon and, like it or not, we had no alternative but to accept him. Providing he refrained from trying to impress the nurses with a tissue of lies I would not complain.

Our uninvited guest quickly made himself comfortable and ordered Bepe to keep still. Declining the offer of lemonade and sandwiches Windsor produced a little flask and took a gulp. Like Dave, he too was fond of whisky. Windsor quietly listened as we discussed the recent tragic suicide of Marilyn Monroe.

A little later, Mary asked Windsor what type of work he did. Before he answered her, Bepe spotted another poodle close by. Ignoring his master's order to lie down, Bepe bolted across the grass to check out the stranger, followed by an angry Windsor. I hoped that when he returned after retrieving his pet he would bear in mind that he was a guest of ours, albeit an unwanted one, and hold back from telling fibs. Also it would be an ideal opportunity for me to see if Dave's theory about Windsor's motives were correct.

As soon as Windsor sat down, he fastened Bepe's lead around his wrist and replied to Mary in a clear crisp tone. 'You see, my dear, I don't need to work nowadays. I originally had an insurance business, but sold out when I received a substantial allowance from my parents who live overseas, although I do occasionally buy and sell gems, whenever I am in the mood.'

I was in the mood to give this fraud a thump for lying to Mary. He should have been honest and admitted that he was permanently unemployed and receiving dole money.

When Dave noticed that I had become visibly agitated, he discreetly signalled to me to relax. He also produced his little flask and began to pour its content into my cup. As he did so he grinned and whispered, 'Enjoy the charade, Alf; he will leave soon.'

Ann the younger of the two nurses whom I suspected may have realised that Windsor was not genuine, enquired if he was Welsh.

'Oh deary me, how did you guess? Swansea originally.'

This of course was another untruth. This boyo liked to conceal his mixed-race Calcutta background preferring to give the impression that he was a Welshman. He carried the guise very well with his dark features and Anglo-Indian accent that sounded extraordinarily similar to a Welsh accent.

Having now resigned myself to the fact that Windsor was in no hurry to leave, I decided to try and be less irritable and adopt Dave's attitude of not taking this smiling boyo too seriously. It was obvious that Windsor was incapable of being honest.

Enjoying the attention from the girls Windsor continued. 'Next you will be asking me about my abode. In fact, as David and his colleague Alfred can confirm I live in a town house just off Sloane Square. I also own a small cottage in the New Forest where I sometimes retreat to at weekends.'

Dave could hardly contain himself from laughing; I knew that he had once visited Windsor at his tiny bed-sitter on the top floor above a brothel in Soho where he had been living for the last four years ever since he jumped ship at Tilbury.

Windsor continued with his hogwash for a further five minutes. After standing up, he excused himself and took Bepe for a walk promising to return in half an hour with ice cream. I was glad that he was leaving, albeit temporarily. At least we could have thirty minutes of peace.

Following Windsor's departure, Dave immediately laid back and rested his head in Mary's lap and started to yawn.

Ann who had been listening to Windsor in disbelief directed her criticism of him at me. 'I don't believe a single word of what your friend Mark has said. He was just trying to impress us.' She added cynically, 'Just like all men.'

'Ann, how you dare say that?' said Dave teasingly.

Declining to drink from Dave's whisky flask, Mary playfully slapped his hand. 'David you promised me you would not drink in the park.'

'I know darling, only this once I promise.' After taking another sip of whisky, he began to recite his favourite Omar Khayyám poem:

> When dawn's left hand was in the sky
> I heard a voice within me cry
> Come drink my love from the cup of wine
> Before love's wine runs dry.

'What a lovely verse,' remarked a smiling Mary who promptly rewarded him with a kiss on the forehead.

Unperturbed by Windsor's lack of veracity Dave raised himself up from Mary's lap and looked at me with half closed eyes. 'Relax Alf, just ignore Mark and don't be a spoilsport; just enjoy the afternoon.' After yawning yet again, he lay back down and kept perfectly still while Mary caressed his brow.

How I envied my friend's unconcern at the presence of the intrusive Windsor.

I suspected both nurses had now realised that Windsor was a fraud. Thankfully, they had made no attempt to challenge him. Dave would not have wanted an unpleasant scene within our coterie. But what concerned me was if the nurses, whom we had only met about a month previously, knew that an acquaintance of ours was not to be believed; would they have doubts about Dave and me and question our sincerity and decide to stop seeing us? If that did happen, Dave would be partially to blame. Although he had a soft nature and would never hurt people's feelings, he should have had the foresight to avoid Windsor or at least to keep him at arm's length, especially when we were in the company of women.

Because I was somewhat annoyed with Dave over the possibility that our blossoming relationship with the nurses might be placed in jeopardy, I dismissed his theory that Windsor was trying to learn from us. This boyo had had an opportunity to speak honestly about himself and also to note how Dave and I conducted ourselves with young women, but he chose not to. Moreover, if the nurses had, from just one meeting, seen through his guise then surely the Knightsbridge ladies whom I presumed were older and much wiser must have too. Perhaps Windsor was not so successful in the West End as he claimed.

Mary must have noticed that I was ill at ease. She smiled and spoke kindly. 'Don't worry, Alfie, we don't judge people by the company they keep.'

Before I could explain that Windsor was no friend of mine, we were suddenly disturbed by the arrival of Bepe. The poodle instantly leapt on top of Dave's outstretched body where with its hind feet on my friend's head it frantically attempted to lick Mary's face. When the startled Dave attempted to remove the little dog it growled aggressively at him.

Windsor arrived moments later; after sitting down he immediately apologized for his pet's 'naughtiness'. He also apologised for forgetting to buy the ice cream. Now that this boyo was going to spend the rest of the afternoon with us, we had no option but to be prepared to listen to his continuous fabrications. Dave would be spared much of the ordeal because he had fallen asleep.

The nurses concealed their disbelief as they quietly listened to Windsor listing the names of several well-known film stars whom he claimed were his friends. 'One young starlet, who shall remain nameless, visited my cottage in the Forest of Dean.'

A little later Ann, who during Windsor's absence had described him as a 'harmless cad', could not resist finally putting Windsor in the dock. 'Mark, I don't understand; earlier you said that your cottage was in the New Forest but now you are referring to your cottage in the Forest of Dean.'

Windsor realised that he had made a slip up. 'My dear, there is a little confusion here; I actually own two cottages, but have leased the larger one in the Forest of Dean to relatives.'

Dave had now woken up. Shivering and complaining of feeling cold, he suggested that we should leave the park. Windsor was the first to get up from the grass. He tucked Bepe under his arm, thanked us for an enjoyable afternoon, and looked at his watch, 'Cocktails in Chelsea and supper in Soho; I really must dash, see you good people anon.'

As he walked briskly towards the gate, Dave apologised to Ann and Mary for having to tolerate Windsor all afternoon, but far from being displeased the girls had found the boyo quite amusing.

Dave and I were only to see Windsor once more that year before he disappeared abroad. In late summer we found him sitting alone on a bench by the bandstand, he looked tired and dejected. Bepe was nowhere to be seen and the confident smile of the suave impostor had gone. His smile was now replaced by a joyless stare.

'What's wrong mate?' said a puzzled Dave.

'I lost Bepe,' replied a tearful Windsor.

Dave paused for a second then said, 'What do you mean lost Bepe?'

Windsor clasped his handkerchief to his eyes before speaking softly. 'We were in Hyde Park last Sunday when a vicious Doberman attacked him. Bepe did not stand a chance; my little dog was only three years old and now he has gone.'

Dave took out his flask and offered him a drink.

Windsor shook his head sideways and answered him in a whisper. 'No thanks, boyo, I have my own.' After reminiscing about the love and loyalty his pet gave him, he suddenly said, 'Have you boyos ever been to Florida or California?'

When we said no, he became agitated and snapped at us. 'Don't you two Casanovas ever leave London, for Christ's sake?'

Dave and I were surprised at this sudden change of tone in his voice. Windsor had many faults, but he was rarely rude.

Windsor again shook his head from side to side and gave a deep sigh. 'I am sorry boyos, I have had a very bad week.'

We sat down on the bench with him and the ever-patient Dave attempted to raise Windsor's spirits by recalling a conversation that we once had with a merchant seaman in a nightclub at Cable Street. The seaman had claimed that whilst on shore leave in America he had visited Miami and the Florida Keys where he met and befriended an extremely rich divorcée whilst walking on the beach. The woman eventually gave him a large gift of money for certain 'services rendered' that he chose not to mention. Within a week, he rejoined his former ship the *Queen Mary* in New York and sailed home to Southampton, not as a member of the crew, but as a first class passenger, much to the envy of his old shipmates.

Windsor's ears pricked up with delight and he wanted to hear more. Dave explained that the seaman thought the wealthy divorcées and widows of

Miami were always on the lookout for eligible British men, whom they often found attractive.

With his confident smile now returned, Windsor sprang up from the bench. 'You have to excuse me, boyos, I must dash,' and with his customary, 'See you good people anon,' he walked quickly towards the gate.

As we watched him disappear beyond the trees, Dave said it was unlikely that we would ever see boyo again, although the following year my friend did receive a postcard from Windsor with a Miami postmark. The message was brief. He loved the sunshine and Bepe number two was responding well to his instruction.

The tiny flat in Grosvenor Buildings on Cotton Street, Poplar, which Dave shared with his mother was far too small for their needs. He confided in me. 'What should I do, Alf, try and buy a house, but that means a mortgage and hassle, or wait until the council rehouses us?'

I advised him to wait until he was rehoused. It was obvious that Grosvenor Buildings were in a poor condition and were earmarked for demolition as part of the Poplar council's slum clearance programme.

Dave's concern about future suitable accommodation was eventually resolved. In December 1963 the council offered him a new fifth floor flat in Lathem House in Stepney.

Early in 1964, Dave, a highly skilled bench worker at D&W Handbags, was promoted to acting foreman. With his mother at home, now joined by Barbara, his attractive and gregarious sister, who bore a striking resemblance to the film star Olivia de Haviland, he now had more responsibilities. So the old aspiration to rejoin the Merchant Navy had to be put aside, perhaps permanently.

Dave and I had a great social life in the 1960s; for us it really was a decade of 'wine, women and song'. Fortunately it was also a period of full employment. Although we usually worked a six-day week, often in poor factory conditions and for little pay, we were reasonably satisfied.

In the same period, I managed to have a few holidays. But Dave hated holidays; he much preferred to work continuously throughout the year, maintaining that as long as he had a rest day on a Sunday he was contented. However, problems sometimes arose when he was unable to find temporary work when his employer closed the handbag factory for the annual holiday.

Having unwanted free time, he quickly became bored. For Dave there was only one remedy for boredom: he would seek out amusement in the pubs, which resulted in him squandering much money on women and alcohol.

During these forced breaks especially in the early 1960s, Dave would be hired to frame bags for his friend the Wapping-born handbag maker Frank Davies. Davies had set up a small workshop at his home at Riverside Mansions adjacent to the Shadwell Basin. Not only would Dave work for Davies throughout his holidays, he would often work for him in the evenings

Loathing annual holidays, Dave preferred to work non-stop throughout the year. Problems arose during factory fortnight when he quickly became bored and squandered money on alcohol and women. Frank Davis, an employer of Dave's who suffered from polio, persuaded him to join his family at Camber Sands. The children now had a very popular playmate who spent most of the days entertaining them on the beach.

after work. From 6 p.m. until the early hours of the morning, Dave would be framing the bags. Halfway through his shift, food and drink would be provided by Mrs Davies. After snatching a few hours of uncomfortable sleep on the carpet, Dave would rise early and leave for his regular daytime job at D&W Handbags in nearby Cannon Street Road.

It was the Davies family who were successful in persuading a reluctant Dave to spend a short holiday with them at their large chalet at Camber Sands in Sussex. Because Frank Davies was afflicted with polio it was extremely difficult for him to play with his two young children. Dave, who was very fond of the little boy and girl, would spend hours frolicking with them on the beach. The week that Dave spent at Camber Sands in 1961 was the only holiday that he ever had during our thirty-seven years of friendship.

That same year, Dave also had a third job. Early on a Saturday morning, he would mount his motorbike and ride off to Church Street Market at Paddington where he would spend the whole day helping an elderly Jewish couple who owned a handbag and purse stall. First he would collect the stall from a nearby yard, set it up on the pitch, display the merchandise and serve the customers, which he enjoyed immensely. He soon became an excellent salesman, never pushy or persuasive or relying on cheap sales talk but simply being himself, polite and patient.

During my summer holiday, I briefly assisted him at the stall where twice I saw him sell bags to pensioners below the asking price, then making up the deficit from his own money.

As usual, if there were an opportunity to make contact with young female shoppers, he would seize it. A delicate Chinese student who lived in a small flat near the stall was a regular customer. She would only purchase new designs, which led Dave to believe that she was sending the bags to Hong Kong to be copied and possibly manufactured.

When the student returned a handbag that had a slightly loose frame, she asked Dave if he could repair the bag as it was the last of a particular range. Dave agreed to repair the bag later in the day and also offered to deliver it to her door before he went home.

Dave's smile was that of a contented man. 'The student was so grateful that I had kept my word, she invited me into her flat for coffee.' My friend smiled again. 'The gods were with me; I stayed the night.'

Having three jobs during this period did not seem to be tiresome for Dave; he welcomed being fully occupied from Monday to Saturday. As well as earning and saving money, he was keeping out of the pubs.

At the beginning of 1962, Dave ceased working for Frank Davies. This was good news; I did not like Davies whom I suspected had constantly exploited my friend. My suspicion was eventually confirmed by another framer who had also worked for Davies, who told me that, 'Davies only pays school-leaver wages.'

Dave also lost his Saturday job, much to his regret. Old age and illness had forced the elderly couple who owned the handbag stall to retire.

From 1962 until 1967, Dave continued to work full time at D&W Handbags. Often during the weekdays after work, Dave and I would meet and just have a quick half. However, it was on a Saturday and Sunday evening when the fun started. If, on the rare occasions we were not drinking and womanising in the pubs of Wapping and Limehouse, we would seek out entertainment in the West End. Dave and I disliked nightclubs and discos and the growing drug culture was for lesser mortals. Irish dance halls were a particular favourite of ours, especially The Blarney in Tottenham Court Road and Charlie Mack's at Strutton Ground near St James' Park.

Both Charlie and his son were talented musicians; their small lively band attracted people from all over London. Mrs Mack, a matriarch, kept strict control on the door; alcohol was banned and membership was supposedly restricted to practising Catholics, but somehow Dave and I managed to become members and in due course we met many girls. Charlie was a happy, lovable character who refused to allow anyone to sit or stand alone. He would physically push you on to the dance floor and sometimes bring a pretty girl over to you, if you were without a partner.

Situated just a minutes walk from Charlie Mack's dance hall, there was a girls' hostel, owned by the Catholic Church. The nuns who administered the hostel were very strict, and imposed a curfew that was rigorously enforced. Men, as expected, were not welcome and were barred from the building. If a girl wanted to spend a night away from the hostel she had to notify the Sister Superior in advance and leave a note with the address where she was staying.

Two or three times a year the nuns would supervise a dance that was held in the large basement beneath the hostel. They provided soft drinks, snacks and the use of a record player. Amazingly, on these occasions the nuns were always amiable, unlike the chilly response you received if you arrived at the hostel for a date with one of the residents.

Dave and I rang the hostel doorbell. A scowling nun peered at us through the hatch of the heavy bolted door.

'Come closer,' she growled.

I moved forward, adjusting my tie in the process.

She spoke impatiently, 'Not you, the other man.'

Dave realised she wanted to smell his breath to see if he had been drinking. He stood close to the door, with his head turned sideways.

'Now put your face next to the hatch,' she ordered.

Dave did what he was told, but held his breath.

The nun started to sniff then quickly withdrew uttering, 'Just what I suspected, whisky.' She immediately closed the hatch without saying another word.

A few minutes later, the two girls came out having been severely reprimanded for associating with men 'who are inebriated'. They were also advised to be back at the hostel by 11 p.m. or else face 'serious consequences'. None of us were quite sure what the serious consequences might be. Would the girls be disciplined in some way if they did not arrive back at the hostel by the 11 p.m. deadline and what would the punishment be if they stayed out all night? Did the nuns believe that Dave and I would deflower the girls? This of course was our very intention.

The two girls were annoyed at being treated like 'young school girls'. They mentioned how other residents had to rely on subterfuge to avoid the curfews. Ignoring the nuns' warning, they chose to spend the night with Dave and me. The following afternoon when we took the girls back to the hostel, a nun coldly informed them to vacate their rooms within the next two days. So much for those 'Sisters of Mercy'.

Besides frequenting the Irish dance halls during this period, our dockland pub tours were ongoing. I had lost count of the times that we started our tour at Dirty Dick's in Bishopsgate. Following an easterly route we would often visit The Eastern Hotel and Charlie Brown's at Limehouse and Dan Farson's Waterman's Arms on the Isle of Dogs. Leaving the Waterman's with just an hour left before closing time we would make our way to the wonderful Prospect of Whitby at Wapping for the inevitable singsong.

Although I never owned a car during the early 1960s, Dave always had motorbikes, three-wheel Reliant vans or cars. His first motorbike was a little 171cc Francis Barnet. Later he acquired a powerful Triumph 600 with a sidecar. This combination was much safer and proved extremely popular with the girls on our endless pub tours. Although Dave was a reasonably good rider, over the years he did have three or four accidents, two of them unfortunately drink-related.

On one occasion when he was knocked off his motorbike and lay injured in the road, he did a quick calculation and decided that geographically he was exactly the same distance to the London Hospital in the west and the small Poplar Hospital in the east. Knowing how beautiful many of the hundreds of nurses were at the London and how few in number they were at the latter, he pleaded with the ambulance men to take him to the London Hospital at Whitechapel.

'Sorry mate, we have to take you to Poplar,' came the reply.

Suddenly his injuries seemed more painful and his worst fears were soon realised when he was admitted to Poplar Hospital. A very tall muscular German nurse who would have made an ideal sparring partner for a sumo wrestler was assigned to look after him. She soon curtailed my friend's cheeky antics with her no-nonsense attitude. Nicknamed 'Brunhilda, the beast of Belson' by the other unfortunate patients, she seemed incapable of smiling. When Dave's mother, Barbara and I went to visit him at the hospital, he complained bitterly to us about the big 'SS guard who never seems to leave the ward'.

After Dave was discharged from Poplar Hospital, he began to drink more moderately, but this self discipline lasted only a couple of months.

18

Limehouse and the Great Smog

With so many interesting pubs within walking distance from our homes at Poplar, Dave wisely began to restrict the use of his motorbike. One of our local pubs was the Alma, a tiny inviting pub on the West India Dock Road at Limehouse. Alice Shindler, the Alma's popular landlady, had a kind nature. She genuinely liked her customers and seemed to know most of them by name. Her pub was not only frequented by dockers and seamen, but by off-duty policeman from the adjacent Limehouse Police Station. Because the Alma was so close to the police station, disorderly conduct was rare.

I was in the Alma with Dave, when I recognised two of the policemen drinking at the bar. They were the same two who the previous year had stopped me late at night in Limehouse Causeway. One of the officers who was Scottish politely asked me if I would co-operate and take part in an identification parade. I was not prepared to argue with the officers who were both six-footers.

'Of course I will co-operate with you, Constable,' I replied.

With a policeman on either side of me, I was escorted up the steps of Limehouse Police Station and taken into a large rear room. Assembled in the room were about twelve other men. Not a single man seemed to be older than thirty. A sergeant came into the room accompanied by a small bald man who had cuts and bruises to his face. Apparently he had been violently attacked and robbed outside Charlie Brown's pub. We men were ordered to stand in line and look straight ahead. The victim walked slowly along the line and carefully scrutinised each of us. Satisfied that none of us were the robbers he left the room.

Dave thought it would be 'inappropriate' for me to ask the two policemen at the bar if the bald man's assailants were ever apprehended. I ignored my friend's advice and went ahead and spoke to the policemen. It was a mistake; the Scottish policeman was slightly intoxicated. His conversation was brief and most certainly lacked the politeness that he had shown in Limehouse Causeway.

'Piss off, or I will have you in the nick.' I did what I was told.

Dave and I met for drinks at the Alma during the 'great smog' of 1962. The smog, which was the worst for a decade, blanketed the whole of Limehouse. Despite the appalling cold weather and the inability to see further than just a few feet, the Alma was crowded. In the bar, I counted about fifteen people who seemed to know Dave. Many of them were keen to join his company. They included an inaudible Chinese elder nicknamed 'Pukka-poo', Scotch Lily who was a thin local prostitute (and had the saddest eyes that I had ever seen), and a tall homosexual ex-Army major named Hugh who was cold and incisive but soon became warm and friendly when he sat down at our table. A deformed dwarf drifted towards us, obviously tortured because of his ugliness. He took not one but two of Dave's cigarettes. His presence so close to our group disturbed 'Pukka-poo' who got up and left the pub.

Two lesbians in their thirties, one of whom had a black eye, sat down at the next table and immediately started arguing.

Alice stopped serving and intervened. 'Now ladies, no fighting please.'

The women soon became quieter. Recognising Dave they brought their chairs over to our small table, despite not having been invited, and sat down. One of them appealed to Dave to help them settle their dispute.

Lily raised her eyebrows, glared at the quarrelling pair, nudged me in the ribs and said, 'To each his own, laddie.'

I had no idea what advice Dave had offered them, but it seemed to have had an affect. Without acknowledging us, or offering an apology for their rudeness, they went back to where they sat before.

Others who approached our table that evening were a giant docker who challenged me to an arm wrestle and promptly beat me, a one-eyed stateless Polish seaman and, last and the best, two girls who were flatmates from Pennyfields. They caused great laughter when they arrived still clutching their lighted candles that had guided them through the smog. Unknown to me, Dave had earlier invited them for a drink. The girls squeezed in between us, one pressing against my body in the process. This closeness caused my heart to race in anticipation at this unexpected treat.

Lily smiled and nudged me a second time in the ribs. 'You will be alright tonight, laddie.' How right she was!

Thirty years later, long after the Alma had ruthlessly been demolished along with the world famous Charlie Brown's and The Eastern Hotel that stood close by, I met Alice, now an octogenarian, in the street, aided by a walking stick but still indomitable after surviving a major operation for pancreatic cancer eight years earlier.

Another historical local pub that Dave and I visited was the Marshal Keat that stood opposite Poplar Dock in Blackwall. The Marshal Keat, built in 1841, once had strong links with ships' crews, passengers, dockers and rivermen. Unfortunately, it was later demolished, just because it stood in the path of the London Dockland Development Corporation's relentless drive for new and wider roads in East London.

In the early 1960s when Dave lived in Old Grosvenor Buildings, we periodically drank in the nearby Marshal Keat that was then managed by an ex Chindit. A Chindit or Chinthay was a mythical half lion, half eagle. Replicas of these animals were placed at the entrances of pagodas to warn off evil demons. The name Chindit had been given to daring British troops who mounted guerrilla operations behind the Japanese lines in Burma. Their commander was the famous General Orde Charles Wingate.

It was at the Marshall Keat that I had a rare opportunity to find out more of Dave's wartime experiences. Like Dave, the manager was reluctant to talk about the military campaign in Burma, but one evening when the saloon bar was nearly empty the manager was for once in a garrulous mood and he and Dave started to reminisce about the 'Forgotten War'. Both men agreed that they had taken no joy in killing Japanese servicemen. They respected their enemy and found them to be tough opponents, but war was war and they had been there to do a job.

During their conversation, Dave recalled the time in May 1945 when the small warship that he was serving on along with a sister ship were engaged in a fierce battle with Japanese gunboats in the Burmese Hlaing River.

We had a report from intelligence that as soon as the moon dropped, about ten Jap boats would be coming down the river. We waited all night for them but they did not arrive. About 5.30 in the morning we heard firing in the distance so we slowly proceeded upstream with our guns ready. I was on the bofers, but there was no sight of the Japs, so we decided to practice firing on any water hyacinths that might float towards us. When we came to a bend in the river we trained our guns on the water waiting for the first hyacinths to appear. It was 7 a.m. and we had already given up hope of engaging the enemy. Well, instead of hyacinths that came around the bend, three Jap boats appeared and came straight into my gun sights. For a few seconds, I was so shocked at seeing the enemy so close I hesitated, then the CO smacked the top of my helmet and shouted 'Open fire! Fire!'. At the same time we swung hard to port to give them a broadside. As we were turning the Japs opened fire at us and two of their shells went through our bow and got stuck just above our ammo locker. I swung the gun around. As soon as the boats were in my sights again we opened fire. Our first burst was eight rounds of 40mm high explosives.

The next minute the first Jap boat was ablaze, we started to shout at the top of our voices with joy. We swung to the next boat that our sister ship was already engaging. Our next shot hit the centre of the fuel drums that she was carrying on deck and she instantly blazed up. As each boat caught fire it would head for the bank. Thank God they did not try to ram us with their burning boats. The last boat's engines were still running but she was shattered by a direct hit from a 3-pounder. A few of the Jap survivors from the second boat managed to get ashore. One of them hid in a tree and clung to its branches that were hanging over the water, but he was shot and half the tree was brought down by one of our 3-pounders.

The action probably lasted about 15 minutes all told. Two of the Jap boats had been sunk but the third one drifted into a small inlet. The men from this boat got ashore and hid in a big group of bushes, then the villagers tried to round them up but they failed as the Japs were shooting at them, so we told the villagers to clear themselves from the area and then we mortared the Japs with 3-inch shells.

Dave had other exciting stories to tell and over the years he would sometimes briefly mention an incident or action that he had taken part in. But he steadfastly refused to discuss his naval career at any length and never once did he brag about his wartime service. He often changed the subject if our conversation about the Burma campaign continued too long. I am sure he could have capitalised on his role, but my friend was far too modest and self-effacing to ever consider it. For him, the war had been over a long time ago, and his teenage years had been spent in uniform, which he never regretted. Dave had served his King and Country well. Unquestionably he had been a brave and dedicated sailor who rose from the lower ranks to become an efficient and valued officer.

19

The Isle of Dogs

There were three pubs on the Isle of Dogs that Dave and I would visit from time to time: The City Arms in Westferry Road, The Waterman's Arms in Glengarnock Avenue and the early Victorian Gun Tavern at Coldharbour.

The Gun was never a busy pub, unlike the Waterman's and The City Arms that had entertainments most evenings. Because of little trade, the landlord of the Gun could ill afford the cost of live music, but occasionally he would hire a pianist for the evening. The few clientele were mostly those who lived and worked locally and sailors from the cargo vessels and visiting warships moored in the West India docks. Sometimes, curious strangers would arrive attracted by the pub's quaint structure and riverside balcony that offered superb views of the Thames.

I always found Coldharbour to be an interesting but isolated little area. Halfway down the narrow road and surrounded by old warehouses that were still in use stood the Blackwall River Police Station complete with its reassuring blue lamp. Miraculously, the adjacent nineteenth-century river-frontage houses had survived the Blitz. On appearance, these historical buildings give some credence to the story that Lord Nelson and Lady Hamilton had been former tenants, although I suspect solid research would prove otherwise.

Besides being a time-warped little road, what fascinated me about Coldharbour was the ever-present and attractive smell of tar. I was never sure if the liquid was manufactured locally. Years later, the author James Page-Roberts told me that what I could smell was Stockholm tar used for the preservation of coal sacks.

During the mid-1960s, when a thick smog had descended over the Isle of Dogs and fog horns could be heard repeatedly on the river, Dave and I were in the Gun chatting to some American merchant seamen. Avoiding politics and world news, our conversation was restricted to the two subjects that sailors love most: women and exotic ports. As the last bars of 'Yankee Doodle Dandy' were sung and Dave and I were about to leave, a chef from New Orleans asked me a question. Unable to give a plausible answer, I persuaded Dave to give his explanation of why English girls have such rosy complexions. After

Isle House and Nelson House, Coldharbour, Isle of Dogs.

The Gun Tavern, Coldharbour, Isle of Dogs.

promising to accompany the Americans on a tour of the Limehouse pubs a few days later, we left the Gun.

As we walked down Coldharbour with our visibility extremely poor, an old man emerged from the smog like an apparition. He blocked our path and spoke with a strong Irish brogue.

'Excuse me, gents, can you spare a few coppers towards a pint?'

We both searched our pockets for coins. Dave who was in one of his 'silly bugger' moods, winked at me and said to the stranger, 'I will give you a shilling if you sing *Molly Malone*.'

The Irishman took off his cap and placed it over his heart. 'What a song, I knew the man who wrote it.'

'What blarney,' whispered Dave.

The old man burst into song. Surprisingly, his voice was quite refined. Suddenly, just as he reached 'cockles and mussels alive alive ho,' a window above the blue lamp opened and a policeman leant out. Obviously not a music lover, he shouted down, 'Hoy you! Shut that ruddy noise!'

Our new found friend stopped singing; he took off his hat, looked up at the baldhead at the window and said, 'Yes constable, at once, constable.'

We both gave the troubadour a shilling as he deserved it. Noticing how dark his nostrils were, Dave and I politely refused the offer to sample his snuff. Before we left Coldharbour, the Irishman placed his hand on my shoulder and said, 'Next time I will sing *Paddy McGinty's Goat*. Would you like that?'

The landlord of The Waterman's Arms opposite the slipway at Saundersness Road was Dan Farson, who had temporarily abandoned journalism and making television documentaries in order to concentrate on making his pub a success. Dave recalled meeting Farson for the first time in the York Minster pub in Soho in the mid-1950s. When Farson learned that my friend hoped eventually to go back to sea, he became curious and wanted information about joining the Merchant Navy. Three years later, at the height of his television fame, Farson moved from his home at Pelham Place in the West End to a riverside flat above the Woodward Fisher barge repair yard at Narrow Street Limehouse. With his love of the Thames, dockside pubs and sailors, he quickly settled into his new home and stayed for several years. His affection for the area and its people was genuine. Working-class neighbours soon accepted him as one of their own.

Possessing a flair for recognising local talent, Farson helped to promote the careers of the actress and singer Queenie Watts and Dick Whyte, a likeable ship's rigger who was a gifted amateur artist. Two of his paintings of the West India Docks were hanging on the walls of the Gun Tavern. Old friends were remembered too; like the osteopath and etcher Dr Stephen Ward, who had been a key player in the 1963 Profumo scandal. Ward eventually stood trial for supplying prostitutes.

'A convenient scapegoat for the Macmillan government,' remarked Dave.

In an attempt to support his friend financially, Farson arranged an exhibition for Ward's etchings to be displayed in the rooms above The Waterman's. Unfortunately for the fifty-year-old Ward, the stress of the trial and the thought of being found guilty and a lengthy prison sentence proved too much for him; he took a fatal drug overdose before hearing his sentence.

Because homosexual relationships were a criminal offence in the early 1960s Farson had to show discretion, hardly necessary in Limehouse where dozens of homosexual men were regularly picking up sailors, especially in Charlie Brown's and The Eastern Hotel. Importuning was so well established in the West India Dock Road area that the Limehouse police simply looked the other way.

It soon became evident that Farson had a drinking problem. When sober he was kind and thoughtful, but once drunk, as David Upson observed, he was prone to be abusive.

Farson's perennial dislike of the Salvation Army may have been justified. Soon after moving into Narrow Street it was brought to his notice that the elderly residents of the nearby Salvation Army hostel in Garfield Street always missed having a glass of beer with their Christmas dinner. Kind-hearted Farson immediately contacted the hostel's manager offering every man a bottle of beer. To his surprise and dismay his generous offer was refused. Perhaps Farson failed to realise that the Salvation Army regarded alcohol as one of life's greatest evils. Yet the same Salvation Army had no qualms whatsoever about sending their female members to tour the pubs of Limehouse where they would shake their collection boxes at you. Dave and I were aware of this hypocrisy but we still gave money when it was requested.

Reluctantly we would accept their newspaper *The War Cry*, only to discard it immediately afterwards. Farson never forgot the Salvation Army's heartlessness. Thirty-five years later, while the worse for drink in a North Devon pub, it was alleged that he reacted angrily and spat a mouthful of beer over a 'Sally Ann' girl when she approached him for a contribution.

The previous name of The Waterman's was the Newcastle Arms. Dave and I first drank at the pub in 1961, when it looked rundown and sadly neglected. Finding ourselves the only two people in the bar, we quickly consumed our beer and left. When we returned for the opening night of Dan Farson's renamed Waterman's Arms in late 1962, we could not believe what we saw. It was astonishing; the pub had been completely transformed. Dave correctly described its new look as resembling a music hall. A very busy Farson recognised my friend and they shook hands.

Over the next two or three years, we would visit the Waterman's about once every fortnight, sometimes arriving with two women we had squeezed into Dave's motorbike sidecar. Other friends who accompanied us enjoyed the excellent entertainment that often included surviving elderly troupers from the music halls. Younger artists were also very popular. I can recall the superb singing of tall, fair-haired 'Welsh George'. Dave's favourite was Kim Cordel, a big-bosomed redhead with a powerful voice.

The Waterman's Arms was a huge success. Besides being patronised by East Enders it attracted the rich and famous. Well-known celebrities, often unnoticed, were mingling with dockers, sailors, gangsters and their molls. One night Clint Eastwood stood quietly drinking at the bar. That same week he visited the Prospect of Whitby on two consecutive evenings, politely stepping aside when Dave approached to order our drinks.

Dan Farson remained as the landlord of The Waterman's Arms for about three years. During that period he still wrote the odd article and occasionally appeared on television. Suddenly, in 1964, he vacated the pub and left for the West Country. His reason for leaving still remains unclear. Even today, local people still give different versions of why he left the East End. Some say that the police were harassing him; others maintain that the reason was blackmail or that members of the Kray gang had threatened him. I believe that the truth is not so dramatic. He probably just grew tired of living in London and being in the limelight and simply wanted a quieter lifestyle.

Farson settled in Devonshire in a house by the sea that his late parents had left him. Eventually, like his famous father, the American-born Negley Farson, he was the author of several successful books. Fortunately for those of us who enjoy reading his excellent books, his intermittent bouts of alcoholism did not seem to impair his literary output.

The City Arms in Westferry Road was not one of my favorite pubs but if Dave and I were on the Isle of Dogs we would usually make a brief visit. This pub was probably the most famous venue for drag artist shows in London and would attract customers from all over the capital. I never found the ageing drag queens that funny and I thought that their jokes were unnecessarily crude and distasteful. The sight of a fat female impersonator with a ghastly voice singing 'I enjoy being a girl' and then finishing the act with a partial striptease was to me quite revolting.

An evening's entertainment at The City Arms could in no way be compared with the superb cabaret that the effeminate stewards arranged for the ship's crew on the lower deck of the SS *Orontes* as she sailed across the Indian Ocean. I recall no smuttiness or bad language. Our applauding would attract envious passengers who were only allowed to view the show from the foreword upper decks.

Dave invited two acquaintances to sample the entertainment at The City Arms. One of these acquaintances was Nancy, a middle-aged, seemingly prim and proper Australian. Apparently, during her younger days, Nancy was briefly a missionary. The other acquaintance, Canadian Len Mackenzie, had recently retired from the Merchant Navy. Len had accompanied Dave to bars in Rangoon, Calcutta and Cable Street. When Len drank excessively he had an inclination to fight; his reddish nose had as many knocks and dents as Dave's

Reliant car. Much to my surprise, Nancy seemed to enjoy the atmosphere of the pub; but not Len. The expression of utter indignation on his face was a sign that he wished he was elsewhere.

'I have had enough of these two pansies prancing around,' he remarked scathingly.

Although Dave cautioned her against it, Nancy moved alone through the crowd to the foot of the stage where she removed her glasses. Five minutes later she returned with a grin on her face, quite flattered that at her age she was actually chatted up not by one, but three postmen and even had her bottom pinched in the process.

I joined Len outside the pub for some fresh air while Dave and Nancy decided to stay until the interval. Len was aware that Dave and I were still interested in rejoining the Merchant Navy but he was against the idea. As we strolled along the Westferry Road, he lit up a cigarette and said, 'You know pal, if you want some advice don't ever go back to sea.'

'Why do you say that?' I asked curiously.

'Well it's a kinda lonely life. Believe me, pal, better you stay ashore, find yourself a wife and raise kids. Don't finish up like me, forty years at sea, now I am all alone with no family.' He paused for a moment then chuckled. 'Having said that, there are quite a few widows in Nova Scotia, so I might be lucky yet.'

I explained to Len that Dave and I had no desire to spend many years in the Merchant Navy, just a few voyages would be more than sufficient.

As we continued walking, he returned to the subject of marriage, revealing that he had been briefly married before the war, but that his wife had deserted him for 'a yank from Detroit'. 'While I was away at sea, the bitch was on heat; she took my money and disappeared.' Len suddenly stopped walking. He grasped my arm and swung me around to face Lenanton's Wharf. 'Hey, I know these wharfs; if I remember correctly, thirty years ago our ship delivered timber here.' He scanned the area looking for familiar landmarks. 'Now where was Bullivant's Wharf?'

His mentioning of Bullivant's caused me to reflect on the London Blitz. 'You probably did not realise Len that the basement of Bullivant's Wharf was used as an air raid shelter during the war, and on 19 March 1941 the wharf received a direct hit from German bombs, which resulted in a lot of casualties.'

'Don't talk to me about war,' he said. 'War is terrible, pal; we lost a lot of buddies in the Navy, I was torpedoed in the Med, and then in the North Atlantic. Boy was it cold. God only knows how cold it was.'

I went on to explain that my brother-in-law, big Jim Attwell, nicknamed 'Longboat' by my mother, lived nearby. He was home on leave from the Royal Navy the night Bullivant's was destroyed. Jim along with many local men volunteered to help the search and rescue party, but unfortunately more than forty civilians were killed including several teenagers. On that sad note, we turned around and slowly walked back to the City Arms where a frantic Dave was standing outside on the pavement.

'Nancy's has gone to the Waterman's with some postmen; she clambered into a Royal Mail van and told me not to worry.'

But worry we did. We soon arrived at the Waterman's to find our Australian friend wearing a postman's cap. Ignoring us with a dismissive wave, she laughingly climbed onto the stage. After a few words with the musicians she delighted the large audience by singing self-mockingly 'They call me Second Hand Rose'. When the applause died down, Nancy joined us at the bar quite breathless, admitting that she had never enjoyed herself so much since her college days. Moreover she had a date the following Saturday evening with one of the postman who had invited her to try some 'exotic food *al fresco*'.

Dave and I laughed when she revealed the location of the rendezvous. It was Tubby Isaac's jellied eel stall at Aldgate East.

During the autumn of 1962 Dave had invited me for Sunday lunch at his flat. The fish curry that Barbara had cooked was excellent. As we dined, Mrs Upson suddenly said, 'The world is a very dangerous place at the moment.'

Dave's mother had every reason to be concerned. The Himalayan border dispute between India and China had erupted into heavy fighting with casualties on both sides. Although this incident was extremely serious, it could in no way be compared with the Cuban missile crisis that was gathering momentum. Premier Fidel Castro, in defiance of the United States, had allowed the Russians to send bomber squadrons to Cuba. Aerial photography over the island also revealed that ballistic missile bases were being constructed. President Kennedy responded by sending his warships to blockade the island; he also gave the Russians an ultimatum: if their large freighter fleet carrying missiles and military technicians which was heading for Cuba attempted to break the blockade, they would be sent to the bottom of the ocean. The Russians and Cubans ignored the ultimatum.

Barbara said she too had become concerned at the developing crisis.

'Not to worry, Barbo,' said Dave. (He often called his sister Barbo.) 'The Russian ships will be forced to change course and return to port.'

'And if they don't?' I asked my friend.

'Kennedy's warships will sink them,' he replied confidently.

'Then that will mean war,' I remarked. 'Perhaps even nuclear war.'

'That scenario is possible, but not probable,' said Dave. 'The Americans have no alternative; they must act decisively because their country is threatened.'

Barbara, who had shown little interest in politics in the past, thought Fidel Castro was an 'irresponsible fool'.

Mrs Upson described Castro as an, 'evil dictator, much worse than his predecessor Batista'.

Noticing how anxious his mother and Barbara had become, Dave spoke calmly. 'You will see, at the eleventh hour, Khrushchev will come to his senses;

the Russians will not risk a conventional, and certainly not a nuclear war over a little island like Cuba.'

A few days latter Khrushchev did come to his senses; he agreed, as did Kennedy, to a proposal suggested by the United Nations Acting Secretary General U. Thant. The proposal was that the Americans should end their blockade of the island and the Russians must remove their missiles and launching instillations.

'Thank God common sense has prevailed,' remarked Barbara.

'And thank God too for the Burmese U. Thant. At least my country has produced one outstanding diplomat!' said Mrs Upson.

Dave compared President Kennedy with Winston Churchill whom he had always admired. He went on to say, 'November 1962 will be Kennedy's greatest legacy.'

Exactly a year after the Cuban crisis I boarded a train at Waterloo Station to make the short journey to Clapham Station. I had an appointment with François, my Anglo-French girlfriend. She was preparing a meal for us at her Lavender Hill flat, which was just a few minutes walk from the station. A man sitting opposite me in the train compartment was reading a newspaper. I glanced at the front page and there in bold print were the shocking words 'President Kennedy Assassinated'.

A few days after the assassination, Dave and I were walking along Wapping Wall on our way to the Prospect of Whitby. It was late in the evening and quite dark. In the distance, I noticed a large black car heading in our direction. The car was being driven very slowly; suddenly it stopped near us, the windows were lowered and two outstretched arms appeared holding revolvers, pointing directly at Dave and me.

After whispering, 'Don't panic,' my friend quickly pushed me behind him. I thought we were about to be shot; to die by bullets, just like President Kennedy. At point blank range, the guns were fired at us, but miraculously we weren't hit; it was then that I realised the irresponsible youths in the car were firing starting pistols. We could hear laughter coming from inside the car and obscenities were shouted at us.

As the car was driven away, it began to zigzag mockingly down Wapping Wall before disappearing around the corner. 'Let them enjoy their fun,' remarked Dave. 'Perhaps when they are older, these idiots will be sorry for what they have just done; anyway, this definitely calls for a special drink.' Inside the Prospect I drank a large Scotch whisky, and then another.

20

Dirty Dick's and the King's Head

There was something unique and inviting about Dirty Dick's, which Dave affectionately described as our 'halfway house.' This eighteenth-century tavern, one of the great London attractions, was patronised by the city workers, tourists, the curious and often the lonely. Its famous old basement, which comprised the Long Bar and the small cosy Dustbin Bar in the corner, was a joy to visit. From its coal-black, cobwebbed ceiling hung a variety of muskets, rusty tailors' scissors, dented pewter mugs, one of my socks and many mummified cats and rats that were found in the cellars. The walls were covered with thousands of old and new postage stamps, business cards and hundreds of foreign bank notes were stapled to the wooden walls. Hundreds of coins were nailed on to one of the counters of the Dustbin Bar resembling a huge jigsaw puzzle.

Because the busy Liverpool Street station was near by, you could sometimes feel vibrations from the underground trains. When this did occur the sawdust-covered wooden floor would shake, giving you the feeling of its imminent collapse sending you crashing down with it to the cellars below.

Dave and I always felt totally relaxed at Dirty Dick's where we would enjoy the port wine or sample the different sherries from the huge casks, and the cool draught beer was most welcome after a long day in the factory. Descending into the basement for the first time, the visitor might well feel that he was stepping back in time. It was as if the pub had remained unchanged for over a hundred years.

To complete this link with the past, the bar staff were exceptionally old, especially Harry and Eric. Both barmen were diminutive bachelors who shared a small council flat at Bermondsey. Eric, bald and a little unkempt, was near blind. Cantankerous and half-deaf Harry would sometimes rely on Eric's hearing to serve customers.

Although in their eighties, the two men were still fond of women, particularly Harry, who had a penchant for soft-porn literature that he kept under the counter. There was an occasion when I witnessed Harry with impunity refuse to serve a coach party until he had finished glancing through an unsavoury magazine.

Because of the pub's deliberately neglected appearance, yet cosy atmosphere, it attracted many interesting and eccentric people and over the years Dave and I had ample opportunities to meet dozens of fascinating characters and more than once we dallied with some very delectable ladies.

Often, abusive alcoholics from the nearby Salvation Army hostel in Middlesex Street would sneak into the pub and attempt to consume the leftovers. One persistent nuisance, 'Red Boots Danny' was caught behind the bar attempting to fill up an empty milk bottle with sherry. Fred, a tough, grizzled old man, also a resident from the same hostel, was employed for a time to deal with the menacing alcoholics. Fred always stood by the door at the bottom of the stairs and would forcibly bar the way of any unwanted visitor. His vocabulary was usually restricted to just six words: 'All I want is a dinner.'

It was a freezing Friday evening. Fred, who was wearing a thin ill-fitting jacket, was shivering by the door. When I gave him a double sherry, he stood to attention and saluted me. Dave went upstairs to the buffet bar and bought him two scotch eggs; he saluted my friend too and promptly stuffed the eggs in his jacket pocket to be eaten later.

'Irish John' a bulky seventy-year-old barman only served customers in the Dustbin Bar. John would invite customers, usually women, to stand in front of one of the mummified cats that were fixed to the wall and stroke the cat three times and then make a wish. At the third stroke John would pull a lever behind the bar and the cat, attached by near invisible wires, would jerk forward and give the unsuspecting woman a fright.

This barman became very jealous of Dave one evening when he overheard him relating the sad story of Dirty Dick to some German tourists. Nathaniel Bentley, a rich eighteenth century dandy was supposed to have lived in a house on the site of Dirty Dick's. It was alleged that Bentley never recovered from the shock of hearing that his bride-to-be had collapsed and died on her way to the church for their wedding. In his distraught state, Bentley ordered the bridal chamber to be sealed off and the feast prepared for his guests to be left on the table indefinitely. Over the following years, Bentley became increasingly mentally ill, eventually becoming a recluse. He was rarely seen during the day, but late at night he would venture out to roam the streets dressed in the faded and torn clothes that he had worn for his wedding. Eventually, the tragic Bentley became known as Dirty Dick.

When the Germans had left, soon after Dave's talk, John, who probably thought that he had missed out on a generous tip had he told the same story, refused to serve Dave and me drinks, and he also ordered us to leave the pub. Dave reacted by instantly complaining to Bob Sweeny, the manager, whom he knew valued him as a likeable and regular customer. It was good to see Bob reprimand Irish John over his pettiness. Moreover, Bob gave my friend his blessing to inform any customers if he so chose of the Nathanial Bentley legend. Dave was prepared to forget the unfortunate episode and later that evening, against my advice, he offered the still-sulking John a glass of sherry. To my surprise a reluctant John accepted the drink.

How Dave and I would look forward to flopping down in Dirty Dick's in the evenings after our long shift in a cold and dirty Hackney clothing factory. No matter if we sat on the old creaky pews or the wobbly patched-up couches with their exposed springs we loved it. We surely looked a sorry sight, grubby and unshaven, me with my old and torn donkey jacket and Dave in his 'gor blimey trousers'. We could have been mistaken for latter-day Dirty Dicks.

A group of foreign tourists decided to sit around our table. I was so ashamed of my tattered shirt; I tried to conceal its frayed collar by raising my shoulders and lowering my chin. A Dutch woman sitting opposite leant forward and asked me in perfect English if there was something wrong with my neck.

Dave, detecting my predicament, intervened and said, 'Does anybody know the story of Dirty Dick's?'

'No, but we would like to know,' said an elderly Dutchman.

So Dave obliged and once more repeated the tale while I slowly lowered my shoulders to allow my neck to reveal its full length.

The Dutch, true to their nature, were as always extremely friendly. Another old man in their party was keen to tell us about his experiences of working on the Amsterdam canal barges for over half a century and his eyes lit up when Dave related his own memories of working on the Thames.

When the tourists eventually left, they thanked us for talking to them; they showed their gratitude by giving me sixpence and Dave, who fared much worse, the residue that was left in a half-pint of beer. We laughed so loud the tourists must have thought that we were down on our luck.

The Long Bar had become crowded with scores of smiling Japanese tourists complete with their inevitable cameras. Two of the tourists tried to strike up a conversation with Dave and me, but their English was appalling. After persuading us to take photos of them, then taking our photos they insisted on buying us drinks. By now Dave was in a happy mood and surprised me by uttering out loud some phrases in Japanese that he had remembered from the war.

After the tourists' departure he was deep in thought. I asked him if there was anything wrong.

'Do you know what?' he remarked, 'I am not sure what I had said to those Japs; it was either "Cheers have a happy long life," or "Keep your hands up or I will shoot you!"'

Usually, if we had befriended any girls in Dirty Dick's, we would invite them to the Poor Millionaire, which was a cheap drinking club just a hundred yards away at Bishopsgate. Four girls whom we had met earlier in the Long Bar were debating among themselves whether to accompany us to the club. The two prettiest, Angela and Ruth, were interested but the other two, both lesbians and on leave from the Royal Air Force, were not. Following a further brief discussion the lesbians decided, though hesitantly, to come along to the club.

Once inside the club, Angela and Ruth agreed to dance with Dave and me. As the four of us were dancing, I noticed that one of the lesbians who was tall, masculine and liked to be called Mitch was staring coldly at me.

After the musicians took a break and Dave and I and the girls returned to the table, Mitch leaned across to Dave and said, 'Would you please warn your friend not to dance with Angela in that fashion again, otherwise I will get very cross.' Her voice was just loud enough for me to hear.

Dave, who had been enjoying himself immensely with Ruth, tried unsuccessfully to pacify Mitch who for the next hour scrutinised my every move.

After we left the club, the girls accepted Dave's offer of a lift in his Reliant van. The six of us squeezed into Daisy Two. At a slow speed it took us about twenty minutes to reach Ruth's flat at Highgate. During the journey, there was much whispering amongst the girls in the back of the van and I had the uncomfortable feeling that I was about to be garrotted by Mitch who was sitting directly behind me.

Once we arrived at Highgate, Dave and I were invited in for coffee at Ruth's spacious, three bedroom sixth floor flat. The flat had a large balcony that offered superb views across London. I wondered how she could afford to pay the obviously high rent and service charge and it did enter my mind that she might be a call girl. When Dave told me later that Ruth had inherited the flat from relatives I felt ashamed that I had pre-judged her.

We all sat around in the huge comfortable lounge that had a well-stocked cocktail cabinet. Besides the coffee, sandwiches were prepared and a record player was plugged in. Ruth, like Dave, was fond of country and western music and he was delighted when she played a Slim Whitman record. Dave, now happy as a sand boy, began teasing Ruth who was sitting next to him on sofa.

Some time later, Toni, the second lesbian, disappeared into one of the bedrooms and called out to Mitch to join her. Mitch, who had been drinking rum all evening, slowly got up from the armchair, refilled her glass and left the lounge.

A few minutes later she returned with her glass empty. For a moment she stood by the door and began to clean her spectacles. After she put her spectacles back on, she scowled at me before going over to the cocktail cabinet and again filling her glass with rum.

I was hoping that the rum would have an effect and make her so sleepy she would retire for the night and leave Dave and me to have fun with Ruth and Angela, but Mitch decided to remain by the cocktail cabinet. Again, she glared at me menacingly and I soon began to feel like a convict sitting in the visitors' room being monitored by a prison guard. I half expected Mitch to call out 'no touching, no touching'.

'Is Mitch always so hostile towards men?' I whispered to Angela.

'No, not really,' she replied. 'But she does not always approve if I am in men's company too long. I have told her time and time again that my preference is men not women.'

I pressed on, 'Can I ask you why you stay friends with her? She seems to me to be very possessive.'

Angela looked up at Mitch and gave her a sympathetic half-smile. 'You see, I was in the Air Force too, and when I first joined up, she was very kind to me.'

Suddenly, Mitch pointed a long bony finger at me and barked, 'Stop talking about me you ponce.'

'We are actually discussing human nature,' I unwisely replied. My remark seemed to infuriate her and she immediately let loose a tirade of verbal abuse in such a deep, masculine, threatening tone it was almost comical in its delivery.

Ruth and Dave promptly jumped up and tried to calm her down. She reacted by screaming at Dave, 'and you can piss off too, you old git.'

Toni, who throughout the evening had remained quiet and unassuming, rushed into the lounge and confronted Mitch. She placed her arms around her friend's waist, forced her backwards and ordered her to 'shut up'. When Mitch ignored her, Toni managed to push her out of the lounge and into one of the bedrooms from where we could hear Mitch swearing and cursing. Eventually, all was quiet.

Ruth and Dave had stopped dancing and were now sitting on the sofa. I watched with amusement when Dave pulled Ruth towards him.

He spoke teasingly, 'Now, where were we darling?' She giggled and popped an olive into his mouth. For a few seconds I thought that it might be appropriate if I abandoned my plans to seduce Angela and put on my coat and leave, but she seemed very receptive and Dave was having a good time despite the presence of the repulsive and unpredictable Mitch. I gave the situation a second thought and decided to stay, but I remained alert in case of further problems with Mitch.

An hour passed and feeling confident that the two lesbians were now asleep I suggested to Angela that we should go into one of the bedrooms and leave Dave and Ruth alone. She nodded, smiled and led me by the hand. I looked back at Dave who gave me a wink.

During the night, I visited the bathroom and peered into the lounge. Ruth and Dave were nowhere to be seen. The sight of his brown brogue shoes beside the sofa brought an instant smile to my face. I closed the door and returned to Angela's welcoming arms.

A little later, I heard a noise outside in the hall. Suddenly, the bedroom door opened and in staggered a very drunk Mitch. She came towards the bed with her arm raised grasping what I thought was a hammer; fortunately for me, the weapon was a sink plunger. I jumped out of the bed and used a pillow to fend off her blows. She was so drunk, that her spectacles fell off and she was striking the pillow rather than me. Her screams and shouting caused Dave and Ruth to rush into the bedroom followed by Toni. Mitch, who was now crying, fell to the floor.

I said to Dave, 'That's it, enough is enough, I am going home.' Mitch must have heard me, because she immediately stopped crying and lay motionless on the floor. Her histrionics had the desired effect. I quickly got dressed and left the bedroom. Within a few minutes, Dave and I were speeding south down the Holloway Road and back to the East End.

'Not all is lost, I have Ruth's phone number,' said my friend gleefully.

Although I have mostly happy memories of Dirty Dick's there was one ugly incident that occurred there in the mid-1960s and that I have never forgotten. Dave and I were drinking in the Dustbin Bar when I noticed two men in their thirties standing in the middle of the Long Bar and drinking beer from the bottle. They seemed to be enjoying themselves making sarcastic remarks and rude noises directed at some of the sad-looking, elderly men who were sitting alone.

The presence of these two nasty strangers seemed incongruous amidst the well-behaved regular clientele. Dave had also noticed the pair. I hinted to my friend that I had the impression that the two men, although they wearing smart overcoats and carrying briefcases, were probably ex-villains now employed as foot messengers in the City.

'That's strange,' said Dave. 'I have the same feeling too. It proves that great minds think alike!' As we spoke, a group of foreign teenagers sitting in the alcove at the rear of the bar got up to leave. Instead of walking towards the exit they began to run. As they did so, one of the boys from the group accidentally bumped into the two strangers that caused beer to be spilt onto their clothes. When the boy, who was about seventeen years of age, stopped to apologise, he was shouted at by the taller of the two men.

'You have ruined my overcoat you f*****g idiot!' Suddenly the same man, whose mien was that of a pugnacious nightclub doorman, grabbed the boy. While his accomplice pinned the terrified boy's arms behind his back, the man began to viciously punch his face.

Customers sitting close to the assault, instead of intervening to rescue the victim, quickly left their tables and came running towards the Dustbin Bar where Dave and I stood. Some of the fleeing women screamed and several ran up the stairs to the street. Not content with battering the terrified, defenseless boy to the floor, the two thugs started to kick him mercilessly around the head and body. Sensing that he might be killed, I suddenly experienced that wonderful uplifting, surge of fearless emotion that sweeps through your whole being: cowardliness disappears and is replaced by anger. I hurled myself forward and crashed into the two men who were both knocked backwards.

The boy, whose face was badly cut, sobbed uncontrollably. As I crouched on the floor and tried to console him, I pleaded with a disinterested Harry and Eric to give me something to try and stop the blood flowing from the now semi-conscious boy's head. Harry responded by muttering a few swear words before throwing me a wet dishcloth. Thankfully Dave, with his fists clenched, was standing over me confronting the two evil men. Had my friend not been there, no doubt I would have been punched and kicked too.

One of the thugs began to thump his chest like a gorilla and shouted at the customers cowering in the Dustbin Bar, 'Look what he has done to my overcoat; he has ruined it, the German bastard.'

While I was using the dishcloth to wipe the blood from the boy's head several police officers arrived, having been called out from their station at nearby Bishopsgate. As the police and customers gathered around us and in the ensuing mayhem that followed, Dave and I, not wanting to get further involved, discreetly edged our way out of the crowd. We quickly left the pub and disappeared into the night.

I never knew if the two thugs were arrested and placed on trial for their barbaric act. Dave agreed with me that they deserved to be locked up indefinitely. 'At Devil's Island preferably,' he said angrily.

During the early 1980s, the company directors who owned Dirty Dick's made an unfortunate decision – they closed the pub for 'modernisation'. Their contractors removed the ancient beams and wood paneling adorned with postage stamps and business cards. These fixtures, along with the old benches, pews and barrel tables were dumped in a tip. The coal-black ceiling was scrubbed clean; also gone were the mummified cats and dogs and cobweb-covered weaponry. Not a trace of sawdust was left on the floor. Dirty Dick's was no longer a pub; it had been converted into a wine bar. The Long Bar and the small Dustbin Bar had become a single bar. Smooth artificial paneling covered every wall, art-deco tables and chairs were installed and new bar staff were engaged, none of whom seemed older than twenty. The conversion was a disaster, soulless and insipid. Dave and I and most of the loyal customers stayed away.

The boycotted wine bar survived for a while until the owners realised that they had made a blunder. By destroying the interior of the much-loved timeless basement bars, they had created a white elephant. Dirty Dick's was eventually closed for a second time, but this time, for transformation. Costly efforts were made to recapture its original state, but the resurrection was an inevitable failure; it looked too artificial. Customers visiting the new Dirty Dick's for the first time would leave with no lasting impression, unlike before when after just one drink in the former Dirty Dick's and the memory of their visit would have lasted forever.

I may not have shared Dave's frequent patronage of the King's Head in Commercial Road, Stepney, but I would sometimes join him there for a drink. The pub was very popular with older West Indians, much older and decrepit-looking prostitutes, those who were looking for cannabis, and lone, middle-aged white homosexual men. I clearly remember one evening feeling uncomfortable in the gents' standing next to a sickly-looking Tom Driberg MP and, on another occasion, being none too happy standing so close to the author, Colin MacInnes.

I arranged to meet Dave at the King's Head one Sunday lunchtime. Once I arrived, he would finish his drink and we would leave for Poplar for our pre-arranged date with two divorced sisters. Inside the pub, and sitting by the window, my friend was engrossed in a lively conversation with three effeminate men. Dave, like me, was a rampant heterosexual. Of course, being a regular drinker in dockside pubs, you occasionally made acquaintances of homosexual men; providing that they were aware of our heterosexuality, we were very tolerant towards them. I usually found homosexuals to be kind, artistic and non-aggressive, unlike several lesbians whom we had known over the years. Despite trying to imitate men, lesbians could be vituperative and intolerant towards us males when we were in their company at parties.

Not wanting to join Dave and his acquaintants and concerned about the time, I stood at the bar. Dave immediately spotted me and insisted that I sit at his table. As I listened to the conversation, I learnt that the three men were ship stewards. I also noticed that one of the stewards had become a little tearful. Dave later explained to me that a friend of the stewards, who was a drag artist with the stage name of Von Jurgen, had been found handcuffed and floating in the Thames at Rotherhithe, apparently a tragic suicide.

The oldest of the three stewards had a swollen cheek and cuts to his lips. He claimed that he had recently been beaten up and robbed by an 'Irish navvy' in the WC of Charlie Brown's pub at Limehouse. I suspected what had happened is what usually happened: the steward had made an improper suggestion to the Irishman who had reacted in the only way he knew how, with his fists.

The most talkative of the stewards suddenly asked Dave why he thought, 'some men were queer while others were not?'

Dave appeared slightly embarrassed by this unexpectedly direct question. He sipped his whisky before saying, 'I don't think that homosexuality is abnormal, I believe that it is inherent in all men, but remains suppressed. Of course if the conditions were right, it might manifest itself.'

The three stewards seemed satisfied with his answer. Moments later the same steward who had posed the question to Dave, turned his attention to me and asked if I had an opinion on the matter. My reticence prompted Dave to nudge my ribs, which was his usual method of encouraging me to join in a conversation. 'Come on, Alf, I know you have a view on the subject. Let them hear it.'

Reluctantly I agreed and choose my words carefully. 'For what it's worth, I think that the cause of homosexuality is probably environmental and that your developing sexuality was influenced and shaped from a very early age by people with whom you had come into contact including members of your own family.' On reflection, what I added was insensitive, and possibly even cruel. 'Because a homosexual relationship is an unnatural practice, I cannot see how a relationship can have any permanency and in many cases it is doomed to fail, especially for those who have several partners, and I suspect for many it is an inevitable sad fact that they will be alone late in life.'

Although my opinions were instantly rejected, I was thanked for being honest. The stewards were unanimous in believing that they were born homosexual. 'It is in our genes.'

One of the stewards remarked that they were really, 'Women encased in men's bodies.'

Dave wanted to continue the conversation, but I was forced to remind him of our already late appointment with the two sisters. We had approximately fifteen minutes to meet the sisters at a meeting place of their choice.

Stinkhouse Bridge was the location. The bridge was just a minute walk from where they lived. Stinkhouse Bridge is the name given to the old iron bridge that crosses the Limehouse canal at Upper North Street, Poplar. Adjacent to the bridge on the north bank of the canal was the Frederick Allen Chemical Works. The unpleasant fumes from the factory often permeated the surrounding area.

As Dave and I were about to leave, the youngest steward spoke in a slow, falsetto voice. 'Enjoy yourselves, darlings, I hope that the ladies are wearing strong perfume, ta ta.'

In the summer of 1966, Dave was instrumental in finding me a job. His firm, D&W Handbags, had moved from Cannon Street Road, Stepney to a modern factory at nearby 54 Cavell Street. Dave had noticed that C&H Fashions just a few doors away at number 50 were advertising for an experienced part-time stock cutter. He urged me to enquire about the vacancy. He also said that he had seen some pretty girls going into the factory. I needed no further encouragement.

Cavell Street, which connected Commercial Road in the south to Whitechapel Road in the north, was named after the famous British nurse Edith Cavell, who in 1895 became a probationer at the nearby London Hospital.

At lunchtime, I would invariably leave the C&H factory and make my way to the adjacent Watney Street market to buy pie and mash or sandwiches. On one of these excursions, I saw a film being made in the market. Conversing with the director was the tall American black actor Sidney Poitier.

Seven years after it was announced in the press that Poitier would portray E. R. Braithwaite in a film version of *To Sir With Love*, the producers had finally got the film into production. Many of the scenes for the film were shot in Stepney, particularly Wapping.

During this period in the mid-1960s Dave held regular parties at his flat at Lathem House. As always, his superb punch was much sought after. Besides the punch, Barbara would make endless plates of tasty sandwiches and a delicious Anglo-Indian, mulligatawny soup. The parties were so popular that several local nurses and female teachers would arrive uninvited, and we lucky men often found ourselves outnumbered by women.

At one of the parties, Dave and I met Penny and Beth who were former teachers from Kent. Both girls were temporarily unemployed and living in a Stepney commune. In Dave's kitchen and standing by the almost empty punch bowl, Dave, Penny, Beth and I made an arrangement for the following day to see the film *To Sir With Love* that was being shown in a local cinema.

After the four of us left the cinema, Dave suggested that we should have a drink at a nearby pub. It was inevitable that the conversation would be about the film that we had just seen. I suspected correctly, that because I had been one of Braithwaite's pupils, Penny and Beth would want to hear my version of what actually went on at St George's. I would have none of it. I was so outraged at having allowed myself to see such rubbish I was in no mood to have a rational discussion.

Both Penny and Beth were intelligent enough to know that the film was nonsense. Several years previously Penny had seen the American film *The Blackboard Jungle*. She agreed with Dave that the plot was very similar to *To Sir With Love*.

Beth said, 'The film implied that the head master was weak and ineffectual and had no control over his school; that would never happen, he would have been dismissed for incompetence.'

Dave, a great film buff with a preference for John Wayne westerns, sat quietly listening to their comments. Because I had remained silent, he decided to state his views. 'It really is a question of profit. Film companies are like newspaper owners. They are in business to make money, so you can't always expect them to be careful with the truth. A movie is the end product of a series of changes and alternatives that have taken place from an original idea. The finished movie would have been cut, trimmed and edited from the filmed screenplay. The screenwriter, who is sometimes the director, is often given a reasonable free rein but within defined limits by the producers. He can and will play around with the original novel because he knows that the author, having sold the film rights, has forfeited his right to oppose change. And lastly the author himself; he may not be credible; his work might be exaggerated or even false. I suppose if you want to ascertain the truth of a story you really have to question people who were around at the time and had personal experience, but that of course requires time and money and then for what purpose. No, my friends, when it comes to profit, truth and integrity fly out the window.'

Dave sat back contented and noticing his glass was almost empty he remarked, 'And before Alf flies out of the door, he better buy the next round of drinks.' We all laughed at his perfect timing.

The following Sunday afternoon Dave and I took Penny and Beth on a guided tour of Wapping and Shadwell where the film was made. Like so many of our friends who were strangers to Docklands, they loved the interesting walk from Tower Bridge to Limehouse.

That same evening we planned to visit The Prospect of Whitby for a welcome singsong, but first Dave suggested a lightning pubcrawl around Cable Street. The area was still potentially dangerous. A vicious brawl involving some Somalis in Leman Street blocked our path. As we crossed the road near the Brown Bear pub, its door swung open and two fighting Irishmen were thrown out.

Dave whispered to me as if I was partly to blame. 'The girls must think we are a right couple of burps for bringing them around here.'

Contrary to Dave's assumption, Penny and Beth both thought that Cable Street was an exciting place. They would have preferred to have stayed a little longer, but their safety was paramount so we turned around and headed south for Wapping.

In the spring of 1967 Dave and I thought seriously about going into business together. Our idea was to buy or rent a coach and start up a Docklands pub tours company. We would be the guides and our good friend Ronny Radlet, a keen motorist, would be offered the driver's job. Plans were drawn up, finance was arranged and we even found a garage where we could keep and service the coach, but at the last moment we changed our minds, fearing the partnership might jeopardise our friendship.

21

Dave in Rushden

Later in the year, the owners of D&W Handbags decided to open a factory at Rushden. The town was just a few miles from Northampton that was famous for leatherwear and shoe manufacturing. Dave was asked, or probably ordered by his employers, to move to Rushden for a period of three months and assist in the setting up of the factory.

Unlike the East End, there was no shortage of skilled leather workers at Rushden; the wages were lower than London and the rent for the factory was a pittance. Dave's role would be the opening and closing of the building, security duties and helping with the new staff training programme. Not wanting to be unco-operative he agreed to the move. He was found accommodation with a childless married couple and every two weeks he would return home for the weekend. The arrangements were acceptable to him.

It seemed that the couple had a broken marriage. The husband had several mistresses and the wife would take the occasional lover. Dave quickly detected it was a loveless marriage. No sooner had the husband left for work in the mornings, his wife would cook my friend his breakfast. After chasing her around the kitchen table for a few minutes, Dave would settle down and eat his eggs and bacon.

'Of course,' he said, with that familiar twinkle in his eye, 'As I had been a good boy, there was usually a little treat for afters.'

Once the three-month assignment was over and the factory was on course, Dave returned home. He had received no reward, bonus or extra wages for all of the hard work and long hours he had put in to make the new branch a success.

On the very first morning when he arrived for work at his old factory in Cavell Street, his ungrateful and heartless employer told him to go down into the recently flooded basement, remove all of the damaged stock and mop up afterwards. Dave felt deeply offended by this order and instantly handed in his notice.

When I heard the news that Dave was out of work, I managed to persuade my employer at the Pridewear factory that I managed in Hackney to offer him a position as a trainee garment cutter. My friend accepted the offer at once.

Although slow and methodical at first, Dave eventually learnt to cut clothes and in he proved to be a good asset at the factory and our years of working together were happy.

During this period we still talked of joining the Merchant Navy, but it was only a pipe dream; we knew it would never happen. He continued to mention how one day he would love to sail amongst the Greek islands, stopping at little harbour taverns for drinks and kebabs. He joked that if ever he won the football pools he would buy a huge yacht and hire an all-girl crew; of course they would be topless.

I reminded him of the fate that had awaited the late American film actor Steve Cochrane, who had suffered a fatal heart attack at the age of forty-eight while out sailing on his luxury yacht in the Pacific Ocean. The actor's crew were all topless women.

Dave laughed before saying, 'What a way to go!'

During January 1969, the Upsons invited me for Sunday lunch. After our excellent meal the four of us began to discuss the recent Russian and her Warsaw Pact allies' invasion of Czechoslovakia and the suppression of President Dubcek's liberal government.

Mrs Upson and Barbara were saddened by the death of the twenty-year-old Czech Student Jan Pallack who had set himself alight in Prague's Wenclose Square. It was said that Pallack was protesting over the invasion, but it later emerged that he was actually protesting because of his countrymen's lack of response to the occupation.

About a week after Pallack's self immolation, I was with Dave at the Prospect of Whitby. Suddenly, a large group of students who were in full voice stopped singing and rushed outside to the riverside terrace. Dave and I followed suit. At anchor directly opposite the Prospect an East German freighter was waiting for the high tide to take her into the nearby Shadwell Basin. Our shouting was deafening, 'Dubcek, Svoboda, Dubcek, Svoboda.' The silent German crew with their guiltless eyes just stared back at us.

It was a Friday evening when Dave and I arrived at the Prospect with a strong thirst after spending twelve hours working in a Hackney clothing factory. Never was a beer more appreciated. We quickly perched ourselves on the stairs to view the happy scene below. As usual the bar was crowded with scores of smiling faces.

We were joined on the stairs by two attractive young women. Within minutes we began to chat to the women whose names were Maureen and Mary. They told us that they were helpers at Ave Maria, a Catholic-administrated South London home for teenage girls who were in need of care and protection. Occasionally, after they finished duty late in the evening, Maureen and Mary would arrive at the Prospect to enjoy the last of the sing-a-long atmosphere.

Dave and I left the stairs with our new acquaintances and formed a little circle by the Hawaiian musicians where we spent the rest of the evening

Maureen Broome, Alfred Gardner, Josie Fields and David Upson at the Prospect of Whitby, October 1964.

drinking and singing. I could not keep my eyes away from Maureen and wanted to see her again. I asked her for a date, she agreed and we started to meet on a regular basis. As the weeks went by, I found myself becoming increasingly besotted with her and for a while we became lovers.

Although not tall, Maureen was very good-looking with blue eyes and gorgeous dark wavy hair. Her warm smile was ingrained in Dave's memory; he was extremely fond of her and periodically mentioned her name throughout his life. I was puzzled as to why she was attracted to me; we were different in so many ways. I had little schooling, was not that clever or very ambitious, unlike Maureen who was idealistic, bright, confident and quite capable of expressing herself articulately. I was aware that she had received an excellent grammar school education and had achieved high results in science subjects. I also learnt that she had rejected the opportunity to study at one of several Cambridge and Oxford universities that had offered her a place. Instead she was planning to enrol at a college and train to be a social worker.

Sometimes Maureen's calm mood would change and she would become very volatile and explosive, like the occasion when I casually asked her what was her opinion of Enoch Powell's famous 'Rivers of Blood' speech.

'If I could drive and had a car, I would run him over,' she replied angrily.

I thought her threat was absurd; she was incapable of physically harming an insect, let alone a famous British politician.

Because Maureen despised Enoch Powell, I gained the impression that she could be intolerant to those whose views that were contrary to her own. I soon learnt to avoid mentioning subjects that might enrage her. It was romance and sex I wanted, not endless conversations about the rights and wrongs of the world. Although Maureen was clearly a tomboy, with a voice and walk to match, I never found these characteristics unattractive. In fact, during the first night that we spent together, I was amazed at the intensity of her passion and strong sex drive.

In late February 1970, Maureen suggested that we spend a week at her parent's cottage on Guernsey's north coast. Pierre, her father, known to everyone as 'Pip', was a fisherman who with his wife Sheila supplemented their income by growing freesias. Her parents, as I expected, proved to be exceptionally kind and hospitable. The evenings at the cottage were peaceful. I could relax with Maureen and her parents and enjoy the warmth of a real coal fire.

My obsession with music had no bounds. If during the day the rain prevented us from continuing our walks, I played my opera records that I had brought over especially for such occasions. Thankfully Pip and Sheila turned a blind eye, and probably closed their ears too, whenever I selfishly wanted to listen to music at every given opportunity.

At other times Maureen and I would spend hours walking along the headlands enjoying the magnificent coastal views. I had never seen such scenery before. It was breathtaking. During one of these walks, I felt inspired to write a little poem.

Guernsey Cliffs
The gorse grows thick around the towers.
Along the paths we find wild flowers.
Seagulls circle ahead.
We stop and feed them bread.
Rocks like cinders black and grey.
Brace themselves to face the spray.
The grass moves in almost wave-like motion.
As if combed by winds from the ocean.
On quiet cliff tops we walk a mile.
A gift from God your lovely isle.

When it was time for me to return to London, and having said goodbye to Maureen's parents at their cottage door, Pip suddenly called out to me, 'Come back to see us one day, Alf.' Lowering his voice, he added ominously, 'Before the sea takes me.'

Maureen stayed in Guernsey for another week. When we met in London after her return, she seemed to be less interested in me. I soon become

Alfred Gardner, 'Little Mo', David Upson, Mary Notten and Gary Lacey, the manager of the Prospect of Whitby, November 1969.

increasingly pessimistic about our relationship until I finally accepted that our affair had probably been doomed from the beginning; she was young and had plans of her own that certainly did not include me. I had now become a nuisance, increasingly making demands and wanting a commitment from her that she was unable and unwilling to give.

After Maureen refused to see me again, much to my regret at the time, I felt contrite and miserable. I had never been rejected before. It was normally I who ended relationships.

Dave's advice was welcome and accepted. 'Let it be like water off a duck's back and put it down to experience.' I was soon back in my old routine of sleeping around, which included a wild night of passion in one of the bedrooms at the Prospect of Whitby with Maureen's friend, the buxom Mary Notten.

In 1974, I returned to Guernsey for a short holiday. Although my relationship with Maureen had ended four years earlier, I decided to visit her parents, but I was shocked and saddened to learn that Pip, along with his friend, had drowned while out fishing a few months previously. It seemed that his prophecy had tragically come true.

In 1970 Dave and I left Pridewear. My friend accepted a stock cutting position at a Hackney factory, but I had no immediate plans to start work. I enjoyed being out in the fresh air, which was then exceptionally warm, reminiscent of that glorious extended summer of 1959 when Dave and I first became friends.

With spare time on my hands, I saw more of Danny, my football loving nine-year-old nephew. Although I had no interest in football whatsoever, it was not that difficult for Danny to talk me into taking him several times to see West Ham United play at various London football clubs.

Throughout that lovely Indian summer of 1970, I was still pursuing the female form with great success. Fair-haired and blue-eyed Sue, at twenty-two, was every red-blooded male's dream. Not only was she attractive and an enthusiastic nymphomaniac, she was also an heiress who drove an open-top, white sports car.

'I am fascinated by your lean canine look, but not your attire,' said Sue to me. A few moments later she handed me a cheque for £300, 'To buy new clothes.' I was not offended by Sue giving me money but I did tear up the cheque. I had never accepted money from a woman in my life.

During September, Sue parked her car at the western end of Wapping and we watched the demolition of old warehouses at St Katherine's Dock. It was a sad moment for me. These 150-year-old warehouses were a unique part of Docklands' heritage. Some of the warehouses had sustained bomb damage during the Blitz, but others had not. Much to my regret, the adjacent riverside Irongate Wharf, built in 1848, was also being demolished. Where these magnificent ancient warehouses originally stood, one of London's ugliest buildings was erected, the Thistle Hotel.

Besides my affair with Sue I was having affairs with other women too. Dave warned me to be careful, 'Otherwise your over-indulgence might push you into a pit of permanent dissipation.' I ignored Dave's advice. I was just not prepared to give up the succession of pretty girls I was having affairs with.

My relationship with Sue eventually came to an abrupt end. She had learned from a 'mutual friend' that I was 'bedding' Rita, a lithe, sensuous, guitar playing, Anglo-Portuguese girl. Perched on the pillion of Rita's motorbike, much to Dave's amusement, may not have been as comfortable for me as sitting in Sue's sports car, and Rita's modest *pied-à-terre* at Richmond in Surrey was cramped compared with Sue's large house in north west London, but Rita had an appealing, gentle nature, unlike Sue who was strong-willed and assertive.

After Rita's eventual departure, I had further meaningless and brief affairs with girls from Germany, Spain and Yugoslavia. Later in the year my rampant promiscuity was brought to a halt; I contracted non-specific urethritis, a venereal disease.

Shaking his head Dave remarked, 'Alf, I told you to be careful!'

After successful treatment at the London Hospital's VD clinic, I made the decision that my insalubrious lifestyle must end immediately. Abstaining from womanising was essential, at least for the time being.

Over the next few years, Dave and I worked in several clothing factories in Hackney, sometimes on a freelance basis. Often we would find ourselves working in the same building, but the industry was starting to change. Several old established garment companies were beginning to close down, much of their production being made abroad where costs were lower. It was now a different situation to the old days when you could leave one job at lunchtime and start working in a neighbouring firm the same afternoon. Although I eventually found a secure job in Shoreditch, Dave was not so lucky and for the first time since arriving in London in 1954, he found himself out of work.

During this period of unemployment, Barbara Upson asked Dave if he would decorate their flat. Although my friend had a reputation for being a conscientious and hard-working employee, he was chronically lazy at home. Painting a ceiling, washing the dishes, or carpet cleaning were household chores that he loathed.

Because Dave showed no interest in picking up a paintbrush, I offered to do the decorating over two weekends. My offer seemed to have inspired Dave because he suddenly said, 'If we work together Alf, we can finish the decorating in a single weekend.' I hoped that I had not inadvertently shamed him.

Beginning early on a Saturday, we worked until midnight. We would repeat the same fourteen-hour stint the next day. Not once over that long weekend of decorating would we stop working to have a 'pub break'. Perhaps there was some truth in Dave's belief that unless heavy drinkers were fully occupied, they would always return to the bottle.

Dave was desperate to find a job. Each morning he would set out on foot checking out various East End clothing factories to see if there were any vacancies. He even travelled north to Stoke Newington and Stamford Hill. This searching for work went on for about a month. When his savings began to rapidly dwindle, he was advised to sign on at the local Labour Exchange. Reluctantly, Dave agreed, but he felt guilty about drawing unemployment benefit. It was totally alien to him. I suggested to my friend that he should visit the Star Employment Agency adjacent to Aldgate East Station. This agency only recruited clothing workers. The majority of their vacancies were situated in Stepney and Bethnal Green. The thought of being interviewed by receptionists, whom I described as being 'on the young side and attractive too' appealed to Dave; he visited the agency the next morning.

That evening, I met him at the Eastern Hotel, where he was in a relaxed mood. Just before my arrival, he had attempted to make conversation with three unescorted Scandinavian women; they were crew members from timber ships moored at Montague Myers wharf at the nearby Millwall docks. Not disheartened when he received the cold shoulder from the women, he had turned his attention to two mixed-race girls who had come into the lounge bar and sat near to our table. After several minutes of trying in vain to make contact with the girls using his old 'language of the eyes' routine, he abandoned his efforts.

Smiling broadly he said, 'You tricked me, Alf, enticing me to the Star Agency. Those receptionists weren't young and attractive; in fact they were old and matronly.' His accurate description caused me to smile.

After I bought my friend a large whisky, he forgave me. I was keen to know the outcome of his visit to the Star Agency. 'On a serious note Dave, did they not offer you anything at the agency?'

His answer was disappointing. 'Well, they sent me to a dress factory at Stepney Green for an interview that lasted about ten seconds. I rang the factory bell and the boss opened the door and asked me if I could grade dress patterns. When I said no, he just slammed the door in my face.'

Dave dismissed my suggestion to return to the Star Agency to make a formal complaint. Having doors slammed in your face by rude or arrogant bosses was an experience I particularly detested. Dave and I were always extremely polite when enquiring about vacancies; we expected the same cordiality from employers, but it was not always forthcoming.

It was at Dirty Dick's where Dave introduced me to his Anglo-Burmese musician friend, Basil Short. When not playing his guitar and singing ballads in dockside pubs, Basil, who was tall and dark-skinned, supplemented his income by being a film extra. Using his contacts in the film industry, Basil managed to secure a one-day contract for Dave and me to appear in a historical drama that was being made at Bray Studios in Berkshire. Basil would also be an extra in the film. The three of us would be offered £6 each for the day's work, which would be increased to £7 if we were prepared to wear wigs.

At first Dave seemed interested in being a film extra, saying as it would be 'a bit of fun' but he later changed his mind and decided to refuse the work.

Basil and I met outside Hammersmith tube station where, along with about thirty other extras, we boarded a studio coach that would take us to the film set at Bray. I spoke to some of the extras on the coach. It was explained to me that the film that we were to appear in was entitled *Pope Joan*. According to legend, a ninth-century German prostitute who possessed an ability to teach the Christian faith disguised herself as a man. She somehow managed to be elected Pope. The Norwegian actress Liv Ullman would be playing the part of Pope Joan and an international array of fine actors were given supporting roles.

When Basil and I arrived at the studios we were clothed in the attire of Roman citizens and given banners to hold. Basil opted for the additional £1 and wore a ridiculous, ill-fitting, white wig that resembled a mop head.

'I look like Harpo Marx!' he lamented.

As citizens of Rome we were filmed waving our banners and cheering as the Pope and her procession emerged from a church. The church seemed as if it was constructed from cardboard.

The last scene in which we were involved was meant to be deadly serious, but I found an assistant director's instruction highly amusing. At a given command scores of us citizens were to rush forward and lynch the impostor whom I presumed was Pope Joan. Another assistant director warned me that if I was spotted laughing during the surge, I would be sent off the set and not paid. When 'Action!' was called, we outraged citizens began our stampede towards the impostor.

During the stampede, Basil's wig fell off. The wig was instantly tossed in the air by another extra who probably found the episode hilarious. The brave stuntman who stood in for Liv Ullmann must have been on treble wages. He was surrounded, squashed and physically thrown to the ground, where with our bare hands we pretended to rip his clothes off and tear him to pieces. Too add more realism to the scene, a pile of old and tatty dishcloths was substituted for his clothes and placed on his prostrated body.

More film work was offered to me at Shepperton Studios in Surrey. I was to play a soldier in a film entitled *Young Winston*. The film was to be based on Winston Churchill's early life prior to him entering politics. Unfortunately, I had to refuse the work, because I had already agreed to do some freelance dress cutting at a factory in Hackney.

Basil also refused the offer to work on the same film. He was not interested in dressing up as a Zulu warrior. 'From a white wig to a black wig, not for me, no thanks.'

Besides being a heavy whisky drinker, Basil was also diabetic, a lethal combination. Moreover he ignored his doctor and friends' advice to stop drinking and be careful with his diet. As Basil sat on a stall on the small stage of an East End pub and played his guitar and sang gentle ballads, he suddenly collapsed and died. He was in his mid-fifties.

I explained to Dave that I had contacted the Greek Cypriot Clothing Manufactures Association to see if they had any stock cutting vacancies. There were several on their books, but the factories were all located at North London. To reach these areas would involve much travelling.

The association gave me the addresses of a dress manufacturing firm at Haringey that required full or part-time cutters. I was not interested in being interviewed for the post, but Dave was. We drove to Haringey. While I remained in Dave's van he went for the interview. The factory had been converted from a garage (probably illegally) at the rear of a large detached house, but the cutting room was situated in the house's cellar.

After a few minutes Dave emerged from the house and sat in the van. He sighed as he spoke. 'It seems that our journey to Haringey has been a wasted effort.'

'Why?' I asked, mystified.

My friend explained that he could not see how heavy rolls of fabric could be safely carried down the narrow stairs to the cellar cutting room; also there was no natural light or a fire escape. Dave admitted that because of the high wages offered, plus the promise of 'bags of overtime' he was tempted to accept the stock cutting vacancy, but after further thought he changed his mind. It seems that my prior warning to him about avoiding dangerous working conditions had been heeded.

During this unemployed period Dave was spending several evenings in a little dockside pub where Karen, a voluptuous barmaid, worked. Karen, who knew me slightly, had the kind of personality that appealed to him, a friendly smile, not too serious and enjoyed being teased.

Dave, a perennial flirt, would arrive at the pub smartly dressed. Throughout the evening, he would buy Karen drinks and keep her amused, much to the annoyance of the landlord. This flirtation went on for about a fortnight and it resulted in him foolishly spending more and more of his 'reserve kitty'.

Dave invited me accompany him to the pub to 'assess the situation'. My friend must have inadvertently given Karen the impression that he was a wealthy businessman with an endless cash flow. When Dave looked away for a moment she leaned over the bar and whispered to me, 'Who is he?' Not wanting to spoil the fun, I said that he was in the fashion business.

Karen giggled, 'Every time he orders a whisky, he gives me a wink and asks if he can have it on the rocks.'

After Dave and I left the pub at closing time, he sought my opinion about 'his chances'. I advised him to forget Karen because once she had discovered that he was not a rich man, but just a low-paid garment cutter, she definitely would not be interested.

The following morning, my friend set out once more on his endless rounds of knocking on factory doors looking for work. Later that day, he had to sign on at the labour exchange. Feeling miserable, cold and drenched from the heavy rain, he joined the queue of people waiting to draw their benefit. As he approached the window to sign on, he was amazed to find that the receptionist sitting there was Karen the barmaid who apparently only worked in the pub during the evenings.

When she saw the now embarrassed Dave she laughed and jokingly said, 'Still want it on the rocks?'

Fortunately, I managed to find my friend a position as a stock cutter at an established skirt company near where I worked at Shoreditch.

Dave and I met our mutual friends Ronny Radlet and his wife Myra for drinks at the Prospect of Whitby. Myra became an unintentional matchmaker when she introduced Dave to her friend Susan Walker. Susan was a divorcée who lived at Walthamstow with her five-year-old daughter Samantha. Dave and Susan were immediately attracted to each other and a passionate romance followed.

Because Dave's affection for Susan seemed to me to be so sincere, I thought that his womanising days were finally over. An added bonus to their relationship was Susan's daughter, who became very fond of Dave. Happily seated on his lap and fascinated by his Mexican type moustache that she loved to stroke, Samantha nicknamed him 'Fluff'.

So Fluff now had a ready-made family; his future seemed assured. His mother, Barbara and I hoped that the relationship would blossom and might lead to marriage, but as time went by we started to have doubts about their long-term partnership. Because Dave was so keen to see Susan most evenings, he became increasingly reluctant to go home after work to freshen up, have a meal and change his clothes; instead he would jump into his little Reliant van that was parked outride the factory and drive at great speed to Walthamstow to see her. He boasted to me that the journey from Stepney took him only eight minutes.

I was concerned for his safety when he said that he had driven so fast down the Lea Bridge Road that when he had gone over the top of the little hill the van shot into the air like a plane taking off from an aircraft carrier.

After about nine months Susan and Dave's relationship began to wane, and it worsened when he confessed to her that there was 'no more money left in the kitty'. Dave called at Susan's house on a Friday evening, but she refused to let him inside and complained of being unwell. He left, but became suspicious. Anxious to find out if she was telling the truth, he waited outside the front door for a few moments before climbing into her garden to peer through the window. My friend was shocked to see her on the sofa canoodling with a man whom he recognised as being a local builder. Without bitterness or ill feeling, Dave went home and never contacted Susan again.

Remorseful at first, he soon got over the ending of the relationship and returned to his old self and into the arms of Sally a former girlfriend whom he had not seen for two decades. Sally was to become part of his life for the next few years.

Dave had never mentioned Sally to me before. The first time I saw her was on a Sunday morning. I was on my way to meet Dave at his Lathem House flat. Just prior to going into Lathem House, I noticed a strange woman fast asleep and snoring loudly in the passenger seat of his Reliant van. My first reaction was that she may have been a squatter who was staying in one of the old empty council houses nearby that were waiting refurbishment. Perhaps following a late night party, she had found Dave's van unlocked and got inside to sleep for a few hours. Only the week before, I had spotted two young squatters dozing on the lower stairs of Lathem House.

Once inside Dave's flat, I blurted out, 'Dave, there's a strange woman asleep in your van.'

My friend, who was in his armchair and drinking coffee, looked up at me and yawned before remarking, 'Don't get anxious, Alf, its only Sally.' It was obvious to me that he had just woken up from a heavy drinking session the night before. How amazing he was, no matter how much he had to drink, he never showed any ill effects the next day.

I was not so immune. If I had more than three pints of beer, I would wake up in the morning feeling terrible with an excruciating headache; so severe was the pain that I had no alternative but to become a permanent moderate drinker. I once remarked to Barbara that it was unfortunate that Dave had never experienced a bad hangover. If he had, it's possible that the excessive drinking that sometimes dominated his life may have been less frequent.

During the course of that Sunday morning I learned how he had first met Sally twenty years previously when she was just seventeen. He had lost touch with her soon afterwards until recently when he noticed her in one of his local pubs. It seems that she had fled her North London home after her husband, a violent West Indian, physically attacked her and forced her to take drugs. After arriving in Stepney, Sally became a squatter in Aston Street that was near St Dunstan's Church.

Sally, a seasoned drinker, regularly accompanied Dave to his favourite pubs. After the pubs closed they continued to drink at Dave's flat which alarmed Barbara and her mother, who for the first time found Dave drinking in the mornings before leaving for work.

There was another problem relating to Dave's perennial drinking, which had worsened since being reunited with Sally; he was falling asleep whilst smoking. Mrs Upson was extremely concerned, especially when Dave began coming home late at night in a drunken state. She had found him in the early hours of the morning fast asleep in the armchair with a lit cigarette smouldering on his clothes.

Barbara spoke to me quietly in the kitchen. 'Alfie, please warn David not to smoke when he returns from the pub. Mother and I are becoming increasingly worried that there might be a fire.'

I immediately warned my friend of the dangers of his smoking in the home after spending an evening in the pub; it was not the first time. In the past I had given him similar warnings, and had even shown him a newspaper cutting of a fatal accident where an elderly man had fallen asleep in an armchair whilst smoking. The cigarette had dropped onto the carpet and had set his flat ablaze.

This latest shock tactic of mine seemed to have had an effect on Dave. He gave me an assurance. 'In future, I will behave myself.' To alleviate Mrs Upson and Barbara's ongoing fears, I installed smoke alarms at their flat.

The house in nearby Aston Street where Sally was a squatter had now become overcrowded. One of the other squatters in the house, a tall, black-bearded artist, was prone to beating up Melanie, his five-foot girlfriend. One Sunday afternoon, Dave and Sally were drinking mead in an adjacent room; suddenly they heard Melanie cry as she was being punched. Dave, ignoring Sally's warning not to get involved, burst into the room and pounced on the artist. According to Sally, Dave gave the artist such a 'pasting' that he ran out of the house and never came back. Melanie remained at the house for a few days before moving to a squat in Hackney. Sally thought that she might have gone to Hackney to be reunited with the artist who was known to have previously squatted in the area.

'Some women are so daft, they still go back for more,' remarked Dave with a sigh.

Jobless Sally was to spend a great deal of time at the Upsons' flat. I liked her; she had a pleasant personality and laughed a great deal, but unfortunately was totally irresponsible. Eventually, Dave helped her to secure a suitable council flat in Poplar, only to see her evicted for non-payment of rent. She was later offered another flat in Stepney but again was in rent arrears, preferring to spend her money on alcohol. I even found her a job as a presser at a clothing factory. I mistakenly thought that by working she might become more responsible, but one day she absconded from the factory and refused to return.

It was late in the evening when I met a happy Sally in Stepney's Commercial Road where she was about to board a bus. She pointed to a large ring on the second finger of her left hand, and shouted auspiciously, 'Look, David has bought me a ring.'

'With diamonds?' I shouted back.

With her eyebrows raised her happy face changed to a grimace.

'I should be so lucky, just garnets.'

Unfortunately, her love for Dave was never reciprocated; although he was very fond of Sally, he had no intention of marrying her. Dave admitted to me that 'the ring was not a token of love, just a birthday present'. My friend also told me that Sally had now become a burden. Moreover, he did not have the heart to tell her that their relationship was futile. He hoped that she would eventually leave him on her own accord.

I had no plans to get married either. Fiona, my own girlfriend, wanted our relationship to be more 'secure' but I was unwilling to commit myself. My bachelorhood was too precious to forfeit.

Fiona and I were an odd couple. I was working-class with a liberal attitude and came from Stepney, whereas she was middle-class, very conservative and hailed from Guildford. Fiona also disliked the East End intensely. I would have preferred our affair to end, but like Dave I always found it extremely difficult ending relationships.

During the height of the summer, Sally was keen to have a Sunday picnic in Hackney's Victoria Park. However, there was a problem: at the last moment due to engine problems I was unable to use my car. Not to disappoint Sally, Dave suggested that we should use his now-lopsided, ancient Reliant three-wheel van to make the trip. A very annoyed Fiona had to sit with me in the back of the van on the hard floor, amongst old oily rags, a few empty beer cans and a breeze block that was kept there to help balance the vehicle.

I had some reservations about Dave's driving. I was well aware that he and Sally had been drinking earlier, but he assured me that he had had only a couple of drinks and would be extra careful on the road. Declining my offer to drive, we set out and within fifteen minutes we had arrived safely at the park.

While Fiona and I sat by the lake, Dave and Sally sprawled themselves out on the grass and promptly went to sleep. According to a now-livid Fiona, our hosts' behaviour was 'highly improper and not the way to treat your guests'.

I pleaded with her, 'You know, one day in the future, you will look back at today and it will make you smile.'

My plea had no affect. Fiona stood up to get a better view of Dave and Sally in the distance who were still fast asleep under a tree. 'Your so-called friends have extremely bad manners,' snapped Fiona. She sat back down on the bench and gave me an ultimatum, 'Stay in the East End with your friends or join me and leave London.' I chose the former.

When Sally's father, who was living in North London, became ill, she felt that she had to go and look after him. Dave just managed to conceal his relief when she explained that her absence might be for an indefinite period.

After Sally's departure, Dave immediately went to her now-abandoned flat to rescue her cat. He soon found it a home with a kind neighbour and the Upsons decided to adopt Captain Pug, Sally's friendly corgi. Pug, over the years, proved to be a marvellous pet, loved by all, with the exception of Mrs Upson's cat the spiteful Littlelee. The cat, whose private domain was the kitchen, regarded the docile Pug as an intruder and was inclined to take a swipe at his snout when he ambled past the open door to the kitchen. Captain Pug may have been docile, but he was an intelligent animal who soon responded to Barbara's order to bark at Littlelee if it lashed out at him.

Now that Sally was out of his life, Dave's drinking became less, but still too much by normal standards. I was glad as were his mother and Barbara that he was drinking less. It proved to us that he had some control over his drinking and maybe, just maybe, he could abstain altogether. He soon began to restrict the many pubs that he frequented to just one or two near Lathem House.

One of his favourites the British Prince, a family pub, had become very popular with the hordes of squatters living nearby. With his affable nature Dave soon became well known and accepted by the new arrivals; he also became a regular at their parties that were held most weekends.

I could not but notice that several of the female squatters were pretty and quite artistic. As a perennial optimist, Dave seized every opportunity to put his threepenny bit in. His efforts were successful resulting in a few brief liaisons. Dave had met forty-year-old Lizzie an amateur artist at one of the squatter parties. She was over six foot tall, chained-smoked, continually coughed and had a husky voice.

I subsequently met Lizzie one Sunday lunchtime at the Prince. Lizzie explained to me that she was a former squatter, but had recently moved out of the overcrowded premises when she was offered a small local flat. Shortly after the landlord called last orders Lizzie invited Dave and me to her *pied-à-terre* for beer and sandwiches. On entering the flat, Dave and I were confronted by a small but fierce-looking mongrel that would not stop barking.

Lizzie hissed, 'Quiet, Monty, quiet!' But her pet ignored her. When Monty continued to bark after being ordered a second time to be quiet, Lizzie grabbed his collar and took him into the tiny kitchen and closed the door. Being banished did not stop him barking and he was heard continually jumping up at the door handle. Monty's aggressive behaviour was the complete opposite to Dave's loveable Captain Pug who never barked at strangers and greeted all and sundry with friendly nudges and a persistent demand to be stroked.

Wapping High Street, March 2000.

'Monty is over protective,' sighed Lizzie.

She went on to say that Monty's previous owner, a heartless squatter, had abandoned his pet when he had moved out of the area. Lizzie looked towards the kitchen door before saying, 'I found little Monty tied up to a drainpipe in a back yard. The poor mite was soaking wet and whimpering, what could I do? I just had to save him.' Monty's incessant barking ended when Lizzie went into the kitchen and gave him a can of dog food.

The cheese sandwiches that Lizzie prepared were a disappointment. The bread was too dry and the cheese somewhat hard. I managed to eat just half of my sandwich. Dave took a small bite before replacing his own sandwich on a plate.

After the beer was poured into none too clean glasses, Lizzie opened up a thick portfolio of her paintings for us to browse through. I was instantly surprised how insipid her work was. Each painting, which measured about 24 inches square, seemed to show the human form constructed out of a medley of circles, squares and triangles and all in pastel shades. It was difficult for me to determine what the paintings were meant to illustrate. I discreetly glanced at Dave who indicated with his eyes that we should make no comment. If Lizzie's bland paintings could be described as modern art I was not impressed at all. I preferred lovely landscapes, seascapes and the wonderful paintings that I had seen in Rome twenty years previously. I remember standing in awe as I gazed at Michelangelo's beautiful *Last Judgement* that adorned the walls and ceiling of the Sistine Chapel.

Perhaps Lizzie thought that Dave and I were interested in learning about modern art because she began to describe the differences between Cubism,

Dadaism and Surrealism. I had not a clue what she was talking about; and I found it difficult to believe that people were willing to pay Lizzie for her paintings that she displayed on the pavement along the Bayswater Road.

After an hour or so spent at Lizzie's flat, I decided to go home. When I stood up to leave, Dave gave me a wink. His wink suggested that he intended to try and seduce Lizzie.

The next evening I met Dave at the Prince. He was standing at the bar. I soon learnt the reason why he chose not to sit at our customary table. Dave explained that not long after I had left Lizzie's flat, he had joined her on the sofa, produced his whisky flask and offered her a tipple. 'I was surprised how much she liked the scotch and within a few minutes we had drained the flask dry.'

'But surely, Dave,' I replied, 'the effects of the whisky and beer must have put a damper on your ardour?'

'It did at first, Alf, but after we drank black coffee and I forced myself to eat that awful cheese sandwich, I was quite sober.'

With tongue in cheek I said, 'And did you succeed in your endeavours?'

'Yes, but only just.' My question caused him to chuckle. Dave lit up a cigarette then said, 'While we were entwined on the sofa, Monty, who was still in the kitchen, began to bark and he kept jumping up at the door handle.'

Expressing empathy I said, 'That racket must have been very distracting for you.'

In between coughing and chuckling he said, 'What happened next was much worse than distracting.' Before continuing, he sipped his whisky, cleared his throat and released a smile, but it was an extended smile that was a familiar sign to me that he was amused by his misfortune. I was amused too because I had somehow guessed what he was about to reveal.

'Monty managed to turn the kitchen door handle, he came bounding out of the kitchen, leapt up on the sofa and nipped and scratched my bottom.'

'Ouch!' I yelped, suddenly remembering my own painful experience of being bitten and scratched by an Alsatian dog when I was a boy.

'I didn't ouch, I shrieked,' my friend said, emphasizing 'shrieked'.

I waited until Dave had taken another sip of whisky before asking him if he was planning to see Lizzie again.

'No fear Alf,' he replied adamantly. 'At least not while Monty is still in the flat; besides, there are plenty of other spare women about.'

Dave soon dallied with another squatter. The French girl was quite petite. Fortunately for my friend, she had an abhorrence of dogs.

I too, had a brief affair with one of the squatters. Emily, who described herself as a 'street busker' claimed that she had been celibate for several years. She was obviously lying because, after our affair was over, I discovered that I had contracted non-specific urethritis. Again I visited the VD clinic at the London Hospital and again I vowed that for the foreseeable future I would curtail my promiscuity.

Although I kept my vow of abstinence for several months, I still socialised with women. When my period of abstinence ended, I took precautions whenever I was intimate. Dave, who was as promiscuous as I was, seemed to be immune from venereal diseases. I could recall only one instance during our thirty-seven years of friendship when he thought he may have had 'crabs', but after being examined by an urologist, no parasites were found.

As time went by, I became less interested in being in the company of the squatters. Dave however retained his interest, mainly because of the variety of women he was meeting. Occasionally I would still accompany Dave to a few of the squatters' Saturday night parties and had some interesting conversations with our hosts, but I usually found myself disagreeing with their often left-wing views. Dave managed to avoid discussing politics with them; he feared that if he expounded his liberal beliefs, he would be a *persona non grata*.

One of the local squatters, Julia Mainwaring, later became the Labour leader of Tower Hamlets Council. Dave believed that she was the squatters' unofficial spokesperson. Sometimes, Julia, a trained teacher, would come into the Prince for a late night drink and sit with us at our table. Friendly, loquacious and unobtrusive, she seemed to have a constantly smiling face, even when she was in a reflective mood.

Julia told me about her family background in a Welsh mining area and how fond she was of her father. 'I wish I was born a man,' she remarked.

Julia's comment intrigued me. 'And why is that?' I asked.

'Well, if I had been born a man, I would have been able to have understood my father and talked to him better.'

The presence of the ever-increasing squatters in their midst was resented by many of the local older residents who saw them as 'bloody parasites'. Other aspersions included 'wasted druggies' and 'scruffy layabouts'.

A resident of Lathem House who was drinking at the Prince was unable to control his asperity. 'All of these effing squatters live rent-free and sponge off the state while we work for low wages to pay for ever-increasing council rents. Why don't the effing squatters bugger off?'

I felt that his assessment was ill judged, although similar views were widely held in the immediate neighbourhood. It was true that some of the squatters were determined to squeeze out as much as they could from the state, but several whom I had met were working as teachers in local schools. They had moved into the empty houses in nearby Bromley Street because they could not find suitable accommodation. Occupying the empty houses that were waiting refurbishment seemed an ideal albeit a temporary solution.

22

The Old Soldier

Dave and I had a conversation with Tom, an elderly local ex-soldier in the Prince. He sat at the next table to ours. It was obvious that he had fallen on hard times. From the cigarette stubs he kept in a small tin box he would extract the tobacco and roll the thinnest of cigarettes. I began to feel uncomfortable and a little guilty as I drank my pint of beer; I had noticed that Tom was taking the tiniest of sips from his half-pint. It seemed as if he was just wetting his lips.

Tom had become so incensed at the sight of the ubiquitous squatters that he confessed to Dave and me, 'If only I was young again, I would steal a machine gun and shoot the lot of them!'

Shortly afterwards, he began to describe how terrible life was in Stepney during the 1920s. He came from a family of eight who lived in 'two cold, top-floor rooms and the bloody roof didn't 'arf leak, it flooded'. He spoke proudly when he explained how his poverty-stricken family always kept their 'noses clean and never begged or stole a penny from anybody'. With a chuckle, he recalled how he and his two brothers played in the streets 'with no shoes on and no arse in our trousers'. When the war came in 1939, the three of them joined the Army and were sent overseas to fight in many campaigns and now at the age of seventy he was always struggling to pay his way.

Dave and I felt privileged to sit and talk to this friendly but embittered man. I wanted to offer him a drink, but I knew he would refuse it on the assumption that we were feeling sorry for him. However, a little later I boldly placed a pint of beer in front of him. Fortunately he did not push the beer aside; instead he said, 'Who is that for?' I explained that I had mistakenly ordered one pint too many and would he not mind accepting it. The trick worked and in one gulp he consumed what was left of his original drink.

Whilst we listened to the old soldier's harrowing description of the poverty in the East End sixty years before, a loud-mouthed effeminate snob on the next table was pontificating to his friends, who all seemed to be nodding in agreement, on the art and merit of Andy Warhol and Jasper Johns. So loud was his voice that it was becoming increasingly difficult to hear our elderly friend who had now become very irritable at having to sit so close to the group. I could see that this fearless old man, despite his age, still had some fight in him and was prepared to have a scrap.

Visibly annoyed, he remarked, 'These poofs think that they own the place; lucky they were not in my regiment, we would have throttled them.'

'Calm down,' said Dave. 'Why not move to another table?'

Ignoring Dave's suggestion he turned around to face his noisy thoughtless neighbour and gave him and his friends a disdainful look like that of a sergeant major inspecting a parade of new recruits. Far from having the desired affect the snob took up the challenge and spoke louder and faster than before.

The old soldier, now exasperated, responded by speaking menacingly and even louder still. 'I wish I had a bloody red-hot poker handy.'

His remark brought an immediate silence from the next table. I suspected that the group were familiar with English history and must have realised what a terrible fate awaited Edward II in the dungeon of Berkeley Castle in 1327 with a similar lethal implement. Perhaps, fearing that the old man to be a latter-day executioner, the snob stood up, looked at us disapprovingly and left the pub followed by his entourage.

Dave often made acquaintances with various odd characters in the pubs that he frequented around Docklands. As usual Dave insisted in introducing them to me. Because on occasion I was reluctant to join in the conversation with his new associates, my friend wrongly equated my taciturnity with shyness. The truth was I thought it was safer not to be so amicable to strangers without knowing a little about their background.

Dave and I were drinking in Dirty Dick's when he commented on my reticence. 'I know it can be difficult for you Alf, but try and make the effort to be more open and friendly. Surely we should all be more trusting towards each other. If we don't talk, listen and argue amongst ourselves how are we going to progress? If we respect each other's point of view, there's nothing to worry about.'

Because of the absence of any antagonism or provocative remarks in his conversation with strangers, coupled with his gentle tactful manner and acute understanding of human nature, Dave always felt assured that he could quickly gain the trust of even the most difficult individual. He would never ignore or belittle anyone who tried to strike up a conversation with him; providing they were not sarcastic, a trait that he despised, he would tolerate them no matter what their age, sex or nationality. This liberalism was natural to him but a concern for me and I would often wonder if a few of the characters whom he had met in the pubs and clubs may have had an ulterior or sinister motive, rather than just wanting to have a friendly conversation over a few drinks.

On reflection, my fears proved groundless. Dave survived intact, quite remarkable considering that he spent forty years drinking on a regular basis in some of the toughest pubs in East London. But Dave did not avoid altercations and violence entirely.

During the mid-1950s he was involved in several fights in Dockland pubs and clubs. A particular savage fight in The Golden Lion resulted in him having a chair smashed across his back. His ongoing fascination with those whom he described as 'society's misfits' continued. As always, I sat back and marvelled at his skill at creating an instant rapport with whoever he came into contact with.

Despite my concerns of the possible motives of some of his acquaintances the majority seemed to be genuine, although several of them seemed to have noticeable emotional or personal problems, but that was to be expected, especially if they came from a poor deprived background.

There was a slight risk socialising with 'society's misfits,' but I was always on my guard against the unexpected. One or two awkward situations did occur over the years but there were no serious incidents. Dave was capable of diffusing any acrimony that arose amongst those in our company. He once acted quickly and decisively and calmed down a wide-eyed fidgety African seaman, a paranoid schizophrenic, who had accused me of trying to poison him by dropping an 'evil substance' into his glass of beer, but on the whole such unpleasant scenes were rare.

I can remember explaining to Dave that I thought that there were few people like him who would have had the patience and tolerance to entertain some of the men and women whom he met in the pubs and clubs. My friend seemed a little embarrassed at my long-overdue praise.

He paused for a few seconds before saying, 'Did it ever enter your mind, Alf, that it's possible I might be just an opportunist?'

My reply to this odd question was an emphatic, 'No, never.'

He further added, 'Do you not think that by my trying to gain the confidence and trust of perhaps vulnerable women, it was in reality a devious method of mine whereby I could in fact be trying to take advantage of them, sexually I mean?'

My answer to his second question, like the first, was a definite, 'No.' I went on to say, 'Dave, I don't think it's in your nature to use such means to obtain sexual favours. If a girl was disturbed or in trouble and sought your advice, your first reaction would be to help her, just like you have done on numerous occasions in the past. You certainly would not want to jump into bed with her. Of course, if she was attractive the thought would probably enter your mind, but your strong code of ethics would always prevail. I am sure of it.'

He listened attentively and said, 'It's just lately, Alf, I have been trying to do a self-analysis of my motives and I can't seem to arrive at satisfactory conclusions.'

Although I never doubted his integrity, I was puzzled at this sudden expression of self-doubt. It was totally out of character. I attempted to reassure my friend by mentioning incidents over the years where his gentlemanly behaviour towards women was exemplary. These recollections of the past seemed to help and bring him out of this unusual mood. I concluded by asking him to recall an episode in the not-too-distant past where he could have taken advantage of two girls whom we had met at the Prospect of Whitby. He smiled, but there was a look of uncertainty on his face.

We left the pub and went our separate ways. I needed to try and analyse what Dave had just said. I took my usual route to Poplar, walking briskly through Narrow Street. As expected, the area was peaceful and welcoming. The familiar and reassuring sight of the solitary old lady with the arthritic hip came into view. She was clutching her bottle of stout and swaying from side to side as she slowly walked home from the pub. Whenever I found myself walking behind her at night, I would cross the street in order to overtake her, fearing that my approaching footsteps might cause her to become anxious.

I felt slightly uneasy over what Dave had told me earlier. It was unusual for him to be confused and unsure. Usually, he was extremely positive about his motives. Hopefully, my mentioning to him about a recent episode at the Prospect of Whitby, when he brought a little happiness into the lives of two lonely girls, would help him discard those negative doubts. The girls, both in their early twenties, would regularly be seen standing together drinking quietly at the bar. They always seemed to be excluded from the happy atmosphere that surrounded them. Perhaps because they were neither good-looking nor vivacious they remained unnoticed by the single men who were after fairer game. It seemed obvious to me that they would have liked to have been invited to join in the fun and singing that was so enjoyable, but it never happened. At closing time the girls would leave. The following Saturday they would return to the Prospect and once more spend all evening by themselves. As the evening progressed, their conversation would become less and less until the bell for last orders would ring and they would then go home.

This scenario was repeated for several weeks until Dave suggested that we should try and 'cheer them up'. The two girls did not seem to object when we approached them at the bar and after a little coaxing they accepted our offer of a drink. The younger of the two, and the most timid, seemed a little uncomfortable with us at first, but Dave soon made her feel totally at ease.

As he placed the drinks in front of the girls he made use of his age-old joke. 'I hope you do realise, that was the last of my mum's pension money.'

His funny remark caused the girls to burst out laughing. Dave was at his most exuberant, very witty and a little teasing. After a few more drinks he managed to manoeuvre the girls away from the bar towards a circle of happy singers. A gap opened in their ranks and he politely eased the girls into its centre. The group accepted the encroachment with good humour and the two girls were instantly swallowed up by the revelry. His mission accomplished we retreated to a position on the stairs where we could obtain a better view of the girls who, much to our delight, were now thoroughly enjoying themselves.

It was so typical of Dave's kind nature to be concerned if he had noticed somebody who was downcast, lonely or unwell. I had witnessed his incredible kindness many times over the years. A typical example was the time during the harsh winter of 1962 when he came across an old Jewish 'bubbeh' (Yiddish for grandmother) stranded in a doorway at Brick Lane. Instinctively, he could not ignore her cries for help and immediately asked her what was wrong.

She replied pitifully, 'It's my arthritis, I can't walk, please help me.' Without another word being said, Dave promptly picked her up and gently carried her down Old Montague Street to her home.

On another occasion when, despite my reservations, he insisted that we take an aggressive drunk who had been beaten up to the casualty department at the London Hospital. Despite receiving several kicks by the ungrateful drunk, we persevered and eventually managed to have him examined by a doctor.

H. L. Menken, the famous American writer and critic, also known as 'the Sage of Baltimore' once wrote, 'A large part of altruism, even when it is perfectly honest, is grounded upon the fact that it is uncomfortable to have unhappy people about one.' Menken's observation may have been limited to a few of his altruistic acquaintances. Had he widened his view, no doubt he would have soon discovered that there were many altruistic people like David Upson who not for one moment ever felt uncomfortable coming into contact with unhappy people.

Dave was the most unselfish and modest man that I had ever known; he was also incapable of bearing a grudge. Dave and I were once drinking in the British Prince. As he gazed around the saloon bar he discreetly pointed to at least six people who owed him various amounts of money.

'Don't you think that you should remind them about their loans?' I suggested. 'After all, you work long hours for your wages.'

'I just can't be bothered,' he replied nonchalantly. 'If they want to repay me that's fine, but if they don't it's not important.'

'But it is important,' I emphasised. 'They must keep their promise and pay you.'

He thought for a moment and said, 'Look, Alf, they can cheat me once, maybe twice, but that's it, no more.'

Over the years Dave continued to lend small amounts of his hard-earned money to so-called friends and acquaintances. In the majority of cases he was rarely repaid.

Dave constantly amazed me. He felt no bitterness when his expensive motorbike was stolen or when vandals during the night overturned his new Reliant van outside his home. I was absolutely furious. How could anybody do that to him?

Responding to my anger, his comment was predictable. 'Don't get annoyed, Alf, it's really not worth it; they obviously had too much to drink, saw the van parked there and decided to have a bit of fun. It won't happen again.'

Throughout his long stay in the East End many people had benefited by knowing David Upson. Certainly I did and I like to think that he gained something from our long friendship. I am sure that he was aware that he had a reputation for always being a giver and never a taker, but that was the way he was and always had been and it was unlikely that he would ever change. It may have been a little impertinent of me to have asked him why he was sometimes prepared to do kind favours often for complete strangers knowing full well that they might be taking advantage of his generosity. Possibly his altruism may have had something to do with his early ingrained, but now-neglected Christian faith.

'There but for the grace of God go I,' was one of his favourite sayings.

23

'Mustard Gas, Bloody Mustard Gas'

I remember vividly one evening in the late 1960s when Dave and I were late for an appointment with two Canadian girls whom we had recently met. The arrangement was that we were to meet them at 8 p.m. at the Town of Ramsgate tavern in Wapping and then visit a drag-artist pub on the Isle of Dogs, but due to unforeseen problems at the Hackney garment factory that I managed and where Dave worked as a stock cutter, we were delayed and only had a few minutes to wash and shave.

During the short time it took me to lock up the factory and set the alarm, Dave, impatient for a drink and with parched lips, dashed across the street to the Sutton Arms opposite the factory and gulped down a quick half. As we drove down Stepney's Cannon Street Road on Dave's powerful motorbike combination, he suddenly braked sharply under the railway bridge and stopped. A figure of a man was lying on the edge of the pavement with his legs in the road.

We got off of the bike and went over to him. He seemed to be about seventy years of age, possibly a vagrant. He looked a sad sight with a thin face and watery blue eyes. He was having trouble breathing.

'Are you feeling unwell?' asked Dave.

He responded by clutching his chest and muttering, 'Mustard gas, bloody mustard gas.' When I offered to phone for an ambulance, he replied in a weak voice. 'No sir, just gimme a minute, will yer.' I asked him if he was staying at the Salvation Army hostel in Whitechapel.

'No, the hostel in Limehouse,' he replied still clutching his chest.

'Can we help you to stand up?' said Dave.

'No, just put me against the wall will yer?' Dave and I lifted him up and sat him against the wall under the bridge. He weighed no more than seven or eight stone.

'Look,' said Dave, 'why not sit in the sidecar and we will take you home?'

Again he refused the offer of help. 'Be on yer way lads, God bless yer.' We stayed with him for a few more minutes vainly trying to persuade him to let us take him Limehouse, but he was adamant that he wanted to stay there for a while.

When his breathing became less laborious we got back on to the motorbike. I glanced back at him as we pulled away; he forced a smile and slowly saluted us.

As we were going into the Town of Ramsgate, I asked Dave if he had ever heard of mustard gas.

'Yes,' he said. 'Both the Allies and the Germans used it with great effect during the First World War.'

Still concerned about the old fellow we left the pub with the girls without having a drink and drove straight back to the railway bridge to see if he had recovered. Thankfully he had gone.

This incident brought back memories of an accident that Dave and I witnessed a few years earlier. Almost at the same spot, an elderly man with a walking stick had stepped into the road without looking and was struck and knocked back onto the pavement by a passing car. The driver stopped his car some distance ahead and accompanied by his woman passenger he walked back to the victim who was sitting on the kerb and rubbing his head. On seeing that the man was not seriously injured and without speaking to him, the couple turned around and began to walk back to their car. As they did so, they noticed Dave and me nearby. The driver asked us if we had witnessed the accident.

When we said yes, the woman spoke coldly, 'You do agree that it was not our fault.'

Dave did not answer her. He had crouched in front of the old man and was applying his handkerchief to the man's right temple that had a small trickle of blood. I answered this heartless woman, agreeing with her that it was not the driver's fault. Dave looked up and asked the couple if they had a plaster. The driver walked back to the car presumably to get the plaster, but to my surprise he just sat in the car and remained there.

Still showing no concern for the victim, the woman asked Dave if we would do her 'a favour'.

Dave by now had helped the slightly confused old man to stand up. 'What kind of favour?' he demanded.

'Well, it's just that we are in a hurry.'

Dave did not answer her.

The women quickly added, 'Would you mind if we leave the old chap with you? He does not seem to be hurt, does he?'

I could see that my friend had suddenly become impatient with the woman's callousness. He suggested to her that we should call an ambulance or take him to the hospital ourselves and have him checked out.

On hearing the word hospital the old man grunted. ''Ospital? I am not going to 'ospital.'

I tried to reassure him that he would not be detained; the casualty staff would only clean the cut, but he refused to listen.

Satisfied that he could stand up unaided, Dave turned to the woman whom I suspected had something to hide. 'You know that if somebody is injured in a road accident, it's normal practice to call the police.'

'Please don't call the police,' pleaded the woman.

'And why not?' replied Dave. 'You don't have anything to worry about. The accident was not your fault.'

The woman hesitated before she answered. 'You see, my boyfriend, the driver, has lost his licence recently and is not supposed to be driving. If the police are called, it could mean he might be sent to prison.'

Dave adopted a polite but authoritative tone. 'I suggest that you go and ask the driver to come back here.'

The woman sighed as if her problems were only just beginning. As she walked slowly towards the car she suddenly started to run. The passenger door was already open; in her haste to get into the car, without realising it she had dropped her purse into the gutter. The car at great speed pulled away and headed towards the not too distant highway.

I picked up the purse. Inside were keys, lipstick and fifteen pounds in cash. Dave took the money out and placed the purse with its contents back into the gutter. I knew exactly what was on his mind.

The old man was still refusing to go to the hospital, insisting that he felt 'all right'. As he attempted to walk away I managed to distract him while Dave placed the fifteen pounds in the pocket of his faded and well-worn overcoat. Later that evening, Dave and I sat in the pub and discussed the incident, both wishing we could have seen the surprised look on the old man's face when he discovered the money.

Over the years, Dave had found himself in all sorts of unexpected situations with strangers on the streets of the East End. If he saw somebody who was in danger and needed help, in most cases he would go to their assistance, especially in the early days, but once he reached middle age he thought twice about involving himself in 'dodgy' situations.

One little episode that he related to me with amusement happened in 1954 soon after he had arrived in London. He had left a pub in Cable Street at closing time and was walking back to the Seamen's Hostel in nearby Dock Street when he saw a man and a woman exchanging blows outside a house. When the woman fell to the pavement the man, apparently her husband, began to pull her along the ground by her hair. Dave immediately intervened and pushed the man aside. As he did so, the wife stood up and, to his astonishment, the ungrateful woman punched him on the nose. More blows were aimed at his body.

The assault continued. The husband joined the fray and attacked him too. Fortunately for Dave there was a dustbin close by. He managed to grab the lid and used it as a shield to protect himself; but there was more to come for my friend. The couple's two small dogs run out from their house and snapped at his ankles. He broke free from the mêlée and ran across the road minus his hat. As he walked away he glanced back. To his amazement the couple had their hands on each other's throats and were wrestling on the pavement while the two dogs were having a tug of war with his hat. (He later recovered his hat.)

In 1958 Dave was involved in another incident in Cable Street that always baffled him. After drinking in several pubs in the area, he woke up the next morning in the arms of an attractive blonde girl in the back of a large van. He had no idea who she was, or how he came to be there. When he clambered out of the van, the girl jumped into the driving seat and sped off. Checking his pockets he discovered that his wallet was missing.

These tales, and there were others too, were told to me without the slightest hint of bitterness or regret. His ability to laugh at his own misfortune was remarkable.

My friend's concern for others was not only restricted to people in distress. Dave and I boarded the Northern Line tube at Euston to travel up to Brent Cross for a house party. There were few passengers in the compartment and by the time we reached Chalk Farm they had all disembarked except for an elderly railway man sitting directly opposite us. He had a melancholy look about him, like that of a pallbearer. He sat motionless, robot-like, not blinking an eyelid. I sensed that Dave had decided he would try and bring a smile to his sad, vacuous face. Dave's jokes were always original and with his habit of sometimes speaking loudly in confined spaces he knew that the elderly man would hear his every word, but Dave's efforts were a wasted exercise. The railway man did not seem to be amused.

When the train stopped at Golders Green, an area with a large residential Jewish population, Dave looked over his shoulder at the people walking along the platform and said loudly, 'Look at me, the only Arab in Golders Green'. On hearing Dave's remark the old railway man could no longer keep a straight face; he let out a tumultuous laugh and he continued laughing to himself even after we got out at Brent Cross, the next stop. Dave and I both felt satisfied.

We did not feel quite so good a couple of months later. It was a November evening; we were returning to the East End by tube after visiting The Dove, a historical pub on the banks of the Thames at Hammersmith. Sitting facing us were an elderly couple with poppies in their lapels. The husband who smelled of whisky was vastly overweight and his neck was as wide as his extremely red, bald head; he seemed to have to stop for breath after every sentence. I soon became aware that by the way he was focusing his eyes menacingly at Dave, he clearly did not approve of my friend who was the only non-European in the carriage.

Although the old man whispered to his embarrassed wife, he knew Dave and I could hear every word. 'Foreigners, I can't stand 'em; never could and never will.' He took a deep breath. 'The country is being overrun by 'em.' He paused for a moment to take another breath. 'I will never vote for Labour again. Mosley was right.'

His wife, who must have heard his ranting a hundred times before, ordered him to, 'Shut up for gawd sake.'

Ignoring her, he took several deep breaths before saying, 'If I were Prime Minister, the darkies would be deported.' Again his wife interrupted him, but he brushed her aside and spoke vehemently. 'It was the bloody foreigners who brought the TB with 'em and gawd knows what else.'

Dave had remained impassive throughout, but I suspected that he may have been hurt by the bigot's deliberately offensive remarks.

I said to Dave, 'Listen, let's get off at the next stop and jump into the next carriage.'

He flatly refused my suggestion and remarked, quite loudly, 'You have to understand, Alf, he is an old-aged pensioner; he probably has had a hard life, perhaps fought in the war and now finds himself living on a meagre state pension. In a way, I can understand how he feels and if I do get annoyed with him, in his condition, he could burst a blood vessel and then what?'

Dave took out a packet of cigarettes, before realising that it was a non-smoking carriage. He quickly put the cigarettes back in his pocket and said to me, 'You know, Alf, there is a lot of truth in that old saying, 'Where ignorance is bliss, it's folly to be wise'.'

I don't think the old man had heard Dave's remarks as his angry wife was telling him to move towards the exit. When the couple left the train at Charing Cross and just as the sliding doors closed she could be seen shaking her finger at his face. Ignoring her, he turned around, glared at us through the window and shook his fist provocatively. Although somewhat humiliated, Dave would soon forget the whole affair. He had been on the receiving end of such racist remarks and innuendoes before and knew how to cope with them. No matter how provoked, Dave would never despise or hate the provoker. I thought to myself what a rare character Dave was. If the bigot had suddenly collapsed while delivering his abuse, and judging by his appearance it was a strong possibility, Dave would have been the first to have gone to his aid.

Shortly after this episode, the two young girls whom we had befriended at the Prospect went on holiday to Spain. Within days of their arrival, the youngest was tragically killed when a bus knocked her down as she tried to cross a busy road.

I asked Dave, 'Why is it that a nice young girl's life can be ended in a second?'

He replied immediately, 'Because life is cruel and unpredictable.'

There was more tragic news. Sixty-seven year old Alf Cohen, whom Dave and I had known for many years, was beaten to death. Alf Cohen and his slightly older brother Mick were the proprietors of 'The Hole in the Wall' kiosk in Stepney's Cannon Street Road. The kiosk really was a hole in the wall; it was filled to the ceiling with boxes of fruit, cigarettes, soft drinks and condoms and no doubt mice too. There was no standing room inside the kiosk, so the brothers had to stand at the door to serve customers.

The business was established in the mid-1930s and was open until 4am, seven days a week, 365 days a year. Mick worked the day shift and Alf the night shift. Regular customers included taxi drivers, night workers and patrolling policemen. The Cohens also had a lucrative trade selling condoms to local prostitutes.

Throughout the summer months, Mick could be seen sitting outside the kiosk with folded arms and guarding the fruit that was displayed on a table. There was the occasional theft, mainly from vagrants and groups of school children and I once witnessed an outraged Mick throw a mouldy orange at a scruffy character who was attempting to steal bananas.

It was during the late spring of 1974, I had just bought a packet of three from Alf who seemed agitated. As I was about to leave, he gripped my arm and pleaded with me to, 'hang around for a few minutes.'

A drunken and fractious Somalian was refusing to pay for cigarettes. When the Somalian eventually paid for his cigarettes and staggered away I questioned Alf why he did not employ an assistant to work with him on the night shift. He shrugged his shoulders before remarking, 'Usually I can look after myself.'

I thought his answer odd. He was only about five foot four inches tall and looked unfit; if he were to be attacked, it was unlikely that he would be able to defend himself. Alf was foolish; he should have realised how dangerous the area had become, especially during nightime. A few years earlier, his brother Mick had been attacked and robbed outside the kiosk in broad daylight. He never fully recovered from the beating; twelve months later he was dead.

At 4am on Friday, 27 September 1974, two men brutally assaulted Alf as he was about to lock up the kiosk; he died on the pavement. His assailants grabbed packets of cigarettes and a few pounds from the till and fled. Within days, David MacLean, twenty-five and Andrew Barbour, twenty-two, were arrested and charged with Alf's murder. They were later put on trial, found guilty and received long prison sentences.

When the police searched the cramped kiosk, they discovered a huge amount of cash hidden in cardboard boxes. Many of the wads of banknotes, including old white five-pound notes, were in a poor condition having been badly affected by mildew. It took a team of police officers seven hours to count the money; the final total was a staggering £110,000. Later, the police did a routine inspection of bachelor Alf's sparse council flat in nearby Christian Street. Inside the larder, the shocked officers found just a small tin of baked beans.

Soon after the killing Dave and I sat drinking in the Mackworth Arms, the Irish pub just a few yards from the kiosk. We were saddened, having just heard the terrible news of Alf's death. We both regarded Alf as a kind and inoffensive man who would not have hesitated to give his faithful customers credit. Occasionally Dave himself in the past had made use of this concession. Like my friend I too was a regular customer, having been so since my schooldays in the 1950s.

An Irish acquaintance was sitting with Dave and me at our table in the Mackworth Arms. The three of us began to discuss why Alf should have hoarded a fortune inside the kiosk.

'Perhaps he didn't trust banks,' suggested the Irishman.

Another Irishman, sitting at the next table, overheard his remark. He leant towards us and cruelly said, 'No way, Michael, the old boy was a miser.' He then leant even closer and laughed when he spoke, 'He will be the richest man in the cemetery.'

'Maybe it was tax avoidance,' said Dave soberly.

I had no opinion why Alf felt the need to hide money, but it did seem tragic to me that a harmless little man had spent seven nights a week for the previous forty years standing at his kiosk doorway, in all weathers, and then to suffer a barbaric death. The kiosk remains closed to this day.

In the spring of 1973 I opened a small clothing factory in Shoreditch. Trading as Minuet Fashions I remained in business until June 1979. (An extended chapter of my six years as a garment manufacturer is included in my book *Watch Your Fingers*.)

After I closed my business I was in no hurry to work full time. For the foreseeable future, I was quite content to continue as a freelance cutter. I also had some business cards printed that advertised my services as a cutter and marker-maker.

Because Dave was unemployed, it was an ideal opportunity to see more of my best friend. Each morning, I would happily accompany Dave as he knocked on clothing factory doors enquiring about vacancies. It would also be an opportunity for me to leave my business cards with factory owners. In a way, it was a nostalgic experience wandering the streets with Dave. They were the same streets that we leisurely strolled down twenty years before when we first became friends during that wonderful warm summer of 1959.

Starting early, Dave and I would head for the Aldgate East and Whitechapel area where several clothing factories were located. Some factory proprietors were considerate; they took Dave's 'phone number, assuring him that if a vacancy became available they would notify him. Other proprietors thought that my friend had insufficient cutting and marker-making experience. A few were downright rude and hastily slammed their doors in our faces.

One sympathetic Shoreditch coat manufacturer did offer Dave a job, but there was a stipulation. 'You must assist the other cutters to unload the cloth from the van.'

When Dave and I saw the enormous rolls of fabric under the cutting table we frowned. Dave, who was in mild but constant pain from a hernia that was probably caused by carrying fabric in the past, wisely refused the offer.

At lunchtime a quick half in a Whitechapel pub was usually called for before resuming our search for work. Whilst in the area we also visited the Star Agency. Just prior to going inside my friend remarked, 'It's just a waste of time Alf; they never have any decent jobs on offer.' Our visit, as he predicted, proved fruitless; the agency had no current vacancies for stock cutters.

During a trek around Hackney, Dave managed to secure a two-week engagement as a framer at a small handbag factory. The firm's regular framer was on holiday. Derisory as the wages were, my friend never complained.

24

The Post Office Railway

Fortunately, Dave was soon to be re-employed. Our mutual friend Ronny Radlet came to his aid. Ron, a former dress cutter, hated the clothing trade. In 1975 he had finally abandoned cutting and joined the Post Office Railway or POR as it was known.

The POR operated small driverless trains that carried trolleys full of sacks of mail on an underground network that called at seven stations between Paddington and Whitechapel. Throughout the day and most of the night, the trains would arrive every few minutes at the stations along the route.

When Ron heard that Dave was unemployed, he arranged to meet him at the Prospect of Whitby. In the past, Ron had often suggested to Dave and I that we should give up garment cutting and join the POR. Although Dave and I had never seriously considered leaving the trade, we did realise that there were fewer stock cutting vacancies becoming available; and those that were available the wages offered were usually inadequate. Also, more and more East End clothing manufactures were going bankrupt and others were outsourcing their production to factories abroad where costs were lower.

At the Prospect of Whitby, Ron, Dave and I sat outside on the riverside terrace where Ron confirmed that there were several vacancies at the POR. He suggested that not only Dave but I too should apply for a position.

'If you do,' said Ron 'I am sure that you both will be accepted.'

Ron enthusiastically explained the benefits of becoming railwaymen. 'We get an excellent salary and plenty of overtime; also there is sick pay, generous holidays, subsidised canteen; even your overalls and steel-cap boots are provided free and there is a nice pension too when you retire.'

The more Ron effused, the more interested Dave became, but I began to have reservations, especially when Ron informed us that as railwaymen we, 'Must be prepared to work late and night shifts.' Having to work through the night did not appeal to me at all, neither did it appeal to Ron, but Ron had a remedy. Because of the extra financial allowance you received for the late and night shift, he usually managed to swap his night duty with a railwayman from the early shift that paid a lower rate.

'And why the necessity to wear steel-cap boots?' I asked my friend. He replied by demonstrating with his hands, how, before you pulled the steel trolleys off the trains onto the platform, you first had to bend down and release a catch that secured a heavy twelve inch high steel plate that extended along the base of the carriage. This plate had a dual purpose: it acted as a barrier preventing the train from toppling off the moving train and it became a ramp that enabled you to pull and slide the trolley off the train and onto the platform. Ron further explained that there was always the possibility that without careful handling when you bent down to release the catch, the plate could crash down onto your toes and cause an injury, hence the steel-cap boots. Ron admitted that the work could be very physical and occasionally dangerous; only a few weeks before a railwayman had been killed when he was struck by one of the trains.

Besides working on the platform, there was another duty. Railwaymen had to work at a conveyer belt that continually carried sacks of mail. Ron empathised that at the belt, 'You have to work at a fast rate to remove the sacks that are then thrown into appropriate trolleys.'

It seemed to me that the term 'railwayman' was a misnomer; Dave and I would not be railwaymen but railway labourers.

As I listened to Ron expound the merits of becoming railwaymen, I became concerned. Dave was not exceptionally strong; although he had carried hundreds of often heavy rolls of fabric when he worked in the clothing trade, his untreated hernia was becoming more and more painful. It seemed to me that my best friend was making a mistake by considering joining the railway. I immediately reminded him that strenuous humping would not only aggravate his hernia, but might cause complications and irreparable damage.

His reply disappointed me. 'Then I will just have to wear a hernia brace.'

Ron seemed satisfied that he had persuaded Dave to give up stock cutting. He also thought that Dave was quite capable of overcoming the manual side of the job.

Turning his attention to me, Ron remarked, 'Be realistic Alf; the smutter trade is dying, get out while you can.'

I responded by saying, 'I honestly cannot envisage myself working on the railway, but I am quite willing to give it a try, for a week or two.'

The next day, Ron went ahead and arranged interviews for an enthusiastic Dave and a somewhat hesitant me with a POR recruitment officer.

At the Post Office Centre at Farringdon, Dave and I passed a written English test and completed a questionnaire that included questions on our medical history.

The recruitment officer had a reservation about Dave's application. He told my friend, 'Because of your hernia you may not be able to pull the heavy trolleys off the train.'

Dave sighed disappointedly, but he quickly explained to the officer that in the past his hernia had never inhibited his ability to carry large rolls of fabric on his shoulders and up flights of stairs. As Dave spoke, I could recall us recently frowning at the sight of the heavy rolls of fabric under the cutting table at the Shoreditch coat factory.

After the recruitment officer informed us that we would be hearing from him by letter, Dave and I left the centre. Sitting in a nearby pub, Dave was noticeably despondent. He was convinced that I would be accepted as a railwayman but not him.

'Because of my wretched hernia,' he remarked sorrowfully.

I assured him that if his application was rejected and mine was accepted, I would prefer to remain a stock cutter.

He replied almost before I had finished the sentence. 'You will do no such thing, Alf.'

In an attempt to rid Dave of his despondence I reminded him that we were to meet two women later that evening at the Prospect of Whitby. A further inducement was a large whisky and a toasted cheese sandwich that I placed in front of him. My reminder of our date caused him to perk up, but his perkiness soon disappeared along with his appetite. He left the sandwich half-consumed. Having already scoffed my sandwich and being constantly hungry, I quickly devoured my friend's leftovers.

Dave stubbed out his cigarette and spoke slowly. 'Alf, I really must stop cutting and leave the trade. I did not mention to you in the past but my eyes are beginning to fail. Even though I wear glasses at work, I have had one or two near-accidents, and when I have been drinking the night before, my vision becomes so blurred I can't always cut accurately on a straight line.'

Dave's revelation concerned me. I had no idea that he was having problems with his eyesight. He had obviously made the right decision to give up stock cutting. Using a powerful cloth cutting machine with insufficient eyesight was potentially dangerous; he could be quite easily cut or even lose a finger. Even I, who had perfect vision, had cut my fingers on numerous occasions over the years.

We left the pub and made our way back to the East End. The next morning, I stopped by at Dave's flat at Lathem House and suggested to him that as it was unlikely that we would be working on the railway, we should visit Stepney Labour Exchange at Settle Street and see what vacancies were on offer.

Dave preferred to take the bus rather than walk to the Labour Exchange. As we sat on the bus, my friend predicted that the majority of jobs advertised at the Labour Exchange, 'Would probably be an assortment of low-paid mundane positions like warehousemen, packers and van drivers.' 'If only I could find a job on a Thames dredger.'

At the Exchange, the jobs advertised on the boards were, as Dave thought, low-paid and mundane, but there was one interesting vacancy that he spotted. It was for a bench-worker at a Hackney handbag factory. A clerk 'phoned the handbag manufacturer to see if the position was still available. Unfortunately,

David Upson in the signal box at Mount Pleasant Post Office Railway, *c.* 1986.

for Dave, the handbag manufacturer claimed that only the day before he had engaged a skilled bench-worker and had forgotten to notify the Labour Exchange to remove the vacancy.

Forcing a smile, Dave said, 'Just look at me, Alf, I am fifty-two and have a hernia, a perforated liver and now my eyesight is fading. Maybe the scrapheap is beckoning to me.'

'Then we will land on the scrapheap together,' I joked.

My joke caused him to laugh profusely. He slapped me on the back and said, 'Enough for the moment, Alf, let's go to Limehouse, have a quick half and plan our next move.'

Dave and I took the bus to Limehouse where a quick half in Charlie Brown's became a two-hour drinking session. While we drank, flirted and teased Mavis and Jessie, who were former prostitutes, our next move had already been decided for us, much to Dave's surprise and jubilation. We both received letters from the POR recruitment officer offering us immediate employment as trainee railwaymen.

A few days later, Dave and a slightly cautious Alf reported for work at the POR station at Mount Pleasant in north London. During that first introductory week, Dave and I did not partake in any duties whatsoever. Each day, we were sent to a different railway station to become familiar with the surroundings and be 'shown the ropes'.

From Whitechapel Station to Paddington Station or any of the five other stations along the six mile network, the physical work was always the same:

railwaymen would be pulling off the trolleys from the little driverless trains or standing at the conveyer belt sorting out the sacks of mail.

At each station we were introduced to the manager who was based in the operational cabin on the platform. These cabins reminded me of a miniature railway signal box. Standing in front of the switch-frame with its numerous levers, switches and green and red lights, a railwayman would shunt the trains in and out of the station. Operating the switch-frame required absolute concentration. The manager at Mount Pleasant Station attempted to explain to Dave and me the intricacies of the switch-frame, but I was totally baffled, unlike Dave who seemed to be able to grasp all what was being explained. In due course my friend would become a capable switchman.

When the introductory week was over, I was assigned to the POR station at King Edward Buildings (KEB) at Giltspur Street, quite near to the Old Bailey and Dave was sent to work at the Mount Pleasant Station in Clerkenwell.

It was my first morning at the KEB station. Feeling a little apprehensive, I stepped inside the platform cabin at 8am and signed in. My steel-capped boots were on and I was ready to start work, but to my surprise it was not to be. A railwayman whispered in my ear, 'Slip away for an hour and go and have some breakfast.'

His instruction confused me. I had arrived on time and had expected to begin work immediately; instead I was told to slip away and have breakfast. I did not need a breakfast. I had already had breakfast earlier at my home. Still confused, I reluctantly followed a couple of railwaymen to the subsidised canteen that was located on one of the upper floors. The canteen was crowded with postal staff. While my two workmates tucked into eggs, bacon and sausages, I drank coffee.

Sitting at the table, I began to feel extremely guilty. I had not done a single minute of work and here was I having an hour-long breakfast break. There was obviously something drastically wrong with the system here at the KEB. For the previous twenty-five years working as a garment cutter in East End clothing factories I had to toil away for two hours every morning before being allowed a timed ten-minute teabreak.

When my breakfast period was over, I returned to the platform in the depths of Giltspur Street and began to unload the heavy trolleys from the endless stream of incoming trains. After an hour or so of strenuous humping a railwayman came over to me and said, 'I am your relief, buzz off for an hour.' Again I did what I was told.

In a nearby 'rest room' I sat amongst other resting railwaymen who were watching television. When my rest period was over, a senior railwayman sent me to work on the conveyer belt where time passed very quickly. About an hour later the same railwayman who earlier had instructed me to slip away for breakfast arrived at the conveyer belt. His latest order did not surprise me at all. 'Take an hour lunch break.'

In the canteen I bought a hot cooked meal and sat next to Bill, an overweight switchman. I had met him briefly during my introductory week. With his cropped fair hair and square head, he looked Prussian. Bill had a slightly menacing appearance, but there was nothing menacing about him. He was a softly-spoken, gentle Cockney who, like David Upson, adored American country and western music. Bill explained that for many years he had been collecting records of his favourite singers from America's southern states and, later that year, he would be holidaying in Nashville, Tennessee where he planned to visit the 'Old Opry'.

'Do you wear a Stetson?' I jokingly remarked.

Rather than give him the impression that I was a snob, I declined to mention my love of Italian opera.

As Bill and I chatted, we were interrupted by an elderly Jewish postal worker who attempted to sell us some ballpoint pens. When he failed to persuade us to make a purchase he moved on to the next table.

'Greedy Jew,' muttered a railwayman sitting opposite me.

'Bloody Shylock,' growled his companion.

I thought that their anti-Semitic remarks were offensive.

Bill spoke too. 'Unlike you or me Alf, that Jewish postman is not satisfied with just one wage packet, he wants two.'

I refrained from stating my opinion that would have been at variance with the comments already expressed. Being a perennial believer that if an opportunity arose to make a little extra money, providing that it was within the law, why not seize it? Although it was unlikely that the Royal Mail's rules and regulations would permit one of their employees to conduct a little business venture on their premises.

The second half of my shift was much the same as the morning period. I would work for an hour either on the platform or at the conveyer belt before being told to take the inevitable hourly rest break.

That evening, as arranged I met David Upson at Dirty Dick's pub in Bishopsgate. Dave agreed with me that being a railwayman was physically more demanding than garment cutting. But he admitted that during the day he had only 'humped' for approximately four hours; the remaining four hours of the shift had been spent resting. He did not seem that surprised when I explained that I too had only worked a similar amount of hours.

Sitting upright on bar stool, he remarked, 'Maybe, that's why we are given so many breaks – we need the rest period to rejuvenate our muscles.' To emphasise his point, he placed his hands on his hips and slowly moved his body sideways in an attempt to loosen up any stiffness.

I did not agree with Dave's analysis. I was certain that the long rest periods were not necessary concessions to rejuvenate ourselves, but some kind of unofficial practice that the management had condoned.

I would be on the late shift during my second week at the KEB. I would supposedly work from 2 p.m. until 10 p.m. From 6 p.m. onwards we would be paid an extra rate. The work pattern on the late shift was similar to the early shift; you worked an hour on the platform or the conveyer belt before being told by your relief to, 'Slip away for an hour.' Sometimes these breaks were extended to nearly two hours.

During the late afternoon, an inebriated railwayman informed me that rather than stay until 10 p.m. I could 'slip away at 9 p.m.'. I did what I was told. 'Slipping away' seemed to be the most important orders of the day. I soon learnt that these orders were religiously observed.

Whilst on my late shift I was offered overtime. Instead of finishing at 9 p.m. I could stay and work throughout the night. Apparently, if a railwayman on the night shift was unable to report for duty because of illness, his shift would be normally offered to a railwayman on the late shift. I accepted the overtime that included a lucrative night allowance. As expected, half of my night shift was spent humping on the platform and the conveyer belt. The remainder of my time was taken up by visits to the canteen or the rest room. Unable and sleep and anxious not to disturb sleeping railwaymen, I quietly sat down on one of the comfortable chairs and began to doze.

My third week at the KEB was easier than the previous two weeks. I was on the night shift, but there did not seem to be much work for me to do. In the rest room it was difficult to sleep amidst several snoring railwaymen so I went into the cabin and sat in a corner and watched with interest the switchman at work. Eventually, I was sent out onto the platform, but fewer and fewer trains were arriving. Throughout that night and the remaining four nights I rarely humped for more than two hours, yet I was being paid for eight hours' work.

In due course I became involved in a conversation with some letter-sorting staff in the canteen and learned about their working conditions and salary. It seems that their earnings were slightly less than what a railwayman received; they also worked eight-hour shifts that occasionally included nights. As there were no extended rest breaks for the sorters, I thought it wise not to divulge too much about the railwaymen's daily work routine. Being an ex-factory manager and later a company director, I was able to see that the POR was poorly organised and riddled with unofficial four hour daily breaks that should never have been tolerated. Because this improbity was an accepted practice at KEB and at Mount Pleasant too, as confirmed by David Upson who was based there, there was every reason to suspect that the same unofficial practices were taking place at the other five POR stations.

Bill had explained to me that there were approximately 200 workers employed at the railway. Without question two thirds of that total could easily have operated the network. A typical example of how the system was abused: four railwaymen worked as a team while two of them were based on the platform or on the conveyer belt; the other two were 'resting '. It was often the case that during this rest period one of the railwaymen would leave the station and go home. He would not have been missed. An ideal situation would have been to designate a team of three and not four railwaymen to work a shift. This three-man team could quite easily complete their shift without the unofficial and extended breaks.

As the weeks went by, I became increasingly disillusioned being a railwayman and having to participate in what I perceived to be a dishonest work practice. My disillusionment eventually changed to a loathing. I loathed humping the sacks of mail off the conveyer belt and, much worse, having to unload the trains and work alongside half-drunken railwaymen on the edge of the platform, an experience that could be highly dangerous.

It was amazing for me to discover how much drinking occurred amongst the staff. Many resting railwaymen would venture outside the KEB station and visit the pubs in Giltspur Street. Returning in an inebriated state they occasionally became involved in arguments and scuffles with fellow railwaymen, especially when it came to the allocating of valuable overtime. Resentment often arose if a railwayman thought that he was not being offered his fair share of overtime. Because I had no interest in doing overtime, I was able to avoid becoming embroiled in the ongoing disputes.

I also hated being underground during the warm summer evenings. I would have preferred to have been sitting on the riverside terrace wall at the Prospect of Whitby enjoying a glass of cider and trying to make conversation with the numerous women who frequented the pub. After nine months of working and resting below ground, I decided that a career as a railwayman was not for me, but a career as a garment cutter was still available.

No doubt my future salary from cutting garments would be approximately half of what I was earning as a railwayman; also there would be no benefits like sick and holiday pay, no subsidised canteen or four-hour rest breaks. I would be paid only for the hours worked.

During my period at the Burns & Lux blouse factory at Hackney, my time was calculated to the minute. Not a week went by without three pence or four pence being deducted from my wages, but at least I was involved in satisfactory work. Moreover as an experienced and competent cutter I was usually shown much respect by employers who were only too pleased to give me dockets to cut, knowing that I could always be relied on to produce perfectly cut garments. I had missed making markers too, that in a way was like sketching a picture, and I also missed the long but relaxing hours spent laying up wide fabric and getting to know some of the more interesting characters who were assigned to assist me.

During my last shift at the KEB, I worked alongside Joseph, a diminutive, middle-aged Indian-born Jewish bachelor. We had worked as a team on a previous late shift.

I shared a bad habit with Joseph – we both neglected our appearance. Joseph was constantly ridiculed by vindictive and sarcastic railwaymen who considered him to be a 'scruffy miser'. My little work-mate may have had a propensity for placing cardboard over the holes in his shoes and wore old well-worn trousers and a not always clean shirt, but he had a pleasant nature.

During the five days we worked together he described to me the happy holidays that he had spent in Israel. Each year he would stay with poor relatives in Haifa and help them financially.

'My relatives treat me like a king,' he said proudly.

I later asked David Upson if he thought that any of the spiteful railwaymen who taunted Joseph because of his scruffiness would also send part of their earnings to poor relatives.

Dave gave a resounding reply. 'Not one of them.'

After collecting my final wage packet at the KEB, I left the station in a jubilant state. My tenure at the Post Office Railway had lasted nine months and I detested every moment of it. Within minutes of leaving the station I met David Upson at the nearby Bishop's Finger, a popular alehouse opposite St Bartholomew's Hospital. My friend had already drunk several whiskies and was about leave for his shift at Mount Pleasant Station.

Since Dave had began working on the railway his salary was twice as much as what he had been earning as a garment cutter. With so much spare cash in his pocket to squander in the pubs, he soon became part of a small clique of heavy-drinking railwaymen who regularly patronised the local pubs and bars. Dave has also acquired a taste for toddy that was a spirit mixed with sugar and hot water and very popular with postal and market workers. Before starting his morning shift, he would often seek out those pubs adjacent to Smithfield and Spitalfields markets that had an early morning licence to sell toddy.

I soon became concerned by the huge amount of alcohol Dave was consuming. Several times I warned him that his excessive drinking might cause him to have an accident; he could easily fall off the platform in front of an incoming train or crash his motorbike.

His answer was always the same. 'Don't worry about me, Alf, I will be alright.'

His answer was unsatisfactory. Dave had been my closest friend for thirty years; we were like brothers. I dreaded the thought of him being disabled or killed.

Eventually, the inevitable happened; his motorbike struck traffic lights at Holborn and he received a severe injury to his forehead. To my regret, after he recovered and was back at work he began to drink again with abandonment.

Over the next decade the result of Dave's seemingly uncontrollable drinking, chronic smoking and small appetite began to affect his health. His decision to become a railwayman was proving to be a deadly mistake and might well prove to be his perdition. When he had worked in the clothing trade the wages were of course much lower. After he paid his mother her housekeeping money and his other dues there was less money to spend on alcohol, but still enough to drink on a semi-regular basis. Never one for borrowing money he always kept within his budget, but now his situation was different. With plenty of spare cash available Dave often spent over a £100 a week in the pubs.

I breathed a sigh of relief when he was finally forced to retire at sixty-five. When I reflect on Dave's career working on the railway, it seems incredible that with his slight physique, recurring hernias and increasing reliance on alcohol, he was able to manage to cope with such laborious and irksome work.

Throughout the thirteen years that Dave worked for the POR, I continued to cut garments in numerous East and North London factories. Despite the declining clothing industry, I was always able to find adequate work. Sometimes I worked full-time, other times part-time or freelance.

Towards the end of the first week of my fortnight break from the Burns & Lux blouse factory in Hackney where I regularly worked part-time, I became a little restless sitting on the riverside benches at Shadwell Park. I would usually spend about four hours a day in the park reading and writing or just quietly relaxing.

My restlessness would have been alleviated if there had been a woman to keep me company. Bobbie, my erstwhile Yugoslavian girlfriend, who a few weeks earlier had correctly described me as 'just another Casanova', could have been contacted if I had been prepared to be 'serious' about our relationship, but being serious with any girl at that stage of my life was out of the question. I was too busy enjoying my bachelorhood. Also Bobbie was now living and working at Reading in Surrey, which was too far from the Aldgate pump. This ancient pump, which was originally David Upson's boundary mark, was now my boundary too.

At the beginning of my second week's break, I walked to Stratford in East London with the intention of obtaining a ticket for the Theatre Royal's current production. As I approached the Good Grooming factory on Stratford High Street where Dave had once worked, I paused for a moment and glanced at the company's vacancy sign: an experienced stock cutter was required. A thought entered my mind. To end my restlessness, would it be possible for me to work there just for a few days before I returned to the Burns & Lux factory, although I had never forgotten that, whilst working at the Good Grooming factory, David Upson told me that on Christmas Eve, as he was cutting our a lay of blouses, he heard his name being called. He switched the cutting machine off and saw his boss on the other side of the cutting table throw a packet of ten cigarettes at him.

'Was that your Christmas bonus?' I enquired.

Dave smiled. 'Yes, and it was a cheap brand at that.'

'And now you know why your boss drives a Rolls Royce.' I remarked.

Despite his former employer being heartless, I was prepared to work there just for two or three days. I rang the factory bell of the Good Grooming factory and stepped inside. Standing by the entrance, I was interviewed by the two managing directors. The interview lasted for a few minutes. To the usual questions, that all factory owners ask prospective cutters, I gave my standard answers.

'I have been cutting garments for nearly 30 years, yes I can grade patterns and yes I can make markers too.'

The directors must have been desperately short of experienced cutters because they failed to ask me where I had worked previously and what my reasons for leaving were. My confident answers must have impressed them because the older director suggested that I could start work immediately. No wages were mentioned. At the end of the day the directors would have made an assessment of my capabilities and offer me what they described as 'a salary accordingly'. Whatever salary they offered for the few days work, it would be acceptable.

The partners were very different in appearance. The younger man was tall, slim and dark-haired and he moved about very quickly. Harry the older man was slower and overweight and his facial features were like those of a retired pugilist; it was probably him who had thrown the packet of cigarettes at Dave.

Keith the self-assured production manager was the same Keith whom I had known twenty years before when I worked at the Scare & Lee factory in Stepney and he worked as a stock cutter at a neighbouring gown factory. Keith could remember our mutual friend Johnny Steingold the buttonhole hand, but he had no recollection of me despite us chatting at the same table in Platt's café on numerous occasions.

I followed Keith across the large factory floor to where the cutting tables were situated. The factory was a modern, one-storey building. Approximately two thirds of the floor was occupied by the machining, pressing and dispatch staff. At least thirty women were machining at a fast rate; they may have been piece workers. The remaining floor space was the cutting section. The fluorescent lighting above the two long cutting tables was insufficient. This lack of light gave the area a foreboding gloomy appearance.

Keith gave me a work docket and also a blouse marker, which I presumed he had just completed. We checked the marker together; it was, as I expected, perfectly made. The fabric for the docket was too wide for me to lay single-handed, so Joe, the nimble, middle-aged driver, was assigned to be my assistant. Another cutter worked at a separate table. This cutter made no attempt to acknowledge me, but we did exchange a few brief words at lunchtime.

As Joe and I were laying the fabric, a sour-faced woman brushed past and went into a tiny room next to the cutting tables. She instantly sat down at a desk by the open door and sipped a cup of tea.

Joe speaking quietly, explained that the woman was the wife of one of the directors and she was also, 'Supposedly, the company's designer.'

Throughout the morning, whenever, I glanced obliquely in her direction, the woman glanced back. She did not seem to me to be engaged in any designing; her desk was bare and I could see no sketch or notebook, no pencils, coloured crayons or piles of fashion magazines that she could browse through to induce creativity. She just sat there, hunchbacked, her elbows resting on the desk and her cheeks cupped in her hands, or she sat bolt upright like a silent owl perched on a bough. The woman's eyes seemed to me to be constantly directed at me. I soon began to find her presence increasingly disconcerting and wondered if her real role was not that of a designer, but an overseer. It could be that in the past the company had encountered problems with indolent cutters or even pilferers, but I was neither indolent or a thief. Because of her close proximity, it may have been the reason why the other cutter was reluctant to talk to me during working hours. Two days of being observed by a sentry as I worked became unbearable. I collected my pay and left the company.

I chose not to mention to Dave my experiences of working at the Good Grooming factory.

Now that Dave had retired, I expected that his drinking would be somewhat curtailed as there would be less money available to spend on alcohol. But with retirement there could be problems; he was not in the best of health, he had few interests and no hobbies to occupy his mind, no love of reading or gardening. It was inevitable that he would become more sedentary. Being inactive, he could also become bored; if that happened he might be tempted to return to late-night drinking in the pubs. It was inconceivable that the term 'old-age pensioner' applied to Dave. He was so young at heart; it was as if he had discovered the magic formula of eternal youth.

Barbara and Dave adored their mother Doris, who had lived with them quite contentedly since arriving in London during the late summer of 1961. She had spent months at sea on board an old German freighter. As Dave predicted, his mother quickly adapted to life in Stepney and she soon became well known and befriended by the locals. At lunchtime, she often enjoyed a glass of stout in the Prince at Bromley Street with several elderly ladies whom she referred to as her 'mates'.

Mrs Upson, an avid reader, was extremely intelligent. Her particular interests were philosophy, world religions and mysticism. Whilst living in India, following her flight from the Japanese invasion of Burma in 1942, she involved herself with the women's movement, eventually becoming one of their union representatives; she also became an acquaintance of Mother Theresa and occasionally supported her work financially.

David, Barbara and their mother all spoke beautiful English. For me, to be in their company and listen when they conversed with each other was a constant joy. Always softly-spoken and polite, the Upsons never argued or were rude; their gentle ways were a blessing for me to witness. Sometimes, I would arrive at their home, not always in the best of moods and they would greet me at the door with wide-smiling faces. Their welcome, as always, was overwhelmingly warm; food and drink would be made available and I could, if I wanted to, have their undivided attention all evening. Over the years I dined with the Upsons hundreds of times they were an important ongoing part of my life and I am proud to know that they considered me from the earliest days to be one of their family.

Mrs Upson had expressed an interest in some of my poems. Although she never mentioned it to me she also had written some poetry. It was only after she died in September 1988, at the great age of ninety-two, that I found out and I was extremely pleased when Barbara gave me some copies of the poems. The little verses, which I believed were composed over half a century previously, seemed to express the different moods she was in when she put her pen to paper.

Out of a quartet of four short poems, 'Lost Light', 'Spoken Vows', 'The Scindian Boat Song' and 'Tryst', I prefer 'Lost Light' which I thought typical of her creative writing.

Lost Light

I have put away my sorted threads,
The colour of the plum-bloom,
Green of stagnant water,
The very blue of the sky,
And the mauve skein,
Coaxed from the little tailor,
Who fashioned my wondrous cloak;
The colours have lost their glamour.
They say the tailor died for love of me.

Not long after Mrs Upson died, the local council rehoused Barbara and Dave. Their new home, a little terrace house on nearby Shandy Street, was just a minute's walk from Stepney Green Underground Station. With Barbara's unique touch, she quickly transformed the house into a warm, cosy home, but the garden at the rear, that had a huge deep-rooted tree trunk in the centre, was neglected and overgrown. Because Dave was incapable of removing this formidable obstruction I volunteered to take up the challenge. After nearly five hours of digging, hacking and sawing, I still could not budge it. Wanting to give up, but refusing to be beaten, I carried on until it finally broke free to my loud cry of 'Gotcha!'

My reward was one of Barbara's delicious fish curries. Once the garden was tidied up, Barbara and her green-fingered friends began to plan a pretty oasis.

Shortly after Barbara and Dave had settled into their new home, Dave, to my regret, began to drink again at an increased rate and his asthma attacks were becoming more frequent. Thankfully, Barbara, his ever-patient sister, was at home to look after him, but she was not in the best of health herself. I looked at his future with trepidation.

At this stage of his life it would have been beneficial if some of Dave's old friends and work mates would have found the time to call around to see him, but with the exception of Roger Bullock, our mutual friend, Dave never received a single visit from former friends or acquaintances.

I suggested to Dave that now was the time to write down his wartime experiences. His answer was disappointing. 'That's the past Alf, it's water under the bridge.'

I frowned. 'But it would be a valuable document. You were there, you saw action in Burma.'

'I suppose so,' he replied nonchalantly.

I pressed on and asked him if he still kept the notes that he wrote during the war.

'Of sorts, yes,' he replied, quickly adding, 'but nobody is interested in the war, so let the matter rest.'

I was unable to let the matter rest. For years I had been curious to know more about his life in the Burma Royal Navy Volunteer Reserve, but he remained modest and reluctant to reminisce about his wartime role. Occasionally, I did manage to piece together a somewhat sketchy outline of his naval career. At fifteen years old and pretending that he was eighteen, he volunteered to join the BRNVR. After a few weeks training, he joined his small warship as a rating and found himself operating behind the Japanese lines in the rivers and creeks of North West Burma. He took part in four invasions, and as a gunner on his ship he had blown up Japanese gunboats. Eventually he rose through the ranks to become a junior officer. At the end of the war he was commanding a small naval patrol boat and spent the last six months of his service hunting bandits in the Burmese Delta.

Dave's continued reluctance to reveal details of his naval career is typical of many ex-servicemen who prefer to remain anonymous and keep their wartime memories in their minds rather than record them for posterity.

My worst fears for Dave's wellbeing were soon realised when Barbara had to be admitted to hospital for an operation. Dave very quickly lapsed into a permanently drunken state. I always stopped by at his house during the evenings after work to see how he was. It was heart-wrenching to see him deteriorate into such a shocking state of neglect, rarely eating and consuming huge amounts of beer, whisky and wine. I tried desperately to coax him to eat, but with little result. My greatest worry was that he would fall asleep while smoking and the house would then catch fire and he would be trapped. Finally, sensing my grave concern, and with tears in his eyes, he made me a promise that he would try and eat again and to stop drinking. I realised how much my friend depended on Barbara and that the longer she was away, the worse his situation would become, with possible dire consequences.

After a few weeks in hospital Barbara was well enough to be discharged. Dave kept his promise to me and somehow managed to pull himself out of this dangerous period, but sadly his efforts to eat more and to abstain from drinking were only temporary.

25

Dave is Mugged

A very worried Barbara 'phoned me at midnight. Apparently, Dave had not arrived home from the pub. She pleaded with me to try and find out where he was. I was deeply concerned; I knew that he was going through a heavy drinking session and had recently suffered a savage mugging.

As I drove to Shandy Street, I passed all of his regular drinking haunts; they were in darkness. I began to fear the worse. From Barbara's home, I 'phoned the London Hospital to see if he was there. Fortunately he had not been admitted. I quickly 'phoned Leman Street Police Station. The news was good. We were relieved to be told that he was at the station, unhurt, and that he could be collected. I suspected that a passing police car picked him up when they saw him staggering along the street in a drunken state.

When we arrived at the police station, Barbara stayed in the car while I went inside. A police sergeant brought Dave out from a rear room to the front desk. My friend looked in a rough dishevelled state and still bore the bruises on his face from being mugged. Surprisingly, despite his appearance, he seemed in a jocular mood. The police had decided not to charge him for being drunk and were more than satisfied that somebody had come to take him home.

I asked the sergeant if Dave had told him about the mugging.

'No, he had not,' he replied, quizzically. 'What happened?'

Dave was reluctant to discuss the incident, but when questioned further by the sergeant he decided to relate the story of the beating that he had received from the two men. Characteristically, he expressed no bitterness towards his assailants. 'It was last Saturday evening when I was walking home from the Brewery Tap pub when I was confronted by a Jamaican (Dave always described Afro-Caribbean men as Jamaican) who threatened me and demanded my money. Now, when I was young, I did quite a bit of boxing. When the Jamaican came menacingly towards me with his fists clenched, I put my left hand up towards his face and said to him don't hit me, I will give you the money and at the same time I let him see me put my right hand in my back trouser pocket where I pretended to take out my wallet. Meanwhile, I was still holding my left hand up towards his face. I then brought my right hand up and punched him hard in his mouth and down he went.' Dave paused before continuing. 'What I did not realise was that the Jamaican had an accomplice who came up behind me. I managed to fend him off too but then they both started to punch me and when I was lying on the pavement they stole my wallet.'

This incident seems incredible. Dave was in his mid-sixties, in poor health, and had been drinking for several hours, but because he was such an honest man who was incapable of lying, I knew that he was telling the truth. It was also possible that the same two muggers may have been responsible earlier that evening for attacking and robbing a woman less than half a mile away.

As Dave related the episode, the duty sergeant was making notes. 'These men who robbed you, you said that they were Jamaican? What colour were they?'

Dave looked perplexed; he glanced back at me for a moment; before facing the policeman and saying, 'They were black.'

He was then asked, 'How old were these two gentlemen?'

Again Dave looked back at me. His mouth wide open as if temporarily speechless and his round face suddenly seemed elongated. He turned to the policeman, leaned forward as if to whisper and spoke slowly and emphatically, 'I can assure you sergeant, they were no gentlemen.'

His answer caused me to burst out laughing.

After the sergeant made out his report we were allowed to leave. As Dave and I walked slowly back to my car, where an anxious Barbara waited, my friend looked back at the blue lamp outside the police station and said, 'You know, Alf, it was forty years ago when I was first charged here for being drunk and now after all of these years I find myself back here again.'

'Perhaps you have an affinity with the building,' I joked.

He laughed and said, 'Home James and don't spare the horses.'

> What'er he did was done with so much ease.
> In him alone 'twas natural to please.
> John Dryden

The next year was a peaceful one for Dave. His appetite was restored and his drinking stopped altogether; even his asthma seemed more controllable, and to my total surprise he and Barbara managed to go swimming at the York Hall Baths in Bethnal Green, but it was impossible for him to give up his habit of fifty years, chain smoking.

After Dave was diagnosed with terminal cancer in the summer of 1996, he showed the same kind of courage that he possessed when he faced the Japanese in combat. His resilience was remarkable. Philosophical as ever, he told Barbara and me, 'I have had a good life, I have done everything, been everywhere, and so I can't complain.'

When the ambulance men arrived to take him to St Joseph's Hospice and were lifting him into a wheelchair, he joked with them, 'Now, please be careful, I am not insured.'

As they struggled to carry him down the awkward and narrow staircase, still possessing his legendary politeness and altruism, he apologised, 'I am sorry to be such a nuisance and cause you so much trouble.'

Silently I thought, 'As if this most gentle and kindest of men was ever trouble to anyone.'

Dave joked once more with the ambulance when they arrived at St Joseph's. 'Please don't leave just yet because I want to have a look at the nurses and if they are not good-looking, I shall be back and then you can take me home.'

One of the attendants smiled and said, 'We can assure you that they really are nice.'

Just before Dave died, he said to me, 'Alf, the one thing that I have always wanted was to slip away in my sleep.' A few days later on 11 September 1996, Dave's last wish came true. For a brief moment, I thought that God may really exist.

Not long after Dave died, I mentioned to my girlfriend Linda that I would like her to walk with me along Wapping's riverside. We started our walk, just like Dave and I often did, at the bottom of the stairs of Tower Bridge. My plan was for us to stroll at a slow pace down St Katherine's Way through Wapping and on to Shadwell Park. Although I was unsure at the time why I felt the need to return to Wapping, I now realise that somehow I wanted to try to recapture and preserve some of the old memories of the happy times that Dave and I had spent in that once unique and fascinating part of old London, so busy and lively during the day, yet so quiet and tranquil at night.

Of course, by 1996 much of Wapping's riverside had changed out of all recognition; so many of the historical warehouses had disappeared a long time ago, either swept away by a series of mysterious fires in the 1970s. Was an arsonist at work? Some Wapping folk seemed to think so. Or by property developers who were allowed to mercilessly demolish several nineteenth-century riverside wharfs and warehouses, including the Irongate, the Carron & Continental and the British and Foreign Wharfs. After their demolition, the sites were cleared and expensive, but often soulless apartments and penthouses were erected. Thankfully, other ancient warehouses were saved and have since been sympathetically refurbished, like Gun Wharf, St John's Wharf and Oliver's Wharf.

Limehouse suffered much the same fate as its neighbour Wapping. Many longstanding warehouses, like Dundee, were lost, but the beautifully restored nineteenth-century Dunbar Wharf is a joy to gaze at, and in a way some of the new developments in Narrow Street, like Duke Shore Wharf, seem to blend in with the original character of the area.

Linda and I stopped in the little park by Old Aberdeen Wharf to enjoy the view of the Rotherhithe waterfront opposite. How grey and empty the foreshore looked with only a few rusty old barges chained up together. Dave and I would sit in this park thirty years previously amongst the artists at work and watch the ships going into the pool and wonder what cargoes they were carrying and where was their next port of call. How envious we were of the crew who could be seen moving around on the decks.

We left the park and continued walking east along Wapping High Street. As we approached St Hilda's Wharf, my thoughts went back to October 1964 when Dave and I passed this way most evenings. At that time, there was an aggregate company based at St Hilda's, and always parked at the top of a steep slope was a huge tip-up lorry. I can recall Dave explaining to me that it was dangerous to park the lorry on the slope when it was not being used, especially at night. His concern was soon realised with tragic consequences: the tip-up lorry's handbrake had not been correctly secured. Perhaps vibrations from the street traffic caused the eight-tonne lorry loaded with fourteen tonnes of stone to roll down the ramp where it struck a 3000-gallon fuel tank. The impact demolished a fifteen-foot wall which crashed onto the pavement. Unfortunately the falling bricks buried two men who happened to be were walking past the site. Within minutes the fire brigade arrived from nearby Shadwell and the rescuers dug out the two men from beneath the rubble. Sadly, Roy Edward Bligh, a thirty-six-year-old tally clerk of Bromley was killed and John Angle of Charlton was badly injured.

Shortly after the tragedy at St Hilda's wharf, Dave mentioned to me that he felt 'slightly uncomfortable' about the accident.

'And why should you feel uncomfortable?' I replied.

He spoke glumly. 'Don't you think that prior to the accident, we should have complained to some authority about the possible danger?'

I was unsure how to respond and could only say, 'Do you think anybody would have taken notice of your concern?' But concerned he remained and more than twenty-five years later he would sometimes recall the accident if ever we were in the vicinity of St Hilda's.

As Linda and I walked along Wapping Wall, I suddenly remembered that frightful episode that Dave and I experienced in December 1963 when youths in a car fired starting pistols at us. Although the incident occurred thirty-three years previously, it seemed as if it had happened just a day before.

Linda agreed with my suggestion to visit the nearby Prospect of Whitby for a quick drink. We sat outside on the terrace by the willow tree enjoying the late summer evening. Unfortunately, this charming terrace had lost much of its original character. It was now smaller and cluttered with cheap ugly benches. I wondered what had happened to those green-painted wooden barrel tables and chairs half-filled with concrete that blended so perfectly with the old brick wall. The shoreline opposite had now changed completely too. Bellamy's Wharf, with its huge 350ft jetty, Bull Head Dock Wharf and the Surrey Commercial Wharf were all closed and waiting to be demolished to make way for private housing. Thankfully, Globe Wharf, built in the 1880s, had been spared for the time being, though it too was soon to be converted into apartments.

I glanced around this neglected terrace and could still see the scarred brickwork where the old coalbunkers once stood. It was by the bunkers, that Pat, the elderly, Irish pot-man often stood still for a moment to enjoy his snuff. Besides collecting glasses, Pat would keep the three coal fires inside the bars topped up. Tragically, this diminutive and amiable riverside character, who was liked immensely by Dave and me, was soon to die. During a fit of depression he jumped into the Thames.

Linda and I finished our drinks and left the Prospect. Just a hundred yards away the old bascule bridge had been freshly painted. How I missed the old days when Dave and I would stand contently by the bridge and watch the cargo ships going into or leaving the Shadwell Basin.

Before Linda and I went home we wandered around the nearby Shadwell Park. To my regret, the park had changed considerably. There were fewer flowers and trees and the children's playground, the sandpit and the paddling pool had been removed, as had the tea shed. Fortunately this little oasis of greenery still commands one of the best views of the Thames. Of course, the Thames is quieter now, with little commercial use, a waste of resources considering the ever-increasing volume of traffic on the roads. When you gaze around this peaceful little park of seven and a half acres, you cannot imagine that during the last war, huge barrage balloons were hoisted here in an attempt to prevent German aircraft from bombing London.

At the height of the Blitz, on the night of 24 September 1940, two local children, seventeen-year-old Gladys Clarke and her twelve-year-old brother Edgar were killed in the park's public shelter when it was struck by a bomb. After the war, the park was immensely popular with local school children, especially during their August holidays when children's concerts were regularly performed on a raised stage. In the years that followed the war, many scenes for films were shot there. Famous film stars including Diana Dors, Victor Mature, Robert Mitchum and Dirk Bogarde filmed at the park.

From time to time and always on a Sunday during the summer, Dave and I would bring girls to the park. Either we would picnic on the grass or just sit quietly by the riverside. Sitting there close to the ventilation shafts of the Rotherhithe tunnel had a hypnotic effect. Within a short space of time, the gentle and constant drone emitting from the shaft could lull you into a near sleep.

From 1959 onwards, Dave and I visited the park several times a year; it was a favourite location of ours where we could observe the shipping and dream once more of joining the Merchant Navy.

26

Opposing Views

It was at Shadwell Park that Dave and I would often sit and discuss a wide range of subjects. One particular heated discussion that we had following the 1967 Israel/Arab war was never resolved. He was a defender and admirer of Israel while I was, and still am, sympathetic to the Palestinian cause. Although Dave and I were fond of Jewish people we had opposing views on the ongoing Israel/Palestine conflict.

Dave first took an interest in the Middle East when Israel achieved independence in 1948. Five years earlier, whilst serving with the BRNVR in the rivers of Burma, he had heard about the military exploits of General Orde Wingate's famous Chindits who were operating deep in the jungle behind the Japanese positions. But he was unaware that Wingate was a passionate Zionist who supported a Jewish homeland and that as an Army commander he fought vigorously against Arab guerrillas in pre-war Palestine.

My friend admired Wingate whom he regarded as a brave and daring soldier who used his Chindits to great effect. Dave maintained that if the General, who was killed in an air crash in 1944, had initially received sufficient support from the commander of the 14th Army in Burma, the Japanese might well have been forced to surrender much earlier than the summer of 1945.

Several years after the war, Dave learnt that his hero Wingate was a Zionist. The young Upson believed that as Wingate had 'got it right in Burma, he must have also got it right by supporting a Jewish state in Palestine'.

It was not only Wingate who had influenced Dave. He fervently believed that historically the Jews were a persecuted race who had every reason to want to live in their own country, where they would be free, safe and protected. I wholeheartedly agreed with his view, but I reminded him that the Palestinians, whom in my opinion were the most tragic people of the century, also had an equal right to demand that they have their own state.

As laymen, over the years, Dave and I discussed the Middle East conflict many times. Sitting comfortably in the pub, we imagined ourselves to be international mediators who were capable of devising various ideas and solutions that might pave the way for everlasting peace. There were occasions when fellow drinkers joined us and arguments would occur.

One of Dave's plans seemed to me to have been well thought out. He suggested that a future Palestine state should be centred on the West Bank and become part of a federation with Jordan. The Palestinians should hand over Gaza to the Israelis, who would then allow Palestine to expand into Israel proper and occupy the same amount of land as Gaza. The Jewish settlers on the West Bank would vacate their properties and resettle in Gaza. Perhaps Jordan could, with massive financial backing from the West and the rich Arab states, accept more of the Palestinians from Gaza and the refugee camps scattered around the Middle East.

Although Dave's plan was interesting, I was uncertain how the Israelis would respond, and I was absolutely certain that it would be rejected by the Palestinians who would never agree to thousands of their people being resettled. I also could not see how any Arab country would ever recognise Israel's right to exist until the natural aspirations of the Palestinians were fulfilled.

'Then that means continuing war,' he retorted. 'Perhaps even an apocalypse.'

I totally agreed with his assessment and I made a prediction to my friend that if there were no eventual settlement to the crisis, as sure as two and two equal four, Israel's hostile neighbours will one day possess lethal weapons including chemical and nuclear. 'And who knows what might happen then,' I remarked solemnly.

Because of Dave's enduring affection for the Jews and his belief that they were a force for good in the world, he would oppose any criticism that he considered biased against Israel. He seemed puzzled when I suggested that there was a strong possibility that the majority of the Jews in Israel may not be the descendants of the biblical Hebrews and that their ancestry could perhaps be traced back to several countries.

'And where were these countries?' he replied sceptically.

I mentioned Azerbaijan, North Africa and Ethiopia. Dave, the least arrogant of men, surprised me by instantly dismissing my opinion as an irrelevance, although he reluctantly agreed that many people who consider themselves to be Jewish on appearance do seem to come from a variety of different racial backgrounds.

He added, 'It does not matter if the majority of the Israelis have no direct blood line to the ancient Hebrews or that their forebears had converted to Judaism in other lands, Israel is the historical homeland of the Jewish people and will remain so.'

Even my own plan for a peaceful settlement for the region received a negative response. I thought that Israel and Palestine should merge and become one country.

'Your idea is totally unworkable, Alf ,' he replied scathingly.

Not to be deterred by my friend's scepticism, I proposed that, 'By joint ownership, the two communities would administer the new state as partners, not as rivals, and Jewish immigration should be restricted until all of the Palestinian refugees returned and settled in those areas where their ancestors occupied before.'

Dave made no attempt to question my proposal, so I continued. 'I believe that it is inevitable that the Holy Land will one day become a single nation in which both the Israelis and the Palestinians can call their homeland. The two communities deserve peace. There are two legitimate claims for that much sought-after land, not one. Without true justice for both communities there will be no lasting peace, only war. If the Israelis and the Palestinians accept the idea of a jointly owned, multinational state, fragile as it would be at first, we might finally see an end to the terrible bloodshed and suffering that has engulfed the region for nearly a century.'

Dave suddenly interrupted me. 'Israel would never agree to such a plan, Alf. If she compromised with the Palestinians and allowed them joint ownership of the new state, it would be an irreversible step towards national suicide for the Jews, who within a few years would become the minority and could find themselves at the mercy of the Arabs.'

I believed that Dave's scenario was possible, but not probable and I argued that if the new state was demilitarised, a large force of United Nation soldiers could be permanently stationed in the country ready to intervene if either community was threatened or a belligerent neighbouring country was attacking the infant state.

Dave frowned and repeated what he said earlier, 'I am afraid to say Alf, that your ideas are totally unworkable.'

A few weeks later we sat in the Prince and again came up with different plans and solutions to the perennial crisis in the Middle East and, as before, we reached a stalemate.

Dave enjoyed debating; he always had up-to-date knowledge of world affairs. With his gifts of self-expression and superb command of the English language, he was capable of demolishing many of his opponents. Rarely dogmatic, he could be intransigent and then suddenly pliable, but that was probably due to having lost interest in the subject.

One neighbour of his who also lived in Lathem House and enjoyed debating was the one-time feisty left-wing dockers' leader Jack Dash. Now mellow and retired, Jack spent much of his time painting and writing poetry. He was also the author of his own excellent autobiography *Good Morning Brothers*.

Dave and I agreed that it was economics and containerisation that made the London Docks no longer viable; plus the dockers' readiness to strike and the PLA's lack of foresight were contributing factors that hastened their closure. Chatting to Jack one day at a bus stop, Dave insisted that the docks were far

Jack Dash. Although Dave was quite friendly with his neighbor Jack Dash and occasionally would enjoy a serious discussion with him, he regarded the former Dockers' leader as a Communist agitator who used his position to try and further the aims of socialism. (*Edward Hayes*)

too ancient to handle the modern container ships and I audaciously suggested that if only the dockers would have put in the same amount of effort to keep the docks open as they did when they fought for better wages and conditions, perhaps part of the London docks, possibly the Royals, might still have been operating to this day. Jack listened patiently to our criticism and then spent the next few minutes attempting to give his version of who was ultimately responsible for the closure of the docks. As Dave had predicted, Jack blamed 'greedy port employers' as being the main culprits.

Because of my interest in poetry, I was curious to read some of Jack's and was pleased when Barbara Upson gave me a copy of one that she had. I thought that Jack's poem might be in the same interesting style of that other East End working-class fighter, the ex-boxer poet Stephen 'Johnny' Hicks, but I was to be disappointed. I did not like Jack's poem at all and found it pretty awful. Written in 1972 and entitled *Time*, the first few lines were as follows: 'Time begins with the ending of the embryonic period and the thrusting forward from the vagina into a world of materialism and struggle.'

Linda and I left Shadwell Park and began to walk to Narrow Street where my car was parked. As we walked along the dusty fume-filled highway we passed Free Trade Wharf. During the early 1980s, most of the Victorian-built Free Trade Wharf that stretched 200 yards along the river was unfortunately demolished, and the old dockers' urinal that stood outside the wharf's entrance and where Dave had crashed his motorbike had also been bulldozed away during the same period. The two remaining small warehouses had been converted into apartments, but the new expensive apartments that now occupy the huge site are ugly and austere.

The old Free Trade Wharf should have been preserved and refurbished like Gun Wharf in Wapping and Dunbar Wharf in Limehouse, so in keeping with the area's historical character. Perhaps I am wrong and too sentimental in arguing that old buildings that have been around for generations should be protected and not destroyed. In a way, I regard these structures that have thousands of memories within their walls like faithful old friends. You look forward to seeing them, to know that they are there and hopefully will always be around.

Towards the end of his life, if ever Dave was in a nostalgic mood we would reminisce about the great times that we had in the past, often remembering the many women that we had known and loved and sometimes lost, recalling old friends and acquaintances who were no longer with us; either they had passed away or had moved out of the area. My friend was sorry that we never managed to join the Merchant Navy together and sail away like we always wanted to.

'But there is no reason why you should not embark on a voyage one day,' he said encouragingly.

It was inevitable that our conversations would turn once more towards the subject of the London pubs that we had frequented over the years. During this period of constant reminiscing, just prior to Dave being admitted to St Joseph's Hospice, he told me that he would like to spend an evening in Soho again to see how much the area had changed. Sadly, we never made the trip.

A few weeks after Dave's funeral, Barbara decided to sort through his belongings. She invited me to assist her and we spent a whole evening examining his papers. To my delight, Barbara decided to give me Dave's wartime notes, photos, medal ribbons and other memorabilia. She agreed with my suggestion that I should try to find the time to arrange his notes into a diary and, when I had written it, have the manuscript typed. We would each have a copy of the typescript and with her permission, at a later date, I would send the diary to the Documents Department at the Imperial War Museum at South London.

Dave had been an inveterate hoarder when it came to paperwork. Besides his naval papers, there were dozens of old letters, certificates and notes of past love affairs. During our long friendship, I had no idea that Dave had kept an on-off dossier of his relationships with women. Looking through the notes, I noticed that he did not record many intimate details, preferring instead to describe the women's character, intelligence and sense of humour. I was mentioned too.

'Alf is far too serious and reserved, but the girls seem to like him, especially the older ones.'

In another note, fearing that he had crabs, he wrote, 'If you are promiscuous and don't take precautions, it is inevitable you will get the pox; not Alf though, he is always careful.' My friend seemed to have forgotten I had been diagnosed with non-specific urethritis on two separate occasions.

Amongst Dave's effects I found an uncashed four-shilling postal order in mint condition that was dated January 1961; his winnings from Vernon's Pools.

Barbara, Dave and me at my home at Folly Wall. A few months after this photo was taken in 1996, David passed away in his sleep.

Browsing through his wartime naval papers, I could see that much was written on a variety of different types of paper, on the backs of envelopes and in tiny note books, usually in pencil, and often extremely faded. There were several gaps in the closing stages of the war. I suspect that they were among those papers, letters and references from his commanding officers, including the important ones from his skipper, Captain A. Campbell DSC, that were destroyed by a vindictive girlfriend in 1959.

Writing the 15,000-word diary proved somewhat difficult for me. I spent long hours, often with the aid of a magnifying glass, trying to decipher a paragraph, a sentence and sometimes even a single word. Several months later, the manuscript was finally finished. Although Dave had taken part in four naval invasions, his diary is not a spectacular document of war; but an ongoing record of the endless training, patrolling off the enemy coast, escort duties and the occasional fierce battle with the Japanese navy in the rivers and creeks of Burma. I believe the diary is important because it was written by a teenage boy with no formal education who had decided to try and record on a day-to-day basis his experiences while serving with the BRNVR.

Unlike Dave, who preferred the company of a few friends, Barbara was gregarious. She loved seeing her many friends on a regular basis and kept in contact either by letter or phone to those who had settled in America, Canada and Australia. Before coming to stay with her mother and Dave in Poplar in the early 1960s she lived in Calcutta where she was employed as a secretary at the Dunlop Rubber Company. Soon after arriving in London, Barbara found a position in the offices of J. R. Preston, a Queensway-based engineering firm.

She was eventually promoted to office manager and stayed with the company for twenty-five years until retiring. Prior to suffering a mild heart attack at the age of fifty-five in 1976, she was extremely active and only gave up playing hockey when she reached fifty. After Barbara recovered from her heart attack, she remained reasonably fit until the last ten years of her life, but when her health began to deteriorate, an operation was needed on her leg to improve the circulation.

During Barbara's final years, she became frail and somewhat restricted in her movements, but not totally housebound. Although travelling became a concern for her, sometimes during the summer she would make the effort to sit in the little park in Beaumont Square just yards from her Stepney Green home.

Being so delicate, there was always a danger that Barbara could become a victim of muggers who were operating in the area. One incident that could have had serious consequences occurred just before Dave passed away. Two men posing as Water Board inspectors tried to gain access to their home. Dave immediately suspected that they were thieves. Mustering the last of his strength, he confronted them at the door and barred their entry and in no uncertain terms told them to clear off.

Barbara was fortunate that her loyal friends always found time to visit and I would call at her home two or three times a week. Linda and I were regulars for her sumptuous meals and every few weeks we would bring her to our house for Sunday lunch. She would sit by the window for hours and gaze at the river. Believing that moving water was calming and therapeutic, she often said, 'I could get better just by sitting here.'

Barbara possessed the unique and renowned Upson qualities: intelligence, gentleness and kindness. She also had a witty sense of humour and a warm attractive melodious voice that I found so appealing. Her friends still miss her terribly and mention her name often. Her lovely smile welcoming me at her door is a memory that I will always cherish. When Barbara died in September 1999 at the age of seventy-nine, the final chapter of my close friendship with the Upson family that had lasted for forty years was closed.

From the time Dave and I first became friends in 1959, I had noticed that he suffered from mild bronchitis and a cough that worsened with the years. His asthma came late in life and then finally cancer. I believe that heavy smoking probably caused his illnesses. Like many lifelong smokers, he was totally addicted and unable to give up the habit even when he was very ill. He had smoked every day for over fifty years and did not want to stop now. Painful as it was for me, I still had to bring him his fags when his life was coming to an end. He knew I could not refuse.

Being a non-smoker, I was always puzzled why family and friends had taken up smoking when all the medical evidence proves that cigarettes can severely devastate your health. I remember once suggesting to an intelligent and educated man that he should try and give up smoking whilst his health was still good.

His answer astounded me. 'I would only give up if I knew that the cigarettes were affecting my health.'

'Surely,' I argued, 'it makes sense to give up the habit before you reach that stage?'

He shrugged his shoulders nonchalantly and said, 'Maybe.'

When I recall my relatives who had been afflicted with smoking-related terminal illnesses, I get so angry with the tobacco industry and those who import and market their killer weed. Trying to persuade friends and acquaintances to give up smoking often seems a wasted effort; their addiction is so powerful it always overrides your genuine concern for their health. A middle-aged friend of mine is so typical of many. When his coughing becomes severe he is forced to stop smoking for a day or two, swearing profusely that he will never have another cigarette again. The moment his coughing eases off, he starts to smoke again. As always his habit pulls the strings and seems to win every time. I do realise how difficult it can be trying to advise chronic smokers to abstain. Unless they genuinely want to throw away their cigarettes, no good advice or antidote will ever work, and it saddens me when I see young school children smoking. One wonders where they obtained their cigarettes. You ask yourself, are children not taught in schools the dangers of smoking? If only their young minds were capable of realising what major health problems they could be creating for themselves in the future.

Dave always claimed that prior to enlisting in the Navy he was a regular churchgoer and had no desire to smoke and drink, but in order to conceal his true age he started to smoke and drink rum like the rest of the crew. He had hoped to give the impression that he was at least eighteen years old. Intelligent as he was, I don't think that he ever really tried to analyse why he was so dependent on cigarettes. He always maintained that it was impossible for him to stop smoking.

I remember asking him once why it was so difficult to abstain. His answer was heartfelt. 'Because I just can't stop, Alf, no matter how I try.' He had read somewhere that nicotine severs the nerve endings, which causes an irritation and a craving that becomes permanent. I have no idea if nicotine has that effect, but what is evident to me is a simple truth – your lungs are designed to inhale oxygen and not smoke.

Always keen to do my bit in the war against the cigarette, I readily responded in June 2000 to an appeal by a medical research team at the London Chest Hospital for volunteers to participate in a potentially important research project into the effects of smoking on the lungs. The plan was for tiny samples of tissue to be taken from the lungs of three different types of volunteers:

A. Healthy non-smoking people

B. People who smoke but were otherwise healthy

C. Those who had smoked but had given up

By comparing tissue from these different groups it was hoped that the study would reveal if smoking alone causes sub-epithelial inflammation and the role of the cytokines associated with it. Being a layman, I had not a clue what those medical terms meant, but I imagined it was some chronic respiratory illness.

After an hour walk from the Isle of Dogs, I arrived at the London Chest Hospital at the appointed time. Like most men, I try to avoid doctors and hospitals and it did enter my mind, as I walked along the Mile End Road, that the whole idea of being a medical volunteer might be a mistake. I started to feel slightly apprehensive; this was due to the sudden thought that I might have to have a blood test. Over the years I had shown no fear of injections in my gums, inside my nostrils or even in my eye, but the thought of a needle being inserted into a vein in my outstretched arm and blood being withdrawn filled me with near terror. I comforted myself with the fact that on a previous occasion I had managed to persuade a nurse to take the blood from a vein on my wrist rather than from my arm. No doubt the staff at the London Chest Hospital would do the same.

Dr Liz Gamble of the clinical trials unit was one of the investigators who were conducting the study. Liz was tall, quite attractive and had a gentle nature. After she gave me a brief examination, I was sent off to various departments for a series of tests that included an ECG, a chest x-ray, a skin prick test for allergy, and a small sample of blood was removed from my ear lobe to measure oxygen. In one room I did several breathing tests that involved blowing into different machines. Several patients found this awkward and uncomfortable and I soon found myself becoming irritable at having to repeat the exercise.

Once the staff were satisfied with the results, I was sent away to have the inevitable and dreaded blood test. Sitting in a tiny room I was utterly dismayed that my plea for a blood sample to be taken from a vein in my wrist rather then my outstretched arm was refused. The nurse explained that it was the hospital's strict policy that blood samples must be obtained from the arm and nowhere else and she had no option but to comply. Although the nurse was sympathetic and understood my nervousness, she foolishly explained that only recently a burly ex-soldier was so petrified of the blood test he was actually reduced to tears. Her disclosure made me feel even more nervous. As I sat there, I began to feel like a wimp. A few seconds passed by and I became so anxious, I could feel my heart pounding. I looked up at the nurse patiently standing by me with the needle ready in her hand. I gazed out into the corridor and could see several sick patients being wheeled past, one of whom looked remarkably like Dave. Suddenly, I started to feel a change taking place within my body. My racing heartbeat was slowing down and I was beginning to relax. Perhaps it was endorphins released from the brain or some other unknown factor that caused this calming effect.

With new-found courage, I boldly said to the nurse, 'Okay, I am ready.'

Within a few minutes it was all over and I was up and out of the room and heading back towards Dr Gamble's surgery. I felt so proud that I had finally overcome one of my worst fears.

Dr Gamble handed me a spirometer. This grey plastic instrument measured about 25cm long and 20cm in diameter; it also had a small gauge inserted into a scale. When you took a deep breath and blew into the mouthpiece, the gauge would move up the scale and give a reading of the strength of your lungs. I took an almighty breath and blew hard into the mouthpiece.

Dr Gamble examined the reading before saying, 'You know Alfred, since I have been at this hospital nobody has ever reached 760 degrees.'

I grinned, 'Now come off it Liz, you're only saying that.'

'No, it's true,' she replied.

I joked with her, 'It must be all that walking I do.'

She smiled and asked me if I would take away the instrument that I promptly nicknamed the blowpipe and for the next two and a half weeks blow three times into it during the morning and record the highest score on a chart, repeating the same procedure in the evening. She also asked me if I could bring the results back to the hospital in three weeks time and then, if I agreed, have the bronchoscopy.

I listened patiently as Dr Gamble explained what a bronchoscopy was. It was a test that enabled a doctor to examine the airways and lungs. This procedure involves passing the bronchoscope, a flexible tube the width of a pencil, through the nose or the mouth into the tubes of your lungs. Tiny fibers on the bronchoscope would convey light to give a picture, special forceps inserted into the bronchoscope would remove about six small samples of lung tissue, and the whole procedure would be recorded on film.

'As long as I get the film rights,' I quipped.

Dr Gamble went on to explain that a local anaesthetic would be sprayed in my nose and throat to induce numbness and a sedative into my vein would make me feel sleepy but not totally unaware.

Unlike the blood test, the bronchoscopy posed no problem for me. Three weeks later, I arrived back at the hospital. This time I walked from the Isle of Dogs via the Grand Union canal that was much more pleasant than the busy roads.

I was given a bed in a day ward. Dr Gamble soon arrived and explained that she had the results of my previous tests. Everything was fine; the chest x-ray had shown a slight thickening in one small area. This thickening was caused by the pleurisy that I had when I was a boy, but it was normal and nothing to worry about.

I did not have to spend much time in the day ward before I was called to have the bronchoscopy. Lying on the bed in the clinic I was surprised how quickly the nasal throat spray took effect but felt no movement when I tried to swallow.

'You are swallowing,' said Dr Gamble. 'It's just you can't feel anything because your throat is numb.'

Once the sedative was administered into the vein I soon found myself more asleep than awake and after a short period I was back in the day ward and ready to leave.

Peter Reece Edwards and I sat next to each other when this school photo was taken in 1955. We were both fourteen.

I was glad I had joined the other volunteers in assisting the research team at the London Chest Hospital. Although my role was only a small one, I am sure it was of some value. Dr Gamble told me that it would take about a year before the results of the study were known. Hopefully their findings will help the doctors have a better understanding of the effects of smoking on the lungs.

I had benefited immeasurably by being involved in the project because I no longer have any anxiety about having to have future blood tests.

After I became a medical volunteer I was informed at the hospital I would be offered £100 for having the bronchoscopy. This fee was totally unexpected and unnecessary. Knowing how short of funds St Joseph's Hospice is I sent my fee to the Sister Superior in appreciation of the care the hospice gave to my good friend David Upson during his last days.

On 1 February 2001 Dr Gamble wrote to me explaining that the Clinical Trials Unit at the London Chest Hospital now had the final results of their study. From the biopsies provided by the volunteers, the research team were able to answer a number of important questions. Also they were able to identify a new kind of protein that appears in the airways of people with chronic bronchitis when they have a chest infection. It seems that this protein triggers inflammation in the airways causing lung damage. Dr Gamble added that with increased knowledge obtained from the study, the unit's researchers now had a better understanding of how chronic conditions like bronchitis and emphysema develop. Hopefully these results will enable new treatments to be

Peter and I visiting our old
school St George's.

developed and eventually made available to patients suffering from serious
respiratory illnesses. The American Journal of Respiratory and Clinical Care
Medicine published the research team's findings in late 2001.

In the early summer of 2000, I was reunited with Peter Reece Edwards my
best friend at St George-in-the-East School. On reaching adulthood, Peter had
successfully overcome his chronic shyness and reluctance to talk. Peter and I
went on a nostalgic walk of the Cable Street area and soon found ourselves in St
George-in-the-East churchyard and park that was situated just behind our old
school. The churchyard gardens had fewer flowerbeds than before and several
of the old trees had been lost in the great storm of 1987. It was sad to see that the
tiny nature museum was now a derelict building, and the children's playground
that gave us so much joy when we were young had become a neglected corner
with its swings and roundabout removed. However, the magnificent church of
St George-in-the-East designed by Nicholas Hawksmoor was fully restored. In
our day the church looked a sorry sight with its roof destroyed by wartime
incendiary bombs. In 1966, five hundred old coffins were removed from its
crypt and were transported to a cemetery in Essex for reburial.

During our walkabout, Peter and I were keen to visit our old school that
overlooked the churchyard. The headmistress of St George's, who appeared

at a window, realised that the two middle-aged men standing at the edge of the playground and pointing in every direction were former pupils. She came over to us and after a short conversation kindly took our photo and also allowed her caretaker to take us on a much-appreciated and memorable tour of our old school.

The genial caretaker informed us that he was a relative of the late Stepney boxer-poet Stephen 'Johnny' Hicks, whose poetry I enjoy.

Postscript

I knew from the moment I first met David Upson during that lovely warm summer of 1959 we would become firm friends. Who would not want to be a friend of this totally kind and unselfish man? I can recall few instances of him ever expressing animosity. It seemed to me that the word hate was not in his dictionary. Possessing an extraordinary wit, he could soon bring a smile to the face of the most cynical of men. Perhaps I was occasionally guilty of taking advantage of our friendship but it was never knowingly done for personal gain.

I presume it was a Christian who once said, 'Wanting a friend is a mere human craving, but wanting to be a friend is the spirit of Christ in man.'

That simple analysis may or may not be true. I tend to agree with Dave's definition of friendship, a subject we first discussed as early as 1959. He thought that an enduring friendship could only survive if it was based on compromise and mutual respect. Rather like the old Scottish proverb 'give and take makes good friends'.